PRICES, GROWTH AND CYCLES

Also by András Simonovits

CYCLES AND STAGNATION IN SOCIALIST ECONOMIES

Prices, Growth and Cycles

Essays in Honour of András Bródy

Edited by

András Simonovits
Professor of Economics
Institute of Economics
Hungarian Academy of Sciences
Budapest, Hungary

and

Albert E. Steenge
Professor of Economics
University of Twente
The Netherlands

Foreword by Wassily Leontief

First published in Great Britain 1997 by
MACMILLAN PRESS LTD
Houndmills, Basingstoke, Hampshire RG21 6XS and London
Companies and representatives throughout the world

A catalogue record for this book is available from the British Library.

ISBN 0–333–64165–5

First published in the United States of America 1997 by
ST. MARTIN'S PRESS, INC.,
Scholarly and Reference Division,
175 Fifth Avenue, New York, N.Y. 10010

ISBN 0–312–15970–6

Library of Congress Cataloging-in-Publication Data
Prices, growth, and cycles : essays in honour of András Bródy / András Simonovits and Albert E. Steenge.
p. cm.
Includes bibliographical references and index.
ISBN 0–312–15970–6
1. Prices. 2. Economic development. 3. Business cycles.
I. Bródy, András. II. Simonovits, András. III. Steenge, Albert E. (Albert Eelke), 1943– .
HB221.P723 1996
338.9—dc20 96–13143
CIP

This book is printed on paper suitable for recycling and made from fully managed and sustained forest sources.

10 9 8 7 6 5 4 3 2 1
06 05 04 03 02 01 00 99 98 97

Printed in Great Britain by
The Ipswich Book Company Ltd
Ipswich, Suffolk

Contents

Foreword

András Bródy's scientific contributions are marked by a creative, to some extent, dialectical combination of Eastern and Western streams of economic thought. On the one hand it is rooted in the honourable tradition of classical economics interpreted by Karl Marx but carried forward by a sophisticated use of the analytical tools forged by modern neoclassical, mathematical economics.

Having been brought up in a centrally planned socialist economy, Bródy took full use of many opportunities to acquire first-hand knowledge of the structure and operation of the American economy, i.e. the most advanced of the western capitalist economies. By taking on teaching assignments in Africa he gained familiarity with problems confronting less developed third world countries.

It is possible that his interest with the fundamental structural properties common to all economic systems irrespective of their institutional arrangements that turned Bródy's attention to input-output analysis. He has made important contributions not only to the practical development of that methodology, but also to its practical advancement by serving as the first editor of *Economic Systems Research*, published by the International Association for Input–Output Analysis.

His friends and colleagues in many different countries admiring his work contributed to this volume that is being presented to András Bródy on the occasion of his 70th birthday. The seventeen papers included reflect many different facets of his scholarly interests. Let us hope that some of the ideas contained in them might challenge András to continue to advance further his own original thought.

WASSILY LEONTIEF

Notes on the Contributors

Mária Augusztinovics graduated 1952 from the Karl Marx University of Economics, Budapest. She obtained her PhD in 1956, at the HAS (The Hungarian Academy of Sciences). She is Doctor of Economic Sciences 1980, HAS and Professor of Economics since 1988 at the Budapest University of Economics. She is former head of the Department of Macroeconomic Modelling of the National Planning Office. Her earlier research areas include the theory of money, macroeconomic modelling (mainly input–output and linear programming). Her current affiliation is senior research advisor, Institute of Economics, HAS. Her major research topic since the 1980s is macroeconomics of the human life-cycle.

Pirkko Aulin-Ahmavaara is Director of Statistics at the Finnish Ministry of Labour and teacher in Economics at the University of Helsinki. Her research interests are concentrated in generalizing the input–output dynamics to include the production processes of human capital and of active human time and in measuring the productivity of this comprehensive production system. She has published several articles and monographs on this subject.

Anne P. Carter is Fred C. Hecht Professor of Economics at Brandeis University. In earlier years she served as Dean of the Faculty at Brandeis, Director of Research of the Harvard Economic Research Project and Assistant Professor of Economics at Harvard University, Smith College and Brooklyn College. A Fellow of the American Association for the Advancement of Science, she was founding President of the International Input–Output Association and still serves on its governing board. She is also on the governing board of the International J. A. Schumpeter Society and is Vice-President of the Board of Trustees of the Russel Sage Foundation. She is the author of many articles and of six books including *Structural Change in the American Economy* and three volumes on input-output analysis co-edited with András Bródy. Her most recent articles concern the special features and problems of a knowledge-based economy.

Maurizio Ciaschini is Professor of Political Economy at the Law Faculty of the University of Macerata, Italy. He also taught at the Faculty of Economics and Commerce of the University of Urbino. He participated in the IIASA INFORUM Project at IIASA (Laxenburg, Austria), and was a

Visiting Scholar at the University of Maryland, College Park, Ma. As a NATO Senior Fellow he worked at the Institute of Economic Analysis of New York University. He is a member of the Editorial Board of 'Economic Modelling' and Honorary Fellow of the European Economics and Financial Centre in London. He has published two books, *Input–Output Analysis: Current Developments* (1988) and *Modelling the Structure of the Economy* (1993), and a number of articles on multisectoral modelling.

Erik Dietzenbacher is Assistant Professor of Mathematical Economics at the University of Groningen (The Netherlands). His research interests concern input-output analysis, applied general equilibrium modelling, and matrix algebra. He has published many articles in leading academic journals, including *The American Economic Review, The Journal of Mathematical Economics, The Journal of Regional Science, The Journal of Economics, Economic Modelling* and *Economics Letters.* Currently he is Associated Editor of *Economics Systems Research.*

Richard Goodwin was Professor Emeritus of the Department of Economics, University of Siena, Italy. Previously he taught for many years at the Faculty of Economics, University of Cambridge, and before that at Harvard University. His life-long interests were the study of structure and economic dynamics. He produced pioneering studies on non-linear economic dynamics in the 1950s and has continued to contribute to the field, including chaotic economic dynamics, until his death in August 1996.

László Halpern is senior research fellow at the Institute of Economics of the Hungarian Academy of Sciences, where he has been working since his graduation in 1974 from Karl Marx University of Economics, Budapest. His research interests cover macro-economic issues of open economies, East European stabilization policies, and the behaviour of exporting firms during transition. He is author of several publications in international journals and contributed to volumes on different issues related to the transition. He took part in research programmes on Eastern European Transition financed by the European Committee. He was visiting professor at the Universities of Lille and Paris and a Faculty member in the Salzburg Seminar on transition economies. He served as an independent expert in the First Privatization Programme of the Hungarian State Property Agency.

Branko Horvat was a partisan fighter during the Second World War. He was educated in Zagreb, Manchester, London, Harvard, and MIT in economics and other disciplines. He has received two doctorates. He has published some thirty books in economics, sociology and political science and about 300 articles, altogether translated into 13 languages. He has been a visiting professor in economics and political science at a dozen universities, including Paris, Stockholm, Cambridge, Michigan, Yale and Berkeley. He has been chief methodologist at the Federal Planning Bureau, founder and director of the Federal Research Institute, member of the Federal Economic Council, advisor to several governments, and is at present Professor Emeritus (Zagreb). He is founder and editor of *Economic Analysis*, and founder and honorary life President of the IAFES.

Michael Landesmann obtained his D.Phil. at the University of Oxford. For a number of years he was a Fellow of Girton and then of Jesus College, Cambridge, and also a Senior Research Officer at the Department of Applied Economics, University of Cambridge. At present he is Professor of Economics at the Johannes Kepler University in Linz, Austria, and a Research Associate of both the Department of Applied Economics, University of Cambridge and the Vienna Institute for International Economic Studies (WIIW). He is a member of the Board of Managing Editors of *Structural Change and Economic Dynamics* and an Associate Editor of the *Cambridge Journal of Economics*. His fields of interest are production theory and economic dynamics, industrial structural change and international economic relations.

Bart Los studied econometrics at the University of Groningen. He graduated in 1992 and worked as teaching and research assistant with the Econometrics Institute in Groningen afterwards. In 1994 he moved to the University of Twente (Department of Public Administration) to work on a Ph.D. thesis on economic structure and endogenous growth theory.

György Molnár is a senior research fellow at the Institute of Economics of the Hungarian Academy of Sciences, where he has been working since 1978. He has graduated in mathematics in 1977 at the Eötvös Loránd University, Budapest. His main research field is the study of structural changes in the Hungarian economy. From 1993 he has participated in the COST A7 action of the EC, 'The Role of Some Long Range Regulators in the Integration Process of the East-Central-European Countries Toward the Single European Market'.

Karen R. Polenske is Professor of Regional Political Economy and Planning in the Department of Urban Studies and Planning at the Massachusetts Institute of Technology. Prior to joining the MIT faculty in

1972, she taught in the Department of Economics at Harvard University. In the 1960s, Professor Polenske pioneered in the development of a US multiregional accounting framework comparable to the one used at the national level for the analysis of changes in the gross national product. Currently, Professor Polenske is conducting research on distributional implications of transformations in property rights, factors contributing to the fall of energy intensity in China, and socio-economic impact assessments of air-pollution rules and regulations. She is Vice-President of the International Input–Output Association. Her publications include six books, the latest of which is *Chinese Economic Planning and Input–Output Analysis* (co-edited with Chen XiKang), and numerous articles in key economic and planning journals.

Thijs ten Raa is Associate Professor of Economics at Tilburg University, the Netherlands. He has also taught at New York University and Erasmus University in Rotterdam. He is Associate Editor of two journals and has published numerous articles in economics journals. His book, *Linear Analysis of Competitive Economies*, has recently appeared.

Utz-Peter Reich is Professor of Economics and Statistics at Fachhochschule Mainz II. He previously worked as Research Officer with the German Federal Statistical Office. He took his first degree in physics from the University of Hamburg, and his second degree in political science from the University of Konstanz. Publications concern mainly national accounts and their relationship to economic theory.

Francis Seton is Emeritus Fellow of Nuffield College, Oxford. He has also taught at Osaka University, Japan, La Trobe University, Australia, Columbia University, the Wharton School of the University of Pennsylvania, and the University of the South in the United States on various leaves of absence from Nuffield College. He was economic consultant to the governments of Chile, Iran, and Indonesia and for the Human Rights Commission and Environment Programme of the United Nations, as well as for the European Commission of Statisticians of the EEC in Geneva. His books include *Shadow Wages in the Chilean Economy*, published for the OECD in 1972, and *Cost, Use, and Value*, with its second edition entitled *The Economics of Cost, Use, and Value* (1985 and 1992 respectively). He has published numerous articles and monographs on developmental issues, the theory of value, and social accounting.

András Simonovits is Professor of Economics at the Institute of Economics of the Hungarian Academy of Sciences in Budapest. He has been a visiting professor at various institutions. He has published about two dozen scientific papers in English on various topics of mathematical economics, such as linear models, decentralized control, macromodels of the socialist economies and priority queuing. His book *Cycles and Stagnation in Socialist Economies* was published in 1992. Lately he has been working on theoretical and practical issues of pension schemes and overlapping generations. He is a member of the editorial boards of *Structural Change and Economic Dynamics* and *Mathematical Social Sciences*. Since 1992 he has been the East European representative of the Winter Symposia of the Econometric Society.

Ian Steedman is Professor of Economics, Victoria University of Manchester. He has been a visiting professor or research fellow at Alicante, Carleton (Ottawa), Catania, Graz, ICER (Turin), Nice, Padova, Rome and SCASSS (Uppsala). He is the author of several books and many articles and has played an editorial role in the *Cambridge Journal of Economics*, *European Journal of the History of Economic Thought*, *Manchester School* and *Metroeconomica*.

Albert E. Steenge is Professor of Economics at the University of Twente, Enschede, the Netherlands. He studied econometrics at the University of Groningen, where he also received his Ph.D. on a thesis where stability issues in dynamic Leontief models were discussed in terms of Sraffian Standard commodities. He has published mainly in the areas of input–output models, environmental economics, distributional issues, and institutional economics. Since 1992 he has been on the Board of Managing Editors of *Structural Change* and *Economic Dynamics*.

Reiner Stäglin is researcher with the German Institute for Economic Research (DIW), Berlin and the leader of the institute's input-output group. He is also professor of Economic Statistics at the Free University of Berlin. He is currently President of the International Input–Output Association. He served as an advisor to the German Federal Agency for Technical Co-operation, the Statistical Office of the European Communities and Statistics Sweden, Cyprus, Tanzania and Tunisia for the last ten years. His research interest include structural analysis, national accounts, input–output tables and analysis as well as other statistical instruments in empirical research. He has published a number of books and many articles in leading academic journals. He has been member of the editorial board of *Economic Systems Research* since its founding in 1989.

Robert Stehrer is working as an Assistant at the University of Linz, Department of Economics. He has studied economics at the University of Linz and sociology and philosophy at the University of Vienna. After his graduation he worked at the Institute for Advanced Studies (IHS) in Vienna, where he completed a post-graduate course at the Department of Sociology. His special interests concern the consequences of technological progress and structural change, the modelling of long-term economic and social dynamics, and the application of complex models in economics.

Ernő Zalai is Professor of Economics, Chair of Mathematical Economics and Econometrics, Budapest University of Economic Sciences (BUES), Hungary. He graduated and received his Doctor's degree from BUES and also spent a year as postdoctoral fellow at CMU (Pittsburgh). He has been visiting professor at several American universities and researcher at IIASA (Laxenburg, Austria) on various leaves from BUES. He received his Doctor of Economic Sciences Degree from the Hungarian Academy of Sciences in 1990. He has published four books in Hungarian, *Fixed Points and Equilibria in Economic Models* (1978), *Eigenvalues and Labour Values* (1988), *Introduction into Mathematical Economics* (1989), *Input–Output Economics* (1991) and co-edited one in English, *General Equilibrium Modelling and Economic Policy Analysis* (with W. D. Jorgenson and L. Bergman, 1990) and published a number of papers in both languages.

Introduction

András Simonovits and Albert E. Steenge

When András (Andrew) Bródy's 70th birthday approached, in 1994, it was decided to use the occasion to publish a Festschrift honouring his contribution to economics in general and to input–output economics in particular. This eventually resulted in seventeen papers by renowned mathematical economists. Bródy's scientific career up to now spans almost four decades. Being a prolific writer, he has been working on many different fields. His main themes through the years have remained, however, the theory and practice of input–output analysis, Marxian economics, the measurement of economic change and growth, and the theory of cycles.

Initially, it was our intention to organize this volume into individual sections. This, however, proved to be quite difficult, and therefore we decided to apply only a limited organization. Below, we will try to briefly summarize the gist of the individual contributions. Due to a lack of space we are, however, unable to go into details, so that the influence of or relation to Bródy's work will not be discussed by us here. However, informed readers will certainly notice these connection points themselves.

In Chapter 1 (*Accounting for Duality and Circularity*) Mária Augusztinovics combines concepts and methods inherent to National Accounts, Input–Output Analysis and Social Accounting Matrices, to arrive at an integrated, yet novel way of capturing circularity beyond directly observable economic transactions. She defines a dual accounting system, after which she proceeds to construct four separate symmetrically designed open accounting models (production and income, each by composition and by allocation) on this basis. Choosing the models with their proper counterparts finally results in a single closed accounting model of circularity. The author does not discuss causality assumptions, since her objective is to describe circular flow irrespective of pull–push affects or driving forces.

In Chapter 2 (*Change as Economic Activity*), Anne Carter focuses on an increasingly important problem in input–output representations of economic development and growth. Though this problem is of a fundamental nature, it has been largely neglected so far. Traditionally economists have often concentrated on static equilibrium, while bypassing essentials such as convergence to that equilibrium, growth and change. In real life, however, change has of course always been an important factor, the importance of which is continually increasing due to rapid technological changes and shifting specializations. For example, employment trends in services and in the employment of non-production workers in manufacturing suggest that as much as half of all economic efforts may be focused on change. A major problem here is that the traditional sectoral 'proportions' may no longer represent the type of stable structure that we need to characterize the growth potential of most industrial economies. At the moment we do not yet fully understand the mechanisms that regulate change. Anne Carter tries to take a first step towards the formalization of such issues, by identifying relevant concepts and variables. A major factor is to distinguish between costs of production and costs of change, and also between the costs of change and the benefits of change itself.

In Chapter 3 (*Index Numbers and the Theory of Value*) Utz-Peter Reich poses an intriguing question about the established methodology of economics using the index number problem: It is obvious that the economy is changing, but how do we know that it is growing? To proceed, we need to return to the index number problem. Reich observes that economic science has not fulfilled the dreams of its founding fathers; it is still far from being a 'mechanism' with its own specific and invariable laws. This implies a need for reflection on the current state of affairs, as well as the removal of certain 'dogmas' which may actually hinder the further development of economics as a science. One such dogma is the established priority of the concepts of economic theory over those of statistical practice, which is reflected in the fact that theory often pays very little attention to measurement issues. One consequence of this is that the debate on whether the concepts and measurement assumptions of economic theory are 1) operational at all, and 2) are in line with the system of national accounts, has never been closed. So, following Reich, let us see whether we can start from the opposite direction, and explore how far we can go if we take the concepts of statistics as true and real, and those of theory as possibly false. (Interestingly, Laplace's determinism also has come under fire from another point of view discussed in Chapters 10 and 11, namely via the theory of chaos.)

In Chapter 4 (*Current Uses of the RAS Technique: A Critical Review*), Karen Polenske reviews one of the most popular methodologies for investigating the above issues, i.e. growth and change. She points out that economic analysts have based their use of the RAS procedure on a 'myth of accuracy'. As we know, the RAS procedure is a simple technique for extrapolating a matrix with given column and row totals and a given structure (the constrained bi-proportional matrix problem). This technique is increasingly being used as an alternative to non-survey techniques to adjust national or regional input–output tables, and to approximate trade flows and other types of economic data. An important reason for this is that practitioners more frequently than before lack the financial resources to cover the costs of collecting data or using other data sources. Analysts often justify the use of the RAS procedure by stating that in comparative tests with other adjustment procedures it produces the lowest 'errors'. The author critically reviews the literature dealing with this procedure, while focusing on whether or not errors in the results affect policy analysis. This chapter is concluded with a number of detailed recommendations for additional investigations.

In Chapter 5 (*Bi-regional Input–Output Proportions for Germany – First Results*), Reiner Stäglin goes into perhaps even more difficult issues regarding the measurement of change and the updating of old materials. He describes a historical event that is unique in the practical application of input–output tables, i.e. the fact that in October 1990 the former German Democratic Republic became part of the Federal Republic of Germany. In the new Germany the need for reliable statistics to monitor structural change in particularly the Eastern part of the country became immediately apparent. The unification process required a huge amount of consistent statistical information for both parts of the country. This material was produced in a number of steps. Here an important role was played by a bi-regional input–output table for 1991 compiled at the Germany Institute for Economic Research (DIW). This compilation process was a complicated one, because only a limited amount of data for the New Federal States were available, and these data were often of uncertain quality. Despite the fact that much remained to be improved, the first bi-regional table has already proved very useful in a number of respects.

In Chapter 6 (*Analyzing Decomposition Analyses*), Erik Dietzenbacher and Bart Los discuss a frequent problem in the measurement of change in economic structure: How should we decompose a change between two points in time in one variable – whether a scalar, a vector or a matrix – into changes in the corresponding determinants? In the case of continuous time, this decomposition is unique: $d(uv) = (du)v + u(dv)$. However, in practice we have discrete time data where a third term enters, i.e. $dudv$. In addition, as the number of determinants increases, the number of alternative decomposition formulae also increases. The authors examine how the choice of the specific decomposition formula affects the results. Their main finding is that at a detailed level results may vary widely between the various decomposition formulae. This variation increases when the period between the two points in time is expanded. At the aggregate level, the results show only little variation between the methods, a finding that seems to be independent of the length of the time period.

In much of his work Bródy expressed severe dissatisfaction with the narrow interpretation of production and consumption used in the present national accounting systems. The problem is that one of the most important variables which is used to determine national welfare, i.e. human capital, is generally lacking. In other words, among the range of economic activities included in the systems, the most important one is probably missing. And therefore the grand national totals, such as national product and national income, give only a very limited picture instead of representing the full range of economic activities. This severely hampers our understanding of processes of growth, development or convergence.

In Chapter 7 (*Measuring the Productivity of Nations*), Pirkko Aulin-Ahmavaara introduces a framework for measuring the productivity of nations based on extended production concepts. The model she uses is a dynamic input–output model in which the production of human capital is accounted for. To this end, the production processes of heterogeneous human capital and active human time are separated. As a result the efficiency of producing human capital and active human time can also be considered separately. The author proposes using the rate of change in the balanced growth rate as the summary measure of change in total factor productivity, while using the rate of change in the production price as the corresponding sectoral measure.

In Chapter 8 (*Equilibrium and Disequilibrium in a Disaggregated Classical Model*), further issues of stability are discussed including norming aspects. László Halpern and György Molnár combine Bródy's closed dynamic input–output model and Duménil and Lévy's classical model. Duménil and Lévy examined the stability of the economy controlled by norms. Using Bródy's model, Halpern and Molnár generalized the Duménil and Lévy model from three special sectors to *n* general sectors, and discovered thereby a control mechanism which persistently keeps the economy below the equilibrium path with higher growth rates. This theoretical construction reflects particularities of the Hungarian economy, which even after pro-market economic reforms has remained a centrally regulated economy.

In Chapter 9 (*Structural Economic Dynamics: Catching-Up and the Global Deflationary Bias*), Richard Goodwin, Michael Landesmann and Robert Stehrer discuss the relation between uneven technological change in different sectors and macroeconomic stability in open economies. Two types of economies are distinguished: economies that are techologically advanced and economies that are catching-up. The authors investigate whether the emergence of 'technological rents' can give rise to fluctuations in income distribution which would hamper demand in certain sectors. Trade-offs are found between the speed of structural change on the one hand, and various mechanisms which counteract the risk of an effective demand constraint on the other hand. Both types of economies are faced with a number of options, with consequences for employment levels and domestic demand.

The next two chapters further explore the issues of growth and control within a non-linear framework. In linear dynamic systems, if one doubles the inputs, the outputs are also doubled: two tons of steel require twice as much coke as does one ton of steel. This is not the case in non-linear dynamic systems. To simplify analysis, researchers have often concentrated on linear systems, but during the last two decades this approach has been increasingly called into question.

In Chapter 10 (*Complex Dynamics in Control Models with Bounds: A Review*) András Simonovits reviews a special type of dynamic systems first developed by Hicks. He starts out from a linear control system with state space equations and feedback rules, but truncates the decisions by appropriate lower and upper bounds. The new system is partly linear, i.e. it is in fact a non-linear one, but its analysis is sometimes less complicated than in the case of a fully non-linear system. The main mathematical issues he mentions are: (i) Does local stability imply global stability? and, (ii) Is there a stable equilibrium, a limit cycle or chaos? He then proceeds to examine six different economic models individually. In some of the models local stability implies global stability, while in others this is not the case; models of the latter type are called 'destabilizable economies'. Another distinction is between certain models in which the non-linear dynamics remains simple (stable equilibrium, limit cyle), and others in which chaos occurs.

In Chapter 11 (*Proportions, Growth and Cycles between Constant and Non-Constant Returns to Scale*), Maurizio Ciaschini replaces the traditional assumption of constant returns by that of non-constant returns to scale in the use of intermediate goods. While in a linear dynamic input–output model, instability implies non-viability (such as eventual negativity of certain variables), in a non-linear model viability and instability can coexist. The explanation is simple: apart from the (highly improbable) linear cycles, in linear models instability means an exponential explosion. In non-linear models such an explosion may be easily excluded, but instability may result in limit cycles or chaotic motion. The emerging chaotic paths play a theoretically important role in modern dynamic systems.

In Chapter 12 (*Bródy's Capital*), Thijs ten Raa discusses the structure of the dynamic model itself. He 'carries out a suggestion by Bródy' to dispense with the distinction between flows and stocks in dynamic input–output by modelling the time profiles of the input and output components of the structure of an economy. In the proposed model, activities are distributed input–distributed output, while the lags accommodate capital and depreciation. The traditional dynamic input–output model is retrieved when depreciation is exponential, production is instantaneous, and the flow and stock input coefficient matrices fulfil a well-known capital equation introduced by Bródy.

In the preceding chapters the concept of norms and bounds was introduced. However, norms – or rather, normative aspects – can also be derived for completely different areas of input–output theory. Examples of this are found in the next two chapters.

In Chapter 13 (*Towards a Tenable Concept of 'Warranted Supply'*), Francis Seton raises the question whether certain normative arguments can be derived from the traditional Leontief input–output structure. That is, he asks whether the system allows for the evaluation of a central structure such as Gross National Product (GNP) in terms of its relevance to the enhancement of general welfare, for which it should basically be produced in the first place. For such an analysis, criteria are invariably derived from some welfare function exogenous to the system. So, would it be possible to derive criteria from intrinsic features of the system, making it possible to prefer one final bill of goods to another one and thus enabling a 'screening' of GNP for adequacy in terms of its welfare-generating potential? In the words of the author: 'As may be expected, the adopted criterion has more of the characteristics of an equilibrium than of an optimum, albeit of an equilibrium defined by essental features of the prevailing paradigm reflecting an optimum.'

In Chapter 14 (*The Elusive Standard Commodity: Eigenvectors as Standards of Value*) by Albert Steenge, we again find normative elements. Sraffian analysts, in order to clarify income distribution mechanisms, prescribe using the so-called Standard commodity, an eigenvector of very specific proportions, as a standard of value. That being so, the question is how to proceed in actually modelling such statements. Here, many opinions are found in the literature, none of which is quite convincing. In this chapter, Albert Steenge aims to integrate Sraffian analysis with standard input–output analysis. Focusing on the famous Standard commodity, he proposes a quite different methodology to capture the Sraffian spirit. Starting from a closed, static Leontief system (with Perron–Frobenius eigenvalue equal to unity) he shows that its corresponding eigenvector, if properly standardized, can straightforwardly be interpreted as a standard of value. For the general case of the open static model a transformation is shown to exist which yields the same effect. Essential here is that the system can be written in a specific closed form.

The next three chapters deal with issues concerning the labour theory of value in combination with joint production. In Chapter 15 (*Joint Production in a Two-Sector Model*), Branko Horvat reconsiders this famous issue, which was largely neglected in input–output analysis (although much emphasized in von Neumann models). Using his own pure labour theory of prices and interest, the author is able to strip input–output analysis of its usual complexities, keeping the analysis simple by restricting it to two sectors (consumer and producer goods). Transparency remains intact when fixed capital and an expanding economy are considered.

In Chapter 16 (*Price Scheme Cones*), Ian Steedman generalizes the famous non-substitution theorem. As is well known, this theorem plays only a minor role in linear input–output models, in determining the equilibrium price vector. The author considers a joint production system with k commodities, n production processes, many kinds of labour and a uniform rate of profit. His main result is as follows: if the rank of the labour input matrix is (n–2), then there exists an Euclidean cone, defined entirely by the technical conditions such that the vector of relative prices always lies on that cone, whatever the rate of profit and the vector of wages. The role of the distribution is merely that of determining where on the 'technological cone' the price vector will lie.' Further theories are presented on matrices with lower ranks.

In Chapter 17 (*Production Prices and Proportions Revisited*), Ernő Zalai reconsiders Bródy's closed dynamic input–output model. Bródy augmented the flow and stock matrices by two pairs of row and column vectors, representing the household sector's labor and consumption vectors. However, in doing so he did not take into account the particularity of the household sector in that it does not produce any profits. Zalai proposes two solutions to this problem: (i) either to allow reducible (augmented) matrices or (ii) to condense the household sector to the proper industries. Both solutions are helpful in extending Bródy's results on equilibrium prices and volume vectors.

We feel that the contributions outlined above reflect the importance of Bródy's work, as well as giving an impression of latest developments in fields Bródy is and has been working on. We hope that the reader will enjoy this book as much as we enjoyed working on it.

Budapest and Enschede

A Biography of András Bródy

András (Andrew) Bródy was born in Budapest in 1924. After the turbulent years of fascism and Stalinism he entered the Institute of Economics, Hungarian Academy of Sciences, in 1955, where he had a long career and is now working as an emeritus Research Professor.

Bródy's special field is mathematical economics, particularly theories of economic growth and cycles. He is well known as a specialist on von Neumann's growth and price model, on cycle and chaos theory and on input–output analysis. In his first book, *Input–Output Models*, which was published in Hungarian in 1964, Bródy dealt with the limits and precision of input–output analysis. Applying the same framework, in *Prices, Proportions and Planning* he gave a mathematical form to the labour theory of value. This book, his *magnum opus*, was originally published in Hungarian. The English translation appeared in 1970; several editions followed, including translations into German and Polish. Bródy continued research in this field in his third book, *Cycle and Regulation*, published in Hungarian in 1980. His fourth book, *Slowdown* (originally published in Hungarian) appeared in English and Polish translations in 1985.

In addition, Andrew Bródy published several dozen papers, in several languages. He occupies the second or third place among Hungarian economists as far as the number of citations from his work are concerned. He belongs to that rare breed of Eastern European mathematical economists who in their work were and are capable of combining relevance and sophistication: in his work Bródy forges a connection between internationally developed methodology and application to real world problems in Hungary, Eastern Europe and the rest of the world.

He took part in organizing several conferences on input–output analysis, and edited some of the Proceedings. From 1989 (the year in which it was founded) to 1993 he was Editor of *Economic Systems Research*, the quarterly journal of the International Input–Output Society. He also contributed to the new Palgrave Economics Dictionary. Since the 1960s he has been an Elected Fellow of the Econometric Society.

In his own Institute Bródy organized a great many seminars, workshops, and other meetings. He also gave various courses to students at the Budapest University of Economics (which during the socialist era was called the 'Karl Marx University of Economics'). Several generations of Hungarian mathematical economists have benefited from his teachings, and have collaborated with him. He has often been invited to international institutes and universities, ranging from Zambia to the United States, for research and teaching. As this volume will show, he has been a major influence on many non-Hungarian economists as well.

Above we described the various aspects of Andrew Bródy's life as a scientist. In the following we would also like to mention some of his features as a person.

Both of us have known him for a long time. Albert Steenge met Andrew for the first time in 1979, at an input–output conference in Innsbruck, Austria and for a second time at a conference in Héviz, Hungary. It was Andrew who invited him to visit the Institute of Economics in Budapest, for a period of about six months, during the years 1982 and 1983. Here many of his views on topics such as Sraffa's famous 'Standard commodity' and Francis Seton's eigenprices-concept were discussed and further developed. András Simonovits was introduced to Andrew in 1965. András wrote his first scientific paper, as well as his most quoted one, under Andrew's supervision. In those early years, Andrew helped András to visit conferences held abroad.

Everybody who knows Andrew is impressed by his cordiality. Although he is a man of strong opinions, he is always ready to listen and accept other points of view, and ready to help others disseminate their ideas.

In our busy age, many economists do not manage to do much besides writing reports, papers and books on economics, in addition to teaching and consulting. Although Andrew's scientific production is impressive (and his younger son is following this tradition), he has never neglected other activities. His witty Hungarian style has made him a well-known publicist in Hungary. His knowledge of literature is also reflected in his near-perfect knowledge of English, although he was already in his forties when he first got the opportunity to visit Britain and the United States. Let us also not forget that he loves to play the piano and is an avid skier. (No wonder that one of his elder sons is a famous pop star, who writes, composes and sings his Hungarian chansons.)

Although Andrew has already passed the age of 70, he still seems young. Contrary to many Hungarians, both young and old, he rarely looks back at the past; he is as interested in current political developments as in the latest software.

We wish him an eventful and joyful future.

Budapest and Enschede

ANDRÁS SIMONOVITS
ALBERT STEENGE

Publications of András Bródy in English

1. 'The Unicity of the Prices of Production and of the Average Rate of Profit', *Input–Output Tables: Their Compilation and Use*. Scientific Conference on Statistical Problems, Budapest, 1–5 June 1961, Branch A. Budapest: Akadémia, 1962, pp. 243–9.
2. 'Three Types of Price Systems', *Economics of Planning 1* (1965) pp. 58–66.
3. 'The Model of Expanding Reproduction', *Colloquium on Applications of Mathematics to Economics*. Budapest, 1963. Budapest: Akadémia, 1965, pp. 61–3.
4. 'A Simplified Growth Model', *The Quarterly Journal Economics 1* (1966), pp. 137–46.
5. 'On Linear Models of the Economy', *Acta Oeconomica* 2 (1967), pp. 171–88.
6. 'Dual Concepts of the Economy in Marx's *Capital*', *Acta Oeconomica* 2 (1967), pp. 309–25.
7. 'Methods of Analysis and Forecasting Applied in Hungary', *Acta Oeconomica 4* (1969), pp. 299–314.
8. 'The Rate of Economic Growth in Hungary, 1924–1965', *Is the business cycle obsolete?* (ed. M. Bronfenbrenner). New York: Wiley, 1969, pp. 312–27.
10. *Proportions, Prices and Planning: A Mathematical Restatement of the Labor Theory of Value*, Budapest–Amsterdam: Akadémia–North-Holland, 1970, 194 pages. (Reprinted in 1974 with North-Holland)
11. 'The Logic of Market Behaviour', *Acta Oeconomica 14* (1975), pp. 49–58.
12. 'Marx after Steedman', *Acta Oeconomica 19* (1977), pp. 219–22.
13. 'Planning and Planning: Some Comments on Professor Wassily Leontief's Proposals', *Acta Oeconomica 20* (1978), pp. 179–81.
14. 'A Linearised Model of the Cycles', *Acta Oeconomica 21* (1978), pp. 261–7.
15. 'On Measuring Growth', *Acta Oeconomica 24* (1980), pp. 47–56.
16. 'On the Discussion about Measurement – A Rejoinder', *Acta Oeconomica 25* (1980), pp. 191–8.

17. 'An Economy Controlled by Stocks and Profits', *Non-Price Control* (eds J. Kornai and B. Martos), Budapest–Amsterdam: Akadémia–North-Holland, 1981, pp. 141–61.
18. 'About Investment Cycles and Their Attenuation', *Acta Oeconomica 31* (1983), pp. 37–51.
19. 'Three Waves of Criticism of the Economic Mechanism', *The New Hungarian Quarterly 25* (1984), pp. 132–6.
20. *Slowdown: Global Economic Maladies*, Beverly Hills, California: Sage, 1985, 160 pages.
21. 'Growth, Cycles, Crisis', *IDS Bulletin 16* (1985), pp. 31–5.
22. 'An Essay in Macroeconomics', *Acta Oeconomica 35* (1985), pp. 337–43. Co-authors: K. Martinás and K. Sajó.
23. 'Why Can't We Catch Up', *The Hungarian Observer 1* (1988), pp. 38–9.
24. 'Forms of Economic Motion', *Acta Oeconomica 38* (1987) 361–70. Co-author: M. Farkas.
25. 'Prices and Quantities', *The New Palgrave*, London: Macmillan, 1987, pp. 957–60.
26. 'Defense Spending as a Priority', *Peace, Defense and Economic Analysis* (eds Chr. Schmidt and F. Blackaby), London: Macmillan, 1987, pp. 40–4.
27. 'Physical (Phenomenological) Economics?: A Semi-Centennial for J. von Neumann and W. Leontief', Acta Oeconomica 41 (1989), pp. 257–66.
28. 'Economics and Thermodynamics', *John von Neumann and Modern Economics* (eds M. Dore, S. Chakravarty and R. Goodwin), Oxford: Clarendon, 1989, pp. 227–44.
29. 'Growth Cycles in Economics', *Newton to Aristotle. Towards a Theory of Models for Living Systems*, New York: Springer-Verlag (eds J. Casti and A. Karlqvist), 1989, pp. 227–44 (Hungarian original, 1980)
30. 'About Production Lags', *Economic Systems Research 2* (1990), pp. 322–5.
31. 'Prices and Quantities', *Problems of the Planned Economy* (eds J. Eatwell, M. Milgate and P. Newman), London: Macmillan, 1990, pp. 218–26.
32. 'Observations Concerning the Growth Cycle', *Nonlinear and Multisectoral Macrodynamics: Essays in Honour of Richard Goodwin* (ed. K. Velupillai), London: Macmillan, 1990, pp. 90–5.
33. 'Defense of the Realm', *Acta Oeconomica 43* (1991), pp. 167–76.
34. 'On Measuring Growth', *Structural Change and Economic Dynamics 3* (1992), pp. 93–102.

35. 'Gestation Lags and the Explanation of Socialist Investment Cycles', *Cyclical Growth in Market and Planned Economies*, (ed. C. Hillinger), Oxford: Clarendon, 1992 (German manuscript 1972).
36. 'The Trap of Monetary Equilibrium', *Economic Systems Research 5* (1993), pp. 225–34.
37. 'Money-Flow Computations', *Economic Systems Research 5* (1993), pp. 225–34. Co-author: W. Leontief.
38. 'Old Hungarian prints, or: Does the 200-Year Cycle Exist?', *Acta Oeconomica 46* (1994), pp. 163–81.
39. 'An Essay in Macroeconomics, the Use of Thermodynamic Models in Economics', *Economics and Thermodynamics* (eds Burley and Foster), Boston: Kluwer, 1994, pp. 9–22.
40. 'The Hungarian GDP, as Measured by Proxies (Appraisal of the Short-Cut Method of F. Jánossy', *Acta Oeconomica 47* (1995), pp. 69–94.
41. 'Truncation and Spectrum of the Dynamic Inverse', *Economic Systems Research 7* (1995), pp. 235–47.

1 Accounting for Duality and Circularity

Mária Augusztinovics

'Pooh and Piglet Go Hunting and Nearly Catch a Woozle. It is either Two Woozles and one, as it might be, Wizzle or Two as it might be Wizzles and one, if so it is, Woozle. Let us continue to follow them.' (A. A. Milne, 1957)

BACKGROUND

Double-entry bookkeeping has been one of the most ingenious inventions in economic history. It enabled merchants of the Middle Ages to account for negative balance at a time when negative numbers where not yet known and, more importantly, it grasped the inherent *duality* in economic processes. Most economists despise double-entry bookkeeping and some of them can not even tell the credit-side from the debit-side of a T-account.

Introducing this technique into macroeconomics has thus been a no less ingenious and brave innovation responding to the needs of its own time (Stone and Croft-Murray, 1959). Today we have National Accounts in long time series in practically every country. The reliability of SNA-based intertemporal and international comparisons has often been questioned, but there is nothing better in sight. SNA (in the United States NIPA) has become an institution itself and, like all institutions, has a tendency to resist new concepts and methods.

The pioneering idea of Input–Output (I–O) was set forth much earlier (Leontief, 1936) but it began to spread and flourish in parallel with National Accounts, after World War II. (For a concise history, see Rose and Miernyk, 1989.) Despite the evident mutual relevance, inter-industry accounting has remained alien for SNA. Even in countries where input–output tables are regulary provided, these are usually prepared by a separate agency or by a separate department of the same agency, with the result that the tables are rarely reconciled with the 'traditional' national income accounts.

One of the reasons might have been that I–O techniques are based on matrix calculus rather than on T-accounts. It did not take long, however, for people inspired exactly by the potentials of I–O analysis, to realize that the double-entry National Account system can be easily identified with and expressed by a single-entry square matrix. Thereby a third school of empirically minded macroeconomic thinking branched off, resulting in a stream of Social Accounting Matrices. (For fundamentals, see Pyatt, 1991.) Despite its direct SNA ancestry, SAM has never been accepted, certainly not provided by official National Accounts. One of the reasons might have been that SAM seems to neglect the Gross National Product, this fundamental category of SNA, at least does not explicitly account for it.

Input–Output and SAM go beyond accounting. They both strive to attain the cherished goal of macroeconomics since Quesnay, to capture the *circular flow*. There are overlaps and similarities, nevertheless differences in subject matter and method remain. Despite several pleas for cooperation, we have now two, or rather three, separate 'communities' of I–O, SAM and SNA practitioners.

With respect to *subject matter*, I–O has traditionally focused on production, with final demand and value added as open ends. The 'missing fourth quadrant' was a popular topic in the sixties and several interesting ways of closing the system were proposed. Yet, open or closed, this has still remained a model of the production process. Extensions concerning income distribution, human capital and related topics came later, as afterthoughts. (For example, Miyazawa, 1976; Aulin-Ahmavaara, 1991.)

SAM has traditionally focused on income and consumption, the income–expenditure linkage, sectors (more often called institutions), particularly households. Including detailed blocks of interindustry relations, reconciling the sources of income with their origin in production, stretching the analysis to the production process came later, as afterthoughts. (For example, Roland-Holst, 1990.)

Afterthoughts, however, resulted in some loss of conceptual clarity on both sides. The terms 'output' and 'input' are sufficiently versatile to cover everything yet households remain very different from, say, metallurgy. In SAM the original key concept is income. The sales receipts of industries, however, represent market transactions, the exchange of different forms of the same value, hence not income. Purchasing iron ore is different from buying a dinner and neither is the same as paying taxes, although all three are 'outlays'. If there exists a unique substance at all, the flows of which are accounted for in SAM, then it is money rather than income.

The trouble is that over-generalized terms are convenient but they might become meaningless when applied to economically different concepts within the same model.

With respect to *method*, there are two ways of capturing circularity in a linear model. One is to invert a matrix but then the matrix must not be singular, implying that it does not incorporate the entire system. The other way is to consider an overall, singular matrix and its eigenvector(s) but then the matrix must reflect compound, indirect relationships else it could not account for circularity.

With a non-singular matrix parts of the entire system must be designated as endogenous or exogenous. This comes rather naturally in I–O that is admittedly open, and remains conceptually open even if the inverse is then applied in complex matrix-products that include various partitions, added step-by-step in the process of extending the model.

The stochastic coefficient matrix calculated from the SAM transaction table is singular but it records direct links among sectors rather than indirect, circular relations. Hence SAM analysis must fall back on breaking up the system, 'injections' and 'leakages' must be introduced, so that the internal core could be inverted (Pyatt and Round, 1979). This appears to be somewhat artificial and arbitrary in SAM that claims to be closed, all-embracing. Once this has been done, however, decomposition (additive or multiplicative) of the inverse leads to economically meaningful blocks and matrix-products that can be interpreted, even compared with more-or-less corresponding I–O blocks.

From here the two methods seem to converge. One could say that I–O has been evolving from the interior toward the outside, building more and more annexes around the original, modest inverse, while SAM is proceeding inwardly, breaking down the original, huge complex into more habitable parts. Obviously, if one stretched an I–O model and reduced a SAM model to exactly identical frontiers between endogenous and exogenous, then the multipliers would be conceptually and numerically identical. So, after all, the difference in method does not seem to be crucial, it goes back to the difference in subject matter.

The present paper attempts to build on wisdom inherited from all three branches of the field. Direct links with SNA will be maintained by keeping the concept of GDP intact and explicit. The I–O spirit will be evident in the formulation of the accounting framework and the models derived from it. SAM goals will be achieved by detailed accounting for the sources, redistribution and final expenditure of income. With respect to subject matter, our accounting should be balanced and symmetric, avoiding any particular focus on either production or income. With respect to method, we shall end up combining the advantages of open and closed systems, non-singular and singular matrices.

THE ACCOUNTING FRAMEWORK

Our framework consists of a production and an income system, first presented separately, then jointly. The transaction tables are demonstrated in Window 1.1 to which we shall refer throughout this section.

The *production system* is represented by the standard inter-industry table, expressed in value terms at current prices. Comments do not seem to be necessary. The *income system*, however, is somewhat different from the standard SAM transaction table, although it covers much of the same ground.

1. Sales and purchases by industries are not included. Such money flows may be visualized as reverse streams flowing against commodities along the rows (sales) and columns (purchases) in the production system.
2. The single square SAM matrix is replaced here by three, adjoining but separate matrices, analogously to the production system. The primary income matrix $\mathbf{H_I}$ allocates value added categories (rows) to sectors (columns). The transfer matrix $\mathbf{T}$, the square core of the system, records income redistribution among sectors, generating secondary incomes. After the redistribution process, each sector is left with its final income (expenditure) to be allocated to various final uses, the latter represented by columns in the $\mathbf{Y_I}$ matrix.
3. Less important, but to avoid confusion it should be noted that the income system is transposed with respect to the usual SAM presentation. Sectors receive income down the column and spend it along the rows.

Final product (income) and primary input (income) are endogenous parts of the entire production (income) system, they are merely outside of the square core that represents inter-industry or intersectoral transactions. The $\mathbf{H_P}$, $\mathbf{Y_P}$, $\mathbf{H_I}$ and $\mathbf{Y_I}$ matrixes will be referred to as *external flows*, indicating that (1) their common property is being distinguished from the square cores, they are the open-ended parts of the respective system and (2) they are expressed in value terms, they record the level of flows, as to be later distinguished from coefficients that reflect relative shares.

The column totals of $\mathbf{Y_P}$ and $\mathbf{Y_I}$ are explicitly defined in vector f by categories or *types of final use*, e.g. private and government consumption, gross capital formation, etc. Similarly, the row totals or $\mathbf{H_P}$ and $\mathbf{H_I}$ are explicitly recorded in vector v by *types of value added*, e.g. depreciation, wages, indirect taxes, etc.

The *joint system* is more than the two systems taken together, it requires them to be consistent. Accounting identities I1 and I2 are trivial (although in statistical practice not always observed) requirements for the two separate systems. By I3 the classification of value added types as well as that of final

Window 1.1

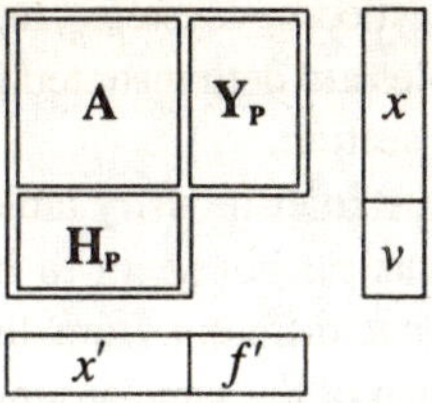

The Production System

x total output by industries

A secondary input matrix

$\mathbf{Y_P}$ final product by industry and type

$y_P = Y_P u$ final product by industry

$\mathbf{H_P}$ primary input by type and industry

$h'_p = u'\mathbf{H_P}$ primary input by industry

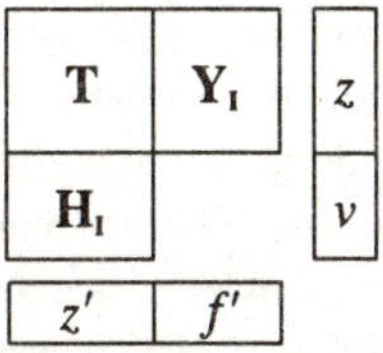

The Income System

z total income by sectors

T secondary income (transfers)

$\mathbf{Y_I}$ final income by sector and type

$y_I = \mathbf{Y_I}u$ final income by sector

$\mathbf{H_I}$ primary income by type and sector

$h'_1 = u'\mathbf{H_I}$ primary income by sectors

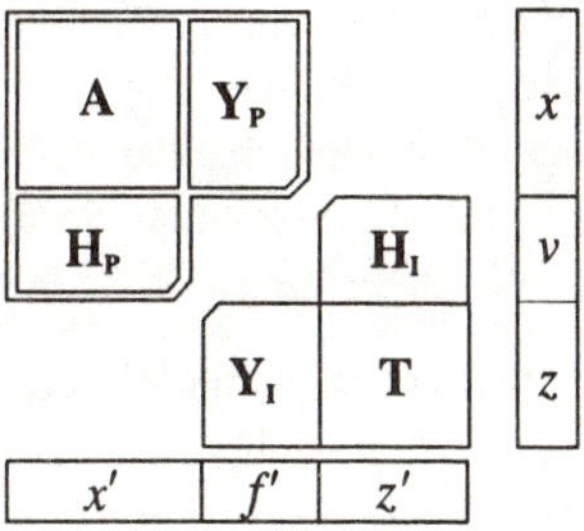

The Joint System

f final use by type

v value added by type

Accounting identities:

$$\mathbf{A}u+\mathbf{Y_P}u=x \quad u'\mathbf{A}+u'\mathbf{H_P}=x' \qquad \text{(I1)}$$

$$\mathbf{T}u+\mathbf{Y_I}u=z \quad u'\mathbf{T}+u'\mathbf{H_I}=z' \qquad \text{(I2)}$$

$$\mathbf{H_P}u=\mathbf{H_I}u=v \quad u'\mathbf{Y_P}=u'\mathbf{Y_I}=f' \qquad \text{(I3)}$$

$$u'v=u'f=\text{GDP} \qquad \text{(I4)}$$

$$u=[1,1,..,1]'$$

The income system is rearranged but not altered in the joint system.

use categories must be identical in the two systems. Moreover, numbers must check, so that vectors v and f provide the links for feasible transition from one system to the other.

Final use vector f is conceptually identical with what SNA practitioners call Expenditure on the GDP, value added vector v is conceptually identical with Cost Components of the GDP, the first two tables in every standard National Accounts yearbook. I4 simply requires that conceptual identity should be implemented numerically.

GDP is not identical with, only a proxy for the *net annual value product of the society* since it includes (1) depreciation, a value component generated by earlier accumulation and (2) indirect taxes less subsidies, not considered factor income because economic theory refuses to recognize the state as a factor of production. Nevertheless, it is a proxy suitable for our purpose. Despite of being called 'gross' (with respect to national income), GDP on the other hand is *net* with respect to total output and total income. It is outside of the square core of both systems, it is the common substance of all four external flow matrices that provide four relevant decompositions of it.

The GDP concept has often been criticized for being narrow, ignoring household production, value added generated by government institutions, investment into human capital, etc. and various proposals for extension have been submitted. (For example, Eisner, 1989.) It should be observed, therefore, that the structure of our accounting framework is not tied to the current definition. Whatever will ever be admitted by SNA as productive activity will find its place in the production system and the accounting identities will hold. Neither is the logic of the framework dependent on actual ways of handling intricate matters concerning the income system, e.g. income gained by the issuance of money, capital transactions with the rest of the world, etc. We simply assume that both systems are technically complete in the sense that they satisfy the accounting identities.

The joint system accounts for the *dual nature* of economic processes, it describes all categories by *origin* as well as by *destination*. With respect to products, there is a deeper interpretation of this duality. Destination (rows) can be associated with the physical properties, the *use value* of the product since this is why users buy it. Origin (in columns) is related to the cost composition of *value*, the basis of price formation (Bródy, 1970). With respect to income, a similarly deep, theoretical interpretation is not available, but where the income of various sectors comes from and goes to tells in itself an important (maybe the most important) story about the structure of a society.

It is important to note that these systems are *not models*. No assumptions have been implied apart from the trivial ones inherent in economics, namely that economic processes are observeable and measurable. Here we only have a systematically arranged, consistent set of data that describes *direct links* among the various accounting units. For the very same reason, while duality is accounted for, *circularity* cannot be treated by the accounting framework itself since circular interdependencies are *indirect*, mediated by long, invisible sequences of successive direct links.

LINEAR ACCOUNTING MODELS

To capture circularity we have to connect destination with origin. The only way to do this is to attribute the *average* pattern of origin (destination) to each and every item of destination (origin), in other words to assume that the accounting units are homogenous.

For the purposes of this paper an *accounting model* is defined as a model that (1) imposes all relevant *accounting identities*, (2) adds only a single assumption to the trivial ones, that of *homogeneity* and (3) returns the *level* in value terms of the complex flows imputed through circular interdependencies. By definition, thus, an accounting model does not seek to reveal causality, it does not say anything on what is cause and what is effect, what is driven, pulled or pushed by what. It simply describes the results of mutual dependencies beyond the directly observeable transactions.

In Window 1.2 we introduce accounting production and income models, based on the respective accounting systems. The average pattern of origin is represented by backward pointing *composition* coefficients, to be attributed to each item of destination. The pattern of destination is reflected by forward pointing *allocation* coefficients, to be applied to items of origin. In our case – corresponding to the arrangement of matrices in the accounting framework – composition coefficients are column-normalized, allocation coefficients are row-normalized. Models on the left (right) side of Window 1.2 are based on composition (allocation) coefficients, respectively.[1]

The composition production model is the standard, open static input–output model. Its allocation counterpart, introduced some time ago (Ghosh, 1958; Augusztinovics, 1970), has also become fairly well known recently as the accounting core of the so-called supply-driven I–O models. Coefficients and the Q_P multipliers (Leontief inverses) are defined by D1–D4. The resulting equations in (1) derive total output from final product or primary input.

The income models are intentionally designed in complete formal analogy with the production models. The composition model traces final incomes back to the primary ones, the allocation model follows the route of primary incomes toward the final ones, both through the Q_I multipliers that represent circular relationships among sectors in the process of redistribution. D5–D8 provide the necessary definitions and total income is derived from final or primary income in (4).

Equations (2) and (5) provide three equivalent forms of the vector that does not figure in the derivation of the totals. The leftmost one follows directly from the definitions. The next one is obtained by substituting (1) and (4), respectively, into this direct form. The substitution yields four matrix-products, denoted by L, to be called *loops*. The rightmost form translates the vector into the row (column) totals of a common (for composition and allocation) nucleus expressed in value terms, $\mathbf{L_P}$ for the production model in (3) and $\mathbf{L_I}$ for the income model in (6), called *level-loops* for brevity.

The loops compress all three matrices of the respective model into one. They provide the mapping from value added types v to final use categories f, or reversely, through the Q multipliers. By their dimensions, all loop-matrices fit into the 'missing quadrant' of the respective system.

Composition $\check{L}_P$ and $\check{L}_I$ run backwards, they derive primary v from final f. Allocation $\bar{L}_P$ and $\bar{L}_I$ proceed forwards, obtaining final f from primary v. Irrespective of the direction, however, in the background there exists the

Window 1.2

Composition Coefficients — *Allocation Coefficients*

Production models

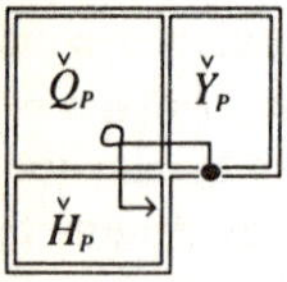

$$\check{A} = \mathbf{A}\langle x\rangle^{-1} \quad \check{Q}_P = (U - \check{A})^{-1} \quad \check{Y}_P = \mathbf{Y_P}\langle f\rangle^{-1} \quad \check{H}_P = \mathbf{H_P}\langle x\rangle^{-1}$$

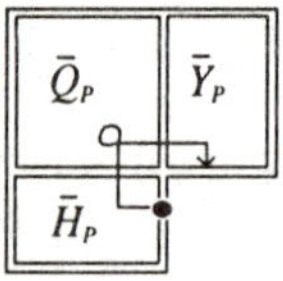

$$\bar{A} = \langle x\rangle^{-1}\mathbf{A} \quad \text{(D1)}$$
$$\bar{Q}_P = (U - \bar{A})^{-1} \quad \text{(D2)}$$
$$\bar{Y}_P = \langle x\rangle^{-1}\mathbf{Y_P} \quad \text{(D3)}$$
$$\bar{H}_P = \langle v\rangle^{-1}\mathbf{H_P} \quad \text{(D4)}$$

$$x = \check{A}x + y_P = \check{Q}_P y_P = \check{Q}_P \check{Y}_P f \qquad x' = x'\bar{A} + h_P' = h_P'\bar{Q}_P = v'\bar{H}_P\bar{Q}_P \quad (1)$$

$$v = \check{H}_P x = \underbrace{\check{H}_P\check{Q}_P\check{Y}_P}_{\check{L}_P} f = \mathbf{L_P} u \qquad f' = x'\bar{Y}_P = v'\underbrace{\bar{H}_P\bar{Q}_P\bar{Y}_P}_{\bar{L}_P} = u'\mathbf{L_P} \quad (2)$$

$$\mathbf{L_P} = \check{L}_P\langle f\rangle = \langle v\rangle\bar{L}_P = \mathbf{H_P}\bar{Q}_P\bar{Y}_P = \check{H}_P\check{Q}_P\mathbf{Y_P} \quad (3)$$

Income models

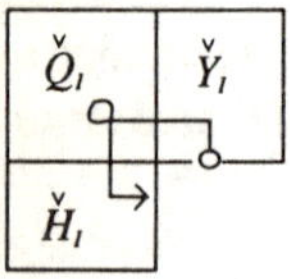

$$\check{T} = \mathbf{T}\langle z\rangle^{-1} \quad \check{Q}_I = (U - \check{T})^{-1} \quad \check{Y}_I = \mathbf{Y_I}\langle f\rangle^{-1} \quad \check{H}_I = \mathbf{H_I}\langle z\rangle^{-1}$$

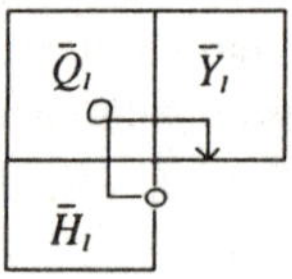

$$\bar{T} = \langle z\rangle^{-1}\mathbf{T} \quad \text{(D5)}$$
$$\bar{Q}_I = (U - \bar{T})^{-1} \quad \text{(D6)}$$
$$\bar{Y}_I = \langle z\rangle^{-1}\mathbf{Y_I} \quad \text{(D7)}$$
$$\bar{H}_I = \langle v\rangle^{-1}\mathbf{H_I} \quad \text{(D8)}$$

$$z = \check{T}z + y_I = \check{Q}_I y_I = \check{Q}_I\check{Y}_I f \qquad z' = z'\bar{T} + h_I' = h_I'\bar{Q}_I = v'\bar{H}_I\bar{Q}_I \quad (4)$$

$$v = \check{H}_I z = \underbrace{\check{H}_I\check{Q}_I\check{Y}_I}_{\check{L}_I} f = \mathbf{L_I} u \qquad f' = z'\bar{Y}_I = v'\underbrace{\bar{H}_I\bar{Q}_I\bar{Y}_I}_{\bar{L}_I} = u'\mathbf{L_I} \quad (5)$$

$$\mathbf{L_I} = \check{L}_I\langle f\rangle = \langle v\rangle\bar{L}_I = \mathbf{H_I}\bar{Q}_I\bar{Y}_I = \check{H}_I\check{Q}_I\mathbf{Y_I} \quad (6)$$

The unit matrix is denoted by U.

Entry points of loops are marked by • and o, exit points by arrows.

common level-loop. The last two forms in (3) and (6) demonstrate that the level-loops can also be derived from either the primary ($\mathbf{H_P}$, $\mathbf{H_I}$) or the final ($\mathbf{Y_P}$, $\mathbf{Y_I}$) external flow. (The Appendix provides a key to these and many forthcoming similar transcriptions.) The identity of the last two forms amplifies the inherent uniqueness of the level-loop.

While composition and allocation loops seem to be one-way streets from f to v or back, actually they are just two, opposite lanes of a two-way road between final use and value added.

Loops capture a higher degree of *circularity* than the Q multipliers since, in addition to interindustry or intersectoral circularity, they also embrace the external flows, the open ends of the models. Nevertheless it is clear that this circularity is yet *incomplete* since it is confined to the production (income) system. No matter which point is taken as the origin of the loop, the way back from the end point is unknown. Therefore we shall have to distinguish them as *open loops*.

Obviously, to obtain complete circularity, production and income loops must be connected. It is important to observe at this point that composition loops can be coupled only with allocation loops and reversely. If a production (income) loop is expected to proceed further from its own exit point towards the complementary income (production) loop then it must meet the entry point of the latter. As the diagrams clearly demonstrate, composition exit v can hit allocation entry v and allocation exit f can meet composition entry f. Therefore, there are only two – and not four, as it could have been expected – ways of combining production with income.

In Window 3 we consider the simplest possible way of cross-linking total output with total income. The leftmost, direct forms of v and f from income equation (5) substituted into production equation (1) yield total output x in (7), the corresponding simple forms from (2) substituted into (4) provide total income z in (8).

Window 1.3

Composition Production *Allocation Income*	*Allocation Production* *Composition Income*	
$x = \check{Q}_P \check{Y}_P \bar{Y}_I' z = \check{Q}_P \mathbf{Y} u$	$x' = z' \check{H}_I' \bar{H}_P \bar{Q}_P = u' \mathbf{H} \bar{Q}_P$	(7)
$z' = x' \check{H}_P' \bar{H}_I \bar{Q}_I = u' \mathbf{H}' \bar{Q}_I$	$z = \check{Q}_I \check{Y}_I \bar{Y}_P' x = \check{Q}_I \mathbf{Y}' u$	(8)

$$\mathbf{Y} = \check{Y}_P \bar{Y}_I' \langle z \rangle = \langle x \rangle \bar{Y}_P \check{Y}_I' = \check{Y}_P \mathbf{Y_I}' = \mathbf{Y_P} \check{Y}_I' \quad (9)$$

$$\mathbf{H} = \langle z \rangle \check{H}_I' \bar{H}_P = \bar{H}_I' \check{H}_P \langle x \rangle = \mathbf{H_I}' \bar{H}_P = \bar{H}_I' \mathbf{H_P} \quad (10)$$

There are two *routes* between x and z. Substitution into the composition models links x with z through final product and expenditure, while substitution into the allocation models connects x and z through primary input and income. On each road we again find an identity in levels, a common (for the two joint models) industry-by-sector mapping, denoted by **Y** and **H**, respectively, to be called *level-routes*. They are expounded in (9) and (10) in various forms.

Level-route **Y** reflects consolidated final product as divided among emitting industries (rows) and consolidated final expenditure as distributed among spending sectors (columns). Similarly, level-route **H** describes consolidated primary input by absorbing industries (columns) and primary income by receiving sectors (rows). Since they both record externals, in other words the GDP, they have to be multiplied by the proper Q multipliers to yield total output x and total income z in (7) and (8), respectively.[2]

The lack of multipliers and loops in **Y** and **H** indicates that the routes reflect *direct* links among accounting units. Although the homogeneity assumption is implied in many ways (not only with respect to industries and sectors but also concerning types of final use and value added), individual components of **Y** and **H** represent – aggregates of – direct transactions between one industry and one sector. Equations (7) and (8) thus do not actually *close* one model through the circular dependencies of the other model, they just reveal the connecting routes.

In Window 1.4 we really close the models, by substituting the loops rather than the direct forms from (5) into (1) and from (2) into (4). Thereby we obtain two, identically looking closed loops illustrated by the diagrams. They run in opposite directions, depending on which of the production models has been combined with which of the income models. Here, however, we shall again discover common nucleuses in value terms, indicating that closed loops are also opposite lanes of a two-way street rather than one-way streets.

The substitution yields further forms of total output x in (11), total income z in (12). Both vectors are now obtained as *eigenvectors* of two singular matrix-products, with unity as the maximal eigenvalue. (Singularity can be proved by previous definitions, using the Appendix for transcription keys.) These matrix-products will be referred to as *circuits* or *closed loops*. Observe that substitution into composition (allocation) models yields right-side (left-side) eigenvectors.

Circuits can again be traced back to common (for the two joint models) nucleuses, $\mathbf{N_P}$ for x and $\mathbf{N_I}$ for z, defined and expounded in (15) and (16). While $\mathbf{N_P}$ provides an industry-by-industry mapping between final product and primary input through the income system, $\mathbf{N_I}$ represents the sector-by-sector mapping between primary income and final expenditure through

Window 1.4

Composition Production
Allocation Income

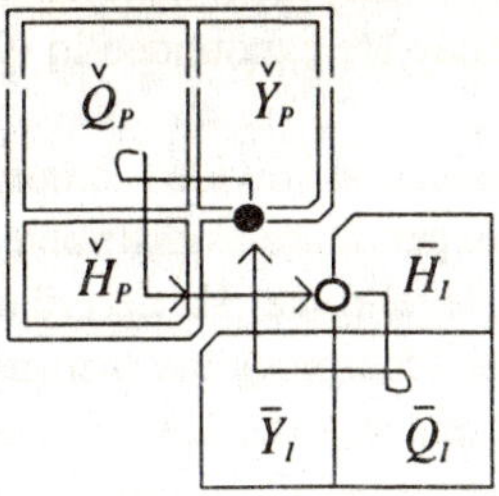

Allocation Production
Composition Income

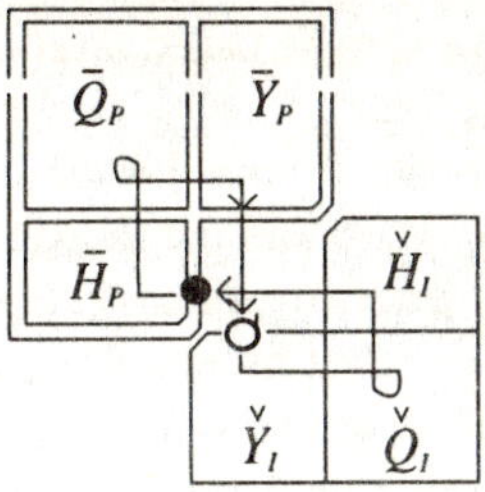

$$x = \check{Q}_P \check{Y}_P \bar{L}_I{}'\, \check{H}_P x = \check{Q}_P \mathbf{N_P} u \qquad x' = x' \bar{Y}_P \check{L}_I{}'\, \bar{H}_P \bar{Q}_P = u' \mathbf{N_P} \bar{Q}_P \tag{11}$$

$$z' = z' \bar{Y}_I \check{L}_P{}'\, \bar{H}_I \bar{Q}_I = u' \mathbf{N_I} \bar{Q}_I \qquad z = \check{Q}_I \check{Y}_I{}' \bar{L}_P{}'\, \check{H}_I z = \check{Q}_I \mathbf{N_I} u \tag{12}$$

$$\check{x}' = u' \check{Q}_P \mathbf{N_P} \qquad \bar{x} = \mathbf{N_P} \bar{Q}_P u \tag{13}$$

$$\bar{z} = \mathbf{N_I} \bar{Q}_I u \qquad \check{z}' = u' \check{Q}_I \mathbf{N_I} = \check{Y}_I \bar{L}_P{}' \check{H}_I \langle z \rangle = \tag{14}$$

$$\mathbf{N_P} = \check{Y}_P \bar{L}_I{}' \check{H}_P \langle x \rangle = \langle x \rangle \bar{Y}_P \check{L}_I{}' \bar{H}_P = \mathbf{Y_P} \check{L}_I{}' \bar{H}_P = \check{Y}_P \bar{L}_I{}' \mathbf{H_P} \tag{15}$$

$$\mathbf{N_I} = \langle z \rangle \bar{Y}_I \check{L}_P{}' \bar{H}_I = \check{Y}_I \bar{L}_P{}' \check{H}_I \langle z \rangle = \mathbf{Y_I} \check{L}_P{}' \bar{H}_I = \check{Y}_I \bar{L}_P{}' \mathbf{H_I} \tag{16}$$

$$f = \bar{L}_I{}' \check{L}_P f = \mathbf{C_f} u \qquad f' = f' \check{L}_I{}' \bar{L}_P = u' \mathbf{C_f} \tag{17}$$

$$v = \check{L}_P \bar{L}_I{}' v = \mathbf{C_v} u \qquad v' = v' \bar{L}_P \check{L}_I{}' = u' \mathbf{C_v} \tag{18}$$

$$\begin{aligned} C_f &= \mathbf{L_I}{}' \bar{L}_P = \bar{L}_I{}' \mathbf{L_P} = \mathbf{Y_I}{}' \check{Q}_I{}' \check{H}_I{}' \bar{L}_P = \bar{L}_I{}' \check{H}_P \check{Q}_P \mathbf{Y_P} \\ &= \bar{Y}_I{}' \bar{Q}_I{}' \mathbf{H} \bar{Q}_P \bar{Y}_P \end{aligned} \tag{19}$$

$$\begin{aligned} C_v &= \mathbf{L_P} \check{L}_I{}' = \check{L}_P \mathbf{L_I}{}' = \check{L}_P \bar{Y}_I{}' \bar{Q}_I{}' \mathbf{H_I}{}' = \mathbf{H_P} \bar{Q}_P \bar{Y}_P \check{L}_I{}' \\ &= \check{H}_P \check{Q}_P \mathbf{Y} \check{Q}_I{}' \check{H}_I{}' \end{aligned} \tag{20}$$

the production system. They include only five factors hence they do not fully close the loop, they might be called *semi-circuits*. Their substance being *external*, the proper multiplier Q is required to complete the circuit for x and z, respectively.

Since $\mathbf{N_P}$ and $\mathbf{N_I}$ are obtained by multiplying by $\langle x \rangle$ and $\langle z \rangle$, respectively, they reflect value terms. It follows that $\check{Q}_P \mathbf{N_P}$ and $\mathbf{N_P} \bar{Q}_P$ for x as well as $\check{Q}_I \mathbf{N_I}$ and $\mathbf{N_I} \bar{Q}_I$ for z also represent levels. they may be called *level-circuits*. Thereby x and z can be expressed as column or row totals of the level-circuits, as demonstrated by the rightmost forms in (11) and (12).

It is perfectly logical, however, to inquire into the *opposite* summation of the level-circuits. When the eigenvector is identical with the vector of row-totals, we derive the vector of column-totals and *vice versa* in (13) and (14).

While the circuits are mappings of x and z on to themselves, the 'opposite-sum' vectors divide consolidated total output $u'x$ (consolidated total income $u'z$) in a novel way. The x_n component represents that part of $u'x$ that has originated from primary inputs absorbed by industry n, x_n reflects that part of the same $u'x$ that has been allocated to the final product of industry n, all the way through the complex circular interdependencies within and between the production and income systems. (The z_n component defines that part of $u'z$ that has originated from primary incomes of sector n, z_n records that part of the same $u'z$ that has been allocated to final expenditure by sector n).

Finally, we complete the joint models by expressing final use vector f and value added vector v within the fully circular framework. Cross-substitution between (2) and (5) yields equations (17) and (18). Here f and v appear as eigenvectors of singular matrix-products derived from the same closed loop illustrated by the diagrams. This time, however, the circuits obtained seem to be simpler (although all circuits include all six parts of the joint system), because both open loops remain intact.

More importantly, in this case even the level-circuits $\mathbf{C_f}$ and $\mathbf{C_v}$, defined in (19) and (20), are common for the two models, they emerge identically from two, seemingly distinct procedures, closing production through income and closing income by production. $\mathbf{C_f}$ is mapping final use onto itself, from final product through route $\mathbf{H}$ to final expenditure *and* reversely. $\mathbf{C_v}$ runs from primary input by way of $\mathbf{Y}$ to primary income *and* the other way round, mapping value added on to itself.

Definitions (9)–(10), (15)–(16) and (19)–(20) display a possibly confusing and seemingly superfluous variety of forms. The point is exactly, however, to demonstrate that

1. Due to the inherent duality, there are several *equivalent forms*. Proceeding from production to income or from income to production, considering composition or allocation, a basic, underlying uniqueness of interdependencies transpires in the absolute levels.
2. Any part of the system, expressed in value terms, the original external flow matrices of the accounting framework as well as the more complex level-loops or level-routes, can be designated to convert any sequence of coefficient matrices into a *level-circuit*.

Circuits capture *full circularity* through the production *and* the income system. Level-circuits represent *circular flows* expressed in the accounting unit of measurement – the ultimate purpose of our exercise.

Circuits have been obtained in two joint models, one that combined composition production with allocation income, the other the opposite. Level-circuits or their crucial level-nucleuses, however, have been proved to be unique in the sense that they are common for the two models. These can be incorporated into a single, block-diagonal matrix to provide a single, concise, closed accounting model of circularity:

$$\mathbf{C} = \begin{bmatrix} \check{Q}_P\mathbf{N_P} & & & & & & & \\ & \mathbf{N_P}\bar{Q}_P & & & & & & \\ & & \mathbf{N_P} & & & & & \\ & & & \mathbf{C_f} & & & & \\ & & & & \mathbf{C_v} & & & \\ & & & & & \mathbf{N_I} & & \\ & & & & & & \check{Q}_I\mathbf{N_I} & \\ & & & & & & & \mathbf{N_I}\bar{Q}_s \end{bmatrix}, c = \begin{bmatrix} x \\ \bar{x} \\ y_P \\ f \\ v \\ y_I \\ z \\ \bar{z} \end{bmatrix}$$

$$r' = [\ \check{x}' \quad x' \quad h_P' \quad f' \quad v' \quad h_I' \quad \check{z}' \quad z'\ ]$$

$$c = \mathbf{C}u \quad \check{C} = \mathbf{C}\langle c\rangle^{-1} \qquad r' = u'\mathbf{C} \quad \bar{C} = \langle r\rangle^{-1}\mathbf{C} \tag{19}$$

$$c = \check{C}c \qquad\qquad r' = r'\bar{C} \tag{20}$$

Vectors c and r are composites of all relevant vectors in the joint system. Level-matrix **C** provides the mapping of them into each other.

Quite analogously to deriving separate models from the accounting framework, composition and allocation coefficients can be calculated from **C** and then, naturally, the composite vectors appear as eigenvectors of the singular, stochastic coefficient matrices $\check{C}$ and $\bar{C}$. Dividing and then multiplying with the bordering vectors does not amount to banality here since the diagonal blocks represent circular imputed flows rather than direct links.

At this point it is important to remember that this is an *accounting model*. It is not suggested that a matrix $\check{C}$ or $\bar{C}$ is 'given' and then the eigenvector is derived as some kind of 'equilibrium solution'. To the contrary, the composite vectors are *known* from the accounting framework and the purpose of the exercise has been to determine the matrixes that reveal the indirect, circular links between them. Following the perfect linguistic hit 'eigenprices' (Seton, 1992), it might be perhaps permissible to speak of the *eigenmatrix* of a given vector – a matrix designed to provide the mapping of the vector onto itself through circular relationships.

Here we concentrated on demonstrating the identities in absolute levels. Eigenmatrix **C** has been constructed to bring home this message. There are of course several alternative ways to design eigenmatrices, some of them are shown in the Appendix.

Window 1.5 offers another overview of the results. That is not a new model neither a new framework, just an illustration of dimensions. It should be noted that the sum total of components in each and every matrix equals the GDP. We have now twelve dual decompositions of the GDP, eight added to the original four external flow matrices. While the latter represent direct transactions, the newly added ones reflect lower or higher degrees of captured circularity.

It is unlikely that anyone would ever want twelve dual decompositions of the GDP at the same time. Most economic models, however, make use of at least one of them, explicitly or implicitly. It can not harm to recognize them in their proper place as parts of a more general pattern.

SUMMARY

We started with four, open accounting models (production and income, composition and allocation) and ended up with a *single closed* model.

Integration of the separate models is based on compound, imputed *flows* (levels) that can be regarded as unique two-way streets between various categories. Uniqueness has transpired in two aspects:

1. When production and income models are defined in a properly symmetrical manner then they are interchangeable as closures for each other. It does not matter whether production is closed by income or income by production, the resulting compound flows are identical.
2. Composition and allocation coefficients are two, complementary approaches to the same substance. This is trivial with respect to the original direct coefficients derived from the accounting framework, it is less trivial with respect to various degrees of captured circularity. Composition and allocation coefficients can be transcribed into each other unlimitedly but both are necessary for connecting production with income.

The resulting single model is completely closed. Drawing arbitrary lines between endogenous and exogenous has not been necessary. This has become possible exactly because *two* systems have been combined:

1. With respect to subject matter, we considered production and income as *two* interrelated but self-reliant systems, each consisting of conceptually different parts. Each is exogenous with respect to the other but, when

Window 1.5

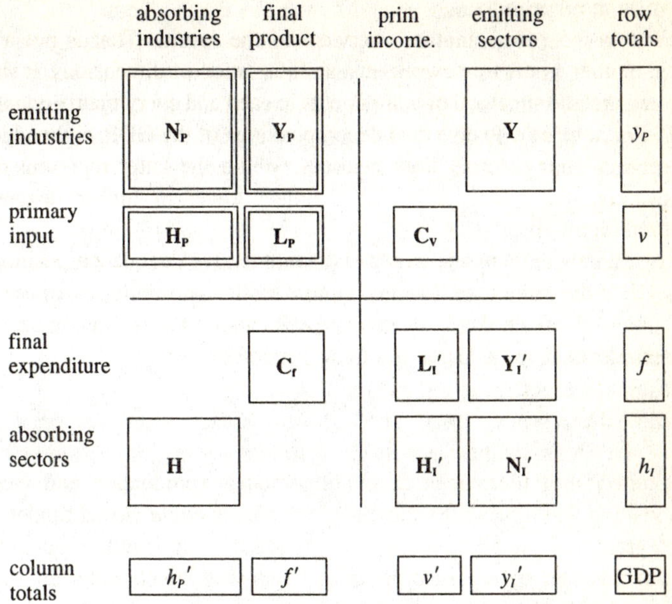

The income system (lower right quadrant) has been transposed and moved apart from the production system (upper left quadrant) in order to make room for loops, routes and circuits.

Matrices in a row (column) block must not be added. The bordering column (row) vectors represent the row (column) totals of each individual matrix and demonstrate that these totals are identical for the matrices in the row (column) block.

Individual matrices are placed in the block-row (block-column) that corresponds to the specification of the rows in the leftmost (columns in the rightmost) factor of the product that defines the matrix. Since the specification of rows and columns of a matrix-product depends on the leftmost and rightmost, respectively, factor of the sequence, the diagram demonstrates the interpretation of individual components.

For example in $\mathbf{C_f}$ rows and columns equally represent categories of final use. Looking at the diagram it becomes evident that rows correspond to final expenditure, columns to final product. Hence component *i, j* reflects final expenditure by all sectors on use-type *i*, originating from income generated by all industries in the production of final product-mix *j*.

combined, together they embrace all parts as endogenous components, without obscuring conceptual differences between them.

2. With respect to method, *two* square cores have been inverted, two partial multiplier matrices have been obtained. Incorporating these in various sequences with the external (to the cores) parts of the systems yielded singular matrix-products. The particular aspect of circularity captured by the singular matrix can be interpreted by observing the order of factors in the sequence.

All this has been achieved without loss of conceptual clarity and without causality assumptions, in true accounting spirit, supported and amplified by the revealed uniqueness of the circular flow. While one-way streets necessarily lead from cause to effect, on a two-way street one is free to choose the direction to be pursued, to decide at will what should be considered the driving force. The lack of causality assumptions makes the whole intellectual edifice less elegant but, in my view, more convincing.

APPENDIX

Key to Transcriptions

Coefficients

$$\check{A}\langle x\rangle = \mathbf{A} = \langle x\rangle\bar{A} \qquad \text{(A1)}$$

$$\check{A} = \langle x\rangle\bar{A}\langle x\rangle^{-1} \qquad \bar{A} = \langle x\rangle^{-1}\check{A}\langle x\rangle \qquad \text{(A2)}$$

$$\check{H}_P = \langle v\rangle\bar{H}_P\langle x\rangle^{-1} \qquad \bar{H}_P = \langle v\rangle^{-1}\check{H}_P\langle x\rangle \qquad \text{(A3)}$$

$$\check{Y}_P = \langle x\rangle\bar{Y}_P\langle f\rangle^{-1} \qquad \bar{Y}_P = \langle x\rangle^{-1}\check{Y}_P\langle f\rangle \qquad \text{(A4)}$$

$$\check{H}_I = \langle v\rangle\bar{H}_I\langle z\rangle^{-1} \qquad \bar{H}_I = \langle v\rangle^{-1}\check{H}_I\langle z\rangle \qquad \text{(A5)}$$

$$\check{Y}_I = \langle z\rangle\bar{Y}_I\langle f\rangle^{-1} \qquad \bar{Y}_I = \langle z\rangle^{-1}\check{Y}_I\langle f\rangle \qquad \text{(A6)}$$

Inverses

$$\check{Q}_P = (U - \check{A})^{-1} \quad \text{i.e.} \quad \check{Q}_P(U - \check{A}) = U \quad \text{further} \quad \check{Q}_P - \check{Q}_P\check{A} = U$$

multiply by $\langle x\rangle$ then apply A1:

$$\check{Q}_P\langle x\rangle - \check{Q}_P\check{A}\langle x\rangle = \langle x\rangle \rightarrow \check{Q}_P\langle x\rangle - \check{Q}_P\langle x\rangle\bar{A} = \langle x\rangle$$

$$\check{Q}_P\langle x\rangle(U - A) = \langle x\rangle \quad \rightarrow \check{Q}_P\langle x\rangle = \langle x\rangle(U - \bar{A})^{-1} = \langle x\rangle\bar{Q}_P$$

$$\check{Q}_P = \langle x\rangle\bar{Q}_P\langle x\rangle^{-1} \qquad \bar{Q}_P = \langle x\rangle^{-1}\check{Q}_P\langle x\rangle \qquad \text{(A7)}$$

Analogous reasoning yields

$$\check{Q}_I = \langle z\rangle \bar{Q}_I \langle z\rangle^{-1} \qquad \bar{Q}_I = \langle z\rangle^{-1} \check{Q}_I \langle z\rangle \tag{A8}$$

Loops (from A1–A8)

$$\begin{aligned}\check{L}_P &= \check{H}_P \check{Q}_P \check{Y}_P = \langle v\rangle \bar{H}_P \langle x\rangle^{-1} \langle x\rangle \bar{Q}_P \langle x\rangle^{-1} \langle x\rangle \bar{Y}_P \langle f\rangle^{-1} = \\ &= \langle v\rangle \underbrace{\bar{H}_P \bar{Q}_P \bar{Y}_P}_{\bar{L}_P} \langle f\rangle^{-1}\end{aligned}$$

$$\check{L}_P = \langle v\rangle \bar{L}_P \langle f\rangle^{-1} \qquad \bar{L}_P = \langle v\rangle^{-1} \check{L}_P \langle f\rangle \tag{A9}$$

$$\check{L}_P = \underbrace{\langle v\rangle \bar{H}_P}_{\mathbf{H_P}} \; \bar{Q}_P \bar{Y}_P \langle f\rangle^{-1} \qquad \bar{L}_P = \langle v\rangle^{-1} \check{H}_P \check{Q}_P \; \underbrace{\check{Y}_P \langle f\rangle}_{\mathbf{Y_P}}$$

$$L_P = \check{L}_P \langle f\rangle = \langle v\rangle \bar{L}_P = \mathbf{H_P} \bar{Q}_P \bar{Y}_P = \check{H}_P \check{Q}_P \mathbf{Y_P} \tag{A10}$$

Analogous substitutions yield

$$\check{L}_I = \langle v\rangle \bar{L}_I \langle f\rangle^{-1} \qquad \bar{L}_I = \langle v\rangle^{-1} \check{L}_I \langle f\rangle \tag{A11}$$

$$\mathbf{L_I} = \check{L}_I \langle f\rangle = \langle v\rangle \bar{L}_I = \mathbf{H_I} \bar{Q}_I \bar{Y}_I = \check{H}_I \check{Q}_I \mathbf{Y_I} \tag{A12}$$

NOTES

1. In I–O literature the term 'allocation coefficient' has become quite standard while the opposite does not seem to be given any particular name. Probably because this had been the original, familiar meaning of coefficients in general.) In our case symmetry and clarity requires that both types of coefficients and models could be referred to by distinct words, although 'composition' may not be the best choice.
   In the SAM transaction table the income system is transposed with respect to our framework. Hence column-normalized coefficients represent composition (origin) for production but allocation (destination) for income. (In SAM analysis they are both interpreted as 'propensity to spend' coefficients, implying that production is seen as *emitting money* in exchange for means of production and *absorbing money* by sales, rather than a system emitting *products* and absorbing *means of production*.)
2. The standard SAM transaction table includes the block **Y** as defined here but presents $\mathbf{H_P}$ and $\mathbf{H_I}$ as separate blocks. The result is that the two factors of **Y** remain unobserved while **H** is not displayed.

REFERENCES

AUGUSZTINOVICS, M. (1970) 'Methods of International and Intertemporal Comparison of Structure', in *Contributions to Input–Output Analysis* (ed. A. P. Carter and A. Bródy), North-Holland Publishing Company, Amsterdam.

AULIN-AHMAVAARA, P. (1991) 'Production Prices of Human Capital and Human Time', *Economic Systems Research*, Vol. 3, p. 345.
BRÓDY, A. (1970) *Proportions, Prices and Planning*, Akadémiai Kiadó, Budapest, North-Holland Publishing Company, Amsterdam.
EISNER, R. (1989) 'Extended accounts For National Income and Product', *Journal of Economic Literature*, Vol. 26, p. 1611.
GHOSH, A. (1958) 'Input–Output Approach to an Allocative System', *Economica*, Vol. 25, p. 58.
LEONTIEF, W. (1936) 'Quantitative and Input–Output Relations in the Economic System of United States', *Review of Economics and Statistics*, Vol. 18, p. 105.
MILNE, A. A. (1926) Reprinted in *The World of Pooh*. E. P. Dutton, New York, 1957.
MIYAZAWA, K. (1976) *Input–Output Analysis and the Structure of Income Distribution*, Springer-Verlag, Berlin.
PYATT, G. and ROUND, J. (1979) 'Accounting and Fixed-Price Multipliers in a Social Accounting Matrix Framework', *Economic Journal*, Vol. 89, p. 850.
PYATT, G. (1991) 'Fundamentals of Social Accounting', *Economic Systems Research*, Vol. 3, p. 315.
ROLAND-HOLST, D. W. (1990) 'Interindustry Analysis with Social Accounting Methods', *Economic Systems Research*, Vol. 2, p. 125.
ROSE, A. and MIERNYK, W. (1989) 'Input–Output Analysis: The First Fifty Years', *Economic Systems Research*, Vol. 1, p. 229.
SETON, F. (1992) *The Economics of Cost, Use and Value*, Clarendon Press, Oxford.
STONE, R. F. and CROFT-MURRAY, G. (1959) *Social Accounting and Economic Models*, Bowes & Bowes, London.

2 Change as Economic Activity

Anne P. Carter

2.1 INTRODUCTION

As late as the 1970s scientists and health care professionals saw the conquest of human ailments as a fixed goal that society was steadily and rapidly approaching. Today they recognize (Harvard Working Group, 1994) that bacteria and viruses mutate and evolve in response to many influences including the curative agents designed to combat them; disease vectors wax and wane in the changing ecologies that accompany human advance; the population of 'ailments' is redefined as options are broadened. Strategy in the battle against disease is now controversial and complex.

This development is a metaphor for the whole economy. We used to see growth as progress in the struggle against poverty. Technical change gave strong exogenous boosts to that growth (Solow, 1957), bringing the world closer to freedom from want. Now we recognize that growth involves metamorphosis rather than simple expansion. Developing new products and processes and adapting to changing opportunities take time and resources. Any given change reverberates throughout the economic system, triggering new challenges. Economic agents – firms, employees, governments, families – face rounds of adjustment as their respective options keep shifting. Anyone who has watched the process of launching a new enterprise or of reshaping an old one must recognize that change itself is a major economic activity.

We economists have focused primarily on the superiority of newer to older techniques of production with little systematic attention to the resources required for transition from one state to another. Happily, there are exceptions of which I cite only a few. Nelson and Winter (1982) see change as an adaptive process; Romer (1990) proposes an aggregative model that treats technical change as endogenous. Neither engages the major challenge of measurement involved. Much earlier Schumpeter highlighted 'creative destruction' but did not treat it explicitly as a cost. Mansfield (1968, 1972), Griliches (1957) and many others consider R&D spending as an economic variable. But R&D is probably only the tip of a very large iceberg of adjustment costs that includes reorganization of production, trial and error, marketing and other learning costs that affect producers, workers and consumers at all levels.

The prevailing ethos holds that rapid technological change and evolution of the division of labor lead to increasing productivity and hence to the 'better life' of plentiful consumer goods and services. Is technical progress always worth its cost? to whom? How does the economic system regulate the rate of change? Does it do a good job? The productivity slowdown of the 1970s and 1980s raised some questions that were never answered. Is it possible that the neglected costs of change can explain the paradox? We can't begin to tackle such questions without recognizing the costs of change, separating them from 'ordinary' costs of production and consumption both in theory and in our basic economic information.

This article is a small step toward more systematic recognition of change as economic activity. It does not articulate a comprehensive new model but identifies relevant variables and some problems of measuring them. First, it shows where costs of change are counted now, reviewing the static concepts of production functions underlying input–output and national accounts and explaining how costs of change are subsumed in these statistics. It then categorizes the costs of innovation and adaptation and raises questions that might be illuminated by separating them from costs of production. In conclusion, it considers special challenges that 'market failures' – informational variables and pecuniary externalities – pose for multisectoral modelling of change itself.

2.2 CHANGE COSTS AND THE STATIC PRODUCTION FUNCTION

2.2.1 The Production Function

Economists' thinking and measurement of production are rooted in the concept of the production function (Hicks, 1939). Conventionally, a production function tells us how much of various resources (inputs), both on capital and on current account, are required to produce any given product or set of products. Thus the output of bread can be seen as a function of inputs of flour, yeast, water, labour and breadmaking equipment. Economists talk about production functions at different levels of aggregation, from aggregate production functions for the economy at large to microeconomic production functions for individual sectors or even firms or establishments.

This paper has a multisectoral perspective, stemming from my own roots in input–output analysis. An input–output model specifies many sectoral production functions simultaneously. Thus the A and B matrices of an input–output system might be seen as a compound production function for the economy as a whole. The disaggregated general equilibrium framework supports a crucial distinction between a change initiated in a given sector and the resulting adaptive changes induced throughout the system. Such a distinction helps us to trace the propagation of change and the incidence of change costs across sectors.

Neoclassical production functions (see Brown, 1966) also specify alternative factor combinations to deliver a given output. These form the basis for computable general equilibrium (CGE), KLEM or other variable coefficient multisectoral systems. In these models, producers can choose among a range of input combinations to produce a given output. However, even in these models, all of the options in the production function are prespecified *ab initio*. Whether some initial choice is prespecified has little bearing on the distinction between costs of production and costs of change now under discussion.

Production functions are seen as exogenously given, dictated by the level of technical knowledge. Actually, of course, there is an enormous distance between technical knowhow and the economist's production function. Modern bread producers use many more inputs than flour, yeast, water labour, and ovens (even the traditional baker did!). If the production function is seen as governing the inputs and outputs of the entire firm, then only a limited portion of that production relation is based on engineering or 'technical' principles. There are two reasons for this.

First, engineers rarely specify production functions even for very narrowly defined productive activities. They solve problems that affect the production function, but their purview is both more general and narrower than the firm or industry. Thus it is left to economists to assemble the 'technical' information that they deem relevant for producers. The complexity of the transition from engineering to economic variables was discussed at some depth by Chenery and others many years ago (Leontief, *et al.*, 1953). Second, the 'core' production activity of any firm is complemented by a significant 'non-technical' component: marketing, sales, communication, packaging, transportation, administration, management and research activities. Each of these activities uses materials and capital as well as labour. We have no explicit theory for what determines the level of these activities nor the inputs used in them. By extension, we might postulate that there is a managerial state of the art, analogous to engineering knowledge, that prescribes them. But many of these auxiliary activities are primarily focused on change. What prescribes their level in a static environment? Would it be minimal?

2.2.2 Change in the Context of the Static Production Function

In today's competitive world, our baker is more likely to be a sophisticated firm like Au Bon Pain or Pepperidge Farm. Such firms do not simply produce bread. They also work on making it taste, look or feel different or last longer by changing the kind of flour used and/or by processing it differently. Perhaps most important, they seek new sales outlets at airport kiosks and special restaurants and in foreign markets.

Finding the right new process requires a certain amount of experimentation that itself uses labour, materials and equipment. To sell more of the new bread than the old, it is necessary to convince prospective customers, at some expense, of the improvement. Yesterday's bread was a white loaf, today's is sourdough French and tomorrow's may be a bagel with Cajun seasoning. New products may render old equipment obsolete. Breadmakers and salespeople must learn to make and present new products. The costs of reinventing and positioning the product, i.e. costs of innovation, easily swamp those of making the bread itself.

The resources required to develop and market new and/or improved products are not part of the conventional production function nor are the replacement of obsolete equipment and other forms of adaptation. This is true whether we focus on 'fixed proportion' production functions of an input–output system or on the neoclassical production functions that specify substitution possibilities. In either case, technological change is considered exogenous, a 'shock', in today's parlance. But in fact firms actively invest significant resources in creating such shocks and in responding to the shocks they face.

Even those who do not actively pursue innovation must adapt to changes in the competitive environment fostered by those who do. In response to Au Bon Pain the neigbourhood bakery serves coffee. Chemical companies develop a packaging medium that preserves without intensifying Cajun spices, or one that keeps bread fresh longer in exposed airport environments. If product and process options didn't change, why would we need engineering, marketing, business strategy, consultants or quality circles? Why would machines and buildings still functional in their old roles be replaced by newer models? What would managers do?

Essentially, production and change are coproducts. To lump costs of change with ordinary costs of production produces distortions on two counts. First, we tend to overlook the study of change itself. Second, we develop a biased view of what it takes to produce conventional goods.

2.2.3 How do National Accounts Deal with the Costs of Change?

Economists depend almost exclusively on published statistics for their data. The information we collect depends on how we see the economy while, at the same time, this information molds our thinking. Our system of economic statistics, including the system of national accounts, is anchored in the basic economic concept of the production function that was just described and its counterpart in consumption. Careful students of history could probably trace these concepts back to concepts of accounting rooted in Mediterranean commerce thousands of years ago.

2.2.4 Measurement of Output and Inputs on Current Account

The basic data for input–output tables and national accounts, which constitute the basis of all but special micro-studies, comes from the economic Censuses, of which the exemplar, the most complete and detailed by far, is the *Census of Manufactures* (US Department of Commerce, 1987). On the input side, the Census tabulates purchases of materials, fuel and electric energy and employment. Additional data on central office functions and the purchase of services are normally estimated in building input–output tables and hence, at least in principle, are allocated to consuming sectors in the national accounts. No distinction between costs of production and costs of change is made in the basic Census information. In the construction of input–output tables, all inputs purchased by a sector on current account are attributed to that sector's measured output (Carter 1989).

Output, in turn, is measured by value of shipments, adjusted where appropriate for changes in inventories. Value added, as an alternative measure of output, can be computed by subtracting intermediate purchases from value of shipments. But neither value of shipments nor value added counts intangible improvements in the firm's market power or future productive potential as an output. Thus a biotech firm that spends several years developing a product registers no output during those years, except insofar as it derives incidental income from grant or contract services or from licensing a patent. Similarly, a software firm that rewrites its programs to run on newer computer or operating systems or a bookseller who launches an expensive advertising campaign to change its image does not count any improvement in its position until it makes a sale. In early January of 1994, Kendall Square Computer made the headlines. Its stock lost heavily in value when auditors discovered that they counted anticipated income from research applications prior to actual receipt of payments (*Boston Globe*, December 1993).

2.2.5 The Capital Account

One important cost of change is increased replacement requirements due to obsolescence. While the Census collects annual information on plant and equipment expenditures there is no attempt to distinguish expenditures for replacement from expansion. In general there is little systematic information on actual retirements, idling of capacity and durability. Normally, firms do not keep records of scrappage. Sometimes assets are retired gradually, becoming standby capacity before they are abandoned completely. In what prices should obsolete assets be measured?

Input–output models generally include estimates of 'normal' replacement in the flow coefficient matrix but these are of necessity very crude because there is no reliable information distinguishing replacement from expansion. Expansion for the individual firm may constitute replacement for the sector. There is even less basis in the data for distinguishing replacement due to wear and tear from replacement due to obsolescence.

Capital coefficients for dynamic input–output models are based on stock/flow ratios. The Bureau of Economic Analysis has published much needed estimates of stocks of capital equipment by sector for the United States, 1925–1989 (US Department of Commerce, 1993). However, the compilers thoughtfully acknowledge the limitations imposed by lack of information about the actual service lives of equipment. With a few exceptions, service lives are fixed by assumption for the entire postwar period. Under these conditions, official estimates of retirements do not provide useful information about replacement and estimates of stocks do not provide a satisfactory basis for estimating capital coefficients.

In sum, Census information on current account combines expenditures on change with costs of production on current account. Replacement costs are not accurately measured at all; the flow coefficients that include them may be understated or overstated in any given year. Finally, capital requirements based on Census information include only physical capital and not intangibles.

2.3 THREE TYPES OF CHANGE COSTS

Costs of change fall into three broad categories. The first includes intangible investments: labour, materials and equipment employed to effect product or process innovations. The second consists of investment to replace capital rendered obsolete by technical change, Schumpeter's 'creative destruction'. The third covers the 'virtual' cost of inexperience as rapidly changing products and/or processes leave producers perpetually high on a shifting learning curve (Hirsch, 1952; Arrow, 1962). While all three categories are important, only the first can be discussed in any detail here.

2.3.1 Intangible Capital Formation as a Cost of Innovation

In addition to plant and equipment, production is supported by an infrastructure of change-oriented investment. Most of it is intangible – general knowledge, specific knowhow, reputations, mutual understandings, 'competences'. Firms acquire intangible capital by hiring appropriate individuals and providing them with whatever materials and equipment they need to acquire information, organize networks, etc. The cumulated expense of these wages, materials and equipment is intangible investment. Whether it is vested in the employees or the firms that hire them is not always clear.

Just as duplicative growth triggers additions to the stock of capital goods, innovation triggers fresh intangible investment. Not all intangible investment is linked to innovation; sometimes duplicative growth may require it too. And sometimes innovation may require the replacement of capital goods. But in general there is no expansion without tangible investment and no innovation without intangible investment.

Research and development is one important type of change-oriented investment that economists have been studying for some time. But change-oriented investment extends well beyond formal R&D to include organizational and reputational investment: establishing and fine-tuning supplier and sales networks, interfirm cooperation and support for complementary products appropriate to the current production set. Innovators may need to search out or even subsidize specialized inputs such as non-standard materials and components and complementary products like software for computers, service and repair networks for equipment, textbooks for schools and colleges.

In high-tech industry intangible investments tend to dwarf both expenditures on plant and equipment and those on production proper. For example:

- Massively parallel computers are so new that producers must devote significant resources to exploring and developing potential markets. One vice-president refers to his firm's investment in software to meet challenges where conventional computing strategies fail as the 'Lourdes to industry' approach. This is in sharp contrast to the old 'build a better mousetrap' assumption.

- Since the costs of duplicating existing software are negligible, writing a new program is essentially developing a new product. One executive software firm mentioned a rule of thumb of allocating 10 per cent of revenue to maintaining old software and the other 90 per cent to writing and selling the next generation of programs.
- Innovators in pharmaceuticals must finance lengthy laboratory and clinical trials to establish the safety and efficacy of the product. Biotechnology startup firms usually 'go public' or sell out to larger firms at this point. The burden of these trials is sufficient to warrant serious consideration of extending the life of drug patents to allow for income foregone in the trial period (Levin, 1986).

Change-oriented costs are by no means restricted to startups, nor are they the exclusive province of frontline innovators. Established firms innovate by developing new products or processes or by acquiring other firms that have done so. Older firms faced with new market or supply circumstances must change to survive. This calls for intangible investment in opening new markets, changing product mix or product design, 'buying out' surplus personnel and searching for new employees capable of implementing a new mission. Stories of attempts to 'downsize' or 'reengineer' on the part of famous companies: IBM, DEC, Wang, Sony, US Steel, Bethlehem, Chrysler, General Motors, AT&T, are too familiar to require repetition here. Under current conditions, small, medium and large firms are pressured to adapt and few are exempt from the costs of change.

2.3.2 Informational Capital and Capacity

Many economic modellers accept the notion that physical capital requirements for expansion are roughly proportional to the amount of capacity to be added. This is implicit in the idea of 'capital coefficients' or capital/output ratios. Much of intangible investment is 'informational' (Arrow, 1974; Carter, 1987). In contrast to equipment it does not have a definite 'capacity'. When research creates a new drug more or less of it may be produced. Similarly, a computer program can be duplicated very cheaply as often as the market warrants. Thus capacity expansion in a given firm may not require any further intangible investment. But these are simplistic examples. A sales network can handle more or less volume, but a different organization is called for at larger scale. Imitators must make their own informational investments. Thus the amount of change-oriented investment in a sector will depend on the number of producers and on information transfer among them. Informational investment is also associated with other significant externalities to be discussed below.

2.3.3 Flexibility of Tangible and Intangible Investment

Generally, innovation will call for change-oriented investment because intangible infrastructure already in place is specific to older technology. Is an infusion of intangible capital needed with all innovations? Generally, yes, but needs will vary with the flexibility of intangible infrastructure already in place. As in the case of capital goods, some intangible investments are more product- or process-specific than others. Machines can be replaced within an old factory building; similarly, an existing sales network can offer a new wonder-drug instead of an older one. Still, a new layout within the factory requires some investment in renovations; salesmen must be supplied with appropriate literature and samples of the new product and must learn its indications, side effects and medical niche.

As management anticipates rapid change, both tangible and intangible investment strategies anticipate future opportunities. Flexible machinery and flexible management configurations minimize the cost of changing the product or process but do not eliminate it altogether. Toyota can change the kind of car it delivers more quickly than General Motors. Citicorp restructures its top management decision making (*New York Times*, January 16 1994) to facilitate quick response to changing market options. IBM considers abandoning its Armonk headquarters to effect a more responsive management style. Clearly, change itself is a process whose efficiency can be improved. The size of efforts in this direction suggests that the costs of change are no longer negligible, if they ever were.

2.3.4 Creative Destruction and Informational Capital

Schumpeter pointed out that new and superior productive capacity would lead to the demise of the old, and labelled the induced obsolescence 'creative destruction'. He saw the replacement of obsolete plant and equipment as the primary cost of change. Innovation also renders intangible investment obsolete, forcing other firms to adapt with change-oriented investments. Creative destruction explains why both tangible and intangible investment will be high under conditions of rapid change.

2.4 CHANGE COSTS IN DYNAMIC INPUT–OUTPUT MODELS

2.4.1 Distinguishing Production and Change Costs in Current Models

Empirical input–output analysis is based on the traditional conceptual and statistical system described in section 2. Under that system, costs of change are subsumed in 'observed' flow and capital coefficients, as if the change activity were part of ordinary production. The idea can be formalized in terms of Bródy's (Bródy, 1970) very general version which captures the spirit of these disaggregated growth models:

$$p^0[I - A^0(t)]x^0 = \mu^0 p^0 B^0(t)x^0 \tag{1}$$

Where μ^0 is the economy-wide growth rate

p^0 and x^0 are the corresponding price and output eigenvectors associated with observed technology, and

$A^0(t)$, $B^0(t)$ are 'observed' flow and capital coefficients. (Note that flow coefficient matrices include allowances for the replacement of capital goods that wear out over time.)

These flow and capital requirements matrices can be divided into two components:

$A(t)$, $B(t)$ denote input and capital coefficients for technology of time t in the absence of further change efforts. These are essentially the costs of producing with static technology,

A^*, B^* are costs of change, including both expenditures on intangible infrastructure and replacement of capital, above the static norm, that results from creative destruction.

(1) can be rewritten

$$p^0(I - A(t) - A^*]x^0 = \mu^0 p^0[B(t) + B^*]x^0 \tag{1a}$$

In the absence of change costs, (1a) would be replaced by

$$p(I - A(t))x = \mu p(B(t))x \tag{1b}$$

where (1b) is the balanced growth equation under the assumption that there are no further efforts to change and that production continues under the technologies of time t.

Since the elements of A^* and B^* are positive the inclusion of costs of change in $A^0(t)$ and $B^0(t)$ lead to computed growth rates and eigenvectors different from those associated with the pure technology of time t. Because costs of change make resource demands on the system, the elements of A^* and B^* will be positive. Devoting resources to product and process improvement presumably serves the ultimate goal of increasing the economy's growth potential. However, no positive effects of such expenditures are specified. Therefore the efforts devoted to change itself decrease the growth rate below what it would be in the absence of costs of change, i.e. $\mu^0 < \mu$. In this perspective, an increasing proportion of resources devoted to change might produce an apparent deceleration in the observed growth rate, even in the face of steady improvement in the basic production system.

Input–output tables tend to register intangible capital outlays in the current account. Therefore, presumably the output proportions associated with $A^0(t)$, $B(t)^0$, i.e. of system (1), will include higher levels of production for goods and services associated with learning, searching, moving and other adaptation to new conditions than those associated with $A(t)$, $B(t)$, i.e. (1b). Similarly, prices of high-tech goods should be lower when the costs of change are removed.

2.5 WHERE DO WE GO FROM HERE?

Distinguishing the costs of change would clarify the interpretation of production statistics. Beyond that, the ultimate objective is to incorporate change into the economy-wide model and implement it with new data. The remainder of the paper scopes out some of the problems that must be solved before that long range objective is feasible.

2.5.1 General Conceptual Problems

In the previous section, A^*, B^* were defined essentially as errors in the measurement of the basic production function. But if change is economic activity, how does this activity fit into the overall system? In a multisectoral context, can we explain how these resources are deployed?

The economist's natural next step might be to try to associate sectoral costs of change with the specific changes that they effect. If C_j^* are sectoral costs to be reassigned from current inputs into change, how is the level of change itself to be measured? One theoretical possibility would be to link sectoral expenditures C_j^* with reductions in sectoral input and investment requirement coefficients, $A(t)_j$ and $B(t)_j$, i.e. to improved sectoral productivity. Symbolically:

$$\Delta A_j, \Delta B_j = f(C_j^*) \qquad (2)$$

If this approach were realistic, reductions in input requirements would become an alternate mode of growth, besides conventional capital accumulation. The multisectoral economy-wide model might then be solved by optimization techniques. Unfortunately it is not as simple as that. As will be explained below, the relation between change costs and change itself is complex and externalities limit optimization.

For input–output and empirical production functions in general, structural parameters are estimated from observations of input and output over time. Could we estimate a production function for the change activity itself by juxtaposing observed costs of innovation against observed changes in input–output coefficients? Associating costs of change with productivity improvements in a multisectoral context presents problems. Three major major issues are explained below.

2.5.2 Is There a Stable Relation between Effort and Innovation?

Production functions are supposed to describe repetitive activities – weekly outputs of aluminium dependent on weekly inputs of bauxite, electricity, labour, etc. Change activities, at least in principle, are unique, even creative, acts. Is it reasonable to expect there is a stable relationship between change, however measured, and the inputs that generate it?

2.5.3 Linking Informational Inputs with their Outputs

Change-oriented infrastructure is information-intensive. As suggested in 2.3.2, it is impossible to assign capacity, in the usual sense, to informational capital. This makes it difficult to specify a quantitative relationship between informational infrastructure and either production or change. A given advance, say the laser, may spawn many new applications. What proportion of laser development costs should be charged to any given application?

Intangible investments may also be targeted to broadening the future range of choice, or to insuring the appropriability of gains, rather than to effecting well-defined cost reductions or increments in a given product. This compounds the difficulty of tying specific outlays to definite productivity advances. Sony's acquisitions in the entertainment industry are a good example.

2.5.4 Externalities and Innovation

Innovation has significant external economies. An innovator does not bear responsibility for capital losses or other costs of adaptation imposed, directly or indirectly, on others; such external effects are not part of the innovator's decision-making calculus. By the same token, innovators do not benefit from spillovers that expand the options facing other firms or sectors. Thus expenditures on change and their effects are not matched: A dollar's worth of expenditure on change may effect more or less than a dollar's worth of improvement economy-wide. If a sector's productivity increases, how much of the increase should be attributed to expenditures on change within the sector, how much to spillovers from other sectors, how much to externally absorbed costs?

Conflicts of interest arise because externalities impose costs on some and benefits on others. Dupont's introduction of nylon led, eventually, to displacement of silk and some forms of rayon, production of nylon by others, changes in how stockings were made, pantyhose and the demise of the garter belt. Dupont did not bear the capital losses in silk, stockings and garter belts, nor did it capture all the surplus in pantyhose or in nylon itself.

A given innovation changes the options facing producers throughout the economy. The new options in any given sector include spillovers of the new technique itself and spillovers of adaptations to the initial change that reverberate throughout the system. Some agents in the long adaptive chain of response to any initial change: competitors, suppliers, customers, producers of complementary goods, employees, may not even know the source of the spillovers that affect them. Thus, while we may be able to estimate expenditures on change in a given sector, it is hard to measure the external costs imposed on others. Perhaps most important, it is difficult to track all the change for which those costs are responsible.

In sum, while we may be ready to begin the task of sequestering inputs into the change process there is much to be learned before we can make change endogenous in the context of a multisectoral model. We need a clearer understanding of how change itself is structured.

2.5.5 Data on the Costs of Change

Because our basic statistical sources do not distinguish costs of change it will take a long time (and substantial resources) to measure them systematically for the whole economy. Porat's work on 'the information economy' (Porat, 1977), tied to the 1967 input–output table, gives some pointers and also indicates how very substantial such an undertaking would be. Porat's work distinguishes information workers from others using a very detailed occupation-by-industry matrix constructed by the Bureau of Labor Statistics and based on Census of Population information. Functional distinctions in employment provide guidelines for splitting out other inputs as well.

Summarizing very detailed estimates Porat concluded that information workers, including both employment in 'primary information industries' and information workers in other industries, comprised 46 per cent of the workforce in 1967. If informational activity occupied 46 per cent of the workforce in 1967, what would the percentage be today?

While there is no update of Porat's study, we know that the information-intensive service sectors have continued to gain relative to manufacturing and agriculture (US Department of Commerce, 1993b, pp. 419–21). The proportion of production workers in manufacturing itself dropped from 73 to 64 per cent between 1967 and 1990 US Department of Commerce, 1993b, p. 742).

While information inputs and inputs into change are not identical concepts, the success of Porat's project suggests that a matrix of change inputs could be estimated by a similar methodology. The task would require substantial research resources and the essential cooperation of government agencies that collect such data.

2.5.6 Next Steps

An economy-wide survey of sectoral costs of change would be a major quest. In the near term, exploratory missions can begin to map the terrain. For example, we know that sectors vary greatly in the proportion of production and non-production workers employed. While production workers constitute about 65 per cent of total manufacturing employment, the proportion varies from less than 25 per cent for computers and office equipment, guided missiles and spacecraft and navigation equipment to close to 90 per cent in textiles and apparel (US Department of Commerce, 1993b, pp. 744–7). What technical and market features characterize sectors that devote a relatively high proportion of resources to change?

What determines the proportions of expenditure on the different components of change costs such as research, development, finance and marketing in individual sectors? How persistent are these proportions and why? Why are some sectors persistently, rather than sporadically, change-oriented? Does the accumulation of intangible infrastructure-building a large research or sales force-predispose a firm toward continuing change? How does the composition of intangible infrastructure differ between new and established firms?

The answers to these questions would be of interest in themselves; they would certainly inform the more general discourse.

2.6 CONCLUSION

At the turn of the century, it was unthinkable that agriculture would some day supply the food needs of the entire nation and of many other parts of the world, while employing only 3 per cent of the workforce. Now manufacturing also shows major shrinkage. The concomitant rise in services is a symptom of stepped up change throughout the economy. Employment in services and of nonproduction workers in manufacturing suggests that as much as half of all economic effort might be focused on change. At this point we don't understand clearly the system that regulates the change process.

Separating out the costs of change is one important challenge; linking change costs to measured benefits is another. Externalities make it hard to infer costs or benefits of change from statistics of observed transactions. Substantively, externalities also limit the effectiveness of markets in guiding technological transformation. The fact that innovators bear only a fraction of the total economic cost of innovation enhances the market's thrust toward greater change. On the other hand, spillovers blunt incentives to innovate by limiting appropriability.

Without knowing what change, and hence what production itself, really costs, we cannot properly measure conventional productivity. Failing that, how can we judge whether improved productivity warrants expenditures on change, also unmeasured?

Economics aside, change has taken on a positive value in itself: we may even be addicted to change. The hypothetical economy that merely reproduces itself, or grows proportionately, would be boring. The real economy brings uncertainty, improvization, frustration and waste but also new and cheaper products, wonder and excitement. Would we be better off devoting more resources to here-and-now production and less to change? Do we really have a choice?

REFERENCES

ARROW, K. J. (1962). 'The Economic Implications of Learning by Doing', *Review of Economic Studies*, 2, pp. 155–73.

ARROW, K. J. (1974) *The Limits of Organization*, New York, Norton.

BRÓDY, A. (1970) *Proportions, Prices and Planning*, Amsterdam, North-Holland Publishing Company.

BROWN, M. (1966) *On the Theory and Measurement of Technological Change*, Cambridge, Cambridge University Press.

CARTER, A. P. (1987) 'Knowhow Trading as Economic Exchange', *Research Policy*, 18. pp. 155–63.

CARTER, A. P. (1989) 'Input–Output Recipes in an Information Economy', *Economic Systems Research*, Vol. 1 pp. 27–43.

GRILICHES, Z. (1957) 'Hybrid Corn: An Exploration in the Economics of Technological Change', *Econometrica*, 25, pp. 501–22.

HARVARD WORKING GROUP ON RESURGENT DISEASES (1994) 'The Emergence of New Disease', *American Scientist*, Vol. 82 Jan.–Feb., pp. 52–9.

HICKS, J. R. (1939) *Value and Capital*, Oxford, Oxford University Press.

HIRSCH, W. (1952) 'Manufacturing Progress Ratios', *Review of Economics and Statistics*, 34, pp. 143–55.

LEONTIEF W., *et al.* (1953) *Studies in the Structure of the American Economy*, New York, Oxford University Press.

LEVIN, R. C. (1986) 'A New Look at the Patent System', *American Economic Review*, May, pp. 199–202.

MANSFIELD, E. (1968) *Industrial Research and Technological Innovation*, New York, Norton.

MANSFIELD, E. (1972) 'The Contribution of R&D to Economic Growth in the United States', *Science*, 175, pp. 477–86.

NELSON, R. R. and S. G. WINTER (1982) *An Evolutionary Theory of Economic Change*, Cambridge, MA, The Belknap Press of Harvard University Press.

PORAT, M. U. (1977) *The Information Economy: Definition and Measurement*, US Department of Commerce Office of Telecommunications, Special Publication, 77–12 (1), Washington, DC, US Government Printing Office.

ROMER, P. M. (1990) 'Endogenous Technological Change', *Journal of Political Economy*, Vol. 98, pp. 71–102.

SCHUMPETER, J. A. (1934) *The Theory of Economic Development*, Cambridge, MA, Harvard University Press.

SOLOW, R. M. (1957) 'Technological Change and the Aggregate Production Function', *Review of Economics and Statistics*, pp. 312–20.

US DEPARTMENT OF COMMERCE, BUREAU OF THE CENSUS. (1987) *Census of Manufactures*, Published quinquenially, Washington, DC, US GPO.

US DEPARTMENT OF COMMERCE, BUREAU OF ECONOMIC ANALYSIS (1993) *Fixed Reproducible Tangible Wealth in the United States, 1925–1989*, January, Washington, DC, US GPO.

US DEPARTMENT OF COMMERCE, BUREAU OF THE CENSUS. (1993b). *Statistical Abstract of the United States, 1993*, Washington, DC, US GPO.

3 Index Numbers and the Theory of Value

Utz-Peter Reich

3.1 METHODOLOGICAL REFLECTIONS ON THE RELATIONSHIP BETWEEN THEORY AND PRACTICE IN ECONOMICS

Economics is rightly called an empirical science today. The claim is based on two developments having taken place in this century, mathematization and national accounting. Mathematization of economics has provided the intellectual means for building interdependent and coherent models of complex economic processes; national accounts have provided a corresponding, equally coherent set of data. Yet, the initial dream under which such kind of 'econometrics' was launched has not become true. Economics has neither discovered specific laws of motion, nor has it determined constants of society, in analogy to constants of nature, which would allow irreproachable forecasts of future economic events. Economics has not become like mechanics.

Looking back at this history, the result might have been expected from hindsight, but it has rarely been reflected. The disappointment was not felt by the generation who began the revolution in economics, because they did not live to see its results. And the generation knowing the results never shared the idealistic expectations of the pioneers. This is a natural cleavage, but for the development of knowledge it may create a fallacy. Each science has its dogmas and rules generated by hopes and expectations of future discovery. If the later disappointment is not reflected, and analytically investigated certain dogmas may be carried on which hinder rather than promote progress, albeit by their being employed unconsciously. One of these dogmas is the priority of the concepts of economic theory over those of statistical practice.

Whenever there is a divergence between the concept that should be measured in terms of theory, and one that is actually measured this is unconditionally counted against statistical practice. The latter is interpreted as a bad, or sometimes good, approximation of the first. The concept as such is not put into question. In spite of the mathematical and empirical foundation it has not occurred, yet, in economics that a theoretical concept has been discarded because it was found to be unoperational. The capital controversy pays witness to the fact. Although the microeconomic concept of capital was proven unoperational on the macrolevel, neither economic theory nor economic practice (politics), nor economic measurement (national accounts) changed in any way. A similar delusion of thought has occurred to the index number problem. The riddle has kept alive an academic community for a hundred years, with minimal effect on statistical practice. Essentially prices are measured today in the same way as they were a 100 years ago. This statement alone reads like a reproach of statistics, a reproach for conservatism, if not theoretical disinterest and ignorance. Why do statisticians not make use of the multiple, and brillant ideas which have been produced since the invention of index number theory?

This is a crucial point. In this paper I reverse the question. Why is it that theory has so little concern about the problems of measurement? It is customary, of course, to formulate hypotheses, subject them to tests and come up with findings. In this sense theory does use data, and is willing to overthrow its hypotheses. But our problem lies one level below. In an economic model there are behavioural equations, and state variables. The first are tested, the second never. For them one uses what is provided by the national accounts, realising that what is compiled does not always fit to what one wants, but for lack of better data, as is then said, one takes what one has, and stops thinking. The debate of whether the concepts and measurement assumptions of economic theory, firstly, are operational at all, and secondly, suit the national accounts is underdeveloped. This is a clear, though negative, legacy of the past.

When the national accounts were at their beginnings there was only theory to draw on in order to design a coherent set of concepts. Hence dates its priority. However, strictly speaking, this theory was always hypothetical, and subject to revision if practice would prove otherwise. Such proof takes time. It can be put into effect only after practice has itself arrived at a certain state of the art with rules, conventions, dogmas, etc. This is the situation today. If statistical practice stubbornly continues measuring variables in a certain way, and one theoretical proposal after another does not find its way into it this is not a question of stubborn people but of stubborn reality. Apparently those whose task it is to describe reality cannot use the proposed concepts, and this is an empirical finding which must reverse theoretical assumptions.

Considering the concepts of statistics as true and real, and those of theory as possibly false is an unusual approach, and difficult, because in our learning of economics, theory comes first. These concepts form our minds. Nevertheless this approach is necessary. So the question is about how you can continue economic reasoning without employing your basic economic concepts. You can, and it is fruitful. In the paper we will explain what understanding can be obtained if the premises under which the index number problem was forced to be treated by unreflected economic theory are relaxed. They are the premises of the microeconomic theory of value. It may seem strange to discard them, and still arrive at numbers of economic substance. But any theory has its limits, and it is the assumption that the microeconomic theory of value does not necessarily hold at the macroeconomic level that helps us solve the index number problem.

We have long been acccustomed to learning, and teaching, only one theory of value. In its different branches, theory of the household, theory of production, or theory of general equilibrium it has formed our minds to interprete economic value as a microeconomic phenomenon above all. Its range of application appears unlimited in spite of the never resolved aggregation problem. But science is not static. There was a time when an alternative to microeconomic value theory, framed in mathematical terms, was at least discussed (Bródy, 1974). Although the aggregation advantages are enticing the intellectual attack did not impress the main stream. But even without an accepted alternative the proposition should be acceptable that every theory has its limits, and that there are fields where its concepts are not useful, so that other concepts must be employed and developed. One of such fields are the national accounts, in particular, and macroeconomics, in as much as they are based on the national accounts, in general.

3.2 DEFINING THE INDEX NUMBER PROBLEM

When Laspeyres published his index of consumer prices in the year 1871 economics leaped a step ahead. When three years later Paasche came out with his index the economics community took almost the same step back. It has been pinned down swaying back and forth between the two formulas ever since. This is the index number problem. Impossible to count the trials, or to measure the effort that has been put into the problem since. Fisher's study (1922) became a classic, although instead of deciding between the two formulas it brought in a third one, which less modest than his predecessors, he propagated under the claim of an 'ideal index'. Since then dates the tradition that authors compete in inventing nice names for their formulas. After the ideal index we had the exact index, the invariant index, and the superlative index. Hedonic indices, although not quite the same, also convey positive feelings. Between these famous brands a whole meadow of nameless indices has grown, and been cultivated, a veritable school of index number research developed around the problem as a subject of its own. But strangely all this passed only in theory (for a comprehensive summary of the state of the art, see Diewert, 1993). In working statistics, it has always been

Laspeyres and Paasche who ruled the field, finding their agreement by practical compromise rather than sharp reasoning, and this being accepted by the public as legitimate. The problem was blown up in theory, and cooked down in practice.

Whether a solution is a solution depends on the criteria which you apply. And these in turn are not arbitrary but should be consistent with the premises on which the solution is constructed. One of the conspicuous premises in this respect, underlying all solutions of the index-number problem called economic, is the statement of constant utility in time. Hicks took note of it (1940, p. 107f.), but ignored it for his treatment, and paved the way for the followers. Thus in index number theory, production may change, goods may change although that strains it to the limits, but the map of preferences is stable over infinity. To a layman the premise is not explicable, less to person well versed in social sciences. It is only understandable as a positon of last resort: If we don't assume constancy of preferences in time, it seems that we have no economic theory at all. And the *horror vacui* of that realization keeps the assumption alive.

There is also what is customarily called statistical index number theory. It does not make use of economic preferences, and thus has more room for manoeuvre to adjust to reality. Here the originators of the problem, Laspeyres and Paasche are at home, and this is also the area within which Chapter XVI of the new SNA (United Nations, 1993) can be called a solution. Consequently, we will not answer the question about what is the best index within given, constant, and consistent maps of individual preferences, because we have no information about such maps from our data in the national accounts. We will answer the question of how to solve the problem statistically. In other words, we work without any assumption about subjective utility or implied preferences. As the statistician says: 'A potato is a potato.' This we measure, and not its unobservable, fluctuating, individual, and, last not least, ordinal utilities. Actually, we do not even measure the potato because we cannot, but that is a point for later.

The task of the index-number studies initiated by Fisher seemed to be simple: to find, of the many formulas that could be invented, the one which is superior to all others. This is a problem of uniqueness. Actually the problem is a little more complex. The pair of Laspeyres and Paasche indices have the mathematical property that, if applied together to price and quantity changes, and multiplied, they yield the initial nominal value. They do not have that property individually. A Laspeyres index for prices, and a Laspeyres index for quantities do not match in this way, nor do Paasche indices. As a result, there is a logical dilemma. Whatever reason be found for preferring one index of the two, the logics of multiplication necessarily demands the application of the other index as well. A Laspeyres index for quantities implies a Paasche index for prices, and vice versa. Consequently, it is impossible to remain consistent in preferring one index over the other. If, for example, the argument of easy availability is used to prefer the Laspeyres index for quantity measurement (values at constant prices), the argument is invalidated if prices are then necessarily expressed in the form of Paasche (values at changing quantities). The implication of its own negation is the logical dilemma on which the index numbers are nailed. It seems to be logically impossible to decide for one of the pair in a consistent way. This is a problem of symmetry, or as Fisher called it, of reversability.

Another problem of index numbers is additivity. The property pertains to a set of interdependent index numbers related by accounting constraints. If an aggregate is defined as the sum of its components additivity requires this identity to be preserved when nominal values are turned into real values. In the language of linear operators one can say that the operator of aggregation, and that of deflation should be commutable. Laspeyres indices having constant weights fulfil this requirement. 'Other volume indices in common use are therefore not additive' (SNA, par. 55). If the applied index is not additive deflation of nominal values will generate new balances which have the peculiar property that they occur only in real, not in nominal values. The creation of 'real balances' drives the national accounts into problems of interpretation.

A third problem, instigated by statistical practice rather than economic theory, concerns the adoption, and the abandonment, of a base year. In constructing time series, much desired by econometrics, the compilation of values at constant prices requires the choice of a base year. However, after a certain time that year is outdated. A new base year must be chosen, and the time series must be adjusted. No recipe on this issue has been elaborated in theory, it being considered as a matter of practical expedience, and left, therefore, to the discretion of the statistician. But this is false modesty. It is well known that the value of the real growth rate of a certain year of observation depends on which year has been chosen as the base period. That is a strange effect of measurement, and it has theoretical implications, because there is an apparent contradiction. Real values are measured as values at constant prices, but ever so often when the price vector significantly changes, the prices are moved on, an odd constancy over the long run. Thus even if index number theory does not cope with the problem of base years a proposal of an 'ideal' index must solve this aspect, too.

3.3 INDEX NUMBER THEORY AND THE ANSWER OF THE SNA

3.3.1 The Failure of Axiomatization

Two options are open in order to generate uniqueness of index numbers. One is the authoritative one: to impose a formula by legal act. The other is the scientific one: to convince of a formula by argument. The new SNA has the authority of imposing. If national accountants want to compare their economies they must find common rules, and the United Nations is the agreed body for the purpose. In this perspective it is evident that the SNA has solved the index number problem, in any case, but it is also trivial. In addition, one can show that there are good theoretical arguments which support the solution. They are not all spelled out in the official text, and may be they are not even all shared by its authors, but they deserve to be presented.

We begin by examining in what sense the required solution should be unique. Here, too, an implicit hope of research has not materialized. Mathematization means axiomatization. As a consequence it could be expected that by studying the logical structure of indices one would find some axioms, which are as evident, and at the same time unproven in economics as those in geometry, and that they would single out the theoretically valid index by mathematical derivation. In another classic study (Eichhorn and Voeller, 1976) this idea is comprehensively disproven. Of the axioms under consideration one can form minimal sets of those which are mutually compatible. But no index conforms to all axioms nor are there any axioms which are so superior that they together would uniquely define an index. The range of axioms studied is so impressive that it is worth naming their list: monotonicity, homogeneity, homotheticity, normalization, additivity, multiplicativity, quasilinearity, dimensionality, internality, commensurability, proportionality, circularity, reversability, determinateness, continuity, symmetry, expansibility, aggregation. It is understandable that no dominating set can be formed out of such diversity. Thus one arrives at a rather general definition:

> An **economic index** is an economic measure, i.e. a function $F : D \rightarrow \mathbf{R}$ which maps, on the one hand, a set D of economically interesting objects into the set **R** of real numbers and which satisfies, on the other hand, a system of economically relevant conditions. (Eichhorn, 1978, p.1)

The lesson is that there is not one index number solution, but several, and that the specific definition depends on what axioms the user is interested in. Not all possibly desirable properties are mutually compatible, they are partially contradictory, but not theoretically dominating one another. Clearly, this is not a satisfactory statement for a theoretician. In this sense the study by Eichhorn and Voeller marks the end of the research road opened up by Fisher.

3.3.2 The axiom of Temporal Identity

It is the empirical angle from which one might gain a new perspective. Returning to the problem of the base year, mentioned already, we are concerned with measurement. It is clear that any measurement, be it economic or otherwise, is the determination of a number in space and time. Whatever figure we compile its temporal as well as its spacial identity must be unique. Let us stay with the first. If we measure real value by means of a Laspeyres index we employ two points in time, the base period and the observation period. Consequently, the result, depends on the choice of the base period. The real growth rate between two periods 1 and 2 is different for each different period 0 chosen as the base year. Economists have long become accustomed to the fact, but not without loss of rigidity on the theoretical side. Imagine that in some other science the measurement of a variable depended on what arbitrary choice you take for a required reference period. Be sure to distinguish. The question is not about the fact that the behaviour at time t depends on all times $t - i$ before (causality). The question is about its measurement. Should the perimeter of a triangle today be dependent on whether you compare it to its perimeter of yesterday, or of the day before? The most striking effect of this definition is that real value is identical to nominal value if the base and the reference period coincide. Is real value then a fiction?

Indeed it is because the correct intepretation of a Laspeyres index is conditional: What would the value of a commodity basket be if prices of the base period prevailed? No other interpretation is possible (Fisher and Shell, 1972). A Laspeyres index is not a statement of fact, nor is the Paasche index for that matter.

The uneasiness of this procedure is articulated, and taken care of, in practical statistics. One says that 'after a certain time' (a typical pragmatic phrase) the base period becomes obsolete, and must be exchanged for a more recent one, the connection being made by means of chaining. In spite of the thinking in terms of constant weights, all indices have at some point or other been chained, the time lag of rebasing being roughly inversely proportionate to the volatility of the observed time series. This is a practical proof of the fact that a criterion of what we might call temporal identity (Reich, *et al.*, 1977,

p. 62) is observed in practice. We need to take it up, and introduce it formally in theory.

Let us recapitulate. Measurement is an assignment of a number to time and space. Such assignment applies to nominal values quite simply and directly. The question is how it applies to real values and price indices. If they are to be well defined in time they must be independent in their measurement of values at any other point of time. They must be unique and determinate for one point in time only. Thus we base our index definition on the axiom of temporal identity:

$$P(t) = f(q(t), p(t)) \tag{1}$$

Temporal identity is not a criterion looked at in index number theory, but it has unconsciously always been observed in practice. We call it an axiom, because it applies to any empirical variable, even before it is called economic. It is an axiom of measurement. Any measurement process must have this quality, and if it has gone unnoticed for so long this is because economic circumstances change slowly, and their measurement is inexact for many other reasons, anyhow. But the theory of measurement demands it nevertheless. Thus our definition is the following:

> An **economic index** is a function which maps prices $p(t)$ and quantities $q(t)$ into the set **R** of real numbers, and which complies with the axiom of temporal identity.

This is a more specific definition than the one given by Eichhorn and Voeller in that it explicitely mentions quantities and prices as the operational data from which an economic index starts, and the one criterion which must apply. As we will see the criterion of temporal identity singles out one index. This is shown by the SNA solution.

3.3.3 Deriving the Divisia Index

In its Chapter XVI, the new SNA first treats comparison in time and then in space. We restrict ourselves to the first. The best summary of the SNA recommendations is found in the SNA itself (Ch. XVI, par. 73):

(1) the preferred measure of year to year movements of real GDP is a Fisher volume index, changes over longer periods being obtained by chaining: that is by cumulating the year to year movements;
(2) the preferred measure of year to year inflation for GDP is therefore a Fisher price index, price changes over long periods being obtained

by chaining the year to year price movements: the measurement of inflation is accorded equal priority with the volume movements;

(3) chain indices that use Laspeyres volume indices to measure movements in real GDP and Paasche price indices to measure year to year inflation provide acceptable alternatives to Fisher indices;

(4) the chain indices for total final expenditures, imports and GDP cannot be additively consistent whichever formula is used, but this need not prevent time series of values being compiled by extrapolating base year values by the appropriate chain indices;

(5) chain indices should only be used to measure year to year movements and not quarter to quarter movements.

All through the paragraphs preceding this conclusion emphasis is placed on the chaining procedure. Chain indices 'have a number of practical as well as theoretical advantages' (par. 41). One obtains a better match between commodities in consecutive time periods than between periods which are far apart, remembering the fact that commodities are continuously disappearing from markets and replaced by new commodities, or new qualities. What refers to each individual commodity also refers to their weights in the commodity basket. These, too, are changing continuously, and a chain index assures that the weights are up-to-date. Summarizing these statements it seems that the principal argument brought forward in different variations in support of the chain index in the SNA is based upon the axiom of temporal identity introduced above. It is never explicitely mentioned, but it seems to lie at the heart of the matter. If you want to measure a change of variables aggregated by means of weights, and the measure is to be independent of the variables at other points of time, and to depend only on the variables at the time of observation, or, stated in practical terms, if you want the weights to be up to date with the variables you implicitely apply the criterion of temporal identity. Its proper, and only, operationalization is the chain index in practice, and, to draw a first conclusion, its proper theoretical concept is the Divisia index so that instead of formula (1) an empirically more precise definition of a price index reads

$$dP(t) = f(q(t), dp(t)) \tag{2}$$

the differential price changes being aggregated rather than the absolute prices.

If chaining is the preferable method the choice of a particular formula to be chained is of secondary importance (par. 30). Then the discrepancy between the Laspeyres index and the Paasche index relates to a short period of time only, and in the theoretical limit of a zero time interval it fully disappears. Still it is there, of course, in practice, but only because measurement needs a finite span of time, and not because of some theoretical reason. For each small time period, the weights of the beginning could be used, Laspeyres, or those of the end, Paasche. More plausible it is, of course, to use weights which occur in the middle, and if you don't have them take a symmetrical index between beginning and end as an approximation. In the SNA, the Fisher index and the Tornquist index are considered for the purpose, preference being given to the first.

The SNA choice of the Fisher index for the small time periods to be chained reveals another criterion. As it is not mentioned in the official text it must be inferred. The Fisher index satisfies reversability, the Tornquist index does not. If

$$Q(p^0,q^0,p^1,q^1) = \mathrm{P}(q^0,p^0,q^1,p^1)$$

is the aggregating function of the volume change Q, derived from an aggregate price change formula P by means of a reversal of the prices p and quantities q, and if

$$P^F = \sqrt{\frac{\sum q^0p^1}{\sum q^0p^0}\cdot\frac{\sum q^1p^1}{\sum q^1p^0}}$$

is the Fisher index for price aggregation then

$$P^F \cdot Q^F = \sqrt{\frac{\sum q^0p^1}{\sum q^0p^0}\cdot\frac{\sum q^1p^1}{\sum q^1p^0}}\cdot\sqrt{\frac{\sum p^0q^1}{\sum p^0q^0}\cdot\frac{\sum p^1q^1}{\sum p^1q^0}} = \frac{\sum q^1\cdot p^1}{\sum q^0\cdot p^0} = \frac{\sum v^1}{\sum v^0}$$

Multiplication of prices and quantities yields nominal values v^0 and v^1. If, on the other hand,

$$P^T = \prod\left(\frac{q^1}{q^0}\right)^{0.5(s^0+s^1)} \text{ with } s^0 = \frac{q^0p^0}{\sum q^0p^0}, s^1 = \frac{q^1p^1}{\sum q^1p^1}$$

is the Tornqvist index then

$$P^T \cdot Q^T \text{is not equal to} \frac{\sum v_1}{\sum v_0}$$

The factor reversal test expresses an idea of symmetry. If an index formula is used for prices it is logical to use the same formula for aggregating quantity changes. We already discussed the point. The logical relationship within the pair Paasche–Laspeyres is such that suppose you arrive at some convincing argument for using the Laspeyres index, say for quantity changes (measurement 'at constant prices'), it is difficult to argue why for the change in the other variable the same argument does not apply; why if you measure quantities at constant prices you do not also measure prices at constant quantities, while if you do so, the product between the two aggregates does not yield the original nominal values. Similarly for any other unsymmetrical index, and the habit of looking only at one component, disregarding the implied definition for the other, means to ignore a logical problem, and does not define away the inconsistency of argument. There is nothing in the concept of quantity and price that would warrant a different aggregation formula for one than for the other.

If a chained Fisher index is proposed as the solution of the index number problem for national accounts one major criticism must be dealt with. By definition, neither the Divisia index nor its chained approximation are independent of the path of integration. The same mathematical property is stated somewhat differently by saying that the Divisia index is not a total differential the integration of which yields some well-defined explicite function of prices and quantities. From this follows that the result of the index between two years 0 and n depends on the way in which prices and quantities move in the years between. In the extreme it may happen that prices and quantities describe complete circles each returning to its original value of time 0 at time n, and, yet, the aggregated index shows a non-zero value. 'Even if the prices and quantities for a particular month, or quarter, were to be identical with those in the previous year, a chained Laspeyres volume index could not be expected to return to its previous level' (SNA, par. 49). We may add that this holds not only for the Laspeyres index but for any other chained index. It is a property of chaining, not of the formula chained.

Also, as the SNA itself notes, a chained index is not additive. Two aggregates deflated by means of their individual, chained price indices yield a different sum than if their nominal sum were deflated by means of the combined index. The position taken in the SNA is reasonable: the transparent procedure is not to force additivity through some model or assumption between the aggegrate and its components, but 'simply to publish the non-additive data without adjustment leaving it to users to decide whether, or how, to deal with the resulting discrepancies' (par. 59). Nevertheless, the problem requires discussion, because a Laspeyres index with truly constant weights would be additive in the accounts.

3.4 THE CONCEPT OF ADDITIVITY

3.4.1 What Can Be Learned from the Quality Problem

It is a tenet of index number theory to begin under the assumption that commodities are homogeneous in time and space, and to consider the non-homogeneous case as an exception to the rule. Thus the quality problem is treated as an appendix to the index number problem. It comes in after the index number problem has been elaborated. This order of affairs is so common that it is never discussed, and the new SNA also applies the norm. While it is true that beliefs cannot be proven it is advisable that they should at least be unravelled and brought to the surface of conscious deliberation. Is the assumption of homogeneous commodities really justified? The answer to the question cannot come from the investigation of index number theory, because there the assumption of homogeneity serves as a premise of deduction. We must look at the quality problem, and its treatment in practice. And this must be done before we enter into index number theory, because the indices are methods of aggregation, and aggregation depends on the qualities of the variables aggregated. It is not difficult to imagine that the standards applied to an aggregation method will differ if commodities can be taken as homogeneous or if they cannot. Which of the two is then the more pertinent assumption?

To begin with a familiar observation, it is well known that in terms of macroeconomic statistics we rarely observe true quantities. Even if commodities were homogeneous their number exceeds any scale that could possibly be operationalized in statistics.[1] As a result, commodities are collected and classified in some thousand groups only. Prices are then observed for specific commodities picked out from, and representing, each group so that what we leniently call quantity (q_i), is determined by dividing the price of the representative good (p_i) into the nominal value of the group total (v_i),

$$q_i = \frac{v_i}{p_i}, i = 1, \dots, n \ (n \sim 5000)$$

Thus we necessarily have an effect of structure. The 'quantity', better to say, the volume of a commodity group may increase just because the prices of some other goods in the group than the price representative increase, all quantities remaining the same. In other words, within each commodity group price differences and price changes relative to the price of the group representative are measured as quality differences, by definition. If it were otherwise, if really pure quantities were summed the corresponding prices would be what is generally called unit values, and these are not accepted as valid measurement in general. Quantity contains quality so to speak, or, more precisely, quantity is a deflated value of an observed sum of nominal commodity values, at the macroeconomic level.

The measurement of prices involves the question of what is the quality of a product. The fabric of a shirt constitutes a difference in quality, but not its color for example. We must enter into the concrete rules of monthly price observation. Remembering our methodological approach stated at the beginning of the paper we will not assume any theory in advance in order to pronounce prescriptions of how quality change should be observed, but we go into the field of price surveys and observe what people do when they deal with the quality problem in practice; we take the inductive instead of the deductive approach. The SNA representing a guide for, and summary of, such practice can be used here as a convenient codex.

Its first statement is already significant: 'In general, most types of goods and services, whether simple food products such as potatoes or high technology products such as computers, are available on the market in many different qualities whose physical characteristics differ from each other' (par. 105). And next: 'Goods and services, and the conditions under which they are marketed, are continually changing over time, with some goods or services disappearing from the market and new qualities or new goods or services replacing them' (par. 118). This is an unbiased observation of reality. It says that goods are not homogeneous on the market, but that they come to the market in all their facets and are made homogeneous there. They are different before valuation and homogeneous thereafter. Consequently, 'differences in prices at the same moment of time must be taken as a *prima facie* evidence that the goods or services concerned represent different qualities of the same general kind of good or service' (par. 110).

Thus quality differences are measured by their prices. The SNA adds the warning that this holds 'in most cases', and takes some care to spell out the exceptions. There may be lack of information on the side of buyers, price discrimination on the side of sellers, or some parallel market existing, under which conditions the observed price is invalid as an adequate measure of quality. Let us summarize this by stating abstractly, that in order to measure quality correctly, the observed market must be in equilibrium.

We have inhomogeneous commodities and the market homogenizes them by assigning a price to each. Money is the truly homogeneous good which disperses homogeneity of value among the physical goods. If we accept inhomogeneity as the premise the quality problem does not disappear, but it is also not considered an exception. It is considered the normal state of affairs and it implies continuous formation of judgement. Every recording of a price is preceded by a judgement of whether the observed good is the same as before or not. The judgement is based on the four well known possibilites (SNA, par. 118):

(1) To ignore the change in quality and compile a price relative as if no difference in quality existed;
(2) To omit the item in question and not compile a price relative for it;
(3) To adjust the observed price of a new quality for the change in quality which has taken place;
(4) To treat the two qualities as if they were two separate goods and to estimate their prices in the periods in which they are not sold.

The SNA warns against option (1) because ignoring quality change introduces a bias. The second option is not recommended for the same reason. The recommendation is to confront the change in quality, and to estimate its value on the basis of given prices. One operationalization of this rule may be to install a deliberate change of the price representative at a time when both sell well, and are strong in the market (cash cows) so that their prices are in mutual equilibrium. This is what we would probably call a pure quality difference. Equilibrium of a market being difficult to determine we also work with the complementary concept of a pure price change, and this is where homogeneity comes in, namely a price difference which cannot be explained by changes in physical or economic conditions so that the underlying commodity must be considered homogeneous in quality.

In terms of market dynamics we can interprete the statistical terminology as follows. A pure quality or quantity change is a change due to market forces of supply and demand whereas a pure price change is a change in the value of money alone. Thus in distinguishing between quality and price change we try to single out monetary from real phenomena at each instance of a price measurement. This has interesting implications for the measurement and definition of real values which are worth being spelled out.

Before we do so a brief mention of hedonic price indices is in order. These methods have been developed in depth but applied only at a few cases namely where prices have changed dramatically on the one hand, but depended only on a few basic physical characteristics, while a sufficient variety of such characteristics was on sale at the market (computers, cars, houses). The method is useful, but does not alter the problem. It is based on ad hoc assumptions (choice of characteristics, functional form of combination) just like a direct, and non-mathematical quality estimate. Therefore we need not go into it here.

3.4.2 Accounting for Inflation: The General Price Deflator

An interesting, and new position of the SNA is found in the statement quoted above that the measurement of inflation is put at 'equal priority with the volume movements'. This is a change from the third revision, deserving explicit recognition and development. The position reinforces the criterion of symmetry between price and volume aggregation, and thus indirectly, the Fisher index. But it also sheds a new light on the definition of real value. In traditional accounting the volume component is considered as some approximation to a quantity. An accounting in real values, therefore, seems to require an accounting in quantities, which in practice means that each nominal value is deflated by means of it own individual price index. This works well as long as one deals with commodities. But a national accounting framework has other flows to show as well, and must reconcile these with the commodity flows. All kinds of double, or approximate, deflation methods have been invented in order to deflate taxes, income, profits, non-market output, etc. (for an intersting new method of deflating, based on market shares, see Durand, 1994). They are not satisfactory.

If looked at under a different angle of recognizing that quantities are not the aim of observation, one may arrive at the position that the primary problem of deflating is to correct for the change in value of the accounting unit money, and that the first task deflation must solve is to correct for the loss of purchasing power, which the unit of measurement undergoes. The practical implementation of this approach is simple, indeed. Price indices are aggregated to a measure of inflation, usually operationalized as the consumer price index. All nominal aggregates in the accounts are then divided into this one and the same general deflator. Whether purchases of commodities are concerned, or payments of taxes, or undistributed profits, all nominal values are gauged to the specific norm of general purchasing power, so that instead of defining real value as a measurement at constant prices, a presumption which cannot really be applied to all flows recorded in the national accounts, one would speak of its measurement at constant money value. The interpretation is not less illustrative, and comprehensible. In addition it is a most straightforward way of avoiding non-additivity in the deflated accounts, because a proportionate shrinking of nominal values preserves additivity, naturally. The SNA does not argue for this position, but it seems to be a logical extension of the concern laid upon the measurement of inflation as part of national accounting.

If the national accounts are deflated by the overall rate of money inflation this does not imply that the same has to hold for other systems. On the contrary, in terms of analysis of production of branches, in input–output tables, where distributive transactions do not play a role, volume measurements by means of specific price deflators are useful and the resulting value added changes can be interpreted meaningfully (e.g. as productivity gains). What we dispute is that these volume measurements should also form the model for deflating non-commodity flows in the national accounts.

3.5 INTERPRETATION OF PATH DEPENDENCY

It would be stimulating and challenging to investigate the different methods which are in use world wide for forming a sound judgement on the side of the price observer. Here it suffices to realize that such judgement is the parent of our data. What we are supplied with from the microlevel of observation are not quantities, but money values corrected by means of judgement for price and quality change. The difference is important, because it bans, or rather makes obsolete, certain criteria which we might want to apply to aggregation formulas.

Repeated observation of prices p and resulting 'quantities', as interpreted above, q leads to time series of each, $p(t)$ and $q(t)$. These have an interesting property, illustrated by means of an example. When nylon was invented, cotton shirts were in use. They also were the price representative of shirts. As demand and technology developed cotton shirts became out of fashion and devalued, the wash-and-wear quality of nylon shirts commanding a superior price and acceptance at the market. As demand and technology developed further cotton shirts disappeared and nylon shirts became the price representative. The change from the one price representative to the other was noted as an improvement in quality (no price change). A decade later, health concerns and a new marketing brought back the cotton shirt. This time it overtook the nylon shirt in price. Again this is rightly interpreted as a expression of higher quality.

In physical terms the result is paradox. The economy seems to have moved in a circle. And an index theory based on quantities as elements will describe just this. But in economic terms this chain of events is meaningful and a sign of progress. The value of a commodity is a historical and social characteristic, not a physical one because it is determined by a social mechanism, the market. If market conditions change the quality of goods change even if physically they remain the same.

The possibility of going in circles is called path dependency in index number theory. Investigation of the quality problem leaves us with the impression that the very elements of our economic indexes, the individual market functions $p_i(t)$ and $q_i(t)$ are path dependent. So the question is not how to avoid path dependency in an aggregating index, but how to interpret its factual existence in our data. We begin with production. A common device to picture production in microeconomic theory is the transformation curve (see Usher, 1974, for details). The curve shows a function $Q(q_1, q_2)$ interpreted as an abstract measure of total output ('isoquant') combined from produced quantities of goods *A* and *B*. Economics has not come to determine the function, mathematically. Usually one is satisfied by drawing a picture of it in qualitative terms (Figure 3.1). Growth is then interpreted as a move to a higher isoquant.

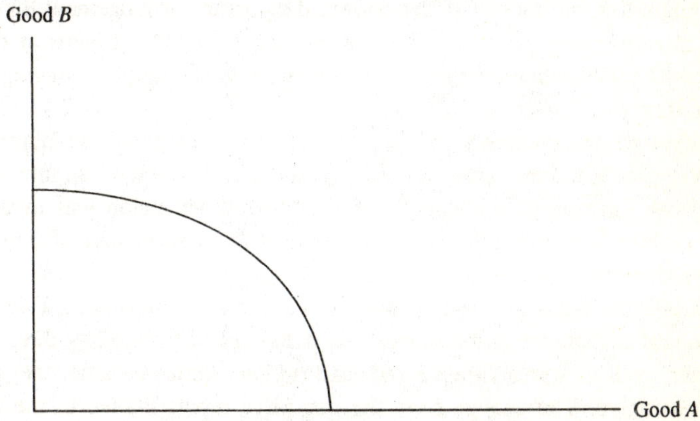

Figure 3.1 Transformation curve between two products

There are two reasons why this intepretation of growth is inadequate. The first is the unavoidable shift of the transformation curve in time. Statistical observation cannot rely on the ceteris paribus asssumption, so convenient for exercises in microeconomics. On the contrary, it must be assumed that at least some conditions change, so that the transformation curve must be written $Q(q_1, q_2, t)$. Then, although it may be reasonable to assume non-intersection of isoquants at each moment of time, this is not so between moments when the 'production mountain' is recognized to move. Since we do not know the functions anyway the issue of whether they intersect or not is like discussing whether the color of an individual electron is red or blue. The question is equally beyond operationalization. Nevertheless, we can imagine that technology shifts in making good *B* cheaper (nylon shirts) while at the same time disinvesting in good *A* (cotton shirts), which then becomes more expensive. Or that the technology of steam engines is less developed today than it was 100 years ago. Generally speaking, technical progress is accompanied by technical losses in history. The result is a crossing of transformation curves in time (Figure 3.2):

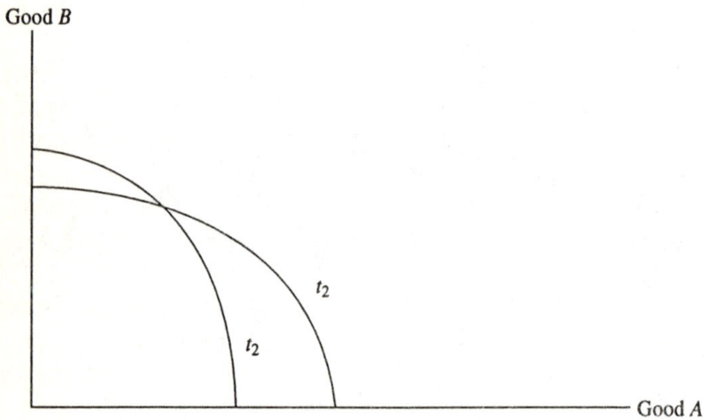

Figure 3.2 Likely effect of growth

The second argument against growth interpretation in terms of transformation curves is that we actually measure and compare just two points in the commodity space which have become realized at times t_1 and t_2. We have no empirical evidence that the new transformation curve runs parallel to the old one, at the macroeoconomic level. Even if a belief in perfect markets determined the first derivatives of the transformation curves at the point of observation this is not enough to determine an entire function (Figure 3.3).

Microeconomic theory needs the assumption of non-intersection. This is because it derives observable prices as derivatives from some postulated but unobservable aggregating function like the transformation curve. Evidently

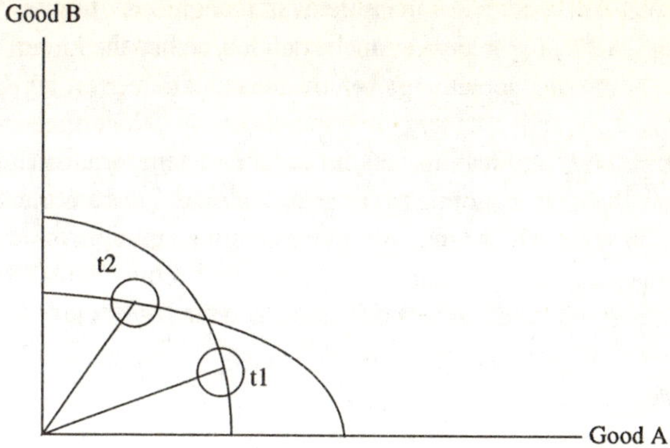

Figure 3.3 Realized points at transformation curves

this is meaningful only in as much as these curves do not intersect. Once we discard the necessity of looking for a transformation curve we are free to deal with prices as not being first derivatives of such a function, and we can interprete a path in time (t_1, t_2) which does not measure an increase in absolute production, like 'growth', but an economic development, an 'acceleration' of production, as we might say instead. This interpretation produces quite different analogies.

Growth means that we are situated at a certain 'height' and have 'climbed up'. It is a variable in Newton's absolute space. Speed means that we are not able to determine our position in commodity space, but only the speed with which we are producing and consuming commodities. It is a local variable, tied to the point of observation, and not to an absolute system of coordinates, and its rate of change is then an acceleration of production. There is no mountain of aggregate output which we climb, but an effort of faster production. We produce today in one year what 20 years ago we produced in two.

On the price side the same rule applies. An ordered set of utility curves is a necessary assumption for microeconomics. Lines of equal utility do not intersect. Utility is thus pictured as the mountain the height of which a price index is to reveal. It is clear that path dependent indexes have no place in this framework.[2] But as the economy changes in time this assumption is also unlikely. We do not know whether utlity levels between two points of time intersect, and if we admit it, we have discarded a major obstacle agains path dependency on the side of demand.

The lesson of economic index number theory seems to be that if you want to measure a function by means of an index, the index must be that function. The empirical procedures of price measurement demonstrate that an aggregate function of prices or of volumes cannot be defined, so that the idea of isoquants and utility levels as something behind index figures is an inadequate interpretation of the index figures.

After the critical implications of the axiom of temporal identity for the interpretation of macroeconomic aggregates in terms of microeconomic theory it is necessary to explain what positive economic interpretation might be employed, instead. This point brings us back to Bródy (1980, 1992). What does it mean if an economy moves in a circle, and the Divisia index then shows

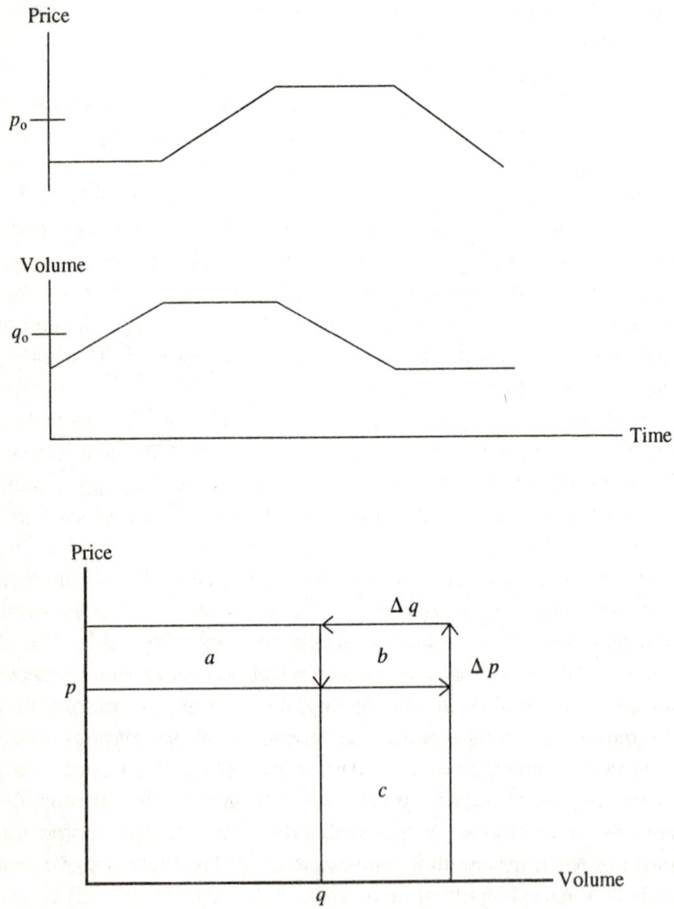

Figure 3.4 Circular movement of an economy

non-zero production change and inflation in the aggregate variables while the the time integrals of the individual price and volume indices sum to zero (Figures 3.4a and 3.4b)?

The interpretation follows the value movements engendered by the market. If price and volume move exactly opposite to one another, nominal turnover changes according to the market elasticity, but the area of the circle is zero. The price increases in the same proportion as the volume decreases. This may be the expected behavior if no lags of production or information exist (perfect market). If volumes precede prices there will first be an increase in turnover due to a volume increase at a low price ($p\ \Delta q$ = area c in Figure 3.4b), then at the higher volume the price will rise, enlarging the turnover by the amount $\Delta p(q + \Delta q)$ = areas $(a + b)$. At the high price volume decreases by the same amount by which it increased before, but the price at which it is valued is now higher, $p + \Delta p$. As a result real product decreases by $(b + c)$. In the last phase price decreases at low volumes $(-a)$. The effect for the volume side is thus $+c - (b + c) = -b$, and for the price side $a + b - a = b$. We have a negative volume component and positive price component.

The interpretation can rely on familiar, practical concepts as they are in use on the stock market, for example. The market is in disequilibrium, circling around its equilibium values, and inviting speculation. In the product market the phenomenon is known as the pig cycle – except that pigs are not a convenient property for speculation – and it supports the SNA rule to exclude such cycles from measurement by an appropriate length of the observation period. In fact, it is an argument in support of the long standing practice of constant prices, or of constant commodity baskets, because it actually means to work with a period of about 5 years, and then to update by chaining. This procedure could be considered as a Divisia index averaged over the business cycle.

For the non-cyclical component of path dependency we may say that it shows the limits of comparability. The higher the possible difference is due to path variation the less the two time periods are comparable. This is nothing but the well known Laspeyres effect, which has never found recognition as a meaningful variable in microeconomics, but as a measure of long-run disequilibrium might well be used to assess comparability in time.

Let us summarize our argument. Index number theory has not produced axioms that determine a single index formula. Statistical practice actually adheres to one axiom, which if theoretically accepted defines the Divisia index as the only one that conforms with it. The underlying axiom may be called temporal identity of measurement. This combined with the property of additivity, desirable for an accounting framework, leads to the recommendation of a general deflator correcting for the change in the value of the unit of account proportionately for all entries. The unavoidable path dependency of the index is a sign that microconcepts such as utility functions or transformation curves do not necessarily hold in this area, and it can be positively interpreted as a result of market disequilibrium in time.

We leave the subject here, recalling a small historical point. Gossen's laws are said to have solved the puzzle of water and diamonds, in that they explain why diamonds are more expensive than water although they are less useful. And the explanation is that marginal utility diminishes with quantity so that where water is plenty and diamonds are few the first is cheap and the second is expensive. Actually the parable is inexact. Absolute prices cannot be compared between commodites. Consider the comparison of flour and flowers, to take some less spectacular goods. The question of which of the two has the higher price is not operational, because dimensions differ. It is not clear how many pounds of flour would have to be compared to one flower. In the same way, measure water in million cubic feet and diamonds in milligrams and the price of water will be higher. Marginalism explains the change of price within one and the same commodity as more of it is supplied, but not the difference of prices between commodities. What you can compare between commodities are relative price changes rather than absolute price levels, and these again can be aggregated to a macroeconomic variable of general price change, the integral of which, however, is not an absolute price level. We have tried to show some implications of index number practice for the theory of value, in order to clear the road lying before us. It needs further effort; value theory is not finished, yet.

NOTES

1. Under this aspect Debreu's general equilibrium is parallel to the spirit of Laplace in physics. If the spirit knew all positions and speed of all particles in the world it would produce a perfect forecast. In the same way knowing all preferences and technologies would yield the perfect measure of value. Both propositions are unoperational, and thus can be believed or not. They cannot be decided.
2. Allen writes that the Divisia index 'takes the heat off the need to assume an unchanged preference map. Each differential change is on a momentarily frozen preference map and integration can proceed whether or not the map shifts over time' (Allen, 1975, p. 178). Actually this is not exact. Even at the differential level the Divisia index measures a different utility change if the map moves than if it remains fixed. If $U = f(q_i)$ we have $dU = \Sigma \frac{\partial u}{\partial q_i} dqi$ while if $U = f(q_i, t)$ we have $dU = \Sigma(\frac{\partial u}{\partial q_i} dq_i + \frac{\partial u}{\partial t} dt$.

Under the assumption that prices equal marginal utilities the first part of the right hand side is captured by the Divisia index, the second not.

REFERENCES

ALLEN, R. G. D. (1975) *Index Numbers in Theory and Practice*, Macmillan, London.

BRÓDY, A. (1974) *Proportions, Prices and Planning: A Mathematical Restatement of the Labor Theory of Value*, North-Holland, Amsterdam.

BRÓDY, A. (1980) 'On Measuring Growth', *Acta Oeconomica*, Vol. 24, pp. 47–56.

BRÓDY, A. (1992) 'On Measuring Growth', *Structural Change and Economic Dynamics*, Vol. 3, pp. 93–102.

DIEWERT, W. E. (ed.) (1978) *Essays in Index Number Theory*, North-Holland, Amsterdam.

DIEWERT, W. E. (1993) 'The Early History of Price Index Research', in W. E. Diewert and A. O. Nakamura (eds.) *Essays in Index Numbers*, Vol. 1, pp. 33–65, North-Holland, Amsterdam.

DURAND, R. (1994) 'An Alternative to Double Deflation for Measuring Real Industry Value Added', *The Review of Income and Wealth*, 40, pp. 303–16.

EICHHORN, W. and VOELLER, J. (1976) *Theory of the Price Index*, Springer, Berlin-Heidelberg-New York.

EICHHORN, W. *et al.* (ed.) (1978) *Theory and Applications of Economic Indices*, Physica, Würzburg.

FISHER, F. M. and SHELL, K. (1972) *The Economic Theory of Price Indices – Two Essays on the Effect of Taste, Quality and Technological Change*, Academic Press, New York and London.

FISHER, I. (1992) *The Making of Index Numbers*, Houghton Mifflin, Boston.

HICKS, J. R. (1940) 'The Valuation of Social Income', *Economica*, pp. 105–24.

REICH, U. P., SONNTAG, Ph. and HOLUB, H. W. (1977). *Arbeit-Konsum-Rechnung. Axiomatische Kritik und Erweiterung der Volkswirtschaftlichen Gesamtrechnung*, Bund-Verlag, Köln.

UNITED NATIONS (1993) *A System of National Accounts*, 4th rev., New York.

USHER, D. (1974) 'The Suitability of the Divisia Index for the Measurement of Economic Aggregates', *The Review of Income and Wealth*, 20, pp. 273–88.

4 Current Uses of the RAS Technique: A Critical Review

Karen R. Polenske[1]

4.1 INTRODUCTION

Many analysts are using nonsurvey techniques to estimate national and regional input–output tables, interregional trade flows, and other types of economic data. Analysts' extensive use of these techniques reflects the delicate compromise they must make between the cost of collecting actual data and the accuracy of the models with which they work. For adjusting and/or updating input–output tables, analysts most widely use the RAS procedure. Based upon the structure of a national or a different, but supposedly similarly structured, regional table, they employ the technique both to update national (regional) tables and to estimate regional tables. They use a base national (regional) table, *A*, and separately estimate marginal row (*r*) and column (*s*) controls for the predicted year. They then iteratively adjust the flows in A first to sum to the respective *rs* and then to the respective *ss* until the new row and column totals in the new matrix are as close as designated to marginal (actual) totals. Thus, the analyst tries to find a new matrix A*:

$$A^{\star} = \hat{r}\, A\, \hat{s}, \tag{1}$$

$$X^{\star} = A\, \hat{q}^{\star}, \tag{2}$$

$$X^{\star} = (\hat{r}\, A\, \hat{s})\; q^{\star}, \tag{3}$$

$$u^{\star} = X^{\star}\, i, \tag{4}$$

$$u^{\star} = \hat{r}\; (A\; q^{\star})\hat{s}, \tag{5}$$

$$v^{\star} = X'^{\star}\; i, \tag{6}$$

$$v'^{\star} = i'X^{\star}, \tag{6'}$$

$$v^{\star} = \hat{r}'(A\; \hat{q}^{\star})\; \hat{s}, \tag{7}$$

where

A = matrix of technical coefficients for the base year (region),

A^* = matrix of technical coefficients for the estimated year (region),

$\wedge$ = a diagonal matrix,
r = column vector of 'substitution' multipliers,
s = row vector of 'fabrication' multipliers,
X^* = matrix of intermediate flows in the estimated year (region),
q = column vector of gross output in the estimated year,
i = column unitary vector,
u^* = column vector of total intermediate output in the estimated year (region), and
v^* = row vector of total intermediate inputs in the estimated year (region).

If vectors u^*, v^*, and q^* are known, the analyst can solve the $2n$ equations with $2n$ unknown multipliers represented by equations (1) and (7). S/he can obtain the solution either by using an iterative procedure or by solving simultaneously the system of equations. Additional information about the solution of the constrained biproportional-matrix problem and a short-cut procedure is provided by Stone, Bates, and Bacharach (1963, pp. 27–9) and United Nations (1973, pp. 67–8).

In this paper, I will make two arguments about how economic analysts are basing their use of the RAS procedure on a myth of accuracy. First, I will show that although analysts sometimes obtain very low errors of estimation, they do so only under relatively restrictive conditions. Second, I will review a number of studies to illustrate that although analysts have often found the RAS procedure to be more accurate than other adjustment procedures, it seldom provides errors of less than 30 per cent. I emphasize the myth of accuracy, because many users fail to recognize that the RAS procedure, if employed without careful and extensive adjustments to the base data, frequently results in 30–50 per cent, or higher, overall errors. Errors in individual elements in a table may, of course, be even higher.

Work on the constrained biproportional matrix problem has been conducted by analysts in several disciplines, as summarized by Lecomber (1975). Here, I focus only on the research most directly related to the economics and regional science disciplines. I will begin by providing a brief history of the first uses of the RAS technique, which seem to have helped lead to the myth of accuracy; then, I will critically review selected major early uses of the technique for adjusting input–output and interregional-trade tables in order to illustrate my two arguments.

4.2 ORIGINS OF THE RAS TECHNIQUE

The roots of the RAS procedure can be traced from Deming and Stephan (1940), Leontief (1941), and Stone and Brown (1962). While working at the

US Bureau of the Census, Deming and Stephan first proposed the simple iterative procedure – later known as the RAS procedure – as a means of adjusting the then upcoming 1940 Census of Population data. They were also the first to use the letters *r* and *s* to designate the multipliers. They tested the iterative procedure and a least-squares method, obtaining almost identical results from both. The 6 × 4 matrices of artificial population characteristics they used as illustrations had marginal totals that were less than one per cent different from the control totals, had positive entries for all cells in the matrix, and had entries in the matrix cells that ranged from a minimal value of 120 to a maximum value of 10,476, all of which helped them to achieve a final solution that seemed to be fairly reasonable after only two complete iteration cycles.

At about the same time, Leontief (1941, pp. 61–4) also proposed using the method of least squares and discussed two sets of row and column multipliers – 'the productivity coefficient of commodity *k*' and 'the productivity coefficient of industry *k*', respectively, that he hypothesized would account jointly for input–output coefficient change. The ideas of Leontief and Deming and Stephan were not widely noticed for some twenty years until Stone and Brown (1962, pp. 294–6) proposed the so-called RAS model for use (instead of a least-squares method) on constrained biproportional matrix-estimation problems. Its first important application in the United Kingdom was at the Cambridge Growth Project, by Stone, Bates, and Bacharach (1963), who also were the first to use the term 'RAS method'. They started its use by national and regional economic analysts.

In a very good survey paper, Lecomber (1975) provides a detailed description and critique of the RAS and four alternative adjustment procedures used to update and/or project national input–output data. Matuszewski, Pitts, and Sawyer (1964) devised a linear programming procedure, Almon (1968) and Johansen (1968) incorporated additional information concerning the statistical confidence of each coefficient into a national table prior to adjusting, and Friedlander (1961) and Theil (1967) each devised alternative quadratic programming procedures. At the regional level, analysts have tested other procedures, such as entropy methods (Wilson, 1970), Lagrangian multipliers (Morrison and Thumann, 1980), and both the pure nonsurvey and other partial survey methods, as reviewed by Sawyer and Miller (1983). On the one hand, the RAS procedure has the virtue of providing estimates that are as accurate as, or in some cases more accurate than, the other procedures. It also requires a minimal amount of data, is one of the simplest procedures to apply, and preserves the signs of the initial elements. On the other hand, unless extensive adjustments are made, the RAS procedure may result in large errors of estimation and unreasonable estimates for some of the elements, and, in a few cases, the iterations may not converge.

In the early 1960s, two adjustment procedures were developed for use in updating national input–output tables: the RAS procedure by Stone and Brown (1962) and a linear-programming procedure by Matuszewski, Pitts, and Sawyer (1964). Both were viewed as having a decided advantage over previously used single-constraint balancing procedures in that both procedures were used not only to balance demand adjustments for each row, but also to balance supply adjustments for each column – the matrix to be adjusted was therefore subject to two sets of constraints.

Stone, Bates, and Bacharach (1963) at Cambridge University applied the RAS procedure that had been set forth by Stone and Brown to update the 32-sector 1954 input–output table for the United Kingdom to 1960. They then used the updated table to estimate a projected 1966 input–output table. They actually used the RAS procedure twice. In the first round, they used it on the Make matrix, which is a sector-by-commodity table showing the composition of output of each sector. They made an identical type of calculation, referred to as LUL, to the Use matrix,[2] which is a commodity-by-sector table showing the inputs used by each establishment. Because marginal controls were only available for 1958, rather than for 1960, they projected the *r* and *s* multipliers obtained with those controls to 1960 in order to estimate the final Make matrix. In the second round, they used the RAS procedure to project the 1960 coefficients to 1966.

Stone and his colleagues focused their attention on the accuracy of each coefficient. They were interested in developing a technique that could be used not only to project the individual coefficients, but also to predict them accurately for the intermediate year, hoping that the RAS updating procedure could extend the life of compiled input–output tables by as much as ten years. Three points relevant for the later discussion should be noted. First, the marginal totals were not actual data but were estimated by a residual method. Second, the projection from 1960 to 1966 was made with the use of the square of the *r* and *s* multipliers, because the difference in years between 1960–6 was the same as between 1954–60. When the square is used, the assumption is that there is an exponential trend in the values of the individual elements of the matrix, an assumption that is questioned by Lecomber (1975, pp. 10–11) because it causes the column sums of the matrices to augment at an increasing rate, which is not usually plausible. Third, there was no input–output matrix for 1960; therefore, Stone, Bates, and Bacharach could not calculate errors between the estimated and an actual matrix. They justified the use of the RAS procedure (1963, pp. 30–2) based upon the testing of the accuracy of the procedure that had been conducted by Paelinck and Waelbroeck (1963) with Belgian input–output data, which I discuss later.

Czamanski and Malizia (1969), Morrison and Smith (1974), and McMenamin and Haring (1974) conducted the first regional RAS studies. In the first two cases, the analysts based the regional input–coefficient estimates upon national coefficients. For their 1969 study, Czamanski and Malizia used the 1958 US input–output data to obtain an estimated set of 1963 data for the state of Washington. Morrison and Smith, who were the first to use the RAS technique for an urban area, applied the technique to data from a 1968 national table for the United Kingdom to estimate a 19-sector 1968 table for the city of Peterborough, England.[3] They found that the RAS procedure ranked first, ahead of seven other methods. They incorporated some survey information into the RAS calculations and were therefore not surprised that the RAS procedure ranked first, but they did make special note of the 'degree of superiority' of the method.

McMenamin and Haring (1974) used an approach that differed in two respects from previous regional RAS studies. First, they used the technique to estimate a 1967 table for the state of Washington based upon the full-survey 1963 table for the state, rather than on the national 1963 US table. Second, they constrained the data in the table to sum to total gross output and total gross outlays, rather than to intermediate outputs and inputs. They concluded that the 'error comparisons of the technical coefficients obtained by the H–M [Haring–McMenamin] method were no better (or worse) than those from the [usual] RAS method at this level of aggregation' (McMenamin and Haring, 1974, p. 204).

After these first applications of the RAS technique at the national and regional levels, many analysts wrote papers in the 1970s and 1980s, including Allen (1974), Allen and Lecomber (1975), Almon (1970), Almon, Atkinson, and Reimbold (1972), Bacharach (1970), Davis, Lofting, and Sathaye (1977), Drabek (1981), Fontela, Duval, Gabus, Borlin, and Velay (1970), Geary (1973), Gretton and Cotterell (1979), Henry (1973a, 1973b), Lamel, Richter, Teufelsbauer, and Zelle (1974), Martin (1972), Minujin and Beccaria (1978), Parikh (1979), and Stäglin (1970). Even today, most users of the RAS technique, however, refer only to the papers by Paelinck and Waelbroeck (1963) and Harrigan, McGilvray, and McNicoll (1980) to justify its use.

4.3 MYTH OF THE ACCURACY OF THE RAS TECHNIQUE

Many analysts using the RAS adjustment technique do so because they claim that it is more accurate than other adjustment techniques. I will show first that, although the RAS procedure may be more accurate than other techniques, the technique is accurate only under certain rather restrictive conditions, and second that unless those restrictive conditions hold, it often results in very inaccurate estimates.

Stone, Bates, and Bacharach (1963) and various succeeding analysts cite the work by Paelinck and Waelbroeck (1963) as verification of the accuracy of the RAS technique. Paelinck and Waelbroeck used the 21-sector Belgian input–output tables for 1953 to estimate a 1959 table and compared the data in the estimated table with 1959 data compiled by direct observation. In the final set of comparisons, after prespecifying six dominant coefficients, only one of the 270 nonzero elements was 'in error' by more than one per cent (1963, p. 111). At least four reasons seem to have contributed to this apparent low error: (1) Very little change occurred between 1953 and 1959. The table presented by the authors (1963, p. 111) shows that 238 of the 270 nonzero coefficients changed by only 0.0–0.5 per cent between 1953 and 1959, that only 17 of the coefficients changed by more than 1.0 per cent, and that 132 of the coefficients showed no change. (2) Actual 1959 data were used for six major cells that did change. The six values used in the table and control totals in place of six deleted elements were actual 1959 data, rather than estimated figures. (3) All control totals were actual rather than estimated data. Actual vectors of total gross output, total intermediate output, and total intermediate input from the 1959 survey table, rather than estimated vectors, were used as control totals. (4) The 1959 table was not a survey table but was itself partially based upon estimates made by industry experts. This latter point leads Barker to conclude that the RAS procedure with supplemental information does no better than industrial expertise. He says:

> It is misleading to imply that RAS as a method can do almost as well in providing an up-to-date table as taking a census of production. Rather it does almost as badly, judging from British evidence, as using partial information on particular flows. (Barker, 1975, p. 66)

As to the errors that did occur in the Belgian tests, Stone, Bates, and Bacharach (1963, p. 31) indicate that there were three causes: (1) The input–output table was highly aggregated. (2) Variations occurred in the substitution effect along the rows, contrary to an assumption that such variations were not present. (3) A ripple effect resulted in which an erroneous RAS estimate in one of the elements can generate errors throughout the rest of the table, especially if the cells in the matrix are connected (if all, or most, of the cells in the matrix contain nonzero entries). Additional discussion of the errors can be found in the Paelinck and Waelbroeck (1963), Barker (1975), and McMenamin and Haring (1974) articles. From my review of these studies, I conclude that the RAS procedure is accurate only under relatively restrictive conditions.

When analysts use the RAS technique without constraints, they often obtain very large errors. Harrigan, McGilvray, and McNicoll (1980) made one of the most comprehensive regional tests, comparing the RAS with five other methods. They estimated a table for Scotland, based upon the 1973 input–output table for the United Kingdom. They then tested six adjustment methods: RAS partial survey, location quotient, cross-industry location quotient, adjusted cross-industry location quotient, logarithmic cross-industry location quotient, and commodity-balance techniques. The RAS procedure in each case outranked the five other estimation techniques. Even so, the errors were not inconsequential, with individual coefficients having, on the average, mean errors that were 30 per cent or more.

Although Harrigan, McGilvray, and McNicoll did not mention the size of the tables, they are otherwise exceptionally thorough in their analysis. They used seven different measures to test the errors: mean absolute difference, Euclidean metric difference, Isard/Romanoff similarity index, sum of Chi-Square distribution terms, absolute mean relative difference, information index, and correlation coefficient. In justifying use of the RAS technique, regional analysts usually refer to the Harrigan, McGilvray, and McNicoll article, noting only that the RAS technique produced lower errors of estimation than any of the other five techniques, which is a true statement. Analysts usually neglect, however, to note that the errors from the RAS technique were sizeable.

In the next section, I show that both of my concerns about accuracy are verified by reviewing a selected number of the many articles on the RAS procedure. I also indicate why analysts need in addition to be concerned with convergence and structural distortion issues.

4.4 EVIDENCE FROM APPLICATIONS OF THE RAS TECHNIQUE

My concern about the use of the RAS technique without making appropriate adjustments is based both upon a careful review of literature and upon the experience my multiregional research staff and I have had in trying to use the technique ourselves. Since the 1960s, most analysts have applied the RAS technique to adjusting or updating input–output tables; only a few analysts have applied the technique to other types of matrices, usually transportation-flow matrices. A sufficient number of analysts have used the technique to draw some general conclusions about the merits and problems with its use. I will focus on the following four issues: (1) errors of estimation,

(2) convergence and speed of convergence, (3) minimum level of discrepancy allowed between control totals and estimated totals, and (4) serious distortions of elements in the table. None of the analysts provided complete information about these aspects in their use of the RAS technique; therefore, some of my conclusions from this review are very tentative.

National input–output analysts have primarily been concerned with the accuracy of the RAS procedure as a means of extending the life of input–output tables. Although this is also an issue for regional input–output analysts, distinctions exist between the use of the RAS procedure for national and regional tables. A major distinction is that national input–output coefficients reflect technical input relationships relating to the production function for the sector. The production function may vary over time as a result of changes in relative prices, technology, or product composition (sometimes called product-mix), none of which need occur proportionally for each input used by a sector. Regional input–output coefficients, on the other hand, reflect the productive capacity of the region. Malizia and Bond (1974, p. 358) maintain that 'basically, regional production capacity can be expected to act on both absorption and fabrication in a manner that will encourage biproportional regional coefficient change'. Such reasoning leads to an a priori assumption that the RAS method may work better for regional than for national input–output tables. As I will show, however, the results to date are mixed. I will review selected comparative information concerning the use of the RAS technique to update and/or estimate national and regional input–output tables and interregional trade tables. Needless to say, I did not include all studies in which the RAS procedure has been applied, but only those that contain information most relevant to this review.

4.4.1 Errors of Estimation

Because of the significant variations in the types of data used and the modifications made to the RAS procedure, I had difficulty making any comparison of the errors in the different studies. Many more of the regional analysts than national analysts have tested for errors, but once again the methods and results vary widely. As shown in Table 4.1, many alternative measures of the errors of estimation have been used. Regardless of the measure used, however, analysts have often found very large errors of estimation. Strangely, only a few analysts, such as Lecomber (1969), Malizia and Bond (1974), Hinojosa (1978), Butterfield and Mules (1980), and Lynch (1986), note how large the errors are, but their results and warnings about the potential errors in the use of the RAS technique are almost never referred to by other analysts.

Table 4.1 RAS adjustments of selected national and regional input-output tables and interregional trade tables

Authors	*Matrix Characteristics* *Region (Country)*	*Size*	*Base Year and Region*	*Estimated Year*	*Errors*	*Comments*
			NATIONAL INPUT–OUTPUT TABLES			
Stone, Bates and Bacharach (1963)	United Kingdom	32-sector	1954 United Kingdom	1960	No actual data were available for error estimation.	Used RAS Procedure. Estimated Make and Mix matrices separately.
Paelinck and Waelbroeck (1963)	Belgium	21-sector	1953 Belgium	1959	Prespecified 6 large coefficients; only 1 of remaining 270 nonzero elements had an error greater than one per cent.(Refer to text for reasons.)	Used the RAS and a modified RAS procedure. 'Actual' 1959 table partly estimated by industry experts.
Schneider (1965)	United States	6-sector 24-sector	1947 United States	1958	Used counts of errors and other measures.	Compared results of RAS and linear programming procedures.

Table 4.1 Continued

	Matrix Characteristics					
Authors	*Region (Country)*	*Size*	*Base Year and Region*	*Estimated Year*	*Errors*	*Comments*
Tilanus (1966)	Netherlands	27-sector	1948 1951 1954 1957 Netherlands	1951 1954 1957 1960	40 percent of matrix elements were zero.	Compared results of RAS and a statistical correction method. Number of sectors not clearly defined.
Lamel, Richter, Teufelsbauer, and Zelle (1974)	Norway	51-sector	1964 Norway	1968	Stopped iterations when absolute deviation from margins was $\leq$ 5.0 per cent for all sectors.	Compared results of RAS and Almon procedures. Developed a new updating procedure called DYMOD.
Barker (1975)	United Kingdom	70-sector	1954 United Kingdom	1963	Model produced errors in 20 to 49 per cent range.	Compared actual 1963 U.K. coefficients with those projected with the RAS technique, incorporating exogenous information.

Table 4.1 Continued

	Matrix Characteristics					
Authors	*Region (Country)*	*Size*	*Base Year and Region*	*Estimated Year*	*Errors*	*Comments*
Davis, Lofting, and Sathaye (1977)	United States	50-sector	1963 United States	1967	Used simple counts to indicate which of two procedures produced coefficients closer to actual 1967 values.	Compared results of RAS and linear programming procedures.
Miernyk (1976)	United States	79-sector	1963 United States	1967	Mean difference was 127 per cent.	Used the RAS procedure. Number of sectors not clearly indicated. Only a brief description of results.
Lynch (1986)	United Kingdom	69-sector	1963 United Kingdom	1968	Can reduce percentage errors to less than 10 percent only on aggregate tables or by using exogenous information on 60 per cent or more of nonzero cells.	Used the RAS procedure on 1963 absorption matrix. Tested effects of aggregating data and of incorporating exogenous information.

Table 4.1 Continued

	Matrix Characteristics					
Authors	*Region (Country)*	*Size*	*Base Year and Region*	*Estimated Year*	*Errors*	*Comments*
			REGIONAL INPUT–OUTPUT TABLES			
Czamanski and Malizia (1969)	Washington State	43-sector 36-secto 28-sector	1958 United States	1963	Mean percentage errors ranged from 39 to 81 per cent. Values of the information coefficient ranged from 0.779 to 54.262.	For best results, excluded tertiary sectors and used field-survey information for primary sectors and sectors in which region specialized.
Morrison and Smith (1974)	Peterborough, England	19-sector	1968 United Kingdom	1968	Estimated mean similarity index; mean absolute difference; chi-square; information content; correlation coefficient.	Compared RAS with seven other non-survey methods. Concluded that RAS procedure was 'overwhelmingly' superior.

Table 4.1 Continued

	Matrix Characteristics					
Authors	*Region (Country)*	*Size*	*Base Year and Region*	*Estimated Year*	*Errors*	*Comments*
McMenamin and Haring (1974)	Washington State		1963 Washington State	1967	Errors of estimation no better or worse using Haring–McMenamin method than using usual RAS procedure.	Constrained data to sum to total gross output and total gross outlays.
Malizia and Bond (1974)	Washington State	52-sector 43-sector 27-sector 22-sector	1963 Washington State	1967	Mean errors were 124 (52-sector)-regional; 133 (43-sector)-technical; 105 (27-sector)-regional; 118 (22-sector)-technical.	Measured divergence between predicted and survey-based estimates; gross output, intermediate demand, and value added.
Hewings (1977)	Washington State Kansas State	29-sector	1963 Washington State, 1965 Kansas State	1963, 1965	Obtained absolute and percentage differences in output.	Tried to determine possibility of using survey-based regional tables from one state to estimate coefficients in a second state.

Table 4.1 Continued

Authors	*Matrix Characteristics*				*Errors*	*Comments*
	Region (Country)	*Size*	*Base Year and Region*	*Estimated Year*		
Hinojosa (1978)	Washington State	27-sector	1963, 1967, 1972 Washington State	1963, 1967, 1972	Compared direct and direct and indirect coefficients; made distribution of frequencies. Lowest mean error was 34 per cent.	Took 11 to 21 iterations to converge. Evaluated relative differences between 12 pairs of matrices.
Hewings and Janson (1980)	Hypothetical	5-sector	n.a.	n.a.	Fixing coefficients provided little improvement in multiplier estimation.	Addressed some of the issues raised by Thumann (1978) and investigated effect of predetermining certain coefficients.
Hewings and Syverson (1980)	Washington State	49-sector	1963, 1967, 1972	1963, 1967, 1972	Percent differences between estimated and observed outputs ranged from 0 to plus or minus 50 per cent. No statistical tests were performed.	Required 7–10 iterations to converge. Modified RAS procedure used, by identifying a priori inverse-important coefficients.

Table 4.1 Continued

	Matrix Characteristics					
Authors	*Region (Country)*	*Size*	*Base Year and Region*	*Estimated Year*	*Errors*	*Comments*
Harrigan, McGilvray, and McNicoll (1980)	Scotland	46-sector	1973 United Kingdom	1973	Estimated mean absolute difference, Euclidean metric difference, similarity index, sum of chi-square distribution terms, absolute mean relative difference, information index, and correlation coefficient. Mean errors were 30 per cent or more.	Tested RAS against location quotient, adjusted cross-industry location quotient, logarithmic cross-industry location quotient, and commodity balance. Concluded that RAS procedure was best.
Butterfield and Mules (1980)	Western Australia	27-sector	1958–59 Australia	1958–59	Nonparametric test of column sums, regression analysis, chi-square test, mean absolute deviation, standardized mean, absolute deviation. Latter error was 33 per cent.	Tested RAS with intermediate sector and total transaction table. Tested against naive estimate.

Table 4.1 Continued

	Matrix Characteristics					
Authors	*Region (Country)*	*Size*	*Base Year and Region*	*Estimated Year*	*Errors*	*Comments*
Sawyer and Miller (1983)	Washington State	50-sector 28-sector	1967 United States	1972 Washington State	Estimated mean absolute deviation and mean absolute deviation as percentage of mean coefficient. For open models, the latter error ranged from 42 to 83 per cent. For partially closed models, the range was from 16 to 42 per cent.	Tested RAS against simple location quotient and supply–demand pool techniques. Concluded that RAS procedure was best. Measured regional coefficients and results of Leontief inverse coefficients.
INTERNATIONAL AND INTERREGIONAL TRADE TABLES						
Bénard (1964)	Capitalist Industrialized Countries	5-region	1953 1957	1957 1960	Mean square relative error was 17 per cent for four-year period and 20 per cent for seven-year period.	Convergence achieved in six to seven iterations.

Table 4.1 Continued

	Matrix Characteristics					
Authors	*Region (Country)*	*Size*	*Base Year and Region*	*Estimated Year*	*Errors*	*Comments*
Waelbroeck (1964)	Entire World	9-region	1938	1948, 1951–52, & 1959–60	n.a.	No information on convergence provided. Only 4 of 81 cells were zero.
Grandville, Fontela, and Gabus (1968)	No Test	–	–	–	–	Proposed use of Dutch Method of Virtual Exports and a gravity model as potential alternatives.
Möhr (1975)	United States	51-region	1963 unadjusted trade data	1963 adjusted	n.a.	Lack of initial convergence for 11 of 79 matrices adjusted. Used a linear-programming procedure to help identify critical zero cells in the trade-flow tables.

Source: Review by the author.
n.a. = not available
– = not applicable

Lecomber (1969), for example, argues that the RAS method should be used when only one table exists. He maintains that if two or more tables exist, other statistical estimation techniques, such as those employed by Johansen (1968) for Norway or by Almon (1968) for the United States that incorporate exogenous information concerning the statistical confidence placed on each interindustry coefficient, provide more accurate results.

Using the 1963 Washington tables as a base, Malizia and Bond (1974) constructed four sets of tables for 1967: 52-sector and 27-sector regional coefficient tables and 43-sector and 22-sector technical coefficient tables. Although they based the regional coefficients upon intraregional (gross flows) only, they based the technical coefficients upon total purchases (gross flows plus domestic imports). They made two major conclusions: First, 'that the RAS method, used without additional exogenous information on interindustry flows for the projection year, is not powerful enough to generate satisfactory forecasts of interindustry coefficients' (Malizia and Bond, 1974, p. 360). Over the four-year time span, their mean errors were greater than 100 per cent for each of the four sets of tables. Second, they concluded that the RAS method was better for regional coefficient tables and for aggregate tables than for technical coefficient tables and disaggregate tables.[4] This latter conclusion, however, must be viewed in the context that the mean errors for the disaggregated tables were 124 (52 sector, regional) and 133 (43 sector, technical) per cent compared with 105 (27 sector, regional) and 118 (22 sector, technical) for the aggregated tables. Their explanation of this latter conclusion is that the RAS method is the most viable 'when input–output relations are viewed as allocative functions based on market factors such as local capacity rather than as production functions based on technical relations' (Malizia and Bond, 1974, p. 362).[5] Given the large size of all of the mean errors, the viability of the technique may be in question regardless of the level of aggregation.

Hinojosa (1978) used the RAS procedure to estimate two 1972 matrices for Washington state, the first with the 1963 tables as the base and the second with the 1967 tables as the base. When he compared the differences in the actual versus estimated direct and direct and indirect coefficients, the mean error of estimation was at best 34 per cent.

Butterfield and Mules (1980) compared a 1958–9 input–output table for Western Australia with tables estimated from the 1958–1959 Australian national tables. They compared both the RAS procedure (including the Haring-McMenamin method of adjusting the entire transactions matrix) and a naive estimate. The tables had 27 sectors. They made a nonparametric test of column sums to determine whether there was consistent overestimation or underestimation. They also did a regression analysis, chi-square test, mean absolute deviation, and standardized mean absolute deviation. In the latter case, the error was 33 per cent (1980, p. 306), which is approximately the same as the lowest levels of errors obtained by other regional analysts.

Lynch (1986) used the RAS method to update the 1963 United Kingdom absorption flow matrix to 1968. In summarizing his research, he emphasized the inaccuracies that arise from use of the method. He concluded that percentage errors could be reduced to less than 10 per cent only by working with a very aggregate table (six or fewer sectors) or by incorporating exogenous information into 60 per cent or more of the nonzero cells.

In other early 1980s studies, analysts still seemed to show little concern with the errors of estimation, often focusing on other information. Hewings and Janson (1980, p. 847), for example, note that one of the largest uses of input–output models is for the analysis of economic impacts. As a result, they correctly maintain that the use of error measures such as the mean percentage error for individual coefficients may not be as relevant as estimations of errors for the outputs, income, or employment calculated from the coefficients. Once again, however, few analysts provide such information. They extended the RAS procedure by fixing selected coefficients a priori and reached two major conclusions: (1) Analysts should make prior estimates for the largest 10 per cent of the coefficients, substantiated by Jensen's (1980) proposal that these are the most important coefficients to consider when updating regional input–output tables; and (2) Analysts should assure that the two sets of constraints (intermediate demand and supply) are accurate.

In a 1982 study, Hewings and Syverson tested Jensen and West's (1980) statement that it is important to focus attention in input–output analyses on major aggregates rather than individual coefficients. Hewings and Syverson applied the RAS procedure to the 49-sector Washington state tables for 1963, 1967, and 1972, first identifying the inverse-important coefficients. Although no statistical measures of errors were obtained, they concluded that 'the contribution of the inverse important parameters to vector accuracy in cases where the RAS algorithm is applied provides minimal additional benefits' (Hewings and Syverson, 1982, p. 5).

One of the latest tests of the RAS procedure at the regional level was by Sawyer and Miller (1983). Like over half of their US predecessors, they tested the RAS procedure using Washington state data. They used 1967 US data to estimate 1972 Washington state data. They tested the effects of aggregation on the accuracy of the estimated tables, using alternative versions of the simple location quotient, supply-demand pool, and RAS techniques on models that were open and partially closed with respect to households. For the RAS tests, the error represented by the mean absolute deviation as a percentage of the mean coefficient (MPMC) was less for the

28-sector data than for the 50-sector data. Even so, the MPMC errors ranged from 42 to 49 per cent for the 28-sector data to 49 to 59 per cent for the 50-sector data for the open model. For the partially closed model, the range was from 21 per cent for the 29-sector model to 26 per cent for the 51-sector model.

In comparing the RAS method with alternative procedures, Sawyer and Miller concluded that 'those approaches that embody the RAS technique provide the best estimates of regional coefficients' (Sawyer and Miller, 1983, p. 1508). They also conducted tests of accuracy of nonsurvey-generated multipliers for both models, obtaining lower errors than for the regional coefficients. For the open model, the MPMC errors were 8.6 per cent for the 28-sector model and 10.6 per cent for the 50-sector models; for the partially closed model, the errors at both levels of aggregation were approximately 19 per cent. The authors also examined effects of value-added coefficients. Finally, they concluded their very thorough review by comparing their results with those from a few of the other studies.

Analysts have also used the RAS procedure to adjust and/or project interregional trade data. As shown in the last part of Table 1, four groups of analysts have used the procedure for international/interregional trade studies. The first three studies related to adjusting international trade figures; adjustments of interregional trade figures with the RAS procedure has been the focus only of the research conducted by Möhr (1975).

Two European studies were published in the early 1960s, one by Bénard (1963) and the other by Waelbroeck (1964), who conferred with one another on their work. Bénard conducted his research at the Centre d'Etude de la Prospection economique a moyen et long terms (CEPREL). He combined export and import data for the capitalist industrialized countries into five groups for each of three years: 1953, 1957, 1960. Using these data and the RAS procedure, Bénard updated a 5 × 5 matrix of international trade flows from 1953 to 1957 and from 1953 to 1960. For the four-year period, the mean square relative error was 17 per cent; for the seven-year period, it was 20 per cent.

Waelbroeck tested a modified RAS procedure on trade flows for the entire world (including socialist countries), with the flows grouped into nine regions. Using 1938 trade flows as a base, he estimated 1948, 1951–2, and 1959–60 flows, using the RAS procedure. He conducted his analysis as part of an attempt to measure the effects of the Common Market on trade between the countries. He did not calculate errors of estimation, nor did he provide information concerning the number of interations required for convergence to occur. It should be noted, however, that because of the highly aggregated nature of the data, only 4 of the 81 cells contained zeros, and the nonzero cells for 1938 only varied in value from 6 to 1534; consequently, convergence probably occurred very rapidly.

Grandville, Fontela, and Gabus (1968) proposed a modified RAS procedure, which they called RAST, that had three multipliers instead of two. It is specified as

$$a^{gh}{}_{i(t)} = a^{gh}{}_{i(0)} \;\star\; R^{g}{}_{(t-0)} \;\star\; S^{h}{}_{(t-0)} \;\star\; T_{(t-0)}$$

where

a^{gh} = trade flow from country g to country h of commodity i
R^g = row multiplier for row g
S^h = column multiplier for column h
T_i = total trade multiplier for commodity i
(t–o) = year t minus year 0.

They did not supply the empirical results from their calculations. They state that a 'retrospective verification' of the procedure was made by CEPREL (Grandville, Fontela, and Gabus, 1968, p. 596). This probably refers to the research Bénard discusses in the article just reviewed. Their RAST method appears to be indentical to the Kouevi (1965) method briefly discussed in Lecomber's article (1975, p. 17). Kouevi published his study in a CEPREL bulletin. Grandville, Fontela, and Gabus also presented two other methods that could be used to estimate the trade flows: the Dutch Method of Virtual Exports and a gravity model. There are obviously several similarities and differences in the use of the RAS procedure for international/interregional trade tables versus its use for input–output tables. Only a few of these have been noted in the literature.

The multiregional planning (MRP) research staff encountered special problems when they estimated the interregtional trade data for the multiregional input–output (MRIO) model (Polenske, 1980, pp. 189–207). The sources of data for the regional input–output and interregional-trade data differ. Both sets of data are assembled primarily from census data; however, in the United States, the census sources differ. The interregional trade data are obtained from the Census of Transportation and other transportation publications, while regional input–output data are obtained mainly from the various Censuses of Agriculture, Construction, Manufacturers, and Trade (Wholesale and Retail). The regional production and consumption totals for each sector in the input–output tables, therefore, differ from those in the interregional trade tables. In order for the MRIO model to operate, the two sets of control totals must be identical. For the 1963 model, the 79 tables of interregional trade data, which were 51 × 51, were adjusted so that the controls from those tables matched the ones from the 51 regional input–output tables, because the interregional trade data seemed to be less reliable than the input–output data assembled for each state. For 11 of the 79 tables, convergence did not occur until special estimates were made for selected cells (Polenske, 1980).

In summary, concerning errors of estimation, some authors, such as Stone, Bates, and Bacharach (1963), could not make error tests, because actual data were not available. Others used a broad range of different error measures, making comparision among the different studies difficult. Davis, Lofting, and Sathaye (1977) and Schneider (1965), for example, used counts of errors and other means of providing information on the errors, while Harrigan, McGilvray, and McNicoll (1980) used seven different error measures. Finally, I re-emphasize that although very low errors of measurement were obtained by Paelinck and Waelbroeck (1963), they were the result of incorporating independent estimates for specific cells in the table. They then applied the RAS procedure only to the remaining cells. Even the data in their actual 1959 table were partially based upon estimates by industry experts. If the RAS procedure is used without making independent estimates for some of the cells, the errors in specific cells can become very large.

Based upon my review of the literature, I conclude that the errors from use of an unadjusted RAS procedure on input–output tables are sufficiently large to cause any analyst to use information obtained with the procedure only with extreme care unless s/he makes extensive adjustments to the most critical cells in the table. No error estimates have been made for its use with interregional trade tables; therefore, I can only assume that the same words of caution are necessary.

4.4.2 Other Important Considerations

As I noted earlier, in addition to errors of estimation, analysts should consider at least three other issues concerning the use of the RAS technique, namely: (1) convergence and speed of convergence, (2) minimum level of discrepancy allowed between control totals and estimated totals, and (3) serious distortions of elements in the table. Because information concerning these issues is so limited, I will refer to them only briefly here. I raise these issues mainly from the personal experiences our MRP staff has had with them.

Convergence seems, on the one hand, not to be a major issue for RAS adjustments to most input–output tables for two main reasons: (1) the tables have the mathematical property of large nonzero diagonal elements, (2) the small size of many of the tables creates very aggregated tables with few zeros. Both of these properties helps to assure that the iterative RAS procedure will converge and will do so relatively quickly. On the other hand, convergence does become a significant issue for interregional trade tables. Möhr (1975) used the RAS procedure on the 1963 MRIO interregional-trade tables. As noted earlier, for 11 of the 79 trade-flow tables, he found that the RAS procedure failed to converge or convergence occurred extremely slowly. Möhr showed that Bacharach (1970) had proved only the necessary, not the sufficient, conditions for the iterations of a biproportional matrix problem to converge. In fact, Möhr developed a linear-programming method for determining which critical cells in the matrix were causing the procedure not to converge.

Both convergence and the speed of convergence are issues that emerge as important ones for the adjustment of interregional-trade data in the MRIO model. Many interregional trade tables do not have the unique mathematical property of strong diagonal elements common to input–output tables, and they may have numerous zero rows and/or columns, because certain goods are produced/consumed only in particular regions. As a result, the MRIO staff found that convergence of the iterations on interregional trade tables was never assured. These issues are thoroughly discussed in the paper by Polenske, Crown, and Möhr (1986).

The speed of convergence, of course, is dependent not only upon the mathematical properties of the table, including the number of nonzeros cells. It also is very closely tied to the minimum level of discrepancy between control totals and estimated totals that the analyst will allow. If the analyst, for example, requires that the two totals must be within 0.1 per cent of each other, the convergence will naturally take longer than if s/he sets a much larger level of discrepancy, such as 5.5 per cent.

Previous to Möhr, most analysts did not seem to encounter cases of nonconvergence. Stone, Bates, and Bacharach, (1963); Bénard (1963); Tilanus (1966); and Hinojosa (1978)) have noted the number of interations required for convergence to occur. Each analyst seems to assume that convergence will always occur. The number they cite varies from about six to about twenty. In 1966, for example, Tilanus found that convergence occurred after 20 iterations[6] and determined that projections made with the RAS procedure were no better than those obtained by a statistical correction method (SCM) applied to an original matrix, noting that the 'RAS procedure takes more computing' time than the SCM due to iteration and inversion' (1966, p. 121). Bénard, who used very small interregional trade tables, obtained convergence in six to seven iterations. Hinojosa (1978) in working with regional input–output tables indicates that convergence occurred with 11 to 21 iterations.

Hewings (1977) is one of the only analysts to discuss the issue of the accuracy of the RAS procedure in estimating individual coefficients compared with the accuracy of the marginal vector. Barker (1975, p. 67) states that 'what clearly emerges from this [British] study is the importance of providing the correct row and column constraints in the provisional table'.

Finally, almost no systematic information is available in the literature as to the distortions that the RAS technique may cause to the structure of a matrix. The nature of the iterative procedure is such that a very small cell may become gigantic unless specific limits are set (Schneider, 1965). Some analysts set limits as to how much any individual cells may change (for example, Matuszewski, Pitts, and Sawyer (1963)).

4.5 CONCLUSION

The RAS method is still widely used to adjust national and regional input–output data. Its limited application to interregional trade data is probably because such data are difficult to obtain and because very few regional analysts use the available data. Most analysts justify the use of the RAS procedure by the fact that in comparative tests with other adjustment procedures it produces the lowest errors. The analysts, however, fail to note that errors of 30 per cent or more are not uncommon with the use of the RAS procedure. Only in a few cases, such as Paelinck and Waelbroeck (1963), are extremely low errors of 1–5 per cent recorded; however, these low errors are attributable to special situations, such as the a priori introduction of large amounts of actual data, and to favourable economic conditions, such as a small degree of structural change. These factors cannot be expected to pertain to most applications.

Seven general conclusions can be made from the studies I reviewed. First, even though when analysts compared the RAS procedure with other techniques, they determined that its use resulted in more accurate estimates than other nonsurvey techniques, it still often produces very large errors of estimation. The overall mean errors from the RAS procedure are, on the average, 30 per cent or more even under the best of conditions. These errors, while less than those obtained from other nonsurvey techniques, are still unduly large. Thus, analysts should always try to construct up-to-date input–output tables with actual, rather than with these estimated data, or they should make extensive adjustments to the data as they apply the technique.

Second, analysts have generally obtained the most accurate estimates by taking a regional (national) input–output table for one year and applying the RAS procedure to estimate a table for the same region (nation) for a later (4–10 year) period. The estimates are less accurate when a regional input–output table is estimated from a national one or where the years of the base and the estimated table are far apart. A relatively recent base-year table for the same region (county) is therefore preferred.

Third, the column sums derived from the inverse of an RAS-estimated table are usually more accurately estimated than the individual coefficients in the table.

Fourth, an unambiguous, objective means has yet to be determined for evaluating the difference between the flows (coefficients) in the matrices. Methods employed have included frequency distributions of the errors in individual coefficients (classified by size), mean similarity index, information content, Chi-square statistic, mean absolute difference, and regression.

Fifth, in measuring the errors, the analysts vary as to whether or not they account for the number of cells for which little or no change occurred between the base and the estimated year in the actual data. They also vary as to whether it is the accuracy of individual coefficients or accuracy of estimates made with the coefficients that is important. In discussing the results, the analysts also generally fail to mention other factors such as the size of the matrix, the span of years over which the estimates are being made, and possible structural changes in the economy, such as recessions or inflation, all of which may affect the results.

Sixth, the input–output tables tested have unique mathematical properties, such as dominant diagonals and only a few zero entries, which means that the RAS procedure not only converges, but converges rather quickly (say, after 5–20 iterations) for most input–output tables. Matrices with data for other economic activities, such as interregional trade flows, do not always have these properties; therefore, the questions of existence, uniqueness, convergence, and speed of convergence become important issues for the use of the RAS procedure with these other data.

Seventh, because of the different properties that noninput–output tables may have, analysts have no assurance that the RAS procedure will produce similar results when applied to them.

Given that the RAS procedure will continue to be used, I recommend research on five issues:

1. *Distortions in structure of data.* Analysts need to understand well the repercussion effects to determine how a large error in one cell can be

quickly disseminated throughout a matrix when it is inverted. Here, the work of Jensen and West (1980) and West (1983) on important cells needs to be considerably extended. Knowledge of these effects can help analysts identify critical cells for which actual data should be assembled.

2. *Acceptable levels of accuracy.* Errors from use of the RAS adjustment procedure that are 30 per cent or more are not acceptable for national or regional research even if these are lower than errors obtained from other nonsurvey adjustment procedures. Analysts need to determine levels of acceptable accuracy.
3. *Standardization of information presented.* Analysts present nonsystematic information concerning results of the use of the RAS procedure and of comparisons with the use of other techniques. At a minimum, analysts should provide the following information: size, year, and type (name of region, nation, etc.) of base-year and estimated matrices; year and source of control tables; error estimations, using several alternative measures relevant to the problem being discussed; number of iterations required to reach convergence; and minimum level of discrepancy allowed between control totals and estimated totals. Most articles currently lack such basic information.
4. *Tests using data from different regions.* Over half of the regional studies of the RAS procedure in the United States have been conducted using Washington state tables. To understand the full range of problems that may be confronted in applying the procedure, regional analysts should conduct comparative studies on three or more tables from different regions.
5. *Effects of mathematical properties of matrices.* Additional analyses are required, along the lines of the research the multiregional planning staff has conducted (Polenske, Crown, and Möhr, 1986) of the relationship between the mathematical properties of matrices and the influence these have on the issues of existence, uniqueness, convergence, and speed of convergence when the RAS procedure is applied to different types of matrices.

From my review of the use of the RAS procedure, I conclude that analysts need to use the procedure with considerable caution, being fully aware of the large errors, especially for individual coefficients, and distortions in data structure that may be introduced. Wherever possible, actual data should be used, particularly for critical cells. The procedure will never be a substitute for actual data. Finally, and most important, all analysts therefore need to spend more time than they do now trying to convince funding agencies to sponsor the assembly of real data rather than to rely on relatively crude data-estimation procedures.

NOTES

1. I sincerely thank Drs Malte Möhr and William H. Crown, with whom I discussed these views in the early 1980s, and Dr Xiannuan Lin, who gave me very helpful comments on this paper. Polenske, Crown, and Möhr (1986) and Möhr, Crown, and Polenske (1987) contain supporting information concerning the important issues I review here.
2. They referred to it as a 'Mix' matrix.
3. Because the national and regional data were for the same year, they did not need to adjust the data for temporal relative price changes; however, they should have made adjustments for differences between regional and national prices. They used five methods to evaluate eight alternative techniques of obtaining the estimated data.
4. In this paper, I use the term 'regional input–output coefficients' to refer to state or city tables of input–output coefficients and the term 'trade coefficients' to refer to region-to-region commodity-flow tables of coefficients. Note that Round (1983) refers to regional input-output coefficients as regional trade coefficients.
5. Ghosh (1964, pp. 111–13) discusses the question of technical factors being expressed by the production function, while market factors are expressed as allocations.
6. It is interesting to note that because of the now-primitive type of computers available in 1966, the iterations by Tilanus on a 27-sector table required 2.5 hours of computer prime time, and the inversion of the table required another 1.0 hours, even though time was saved because 40 per cent of the matrix elements were zero (Tilanus, 1966, p. 121).

REFERENCES

ALLEN, R. I. G. (1974) 'Some Experiments with the RAS Method of Estimating Input–Output Coefficients', *Oxford Bulletin of the Institute of Economics and Statistics*, vol. 36, no. 3 (August).

ALLEN, R. I. G., and J. R. C. LECOMBER (1975) 'Some Tests on a Generalized Version of RAS', in R. I. G. Allen and W. F. Gossling (eds), *Estimating and Projecting Input–Output Coefficients* (London: Input–Output Publishing Company), pp. 43–56.

ALMON, Clopper (1968) 'Recent Methodological Advances in Input–Output in the United States and Canada', paper presented at the Fourth International Conference on Input–Output Techniques, Geneva (January).

ALMON, Clopper (1970) 'Investment in Input–Output Models and the Treatment of Secondary Products', in A. P. Carter and A. Bródy (eds), *Applications of Input–Output Analysis*, vol. 2 (Amsterdam: North-Holland Publishing Company), pp. 103–16.

ALMON, C., L. ATKINSON, and T. C. REIMBOLD (1972) 'Dynamic Interindustry Forecasting for Business Planning', in A. Bródy and A. P. Carter (eds), *Input–*

Output Techniques (Amsterdam: North-Holland Publishing Company) pp. 518–30.

BACHARACH, Michael (1970) *Biproportional Matrices and Input–Output Change* (Cambridge: Cambridge University Press).

BARKER, T. S. (1975) 'An Analysis of the Updated 1963 Input–Output Transactions Table', in R. I. G. Allen and W. F. Gossling (eds), *Estimating and Projecting Input–Output Coefficients* (London: Input–Output Publishing Company), pp. 57–67.

BÉNARD, Jean (1963) 'Réseau des échanges internationaux et planification ouverte', *Économie appliquée*, vol. 16, no. 2 (April–June), pp. 249–76.

BUTTERFIELD, Martin, and Trevor MULES (1980) 'A Testing Routine for Evaluating Cell-by-Cell Accuracy in Short-Cut Regional Input–Output Tables', *Journal of Regional Science*, vol. 20, no. 3, pp. 293–310.

CZAMANSKI, Stanislaw, and Emil E. MALIZIA (1969) 'Applicability and Limitations in the Use of National Input–Output Tables for Regional Studies', *Papers of the Regional Science Association*, vol. 23, pp. 65–77.

DAVIS, H. C., E. M. LOFTING, and J. A. SATHAYE (1977) 'A Comparison of Alternative Methods of Updating Input–Output Coefficients', *Technological Forecasting and Social Change*, vol. 10, pp. 79–87.

DEMING, W. Edwards, and Frederick F. STEPHAN (1940) 'On a Least Squares Adjustment of a Sampled Frequency Table When the Expected Marginal Totals are Known', *Annals of Mathematical Statistics*, vol. 11, pp. 427–44.

DRABEK, Zdenek (1981) 'The Product Substitution and Technological Change in Czechoslovakia and Austria', *Greek Economic Review*, vol. 3, no. 3 (December), pp. 325–46.

FONTELA, E., A. DUVAL, A. GABUS, M. BORLIN, and C. VELAY (1970) 'Forecasting Technical Coefficients and Changes in Relative Prices', in A. P. Carter and A. Bródy (eds), *Applications of Input–Output Analysis*, vol. 2 (Amsterdam: North-Holland Publishing Company), pp. 331–45.

FRIEDLANDER, D. (1961) 'A Technique for Estimating a Contingency Table Given the Marginal Totals and Some Supplementary Data', *Journal of the Royal Statistical Society*, series A, vol. 123, part 3, pp. 412–20.

GEARY, R. C. (1973) 'A Method of Estimating the Elements of an Interindustry Matrix, Knowing the Row and Column Totals', *Economic and Social Review*, vol. 4, no. 4 (July), pp. 477–85.

GHOSH, A. (1964) *Experiments with Input–Output Models* (Cambridge: Cambridge University Press).

GRANDVILLE, O. de la, E. FONTELA, and A. GABUS (1968) 'A Note on European Projections of Foreign Trade', *Economia Internazionale*, vol. 21, no. 4 (November), pp. 593–609.

GRETTON, P., and P. COTTERELL (1979) 'The RAS Method of Compiling Input–Output Tables: Australian Bureau of Statistics Experience', paper prepared for the Fourth Annual Meeting, Australian and New Zealand Section, Regional Science Association (Canberra, Australia: Australian Bureau of Statistics).

HARRIGAN, F. J., J. W. McGILVRAY, and I. H. McNICOLL (1980) 'Simulating the Structure of a Regional Economy', *Environment and Planning A.*, vol. 12, no. 8 (August), pp. 927–36.

HENRY, E. W (1973a) 'A Note on the Logarithmic Transformation of the RAS', *Economic and Social Review*, vol. 4, no. 4 (July), pp. 487–492.

HENRY, E. W. (1973b) 'Relative Efficiency of RAS Versus Least-Squares Methods of Updating Input–Output Structures, as Adjudged by Application to Irish Data', *Economic and Social Review*, vol. 5, no. 1, pp. 7–29.

HEWINGS, G. J. D. (1977) 'Evaluating the Possibilities for Exchanging Input–Output Coefficients', *Environment and Planning A.*, vol. 9, pp. 927–44.

HEWINGS, G. J. D., and B. N. Janson (1980) 'Exchanging Regional Input–Output Coefficients: A Reply and Further Comments', *Environment and Planning A.*, vol. 12, no. 7 (July), pp. 843–54.

HEWINGS, Geoffrey J. D., and William M. SYVERSON (1982) 'A Modified Biproportional Method for Updating Required Input–Output Matrices: Holistic Accuracy Evaluation', paper presented at the European Congress, Regional Science Association, Gröninger, The Netherlands (August).

HINOJOSA, R. C (1978) 'A Performance Test of the Biproportional Adjustment of Input–Output Coefficients', *Environment and Planning A.*, vol. 10, no. 9 (September), pp. 1047–52.

JENSEN, R. C (1980) 'The Concept of Accuracy in Regional Input–Output Models', *International Regional Science Review*, vol. 5, no. 2 (Winter), pp. 139–45.

JENSEN, R. C., and G. R. WEST (1980) 'The Effect of Relative Coefficient Size on Input–Output Multipliers', *Environment and Planning A.*, vol. 12, no. 6, pp. 659–70.

JOHANSEN, L (1968) 'Explorations in Long-Term Projections for the Norwegian Economy', *Economics of Planning*, vol. 8, no. 1–2, pp. 70–117.

KOUEVI, A. F (1965) 'Essai d'application prospective de la méthode RAS au commerce international', *Bulletin du CEPREL*, no. 5, pp. 71–120.

LAMEL, J., J. RICHTER, W. TEUFELSBAUER, and K. ZELLE (1974) 'Comparative Analysis of Mathematical Methods for Updating Input–Output Tables', paper presented at the Sixth International Conference on Input–Output Techniques, Vienna, Austria (April).

LECOMBER, J. R. C. (1975) 'A Critique of Methods of Adjusting, Updating, and Projecting Matrices', in *Estimating and Projecting Input–Output Coefficients* (London: Input–Output Publishing Company), pp. 1–25.

LECOMBER, J. R. C (1969) 'RAS Projections When Two or More Matrices are Known', *Economics of Planning*, vol. 9, no. 3.

LEONTIEF, Wassily W. (1941) *The Structure of American Economy, 1919–1939* (New York: Oxford University Press).

LYNCH, R. G (1986) 'An Assessment of the RAS Method for Updating Input–Output Tables', In Ira Sohn (ed.), *Readings in Input–Output Analysis* (New York: Oxford University Press), pp. 271–84.

MALIZIA, Emil, and Daniel L. BOND (1974) 'Empirical Tests of the RAS Method of Interindustry Coefficient Adjustment', *Journal of Regional Science*, vol. 14, no. 3, pp. 355–65.

MARTIN, B. R. (1972) 'Updating Input–Output Table Coefficients', *Australian Economic Papers* (December), pp. 180–86.

MATUSZEWSKI, T. I., P. R. PITTS, and John A. SAWYER (1964) 'Linear-Programming Estimates of Changes in Input Coefficients', *Canadian Journal of Economics and Political Science*, vol. 30, no. 2 (May), pp. 203–10.

McMENAMIN, David G., and Joseph E. HARING (1974) 'An Appraisal of Nonsurvey Techniques for Estimating Regional Input–Output Models', *Journal of Regional Science*, vol. 14, no. 2, pp. 191–205.

MIERNYK, William H. (1976) 'Comments on Recent Developments in Regional Input–Output Analysis', *International Regional Science Review*, vol. 1, no. 2 (Fall), pp. 47–55.

MINUJIN, A., and L. A. Beccaria (1978) 'The Measurement of Flows in Social Statistics: An Example from Argentinean Experience', *Environment and Planning A.*, vol. 10, no. 9 (September), pp. 983–1000.

MÖHR, Malte (1975) 'A Consistency Problem of Multiregional Input–Output MRIO, and Existence Conditions of Constrained Biproportional Matrices', Ph.D. dissertation (Cambridge, MA: Department of Urban Studies and Planning, Massachusetts Institute of Technology).

MÖHR, Malte, William H. CROWN, and Karen R. POLENSKE (1987) 'A Linear Programming Approach to Solving Infeasible RAS Problems', *Journal of Regional Science*, vol. 27, no. 4, pp. 587–603.

MORRISON, W. I., and P. SMITH (1974) 'Nonsurvey Input–Output Techniques at the Small-Area Level', *Journal of Regional Science*, vol. 14, no. 1, pp. 1–14.

MORRISON, W. I., and R. G. THUMANN (1980) 'A Lagrangian Multiplier Approach to the Solution of a Special Constrained Matrix Problem', *Journal of Regional Science*, vol. 20, no. 2, pp. 279–92.

PAELINCK, J., and J. WAELBROECK (1963) 'Étude empirique sur l'évolution des coefficients d'input–output', *Economie appliquée*, vol. 16, no. 1 (Jan.–Mar.), pp. 81–111.

PARIKH, A. (1979) 'Forecasts of Technology Matrices Using the RAS Method', paper presented at the Seventh International Conference on Input–Output Techniques, Innsbruck, Austria (9–13 April).

POLENSKE, Karen R. (1980) *The U.S. Multiregional Input–Output Accounts and Model*, (Lexington, MA: Lexington Books, D. C. Heath and Company).

POLENSKE, Karen R., William H. CROWN, and Malte MÖHR (1986) 'A Critical Review of the RAS Literature', paper presented at the Second Soviet–American Seminar on Regional Planning, Tallinn, Estonia, Union of Soviet Socialist Republics (January).

ROUND, Jeffery I. (1983) 'Nonsurvey Techniques: A Critical Review of the Theory and the Evidence', *International Regional Science Review*, vol. 8, no. 3 (December), pp. 189–212.

SAWYER, Charles H., and Ronald E. MILLER (1983) 'Experiments in Regionalizing of a National Input–Output Table', *Environment and Planning A.*, vol. 15, pp. 1501–20.

SCHNEIDER, Howard Mark (1965) 'An Evaluation of Two Alternative Methods for Updating Input–Output Tables', BA Thesis (Cambridge, MA: Department of Economics, Harvard University).

STÄGLIN, Reiner (1970) 'Estimating an Input–Output Matrix with Incomplete Information', *Konjunkturpolitik*, vols 2/3, pp. 145–53.

STONE, Richard, and A. BROWN (1962) *A Computable Model of Economic Growth* (A Programme for Growth, vol. 1), (London: Chapman and Hall).

STONE, Richard, John BATES, and Michael BACHARACH (1963) *Input–Output Relationships: (1954–1966)* (A Programme for Growth, vol. 3), (Cambridge, MA: The MIT Press).

THEIL, Henri (1967) *Economics and Information Theory* (Amsterdam: North-Holland Publishing Company).

THUMANN, R. G. (1978) 'A Comment on "Evaluating the Possibilities for Exchanging Regional Input–Output Coefficients"', *Environment and Planning A.*, vol. 10, no. 3 (March), pp. 321–5.

TILANUS, C. B. (1966). *Input–Output Experiments: The Netherlands, 1948–1961* (Rotterdam: Rotterdam University Press).

UNITED NATIONS (1973) *Input–Output Tables and Analysis*, Study of Methods, Series F, no. 14, Rev. 1 (New York: United Nations), pp. 65–80.

WAELBROECK, J. (1964) 'Une nouvelle méthode d'analyse des matrices d'échange internationaux', *Cahiers Économiques de Bruxelles*, no. 21, pp. 93–114.

WEST, Guy Raymond (1983) 'Sensitivity and Probabilistic Analysis in Regional Input–Output Models', Ph.D. Thesis (Brisbane, Australia: University of Queensland, Department of Economics).

WILSON, Alan G. (1970) *Entropy in Urban and Regional Modelling* (London: Pion Limited).

5 Bi-regional Input–Output Proportions for Germany – First Results

Reiner Stäglin

5.1 INTRODUCTION

In October 1990, the former German Democratic Republic (GDR) became part of the Federal Republic of Germany (FRG). The unification process resulted, more or less, in a complete revision of all statistical measurement procedures used in the former GDR until the beginning of July 1990. This date marked the start of the monetary, economic and social union between the FRG and the GDR.

Many new economic statistics were needed to support the German unification process in the short run. Among these were statistics for analysing business cycles and measuring structural development in the so-called New Federal States (NFS), i.e. the Eastern part of the united Germany (Melzer and Stäglin, 1991). Since that time, the first components of a comprehensive and consistent statistical information system were implemented for the unified German economy (Statistisches Bundesamt, 1993). According to this procedure, joint and separate data in aggregated or disaggregated form are published nowadays by the Federal Statistical Office (FSO).

To bridge the gap which continued until official statistics were published by the FSO, the German Institute for Economic Research (DIW) estimated empirical data sets on its own. Among them were: nonofficial national accounts data for the NFS, from 1989 onwards, fully comparable to those for the OFS (DIW, 1990),figures on labour and social aspects of private households in East Germany based on a Socio-Economic Panel for the NFS (Schupp and Wagner, 1990), and a rearranged and recalculated input–output table for the former GDR 1987 according to FRG standards (Ludwig and Stäglin, 1993).

The experience gained from these data estimates could be used when the DIW was asked to analyse the economic interdependencies between the Old and the New Federal States and their impact on the labour market (Filip-Köhn and Stäglin, 1994). For this research work a bi-regional input–output table for the unified German economy was compiled for the first time (Stäglin and Filip-Köhn, 1994, pp. 37). The table which refers to 1991 as the first complete year after unification contributed at the same time to the statistical information system necessary for accompanying the economic process in East and West Germany. Its significance will last until the FSO substitutes its own input–output data for the whole of Germany for the bi-regional table prepared by the DIW.

5.2 A BI-REGIONAL INPUT–OUTPUT TABLE FOR GERMANY 1991

In order to describe the interrelationships between NFS and OFS as well as with other countries a bi-regional input–output table was needed. Such a table must present for each of the two regions the sectoral output flows and the sectoral input flows subdivided according to NFS and OFS, i.e. for each region the intersectoral flows between the industries themselves and between the industries and final demand of the other region must be shown.

As can be seen from the two individual regional input–output tables for OFS and NFS in Figure 5.1, the sectoral exports to the other region of Germany are represented in columns and the sectoral imports from the other region are collected in rows. These interregional flows must be subdivided, cell by cell, to arrive at the intersectoral flows of goods and services between NFS and OFS and vice versa, necessary to complete a bi-regional input–output table. The result of such a subdivision is reflected in the marked cells of the bi-regional table for Germany presented schematically in Figure 5.1, too.

5.2.1 The Design of the Bi-regional German Table

The bi-regional German input–output table for 1991 presented in Table 5.1 distinguishes ten industries, six categories of final demand and three primary inputs. The ten industries represent an aggregation of originally fifteen industries which were used in the DIW research report on the economic interdependencies between OFS and NFS (Stäglin and Filip-Köhn, 1994). The industries are defined by institutional units and reflect a heterogeneous output. Consequently, the bi-regional input–output data are fully consistent with the national accounts totals for OFS and NFS published by the FSO (Statistisches Bundesamt, 1992). The flows of goods and services are valued in billion DM at current (ex factory) prices.

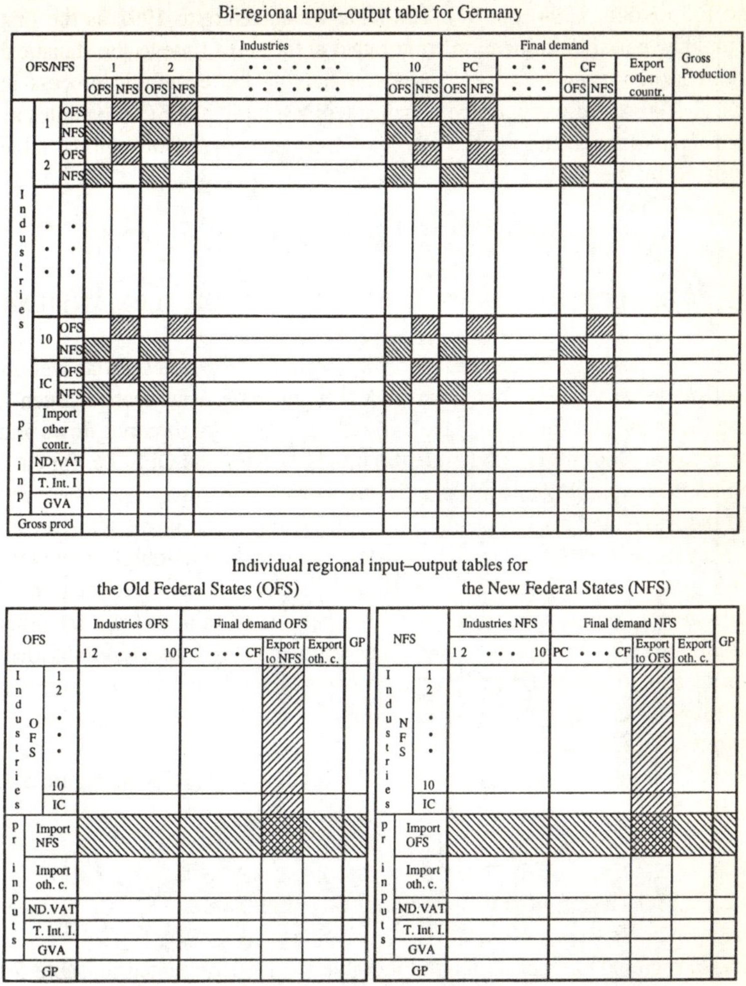

Figure 5.1 Schemes of input–output tables

As can be seen from Table 5.1, all cells – up to the columns for domestic final demand and up to the rows for intermediate consumption respectively final consumption from domestic production – are subdivided into four elements: Two of them represent the intraregional flows, i.e. the intersection of OFS/OFS and NFS/NFS, and two elements represent the bi-regional trade flows, i.e. the transactions between OFS/NFS and NFS/OFS. The bi-regional

Table 5.1 Bi-regional input–output table for Germany 1991 – billion DM, current prices

Industries		1 Agricult.		2 Energy, min.		3 Basic manuf.		4 Capital manuf.		5 Cons. manuf.		6 Food manuf.		7 Construction		8 Trade, transp.		9 Market serv.		10 Non-market serv.	
		OFS	*NFS*	*OFS*	*NFS*	*OFS*	*NFS*	*OFS*	*NFS*	*OFS*	*NFS*	*OFS*	*NFS*	*OFS*	*NFS*	*OFS*	*NFS*	*OFS*	*NFS*	*OFS*	*NFS*
1 Agriculture,	OFS	0.47	0.00	0.10	0.00	3.05	0.00	0.10	0.00	0.63	0.00	40.19	0.00	0.35	0.00	0.28	0.00	4.59	0.00	0.15	0.00
forestry and fishing	NFS	0.00	2.65	0.00	0.00	0.10	0.10	0.00	0.00	0.20	0.20	0.10	2.00	0.00	0.00	0.00	0.00	0.00	0.10	0.00	0.00
2 Energy and	OFS	1.59	0.00	83.81	0.70	29.88	0.00	9.39	0.00	5.44	0.00	3.61	0.00	2.63	0.00	8.69	0.00	12.99	0.40	0.41	0.00
mining	NFS	0.00	0.50	0.05	6.70	0.00	3.50	0.00	1.70	0.00	0.80	0.00	2.30	0.00	0.60	0.00	2.80	0.00	4.50	0.00	0.20
3 Manuf. of basic	OFS	4.46	0.40	10.12	0.85	100.92	3.50	99.01	2.00	35.77	0.80	3.58	0.20	38.71	5.90	17.09	2.00	11.37	4.50	0.93	0.00
and production goods	NFS	0.00	0.40	0.00	0.95	1.60	4.49	1.76	4.36	0.40	1.50	0.00	0.50	0.00	1.80	0.00	0.40	0.00	0.30	0.00	0.00
4 Manuf. of capital	OFS	2.00	0.30	6.78	0.95	11.15	1.60	188.53	4.00	7.44	0.50	2.97	0.00	15.53	0.80	10.74	2.30	13.93	2.00	0.97	0.20
goods	NFS	0.00	0.20	0.00	1.25	0.70	1.00	0.70	5.94	0.00	0.40	0.00	0.50	0.00	1.40	0.00	0.70	0.00	0.70	0.00	0.20
5 Manuf. of	OFS	0.48	0.00	1.44	0.00	11.54	0.00	34.31	0.20	33.66	0.30	9.23	0.00	10.55	0.00	5.58	0.10	21.55	1.00	0.45	0.00
consumer goods	NFS	0.00	0.00	0.00	0.00	0.00	0.00	0.00	0.20	0.20	0.75	0.00	0.20	0.00	0.00	0.00	0.20	0.00	0.20	0.00	0.00
6 Manuf. of food,	OFS	6.16	0.10	0.24	0.00	2.59	0.00	2.32	0.00	1.07	0.00	41.78	3.50	0.22	0.00	2.01	0.10	35.14	1.00	2.27	0.10
beverages and tobacco products	NFS	0.00	0.20	0.00	0.00	0.00	0.00	0.00	0.00	0.00	0.00	0.10	3.00	0.00	0.00	0.00	0.10	0.00	0.90	0.00	0.10
7 Construction	OFS	0.54	0.00	2.66	0.00	2.63	0.00	4.26	0.00	0.55	0.00	0.58	0.00	17.17	1.00	5.01	0.00	15.25	1.20	0.26	0.00
	NFS	0.00	0.00	0.00	0.40	0.00	0.10	0.00	0.10	0.00	0.05	0.00	0.10	0.00	3.00	0.00	0.20	0.00	5.00	0.00	0.00
8 Trade, transport,	OFS	2.35	0.00	5.33	0.00	50.94	0.20	46.88	0.20	17.56	0.05	16.39	0.20	18.43	0.30	129.96	5.50	34.47	1.30	2.12	0.00
communication	NFS	0.00	0.40	0.00	1.75	0.10	1.20	0.10	0.80	0.00	0.30	0.00	0.40	0.00	0.60	0.00	2.70	0.00	2.00	0.00	0.30
9 Other market	OFS	7.00	0.10	7.85	0.40	47.71	0.50	76.60	0.50	34.86	0.10	19.91	0.20	28.61	0.50	80.68	2.00	325.31	4.50	14.34	0.60
services	NFS	0.00	0.10	0.00	0.40	0.00	0.50	0.00	0.80	0.10	0.25	0.20	0.80	0.00	0.90	0.20	1.30	0.60	23.20	0.10	0.40
10 Non-market	OFS	0.60	0.00	0.66	0.00	3.39	0.00	5.88	0.00	2.10	0.00	2.68	0.00	1.62	0.00	3.84	0.00	13.56	0.20	1.08	0.20
services	NFS	0.00	0.00	0.00	0.60	0.00	0.40	0.00	0.35	0.00	0.10	0.00	0.10	0.00	0.20	0.00	0.40	0.00	0.70	0.10	0.40

Intermediate consumption resp. final cons. from dom. product.	OFS	25.65	0.90	118.99	2.90	263.80	5.80	467.28	6.90	139.08	1.75	140.92	4.10	133.82	8.50	263.88	12.00	488.16	16.10	22.98	1.10
	NFS	0.00	4.45	0.05	12.05	2.50	11.29	2.56	14.25	0.90	4.35	0.40	9.90	0.00	8.50	0.20	8.80	0.60	37.60	0.20	1.60
Imports from other countries		9.23	0.10	17.85	0.50	97.60	1.50	133.60	2.11	50.67	0.70	40.36	1.90	13.51	2.00	27.24	1.60	21.63	1.70	1.12	0.10
Non-deductible value added tax		0.00	0.00	0.18	0.00	0.70	0.00	0.92	0.00	0.30	0.00	0.15	0.00	0.20	0.00	2.00	0.00	15.15	1.50	2.20	0.10
Total intermediate inputs		34.88	5.45	137.07	15.45	364.60	18.59	604.36	23.26	190.95	6.80	181.83	15.90	147.53	19.00	293.32	22.40	525.54	56.90	26.50	2.90
Gross value added		32.83	2.45	72.18	21.25	190.03	7.17	377.12	12.08	119.58	3.45	83.18	4.90	141.50	21.00	373.91	34.10	681.52	23.56	335.13	46.49
Gross production (total inputs)		67.71	7.90	209.25	36.70	554.63	25.76	981.48	35.34	310.53	10.25	265.01	20.80	289.03	40.00	667.23	56.50	1207.06	80.46	361.63	49.39

Source: Bi-regional input–output accounting of DIW wherein Germany is divided into Old Federal States (OFS) and New Federal States (NFS).

Table 5.1 Continued

Industries		1–10 Intermed. demand OFS	1–10 Intermed. demand NFS	Private consumption OFS	Private consumption NFS	Government consumption OFS	Government consumption NFS	Capital formation in equipment OFS	Capital formation in equipment NFS	Capital formation in construction OFS	Capital formation in construction NFS	Changes in stocks OFS	Changes in stocks NFS	Domestic final demand OFS	Domestic final demand NFS	Exports to other countries	Total final demand	Gross production (tot. outp.)
1 Agriculture, forestry and fishing	OFS	49.91	0.00	11.19	0.20	1.74	0.00	0.01	0.00	0.77	0.00	–1.00	0.00	12.71	0.20	4.89	17.80	67.71
	NFS	0.40	5.05	0.35	1.25	0.00	0.05	0.00	0.00	0.00	0.20	0.00	0.30	0.35	1.80	0.30	2.45	7.90
2 Energy and mining	OFS	158.44	1.10	37.79	0.20	6.72	0.00	0.37	0.00	2.21	0.00	–0.50	0.00	46.59	0.20	2.92	49.71	209.25
	NFS	0.05	23.60	0.00	8.80	0.00	2.85	0.00	0.00	0.00	0.70	0.00	0.40	0.00	12.75	0.30	13.05	36.70
3 Manuf. of basic and production goods	OFS	321.96	20.15	67.79	0.50	17.79	0.10	2.11	0.00	2.01	0.00	–4.20	0.00	85.50	0.60	126.42	212.52	554.63
	NFS	3.76	14.70	0.10	1.00	0.00	0.50	0.00	0.50	0.00	0.50	0.00	0.80	0.10	3.30	3.90	7.30	25.76
4 Manuf. of capital goods	OFS	260.04	12.65	128.12	10.50	18.50	0.20	153.19	14.01	23.55	0.00	–4.80	0.00	318.56	24.71	365.52	708.79	981.48
	NFS	1.40	12.29	0.10	0.80	0.00	0.30	2.00	10.55	0.00	1.75	0.00	–1.00	2.10	12.40	7.15	21.65	35.34
5 Manuf. of consumer goods	OFS	128.79	1.60	76.63	3.60	8.88	0.30	7.69	0.00	1.30	0.00	–0.80	0.00	93.70	3.90	82.54	180.14	310.53
	NFS	0.20	1.55	0.95	3.20	0.00	0.84	0.00	0.25	0.00	0.25	0.00	0.66	0.95	5.20	2.35	8.50	10.25
6 Manuf. of food, beverages and tobacco products	OFS	93.80	4.80	131.84	6.50	2.74	0.50	0.01	0.00	0.16	0.00	–1.10	0.00	133.65	7.00	25.76	166.41	265.01
	NFS	0.10	4.30	1.00	10.95	0.00	1.45	0.00	0.35	0.00	0.35	0.00	1.50	1.00	14.60	0.80	16.40	20.80
7 Construction	OFS	48.91	2.20	2.50	0.00	12.04	0.10	0.16	0.00	215.40	6.50	–0.11	0.00	229.99	6.60	1.33	237.92	289.03
	NFS	0.00	8.95	0.00	0.40	0.00	1.50	0.00	0.00	0.35	28.60	0.00	0.00	0.35	30.50	0.20	31.05	40.00
8 Trade, transport, communication	OFS	324.43	7.75	224.84	18.00	24.09	1.50	12.49	2.00	4.66	0.00	–2.00	0.00	264.08	21.50	49.47	335.05	667.23
	NFS	0.20	10.45	0.90	28.90	0.20	6.50	0.30	3.00	0.00	0.70	0.00	0.00	1.40	39.10	5.35	45.85	56.50
9 Other market services	OFS	642.87	9.40	407.23	10.86	85.43	4.50	0.02	0.00	20.88	0.19	0.00	0.00	513.56	15.55	25.68	554.79	1207.06
	NFS	1.20	28.65	7.77	31.24	1.50	8.00	0.10	0.20	0.10	0.40	0.00	0.00	9.47	39.84	1.30	50.61	80.46
10 Non-market services	OFS	35.41	0.40	58.35	0.00	256.05	10.17	0.00	0.00	0.43	0.00	0.00	0.00	314.83	10.17	0.82	325.82	361.63
	NFS	0.10	3.25	0.19	2.20	0.30	43.35	0.00	0.00	0.00	0.00	0.00	0.00	0.49	45.55	0.00	46.04	49.39

Intermediate consumption resp. final cons. from dom. product.	OFS	2064.56	60.05	1146.28	50.36	433.98	17.37	176.05	16.01	271.37	6.69	–14.51	0.00	2013.17	90.43	685.35	2788.95	4913.56
	NFS	7.41	112.79	11.36	88.74	2.00	65.34	2.40	14.85	0.45	33.45	0.00	2.66	16.21	205.04	21.65	242.90	363.10
Imports from other countries		412.81	12.21	161.97	42.00	16.13	3.00	77.30	9.00	4.73	2.00	5.90	0.00	266.03	56.00	95.78	417.81	842.83
Non-deductible value added tax		21.80	1.60	101.04	5.60	15.96	0.50	5.83	0.50	26.94	0.50	0.00	0.00	149.77	7.10		156.87	180.27
Total intermediate inputs		2506.58	186.65	1420.65	186.70	468.07	86.21	261.58	40.36	303.49	42.64	–8.61	2.66	2445.18	358.57	802.78	3606.53	6299.76
Gross value added		2406.98	176.45													27.79	27.79	2611.22
Gross production (total inputs)		4913.56	363.10	1420.65	186.70	468.07	86.21	261.58	40.36	303.49	42.64	–8.61	2.66	2445.18	358.57	830.57	3634.32	8910.98

Source: Bi-regional input–output accounting of DIW wherein Germany is divided into Old Federal States (OFS) and New Federal States (NFS).

flows stand for the special case of interregional flows and can be interpreted as elements of two German specific import matrices for OFS and NFS, each.

5.2.2 The Compilation of the Bi-regional German Table

The compilation of the bi-regional input–output table for Germany 1991 in its basic version with fifteen industries was a difficult task. It is caused by the fact that only few data for the NFS were provided by the FSO and that the available data were uncertain. This is not a surprising situation as 1991 was the first complete year after unification and the whole statistical system of the former GDR was in transition.

The compilation of the input–output table started from aggregated national accounts data for OFS and NFS published by the FSO. In order to disaggregate and complete these data for NFS, the results of DIW estimates and calculations were used (DIW, 1993). The interindustrial flows for the NFS part of the bi-regional table could be estimated on the basis of expert judgements and of rearranged as well as revaluated input–output data from the former GDR transactions matrix for 1987; the corresponding intermediate transactions for the OFS part were derived from West German input–output tables for 1986 and 1988 by extrapolation methods.

Most difficult was the 'guestimation' of interregional flows of goods and services between OFS and NFS for the fifteen industries. Basic data on trade flows according to commodity groups were available for the former FRG for the year 1991 (Statistisches Bundesamt, 1991) but they were not sufficient. The data did not cover all trade flows between OFS and NFS due to heavy changes in the statistical reporting system of the NFS; the breakdown of the commodity flows was also not detailed as necessary. Internal material which resulted from the conversion and the revaluation of the input–output table for the former GDR 1987 as well as meanwhile available data on foreign trade pattern of the GDR before the unification came into action and helped to bridge the statistical gap. Additionally, the DIW experiences gained from three decades in compiling consistent input–output tables could substitute some of the missing information. Nevertheless, the intragerman trade flows should be interpreted cautiously and the compilation of the first bi-regional input–output table for a year just after the unification has to be seen as an experiment.

This is also true for the recording of used passenger cars and lorries which are components of the intragerman trade flows and for the distinction between intermediate and final goods originating from the other part of Germany or from other countries. West German private households sold many used cars to purchasers in the NFS in 1991. These flows are recorded in the data on exports from OFS to NFS and also in the imports of NFS from OFS. But the intragerman trade flows of automobiles had no counterpart on the production side in OFS except that the used cars were substituted by new ones. This state of affairs needs to be taken into account when using the bi-regional input–output table for impact analyses, especially for calculating production and employment effects in OFS induced by deliveries to NFS.

The distinction between intermediate and final goods is a general problem in compiling interregional or bi-regional input–output tables. The basic data are not detailed enough to identify the final destination of the traded goods and services from their own kind. This is also the case with the statistics on intragerman trade flows. An additional problem originates from the fact that many commodities are imported by the OFS from other countries though their final use will be in the NFS. Therefore it is difficult to allocate the NFS intermediate and final imports according to their origin from OFS or foreign countries. Only estimates within the balancing consistent input–output system can help to solve these problems.

5.3 AN EVALUATION OF THE BI-REGIONAL INPUT–OUTPUT TABLE FOR GERMANY 1991

The bi-regional input–output table has its own importance independent of any descriptive or analytical evaluation. It represents a snapshot of the economic situation in the Old and New Federal States of Germany in 1991. Among other things, the different role of the ten industries in OFS and NFS with regard to gross production, gross value added, intermediate inputs, intermediate and final demand, etc., can be derived from Table 5.1. Big differences show up in cost structures, output pattern, final demand composition and export/import relations. Nevertheless, for comparing the conditions in West and East Germany one year after unification the calculation of descriptive and analytical input–output proportions from the biregional input–output table will be more favourable.

5.3.1 Intermediate Input and Intermediate Output Proportions in OFS and NFS

The intermediate inputs stand for an important component of industrial cost structures. They can be presented as percentage of total inputs. Additionally, the total intermediate inputs can be subdivided according to their regional origin. The results of such a descriptive evaluation of the bi-regional input–output table for Germany 1991 are presented in Table 5.2. They show the same average total intermediate input proportions for all industries (around 51 p.c.) in OFS and NFS but reflect big differences for the individual ten industries, e.g. for energy and mining and for non-market services. Generally the intraregional and the imported intermediate input proportions are higher in OFS compared to those in NFS. This is compensated by a relatively high percentage of intermediate inputs purchased by NFS from OFS. The proportions range from 2.2 p.c. for non-market services to 22.5 p.c. for

Table 5.2 Intermediate input proportions in Old and New Federal States of Germany 1991 according to regional origin (intermediate inputs as percentage of total inputs)

	Intermediate inputs of OFS				*Intermediate inputs of NFS*			
Industries	*Total* *	*of which from OFS*	*NFS*	*imports*	*Total* *	*of which from OFS*	*NFS*	*imports*
1 Agriculture, forestry and fishing	51.5	37.9		13.6	69.0	11.4	56.3	1.3
2 Energy and mining	65.5	56.9	0.0	8.5	42.1	7.9	32.8	1.4
3 Manuf. of basic and production goods	65.7	47.6	0.4	17.6	72.1	22.5	43.8	5.8
4 Manuf. of capital goods	61.6	47.6	0.3	13.6	65.8	19.5	40.3	6.0
5 Manuf. of consumer goods	61.5	44.8	0.3	16.3	66.3	17.1	42.4	6.8
6 Manuf. of food products, beverages and tobacco products	68.6	53.2	0.1	15.2	76.4	19.7	47.6	9.1
7 Construction	51.0	46.3		4.7	47.5	21.3	21.3	5.0
8 Trade, transport and communication	44.0	39.6	0.0	4.1	39.6	21.2	15.6	2.8
9 Other market services	43.5	40.4	0.0	1.8	70.7	20.0	46.7	2.1
10 Non-market services	7.3	6.3	0.1	0.3	5.9	2.2	3.2	0.2
1–10 All industries	51.0	42.0	0.2	8.4	51.4	16.5	31.1	3.4

* Totals cover the non-deductible value added tax which is not shown separately.

Source: Bi-regional input-output accounting of DIW.

manufacture of basic and production goods. The average for all industries amounts to 16.5 p.c.

A quite different picture shows up when analysing the intermediate output proportions in OFS and NFS according to their regional destination. They are presented as percentage of total outputs. The intermediate exports are neglected because they are part of total exports which represent a final demand category. The proportions shown in Table 5.3 indicate a higher average total intermediate output percentage for all industries in OFS (43.2

Table 5.3 Intermediate output proportions in Old and New Federal States of Germany 1991 according to regional destination (intermediate outputs as percentage of total outputs)

Industries	*Intermediate outputs of OFS*			*Intermediate outputs of NFS*		
	Total	*of which to OFS*	*of which to NFS*	*Total*	*of which to OFS*	*of which to NFS*
1 Agriculture, forestry and fishing	73.7	73.7	0.0	69.0	5.1	63.9
2 Energy and mining	76.2	75.7	0.5	64.4	0.1	64.3
3 Manuf. of basic and production goods	61.7	58.1	3.6	71.7	14.6	57.1
4 Manuf. of capital goods	27.8	26.5	1.3	38.7	3.9	34.8
5 Manuf. of consumer goods	42.0	41.5	0.5	17.1	2.0	15.1
6 Manuf. of food products, beverages and tobacco products	37.2	35.4	1.8	21.2	0.5	20.7
7 Construction	17.7	16.9	0.8	22.4		22.4
8 Trade, transport and communication	49.8	48.6	1.2	18.8	0.3	18.5
9 Other market services	54.0	53.2	0.8	37.1	1.5	35.6
10 Non-market services	9.9	9.8	0.1	6.8	0.2	6.6
1–10 All industries	43.2	42.0	1.2	33.1	2.0	31.1

Source: Bi-regional input-output accounting of DIW.

p.c.) compared to the corresponding one in NFS (33.1 p.c.) though for three industries, i.e. manufacture of basic and production goods, manufacture of capital goods, and construction, just the opposite holds true. The intraregional intermediate output proportions are prevailing in OFS and NFS, both. Only for some industries, e.g. for manufacture of basic and production goods in OFS (3.6 p.c.) and for manufacture of basic and production goods (14.6 p.c.), for agriculture, forestry and fishing (5.1 p.c.) as well as for manufacture of capital goods (3.9 p.c.) in NFS the bi-regional intermediate output proportions are significant.

5.3.2 Final Demand Proportions in OFS and NFS

The analysis of intermediate input proportions has proved the importance of trade flows from OFS to NFS for production. The same is true for satisfying domestic final demand in the New Federal States as can be seen from Table 5.4. The individual expenditures of four domestic final demand categories (exclusive changes in stocks) are presented as percentage of total expenditures in OFS and NFS. Additionally, the final demand expenditures are subdivided according to their regional origin into OFS, NFS and other countries.

The results of Table 5.4 underline the role of West German domestic production for the economic development in East Germany. 27.0 p.c. of total private consumption in NFS and even 39.7 p.c. of NFS capital formation in equipment originate from OFS, and the bi-regional dependence of NFS with regard to government consumption (20.1 p.c.) and capital formation in construction (15.7 p.c.) is also considerable. An analysis by industry brings to light which individual purchases are responsible for the overall proportions. Private consumption in NFS, for example, depends largely on West German capital goods – among them are the used passenger cars on trade, transport and communication, and on other market services from OFS. The high proportions of capital formation in equipment and in construction are mainly caused by the intraindustrial purchases of NFS from OFS.

Another result in Table 5.4 which should be stressed is the percentage of 22 p.c. for NFS imports from other countries in private consumption and in capital formation in equipment. The proportions certify that more than one fifth of the expenditures on the two final demand categories are satisfied by deliveries from foreign countries.

5.3.3 Employment and Productivity in OFS and NFS

Labour coefficients and productivity pattern are the factors to which the different economic conditions in OFS and NFS are mostly traced back. For

Table 5.4 Composition of final demand categories in Old and New Federal States of Germany 1991 according to regional origin (final demand expenditures as percentage of total expenditures)

Industries		*Private Consumption*		*Government Consumption*		*Capital formation in equipment*		*Capital formation in construction*	
		OFS	*NFS*	*OFS*	*NFS*	*OFS*	*NFS*	*OFS*	*NFS*
1 Agriculture, forestry	OFS	0.8	0.1	0.4		0.0		0.3	
and fishing	NFS	0.0	0.7		0.1				0.5
2 Energy and mining	OFS	2.7	0.1	1.4		0.1		0.7	
	NFS		4.7		3.3				1.6
3 Manuf. of basic and	OFS	4.8	0.3	3.8	0.1	0.8		0.7	
production goods	NFS	0.0	0.5		0.6		1.2		1.2
4 Manuf. of capital	OFS	9.0	5.6	4.0	0.2	58.6	34.7	7.8	
goods	NFS	0.0	0.4		0.3	0.8	26.1		4.1
5 Manuf. of consumer	OFS	5.4	1.9	1.9	0.3	2.9		0.4	
goods	NFS	0.1	1.7		1.0		0.6		0.6
6 Manuf. of food,	OFS	9.3	3.5	0.6	0.6	0.0		0.1	
beverages and tobacco products	NFS	0.1	5.9		1.7		0.9		0.8
7 Construction	OFS	0.2		2.6	0.1	0.1		71.0	15.2
	NFS		0.2		1.7			0.1	67.1
8 Trade, transport and	OFS	15.8	9.6	5.1	1.7	4.8	5.0	1.5	
communication	NFS	0.1	15.5	0.0	7.5	0.1	7.4		1.6
9 Other market	OFS	28.7	5.8	18.3	5.2	0.0		6.9	0.4
services	NFS	0.5	16.7	0.3	9.3	0.0	0.5	0.0	0.9
10 Non-market	OFS	4.1		54.7	11.8			0.1	
services	NFS	0.0	1.2	0.1	50.3				
Final consumption	OFS	80.7	27.0	92.7	20.1	67.3	39.7	89.4	15.7
from domestic production	NFS	0.8	47.5	0.4	75.8	0.9	36.8	0.1	78.4
Imports from other countries		11.4	22.5	3.5	3.5	29.6	22.3	1.6	4.7
Non-deductible value added tax		7.1	3.0	3.4	0.6	2.2	1.2	8.9	1.2
Total		100	100	100	100	100	100	100	100

Source: Bi-regional input-output accounting of DIW.

that reason the gross output values of the ten industries from the bi-regional input–output table for Germany 1991 were combined with the corresponding employment data in OFS and NFS. It has to be emphasized that in the computation of labour coefficients and labour productivity the NFS employment figures for 1991 were substituted by those for 1992. That accounts for the high number of short-term workers and for the large reserves of employed persons in East Germany in 1991.

The results presented in Table 5.5 confirm the already known facts. The average labour productivity measured by millions DM of output per person in all industries reflects one third in NFS (0.057) compared to the ratio in OFS (0.168). A comparison by industry shows a wide range between the differences in productivity for non-market services (OFS: 0.064 – NFS: 0.036) on the one hand and for manufacture of consumer goods (OFS: 0.169 – NFS: 0.030) on the other. The highest labour productivities or, synonymously, the lowest labour coefficients appear for energy and mining in West and East Germany, both.

5.3.4 Impact of a Change in Final Demand on Production in OFS and NFS

The proportions which have been analyzed so far are the results of a descriptive evaluation of the bi-regional input–output table for Germany. In order to show the direct and indirect effects induced by a change in final demand the analytical evaluation is needed. It has its origin in the open static Leontief model and in the inverse coefficients which present the general solution of the input–output model (Stäglin, 1989).

Using the inverse coefficients of the bi-regional German input–output table for 1991, it is possible to derive the total (direct and indirect) production effects in OFS and NFS induced by an additional final demand of 100 million DM in each of the ten industries. The results of the computation presented in Table 5.6 bring to light that the induced total production effects in NFS compared to those in OFS are higher in six industries, lower in one industry, i.e. in energy and mining, and more or less the same in two industries, i.e. in construction and in trade, transport and communication.

Consequently, for the purpose of intended repercussions in the economy, it seems to be favourable at the first moment to increase the final demand in NFS. But when the total impact is subdivided into the contributions of NFS and OFS, industry by industry, the volume of induced production effective in NFS decreases heavily. This can be proved with the results of Table 5.6 on the basis of the induced production effects in NFS which are satisfied by the industries in OFS. Neglecting non-market services, the production losses in

NFS according to regional flows from OFS ranges from 15.4 p.c. of total induced effects in energy and mining to 27.6 p.c. in construction. These results reflect an underdeveloped production structure and infrastructure in the New Federal States in 1991 compared to that of the Old Federal States.

Table 5.5 Employment, labour coefficients and productivity in Old and New Federal States of Germany 1991/1992

Industries	*Employed persons in 1000*		*Labour coefficients (persons per million of output)*		*Labour productivity (millions of output per person)*	
	OFS	*NFS **	*OFS*	*NFS **	*OFS*	*NFS **
1 Agriculture, forestry and fishing	963	372	14.2224	47.0886	0.070	0.021
2 Energy and mining	460	176	2.1983	4.7956	0.455	0.209
3 Manuf. of basic and production goods	1805	287	3.2544	11.1413	0.307	0.090
4 Manuf. of capital goods	4594	758	4.6807	21.4488	0.214	0.047
5 Manuf. of consumer goods	1838	340	5.9189	33.1707	0.169	0.030
6 Manuf. of food products, beverages and tobacco products	851	166	3.2112	7.9808	0.311	0.125
7 Construction	1941	640	6.7156	16.0000	0.149	0.063
8 Trade, transport and communication	5545	1206	8.3105	21.3451	0.120	0.047
9 Other market services	5588	1042	4.6294	12.9505	0.216	0.077
10 Non-market services	5634	1389	15.5795	28.1231	0.064	0.036
1–10 All industries	29219	6376	5.9466	17.5599	0.168	0.057

* For NFS the employed persons of 1992 were combined with the gross output values of 1991.

Source: Bi-regional input-output accounting of DIW.

5.3.5 Impact of a Change in Final Demand on Employment in OFS and NFS

Using the labour coefficients for the ten industries in OFS and NFS from Table 5.5, the production effects induced by an additional final demand (see Table 5.6) can be transformed into employment effects. The corresponding results are given in Table 5.7. They confirm the statement on the higher

Table 5.6 Impact of an additional final demand of 100 million DM in each industry on production in Old and New Federal States of Germany 1991

Industries	*Induced production effects in OFS in million DM* Total	*of which attributable to* OFS	NFS	*Induced production effects in NFS in million DM* Total	*of which attributable to* OFS	NFS
1 Agriculture, forestry and fishing	169.1	168.9	0.2	251.6	48.2	203.4
2 Energy and mining	217.0	216.8	0.2	174.9	27.0	147.9
3 Manuf. of basic and production goods	187.9	186.9	1.0	230.0	62.0	168.0
4 Manuf. of capital goods	187.1	186.4	0.7	222.3	57.5	164.8
5 Manuf. of consumer goods	180.9	180.1	0.8	221.3	52.7	168.6
6 Manuf. of food products, beverages and tobacco products	195.4	195.0	0.4	243.3	61.1	182.2
7 Construction	183.2	183.0	0.2	182.2	50.3	131.9
8 Trade, transport and communication	168.3	168.1	0.2	166.4	43.7	122.7
9 Other market services	170.2	170.0	0.2	237.1	61.0	176.1
10 Non-market services	111.0	110.9	0.1	109.6	4.9	104.7

Source: Bi-regional input-output accounting of DIW.

induced effects in NFS compared to those in OFS. But in addition they show a minor decrease in induced total employment effects in NFS than in production effects as a result of the deliveries from OFS. This can be attributed to the different productivities in the two regions of Germany. It can best be exemplified for construction and for trade, transport and communication. Although the two industries show the same volume of induced total production effects in OFS and NFS (see Table 5.6), the

Table 5.7 Impact of an additional final demand of 100 million DM in each industry on employment in Old and New Federal States of Germany 1991

Industries	*Induced employment effects in OFS in persons*			*Induced employment effects in NFS in persons*		
	Total	*of which attributable to OFS*	*of which attributable to NFS*	*Total*	*of which attributable to OFS*	*of which attributable to NFS*
1 Agriculture, forestry and fishing	1775	1772	3	7998	222	7776
2 Energy and mining	631	628	3	1158	118	1040
3 Manuf. of basic and production goods	767	752	15	2244	279	1965
4 Manuf. of capital goods	911	900	11	3403	269	3134
5 Manuf. of consumer goods	1020	1004	16	4700	245	4455
6 Manuf. of food products, beverages and tobacco products	973	964	9	2624	301	2323
7 Construction	1106	1102	4	2303	228	2075
8 Trade, transport and communication	1248	1246	2	2709	250	2459
9 Other-market services	835	832	3	2621	300	2321
10 Non-market services	1619	1617	2	2920	29	2891

Source: Bi-regional input-output accounting of DIW.

appertaining employment effects are quite different in the two regions due to the lower productivity rates (or higher labour coefficients) in NFS.

5.4 CONCLUSIONS

The descriptive and the analytical evaluation of the first bi-regional input–output table for Germany 1991 has offered a brief insight into the economic conditions of OFS and NFS one year after the unification. Using input–output proportions the high dependence of East Germany on West Germany with regard to intermediate and final goods and services could be proved. The productivity gap which is often taken as indicator for the non-expected difficulties in the economic unification process could also be shown. Additionally, the analytical evaluation of the bi-regional German input–output table made possible an impact analysis. Assuming an additional final demand in each of the ten industries in OFS and NFS, the direct and indirect production effects as well as the employment effects could be derived. It came to light that the induced total production and employment effects in NFS have to be reduced by the flows from OFS which contribute to final demand in NFS, too.

All statements are based on the bi-regional input–output table for 1991, the first complete year after unification. Although the input–output proportions have contributed to the growing overall German statistical information system, they describe an economic situation which has changed from year to year. In order to observe the approaching development in East and West Germany over this period, new updated bi-regional input–output tables are needed. These tables should distinguish more industries than presented in the bi-regional input–output table for Germany 1991. But first of all the data base for estimating the bi-regional trade flows between the Old and the New Federal States has to be improved by the Federal Statistical Office.

REFERENCES

ANGERMANN, O. (1994) 'Sammlung, Sicherung und Rückrechnung von statistischen Daten über die ehemalige DDR' (Collecting, Securing and Compiling Retrospectively Statistical Data for the Former GDR), *Allgemeines Statistisches Archiv*, vol. 78, no. 2, pp. 340–9.

DIW (1990) 'Quantitative Aspects of Economic and Financial Reform in the GDR' *Economic Bulletin of the German Institute for Economic Research* (DIW), vol. 27, no. 5 (July).

DIW (1993) 'Sozialprodukt und Einkommenskreislauf – Vierteljährliche volkswirtschaftliche Gesamtrechnung für Ostdeutschland' (National Product and Income Circulation – Quarterly National Accounts for East Germany), *Material of the German Institute for Economic Research* (DIW), Berlin, April.

FILIP-KÖHN, R. and STÄGLIN, R. (1994) 'Im Osten kaufen, im Westen produzieren? Ergebnisse einer Input–Output-Analyse über die Wirkung von Nachfrageimpulsen' (Buying in East, Producing in West? Results of an Impact Analysis using Input–Output), *IAB-Kurzbericht*, no. 13, 23 September.

LUDWIG, U. and STÄGLIN, R. (1993) 'Problems in Comparing Input–Output Tables for East and West Germany', *Economic Systems Research*, vol. 5, no. 2, 1993, pp. 137–47.

MELZER, M. and STÄGLIN, R. (1991) 'The Role of Economic Statistics in the German Unification Process', *Economic Statistics for Economies in Transition: Eastern Europe in the 1990's*, Sponsored by US Bureau of Labor Statistics and Eurostat, Washington, DC, 14–16 February 1991, pp. 407–49.

SCHUPP, J. and WAGNER, G. (1990) 'Die DDR-Stichprobe des Sozio-ökonomischen Panels – Konzept und Durchführung der "Basiserhebung 1990" in der DDR' (GDR Sample Survey of the Socio-Economic Panel – Concept and Implementation of the 'Basic Survey 1990' in the GDR), *Vierteljahrshefte zur Wirtschaftsforschung des DIW*, no. 2/3, pp. 152–9.

STÄGLIN, R. (1989) 'The Input–Output Framework – An Introduction', *Input–Output Applications for Cyprus, Proceedings of the Symposium on Input–Output Tables, 1988*, Edited by E.I. Demetriades and D. A. Petrondas, Department of Statistics and Research, Research Papers and Reports, series II, no. 13, Nicosia, April 1989, pp. 25–58.

STÄGLIN, R. and FILIP-KÖHN, R. (1994) 'Quantitative Analyse der wirtschaftlichen Verflechtung von alten und neuen Bundesländern und ihrer Arbeitsmarktwirkungen' (Quantitative Analysis of Economic Interdependencies between Old and New Federal States and their Impact on the Labour Market), *Beiträge zur Arbeitsmarkt- und Berufsforschung, BeitrAB 183*, Institut für Arbeitsmarkt- und Berufsforschung der Bundesanstalt für Arbeit, Nuremberg.

STATISTISCHES BUNDESAMT (1991) *Fachserie 6, Handel, Gastgewerbe, Reiseverkehr, Reihe 6*, Innerdeutscher Warenverkehr (Intragerman Trade of Commodities), Publication of the Federal Statistical Office, December.

STATISTISCHES BUNDESAMT (1992) *Fachserie 18, Volkswirtschaftliche Gesamtrechnungen* (National Accounts), *Reihe 3*, Vierteljahresergebnisse der Inlandsproduktsberechnung, Drittes Vierteljahr 1992, Publication of the Federal Statistical Office, December.

STATISTISCHES BUNDESAMT (1993) 'Einführung der Bundesstatistik in den neuen Bundesländern' (Introduction of the Federal Statistics in the New Federal States), *Band 22 der Schriftenreihe Forum der Bundesstatistik*, edited by the Federal Statistical Office, January.

6 Analyzing Decomposition Analyses

Erik Dietzenbacher and Bart Los

6.1 INTRODUCTION

Input–output analysis has been used widely for cross-sectional comparisons of economies across time and space. 'The comparison of changes in structure in an economy over time lends itself to more rigour than static structural assessments and cross-country comparisons' (Rose and Miernyk, 1989, p. 245). For this purpose, the methodology of structural decomposition analysis has been applied extensively. According to Skolka (1989, p. 46), 'Structural decomposition analysis can be defined as a method of distinguishing major shifts within an economy by means of comparative static changes in key sets of parameters.'

Early contributions include, among others, Chenery, Shishido and Watanabe (1962), Vaccara and Simon (1968), Carter (1970), and Stäglin and Wessels (1972). For recent contributions, see, for instance, Forssell (1985, 1988, 1989, 1990), Feldman, McClain and Palmer (1987), Blair and Wyckoff (1989), Fujimagari (1989), Kanemitsu and Ohnishi (1989), Barker (1990), Lee (1990), Afrasiabi and Casler (1991), Fujita and James (1991), Karasz (1992), Sawyer (1992), Dewhurst (1993), Lin and Polenske (1993), and Van der Linden and Oosterhaven (1993).

The central idea is that the change in the product of several variables is written as a sum of terms, each of which corresponds to the change in one of the variables. That is, let y be the product of $x_1, \ldots, x_n$. The change in y between time $t = 0$ and $t = 1$ is denoted as Δy. A decomposition of Δy is then given by $\Delta y = \Sigma_{i=1}^{n} x_1 \ldots x_{i-1}(\Delta x_i)x_{i+1} \ldots x_n$. Unfortunately, however, such a decomposition is not unique. The variable x_j ($j \neq i$) may take its value at time $t = 0$ or its value at time $t = 1$. As such, the sources of structural change (i.e. Δx_i) may be given different weights. This feature of decomposition analyses is well recognized in the literature. Nevertheless, detailed sensitivity analyses seem to be lacking and most empirical studies employ only one decomposition. Maybe this is so, 'Because in empirical work, the difference between the ... versions is small', as Schumann (1993) states. The present paper aims at presenting an empirical evaluation of the different versions, for two cases of a structural decomposition.

The plan of the paper is as follows. In the next section we sketch the problem and its background in more detail. Section 6.3 discusses the changes in the Leontief inverse due to technological changes and product-mix changes. The empirical results for this decomposition are presented in Section 6.4. The decomposition of the changes in the value added, into changes in the value added coefficients, the changes in the Leontief inverse and the changes in the final demands are given in Section 6.5. The empirical evaluation of this decomposition follows in Section 6.6. The results are summarized and conclusions are drawn in Section 6.7.

6.2 SKETCH OF THE PROBLEM

Consider the following elementary example of a decomposition of changes in a variable over time. Let the value at time t be given by the price at time t multiplied by the quantity at time t. That is, $v(t) = p(t)q(t)$. When the three variables are continuous functions of t, the change in $v(t)$ may be uniquely decomposed into two additive terms. The first expresses the effects of a change in the price, the second of a change in the quantity. Differentiating $v(t)$ with respect to time and separating terms yields

$$\frac{dv(t)}{dt} = \frac{dp(t)}{dt}q(t) + p(t)\frac{dq(t)}{dt} \tag{1}$$

In most empirical work, however, information with respect to the variables under consideration is only available at discrete points in time. Consequently, the analogous expression of (1) is no longer unique and involves a so-called interaction term. Consider the change between $t = 0$ and $t = 1$, and write $\Delta v = v(1) - v(0) = p(1)q(1) - p(0)q(0)$. Then

$$\Delta v = (\Delta p)q(0) + p(0)(\Delta q) + (\Delta p)(\Delta q) \tag{2.1}$$
$$= (\Delta p)q(1) + p(1)(\Delta q) - (\Delta p)(\Delta q) \tag{2.2}$$

In decomposing Δv, the interaction term $(\Delta p)(\Delta q)$ may be avoided. But this in turn implies that the price change is weighted with the quantity in the one period, while the quantity change is weighted with the price in the other period. That is,

$$\Delta v = (\Delta p)q(0) + p(1)(\Delta q) \tag{2.3}$$
$$= (\Delta p)q(1) + p(0)(\Delta q) \tag{2.4}$$

'It thus becomes obvious that ... there is no single correct method of measuring the relative importance of the two factors ... which explain the ... changes.... The best measure of the relative importance of the two factors would be an average of the answers that result from the two alternative procedures' (Vaccara and Simon, 1968, pp. 25–6). This third alternative is thus obtained by taking the arithmetic mean of the expressions on the right hand sides in (2.1) and (2.2), or equivalently of those in (2.3) and (2.4). Writing $\bar{q} = [q(0) + q(1)]/2$ and $\bar{p} = [p(0) + p(1)]/2$ yields[1]

$$\Delta v = (\Delta p)\bar{q} + \bar{p}(\Delta q) \tag{2.5}$$

'On first blush this all seems straightforward and irreproachable. But, there are difficulties', as Fromm (1968, p. 62) explains in his comment on Vaccara and Simon (1968).[2]

In this paper we take the versions (2.3)–(2.5) as our point of departure. They are simply considered as equivalent alternatives for decomposing Δv, in the sense that there is no preference for one expression to the others, on theoretical grounds. In each of the three alternative expressions (2.3)–(2.5), the first term indicates the effect of the price change and the second term the effect of the quantity change. Decomposition formulae as in (2) have been widely applied also to input–output models. The first question we would like to address in this paper, is whether the results are influenced by the specific expression that is used in an empirical analysis.

Since such analyses are based on input–output tables, it should be taken into account that, in most countries, such tables are not constructed every year. The changes over time therefore relate to a period of several years (i.e. the difference between $t = 0$ and $t = 1$). This time period may differ between different studies but also within the same study (for example, US tables are readily available for 1958, 1963, 1967, 1972 and 1977). The second question we would like to address is whether the results in general and the answer to the first question in particular, are affected by the length of the time period.

6.3 TECHNOLOGICAL AND PRODUCT-MIX CHANGES

In this section we focus on the analysis of changes in the Leontief inverse (i.e. the matrix of direct and indirect input requirements), at an aggregated level. As is well known (see e.g. Afrasiabi and Casler, 1991), these changes may be attributed to changes in the direct input coefficients and to changes in the weights of each sector within the aggregated (or hybrid) sector. The first part is referred to as technological change and the second part as product-mix change.

Consider an $n \times n$ matrix **A** of direct input coefficients, which is aggregated into the $m \times m$ matrix $\tilde{\mathbf{A}}$. Let the aggregation scheme be given as follows (see e.g. Dietzenbacher, 1992).

original sectors	*hybrid sectors*
$1, \ldots, k_1$	1,
$k_1, +1, \ldots, k_2$	2,
$\ldots,$	$\ldots,$
$k_{i-1}+1, \ldots, k_i,$	$i,$
$\ldots,$	$\ldots,$

The matrix $\tilde{\mathbf{A}}$ is obtained as

$$\tilde{\mathbf{A}} = \mathbf{GAH}', \tag{3}$$

with

$$\mathbf{G} = \begin{bmatrix} 1\ldots1 & 0\ldots0 & \ldots & 0\ldots0 \\ 0\ldots0 & 1\ldots1 & \ldots & 0\ldots0 \\ \vdots\quad\vdots & \vdots\quad\vdots & \ddots & \vdots\quad\vdots \\ 0\ldots0 & 0\ldots0 & \ldots & 1\ldots1 \end{bmatrix}, \tag{4}$$

and

$$\mathbf{H} = \begin{bmatrix} w_1 & \ldots w_{k_1} & 0 & \ldots 0 & \ldots & 0 & \ldots 0 \\ 0 & \ldots 0 & w_{k_1+1} & \ldots w_{k_2} & \ldots & 0 & \ldots 0 \\ \vdots & \vdots & \vdots & \vdots & \ddots & \vdots & \vdots \\ 0 & \ldots 0 & 0 & \ldots 0 & \ldots & w_{k_{m-1}+1} & \ldots w_n \end{bmatrix}. \tag{5}$$

The elements w indicate the weights. They express the output of a certain sector as a proportion of the total output of the hybrid sector. That is,

$$w_{k_{i-1}+j} = x_{k_{i-1}+j} / (x_{k_{i-1}+1} + \ldots + x_{k_i}), \tag{6}$$

for $j = 1, \ldots, k_i - k_{i-1}$ and $i = 1, \ldots, m$ with $k_0 = 0$ and $k_m = n$.

Note that (3) may be rewritten as

$$\tilde{\mathbf{A}} = \mathbf{GAWG}', \tag{7}$$

where **W** is the $n \times n$ diagonal matrix as obtained from the vector $(w_1, \ldots, w_{k_1}, w_{k_1+1}, \ldots, w_{k_2}, \ldots, w_{k_{m-1}+1}, \ldots, w_n)$.

In this section we study the changes in the aggregated Leontief inverse. That is, $\Delta\tilde{\mathbf{L}} = \tilde{\mathbf{L}}_1 - \tilde{\mathbf{L}}_0$, with e.g. $\tilde{\mathbf{L}}_1 = (\mathbf{I} - \tilde{\mathbf{A}}_1)^{-1}$.

$$\Delta\tilde{\mathbf{L}} = \tilde{\mathbf{L}}_1 - \tilde{\mathbf{L}}_0 = \tilde{\mathbf{L}}_1\tilde{\mathbf{L}}_0 - \tilde{\mathbf{L}}_0 - \tilde{\mathbf{L}}_1\tilde{\mathbf{L}}_0 + \tilde{\mathbf{L}}_1 = (\tilde{\mathbf{L}}_1 - \mathbf{I})\tilde{\mathbf{L}}_0 - \tilde{\mathbf{L}}_1(\tilde{\mathbf{L}}_0 - \mathbf{I}).$$

Observe that $(\tilde{\mathbf{L}}_0 - \mathbf{I})$ may be written as $\tilde{\mathbf{L}}_0 - \tilde{\mathbf{L}}_0(\mathbf{I} - \mathbf{A}_0) = \tilde{\mathbf{L}}_0\tilde{\mathbf{A}}_0$ or as $\tilde{\mathbf{L}}_0 - (\mathbf{I} - \tilde{\mathbf{A}}_0)\tilde{\mathbf{L}}_0 = \tilde{\mathbf{A}}_0\tilde{\mathbf{L}}_0$. Using these expressions for $(\tilde{\mathbf{L}}_0 - \mathbf{I})$ and, similarly, for $(\tilde{\mathbf{L}}_1 - \mathbf{I})$ yields

$$\Delta\tilde{\mathbf{L}} = \tilde{\mathbf{L}}_1\tilde{\mathbf{A}}_1\tilde{\mathbf{L}}_0 - \tilde{\mathbf{L}}_1\tilde{\mathbf{A}}_0\tilde{\mathbf{L}}_0 = \tilde{\mathbf{L}}_1(\tilde{\mathbf{A}}_1 - \tilde{\mathbf{A}}_0)\tilde{\mathbf{L}}_0 = \tilde{\mathbf{L}}_1(\Delta\tilde{\mathbf{A}})\tilde{\mathbf{L}}_0. \qquad (8.1)$$

In the same way, $\tilde{\mathbf{L}}_1 - \tilde{\mathbf{L}}_0 = \tilde{\mathbf{L}}_1 - \tilde{\mathbf{L}}_0\tilde{\mathbf{L}}_1 + \tilde{\mathbf{L}}_0\tilde{\mathbf{L}}_1 - \tilde{\mathbf{L}}_0$ gives

$$\Delta\tilde{\mathbf{L}} = \tilde{\mathbf{L}}_0(\Delta\tilde{\mathbf{A}})\tilde{\mathbf{L}}_1. \qquad (8.2)$$

Next, $\Delta\tilde{\mathbf{A}} = \tilde{\mathbf{A}}_1 - \tilde{\mathbf{A}}_0 = \mathbf{G}(\mathbf{A}_1\mathbf{W}_1 - \mathbf{A}_0\mathbf{W}_0)\mathbf{G}'$ may be decomposed by using the expressions (2.3), (2.4) and (2.5). This results into

$$\begin{aligned}\Delta\tilde{\mathbf{A}} &= \mathbf{G}[(\Delta\mathbf{A})\mathbf{W}_0 + \mathbf{A}_1(\Delta\mathbf{W})]\mathbf{G}', && (9.1)\\ &= \mathbf{G}[(\Delta\mathbf{A})\mathbf{W}_1 + \mathbf{A}_0(\Delta\mathbf{W})]\mathbf{G}', && (9.2)\\ &= \mathbf{G}[(\Delta\mathbf{A})\bar{\mathbf{W}} + \bar{\mathbf{A}}(\Delta\mathbf{W})]\mathbf{G}'. && (9.3)\end{aligned}$$

Combining the expressions (8.1), (8.2) and (9.1)–(9.3) gives the following six decompositions of $\Delta\tilde{\mathbf{L}}$.

$$\begin{aligned}\Delta\tilde{\mathbf{L}} &= \tilde{\mathbf{L}}_1\mathbf{G}(\Delta\mathbf{A})\mathbf{W}_0\mathbf{G}'\tilde{\mathbf{L}}_0 + \tilde{\mathbf{L}}_1\mathbf{G}\mathbf{A}_1(\Delta\mathbf{W})\mathbf{G}'\tilde{\mathbf{L}}_0 && (10.1)\\ &= \tilde{\mathbf{L}}_1\mathbf{G}(\Delta\mathbf{A})\mathbf{W}_1\mathbf{G}'\tilde{\mathbf{L}}_0 + \tilde{\mathbf{L}}_1\mathbf{G}\mathbf{A}_0(\Delta\mathbf{W})\mathbf{G}'\tilde{\mathbf{L}}_0 && (10.2)\\ &= \tilde{\mathbf{L}}_1\mathbf{G}(\Delta\mathbf{A})\bar{\mathbf{W}}\mathbf{G}'\tilde{\mathbf{L}}_0 + \tilde{\mathbf{L}}_1\mathbf{G}\bar{\mathbf{A}}(\Delta\mathbf{W})\mathbf{G}'\tilde{\mathbf{L}}_0 && (10.3)\\ &= \tilde{\mathbf{L}}_0\mathbf{G}(\Delta\mathbf{A})\mathbf{W}_0\mathbf{G}'\tilde{\mathbf{L}}_1 + \tilde{\mathbf{L}}_0\mathbf{G}\mathbf{A}_1(\Delta\mathbf{W})\mathbf{G}'\tilde{\mathbf{L}}_1 && (10.4)\\ &= \tilde{\mathbf{L}}_0\mathbf{G}(\Delta\mathbf{A})\mathbf{W}_1\mathbf{G}'\tilde{\mathbf{L}}_1 + \tilde{\mathbf{L}}_0\mathbf{G}\mathbf{A}_0(\Delta\mathbf{W})\mathbf{G}'\tilde{\mathbf{L}}_1 && (10.5)\\ &= \tilde{\mathbf{L}}_0\mathbf{G}(\Delta\mathbf{A})\bar{\mathbf{W}}\mathbf{G}'\tilde{\mathbf{L}}_1 + \tilde{\mathbf{L}}_0\mathbf{G}\bar{\mathbf{A}}(\Delta\mathbf{W})\mathbf{G}'\tilde{\mathbf{L}}_1 && (10.6)\end{aligned}$$

In each of the six expressions, the first term indicates the effects of technological change and the second term the effects of a change in the product-mix.

For notational convenience the expressions in (10) are written as

$$\Delta\tilde{\mathbf{L}} = \mathbf{TC}^{(k)} + \mathbf{PMC}^{(k)}, \text{with} \quad k = 1, \ldots, 6, \qquad (11)$$

and for its typical element

$$\Delta\tilde{l}_{ij} = TC_{ij}^{(k)} + PMC_{ij}^{(k)}, \text{ with } k = 1, \ldots, 6 \text{ and } i, j = 1, \ldots, n. \qquad (12)$$

6.4 CHANGES IN THE LEONTIEF INVERSE: EMPIRICAL RESULTS

The results in this section are based on calculations for the Greek economy, for which annual input–output tables in constant prices are available for the period 1958–77 (see Skountzos and Mattheos, 1980). It should be emphasized that it is not our purpose to analyze the results for the Greek economy themselves. It is our aim to test whether different computational formulae yield different results and whether this (in)difference is affected by a varying time lag.

The original tables distinguish 35 sectors which have been aggregated into 12 sectors. Below, we give the 12-sector classification. The number between brackets indicates the number of original sectors that are covered by the aggregated sector.

1 = agriculture, livestock, forestry, fishing (1)
2 = food processing, beverages, tobacco (3)
3 = textiles, footwear, clothing, leather, rubber products (5)
4 = mining, quarrying, plastic products, chemicals, oil refining (4)
5 = metal products, machinery, transport means, other manufacturing (6)
6 = cement, construction materials, construction (3)
7 = wood, paper, printing, glass (5)
8 = trade (1)
9 = electricity, gas, water (1)
10 = transportation, communication (2)
11 = banking, other financial institutions, insurances (1)
12 = other services, housing, public services (3)

Table 6.1 presents the results for the changes in the Leontief inverse between 1976 and 1977, i.e. $t = 0 = 1976$ and $t = 1 = 1977$. The figures denote the average percentage contribution of technical change and, between brackets, the standard deviation. That is, μ_{ij} and σ_{ij}, which are defined as

$$\mu_{ij} = \frac{1}{6}\sum_{k=1}^{6} \mu_{ij}^{(k)}, \text{ with } \mu_{ij}^{(k)} = 100\text{TC}_{ij}^{(k)}/\Delta\tilde{l}_{ij}$$

$$\sigma_{ij} = \sqrt{\nu_{ij}}, \text{ with } \nu_{ij} = \frac{1}{6}\sum_{k=1}^{6}[\mu_{ij}^{(k)} - \mu_{ij}]^2$$

Note that the average percentage contribution of product-mix changes yields $100 - \mu_{ij}$, with the same standard deviation σ_{ij}.

Table 6.1 Average percentage contribution of technical change, 1976–7

μ_{ij} (σ_{ij})	$j=1$	$j=2$	$j=3$	$j=4$	$j=5$	$j=6$
i=1	99.60	94.99	84.50	97.74	101.90	99.61
	(0.04)	(0.42)	(2.42)	(0.50)	(0.20)	(0.20)
i=2	98.76	91.92	53.79	98.15	90.55	98.96
	(0.04)	(0.30)	(2.51)	(0.43)	(2.17)	(0.57)
i=3	206.62	103.62	142.08	109.21	113.33	102.52
	(6.42)	(1.25)	(2.36)	(1.03)	(0.81)	(1.32)
i=4	101.91	110.41	112.85	94.14	22.86	99.95
	(0.11)	(0.27)	(1.00)	(0.72)	(1.83)	(0.23)
i=5	105.49	89.56	42.51	101.20	123.11	100.42
	(0.48)	(0.81)	(5.70)	(0.48)	(0.99)	(0.31)
i=6	100.77	101.49	96.09	101.02	101.47	100.03
	(0.28)	(0.72)	(1.95)	(0.41)	(0.42)	(0.02)
i=7	95.32	72.15	64.45	98.14	246.79	99.79
	(1.47)	(2.93)	(3.96)	(0.42)	(17.20)	(0.08)
i=8	103.07	95.26	–4.92	99.03	105.41	100.04
	(0.37)	(0.21)	(7.41)	(0.34)	(0.33)	(0.08)
i=9	76.71	207.69	75.92	100.52	97.22	99.85
	(10.65)	(2.08)	(3.47)	(0.28)	(2.88)	(0.16)
i=10	100.63	97.08	34.34	99.39	106.96	100.02
	(0.10)	(0.17)	(6.09)	(0.25)	(0.42)	(0.11)
i=11	100.56	93.90	128.94	97.42	100.67	99.94
	(0.11)	(0.34)	(1.52)	(0.48)	(3.94)	(0.19)
i=12	96.97	87.84	79.82	98.94	111.72	100.25
	(0.94)	(0.29)	(2.95)	(0.37)	(1.85)	(0.17)

Table 6.1 shows that the average percentage contribution of technical change to the changes in the Leontief inverse is, roughly speaking, close to 100. It turns out that in 109 out of 144 cases the average contribution falls within the interval (90.00; 110.00). Extremely large (positive or negative) values may be expected when the change in some element of the Leontief inverse is very small (i.e. $\Delta\tilde{l}_{ij} \approx 0$). For the decomposition of 1976–7, the largest average contribution is 246.8 per cent for the element $(i,j) = (7,5)$. For illustration, $\Delta\tilde{l}_{7,5} = -2.95 \times 10^{-4}$ while the average absolute change in the elements of the Leontief inverse amounts to 92.38×10^{-4}. The contributions $\mu_{7,5}^{(k)}$ range between 221.0 per cent and 274.8 per cent. Compared to the maximum values as observed for other years, the observed maximum for 1976–7 appears to be very moderate.

Table 6.1 Continued

$j = 7$	$j = 8$	$j = 9$	$j = 10$	$j = 11$	$j = 12$
97.95	98.77	97.68	90.20	96.88	95.75
(0.61)	(0.24)	(0.49)	(1.33)	(0.64)	(0.77)
101.99	96.26	97.71	86.60	94.38	97.52
(0.88)	(0.31)	(0.51)	(0.31)	(0.53)	(0.23)
102.85	115.44	107.74	121.14	116.16	117.78
(1.18)	(1.14)	(0.92)	(1.61)	(1.17)	(1.21)
66.63	94.64	100.80	129.20	102.03	98.38
(3.17)	(0.36)	(0.07)	(0.11)	(0.30)	(0.14)
98.50	76.85	101.88	104.94	92.86	103.13
(0.74)	(1.26)	(0.33)	(1.59)	(0.60)	(0.50)
99.51	101.01	101.03	101.47	100.94	114.32
(0.27)	(0.28)	(0.38)	(0.34)	(0.16)	(0.87)
94.77	98.96	99.31	97.83	103.46	99.30
(0.37)	(0.36)	(0.26)	(1.10)	(0.18)	(0.18)
97.94	101.40	99.74	100.09	99.96	101.12
(0.27)	(0.16)	(0.20)	(0.58)	(0.25)	(0.19)
114.23	100.47	100.07	112.95	99.76	100.67
(0.33)	(0.25)	(0.09)	(2.65)	(0.09)	(0.16)
99.82	100.58	99.97	98.91	100.13	100.38
(0.15)	(0.06)	(0.07)	(0.54)	(0.05)	(0.09)
164.57	99.54	99.83	105.96	100.00	107.51
(1.60)	(1.24)	(0.05)	(0.20)	(0.00)	(0.23)
103.79	100.82	99.77	105.66	100.02	100.34
(0.27)	(0.15)	(0.17)	(0.14)	(0.00)	(0.04)

The standard deviations in Table 6.1 are small without exception. For only two cases the standard deviation is larger than 10.00. The results clearly show that the percentage contribution of technical change differs only very little between the methods.

Similar tables for other years (all with a one-year lag) sketch very similar pictures. The only exception is that extreme values are observed more frequently. For a major part of the elements, the average contribution of technical change is close to 100 per cent. The standard deviations are small, indicating that the results for the different methods show only little variation. This pattern changes gradually when the time lag is expanded. Still, the average percentage contribution of technical change remains, for most of the elements, in the neighbourhood of 100. The standard deviations, however,

Table 6.2 Assorted results, 1960–70

(i,j)	μ_{ij}	σ_{ij}	min	max
(3,3)	–98.37	38.04	–145.31	–51.39
(4,4)	68.04	20.51	42.87	93.16
(4,5)	15.42	241.07	–283.34	312.07
(4,7)	4515.64	1192.89	2594.68	6017.78
(6,4)	2267.70	605.65	1337.03	3234.55
(6,5)	81.13	75.70	–33.20	191.30
(7,5)	75.39	24.99	43.32	108.30
(7,6)	–15.14	33.54	–59.17	27.84
(8,3)	39.97	28.40	5.01	76.34
(8,4)	59.15	82.16	–41.67	162.35
(10,4)	80.83	39.19	32.34	130.03
(10,5)	–97.13	85.79	–202.74	10.33
(11,4)	216.97	92.24	97.28	340.45
(11,5)	113.73	54.72	45.49	183.67

show a tendency to increase. It is now observed that for certain elements the results differ largely between the methods. Table 6.2 presents some striking results for the decomposition of the period 1960–70. In all of these cases the percentage contribution of technological change varies over a wide range.

The exceptionally large outcomes for the elements (4, 7) and (6, 4) are caused by the fact that the corresponding elements of the Leontief inverse remain almost constant. That is, $\Delta\tilde{l}_{4,7} = -5.93 \times 10^{-5}$ and $\Delta\tilde{l}_{6,4} = 3.03 \times 10^{-5}$, while the average absolute change in the elements equals 16.99×10^{-3}.

In order to visualize the effects of a varying time lag on the standard deviations, we have calculated the average of the figures in Table 6.1. In attempting to avoid misleading results, due to exceptionally large values for specific μ_{ij}s (as caused by $\Delta\tilde{l}_{ij} \approx 0$), we have used a weighted average. That is,

$$\bar{\mu} = \sum_{i=1}^{n}\sum_{j=1}^{n} |\Delta\tilde{l}_{ij}|\mu_{ij} \Big/ \sum_{i=1}^{n}\sum_{j=1}^{n} |\Delta\tilde{l}_{ij}|$$

$$\bar{\sigma} = \sum_{i=1}^{n}\sum_{j=1}^{n} |\Delta\tilde{l}_{ij}|\sigma_{ij} \Big/ \sum_{i=1}^{n}\sum_{j=1}^{n} |\Delta\tilde{l}_{ij}|$$

For example, the very large elements (4, 7) and (6, 4) as reported above, receive weights 2.42×10^{-5} and 1.24×10^{-5}, respectively. The values of $\bar{\mu}$ and $\bar{\sigma}$ have been computed for several years with time lags of 1, 2, 5 and 10 years. The results are given in Table 6.3. Note that the years in the first column indicate the end of the period under consideration, and the length of the period is given by the time lag in years. For example, the results for the decomposition for 1968–73 are presented in row 1973, under time lag 5.

It is clear from the results in Table 6.3 that the average standard deviation $\bar{\sigma}$ increases when the time lag increases. Recall that the values for $\bar{\mu}$ and $\bar{\sigma}$ are obtained by taking, first, for each element the average over the methods and, second, the average over the elements. So six 12×12 matrices are first condensed into a single 12×12 matrix which is then comprised into a scalar. It is also possible, of course, to comprise each of the six 12×12 matrices into a scalar and then to compute the average and standard deviation of these six scalars. That is,

$$\mu^{(k)} = \sum_{i=1}^{n}\sum_{j=1}^{n} |\Delta\tilde{l}_{ij}|\mu_{ij}^{(k)} \Big/ \sum_{i=1}^{n}\sum_{j=1}^{n} |\Delta\tilde{l}_{ij}|$$

Next, $\Sigma_{k=1}^{6}\mu^{(k)}/6$ obviously equals $\bar{\mu}$. The standard deviation of these six scalars yields

$$\bar{\bar{\sigma}} = \sqrt{\nu}, \text{with } \nu = \frac{1}{6}\sum_{k=1}^{6}[\mu^{(k)} - \bar{\mu}]^2$$

The results for $\bar{\bar{\sigma}}$ in Table 6.3 indicate that the percentage contribution of technical change as an average over all the elements shows only little variation between the methods. Moreover, the extent of this variation does not reveal a clearcut pattern across the time lags. Although the contribution of technical change may differ largely from one method to another for the elements separately, these differences apparently cancel each other out when the elements are consolidated into an 'overall' scalar.

Further inspection of the detailed results (which are not reported here), in particular for the 5- and 10-year lags, reveals two interesting features. First, the counterpart of the contribution of technical change is the contribution of product-mix changes. It might be expected that these product-mix changes are the largest for sectors which consist of many original (i.e. before aggregation) sectors. In that case, equations (3)–(5) indicate that the input coefficient is affected the most when the recipient is a large aggregate of original sectors. So, if the percentage contribution of technical change differs considerably from 100, we would expect this to occur for elements

Table 6.3 Results for a varying time lag[a]

	time lag (in years)							
	1		2		5		10	
year	$\bar{\mu}$	$\bar{\sigma}$	$\bar{\mu}$	$\bar{\sigma}$	$\bar{\mu}$	$\bar{\sigma}$	$\bar{\mu}$	$\bar{\sigma}$
1977	101.57	0.69	102.27	1.04	102.87	2.12	101.69	4.23
	(0.19)		(0.46)		(0.64)		(1.12)	
1976	102.12	0.52	100.51	0.58	103.51	2.16	102.39	5.34
	(0.17)		(0.18)		(0.49)		(2.38)	
1975	95.23	0.46	105.89	1.09	104.99	2.47	103.97	4.97
	(0.12)		(0.28)		(0.70)		(2.31)	
1974	107.58	1.11	105.93	1.45	104.71	3.75	103.50	4.49
	(0.24)		(0.45)		(1.65)		(2.04)	
1973	102.54	0.39	101.10	0.81	105.18	3.45	95.12	4.80
	(0.06)		(0.35)		(2.09)		(0.31)	
1972	101.20	0.52	110.27	1.68	104.47	3.53	93.32	4.79
	(0.25)		(0.68)		(2.19)		(0.24)	
1971	94.63	0.75	93.36	1.98	94.22	3.90	94.80	3.21
	(0.21)		(1.06)		(1.16)		(0.25)	
1970	107.20	1.90	106.07	2.06	103.72	3.24	95.99	4.15
	(0.82)		(1.19)		(1.51)		(0.37)	
1969	103.33	0.68	99.49	1.05	93.72	3.23	96.10	2.02
	(0.38)		(0.37)		(0.24)		(0.12)	
1968	100.37	0.91	95.78	1.25	91.43	5.99	98.00	2.27
	(0.09)		(0.04)		(1.61)		(0.14)	

[a] The standard deviation $\bar{\bar{\sigma}}$ is given between brackets.

corresponding to a recipient sector which is strongly aggregated. This observation is illustrated by Table 6.4, using the calculations for the decomposition of 1960–70.

We distinguish two classes of sectors. Each of the sectors 1, 8, 9, 10 and 11 is obtained from an aggregation of one or two original sectors. Each of the sectors 2–7 and 12 consists of three or more original sectors. Consequently, each element μ_{ij} falls in one of the four quadrants in Table 6.4. Next we examine whether μ_{ij} is close to 100 (that is, whether $90.00 \leq \mu_{ij} < 110.00$) or not. These two alternatives are denoted in Table 6.4 as $\mu_{ij} \approx 100$ and $\mu_{ij} \neq 100$. So, all in all, each of the 144 μ_{ij}s falls in one of eight categories. Table 6.4 presents the number of observations in each of these eight categories.

Table 6.4 Frequency distribution for μ_{ij}, 1960–70

Number of observations	*Subsectors in j:* 1 *or* 2	3 *or more*	*Total*
Subsectors in i: 1 *or* 2	$\mu_{ij} \approx 100$: 22 $\mu_{ij} \neq 100$: 3	$\mu_{ij} \approx 100$: 20 $\mu_{ij} \neq 100$: 15	$\mu_{ij} \approx 100$: 42 $\mu_{ij} \neq 100$: 18
3 *or more*	$\mu_{ij} \approx 100$: 30 $\mu_{ij} \neq 100$: 5	$\mu_{ij} \approx 100$: 24 $\mu_{ij} \neq 100$: 25	$\mu_{ij} \approx 100$: 54 $\mu_{ij} \neq 100$: 30
Total	$\mu_{ij} \approx 100$: 52 $\mu_{ij} \neq 100$: 8	$\mu_{ij} \approx 100$: 44 $\mu_{ij} \neq 100$: 40	$\mu_{ij} \approx 100$: 96 $\mu_{ij} \neq 100$: 48

The second feature, that was observed in many cases, is that the larger standard deviations σ_{ij} are observed for average percentage contributions μ_{ij} which differ from 100. In other words, when the average percentage contribution of technical change is close to 100, the variation between the methods is generally small. Large differences are typically observed when the percentage contribution of technical change for the different methods is not unambiguously close to 100. Table 6.5 gives an illustration of this observation, using the results of the decomposition for 1960–70.

6.5 VALUE ADDED DECOMPOSITIONS

In this section we analyze the changes in the value added, both sectoral and total. Let the elements of the row vector $\mathbf{a}'$ denote the value added in each sector. The elements of the row vector $\mathbf{v}'$ denote the value added coefficients, measuring the value added in each sector per unit of this sector's output. That is, $v_i = a_i/x_i$. Let $\mathbf{V}$ denote the diagonal matrix with the elements of $\mathbf{v}'$ on its diagonal. Then $\mathbf{a} = \mathbf{VLf}$ and the total value added (a) is obtained as $\mathbf{e}'\mathbf{a} = \mathbf{e}'\mathbf{VLf} = \mathbf{v}'\mathbf{Lf}$, where $\mathbf{e}'$ denotes the row summation vector, consisting entirely of ones.

Table 6.5 Frequency distribution for pairs (μ_{ij}, σ_{ij}), 1960–70

Number of observations	$\sigma_{ij} < 20.00$	$\sigma_{ij} \geq 20.00$	*Total*
$\mu_{ij} \approx 100$	95	1	96
$\mu_{ij} \neq 100$	33	15	48
Total	128	16	144

The decomposition, along the lines of Section 6.2, of the change in the value added per sector yields 16 different formulae. They are all additive and each of them contains the terms **ΔV**, **ΔL** and **Δf**. Applying (2.3), (2.4) and (2.5) to **Δa** = Δ(**VLf**) yields

$$
\begin{aligned}
\mathbf{\Delta a} &= (\mathbf{\Delta VL})\mathbf{f}_0 + (\mathbf{VL})_1(\mathbf{\Delta f}) && \text{[using (2.3)]}\\
&= (\mathbf{\Delta V})(\mathbf{Lf})_0 + \mathbf{V}_1(\mathbf{\Delta Lf}) && \text{[using (2.3)]}\\
&= (\mathbf{\Delta VL})\mathbf{f}_1 + (\mathbf{VL})_0(\mathbf{\Delta f}) && \text{[using (2.4)]}\\
&= (\mathbf{\Delta V})(\mathbf{Lf})_1 + \mathbf{V}_0(\mathbf{\Delta Lf}) && \text{[using (2.4)]}\\
&= (\mathbf{\Delta VL})\bar{\mathbf{f}} + (\overline{\mathbf{VL}})(\mathbf{\Delta f}) && \text{[using (2.5)]}\\
&= (\mathbf{\Delta V})(\overline{\mathbf{Lf}}) + \bar{\mathbf{V}}(\mathbf{\Delta Lf}) && \text{[using (2.5)].}
\end{aligned}
$$

Each of the six equation above includes either the term **ΔVL** or the term **ΔLf**. These may be decomposed further by using (2.3)–(2.5) again. This yields the following 18 equations of which 16 are different.

$$
\begin{aligned}
\mathbf{\Delta a} &= (\mathbf{\Delta V})\mathbf{L}_0\mathbf{f}_0 + \mathbf{V}_1(\mathbf{\Delta L})\mathbf{f}_0 + \mathbf{V}_1\mathbf{L}_1(\mathbf{\Delta f}) && (13.1)\\
&= (\mathbf{\Delta V})\mathbf{L}_1\mathbf{f}_0 + \mathbf{V}_0(\mathbf{\Delta L})\mathbf{f}_0 + \mathbf{V}_1\mathbf{L}_1(\mathbf{\Delta f}) && (13.2)\\
&= (\mathbf{\Delta V})\bar{\mathbf{L}}\mathbf{f}_0 + \bar{\mathbf{V}}(\mathbf{\Delta L})\mathbf{f}_0 + \mathbf{V}_1\mathbf{L}_1(\mathbf{\Delta f}) && (13.3)\\
&= (\mathbf{\Delta V})\mathbf{L}_0\mathbf{f}_0 + \mathbf{V}_1(\mathbf{\Delta L})\mathbf{f}_0 + \mathbf{V}_1\mathbf{L}_1(\mathbf{\Delta f}) && \text{[which equals (13.1)]}\\
&= (\mathbf{\Delta V})\mathbf{L}_0\mathbf{f}_0 + \mathbf{V}_1(\mathbf{\Delta L})\mathbf{f}_1 + \mathbf{V}_1\mathbf{L}_0(\mathbf{\Delta f}) && (13.4)\\
&= (\mathbf{\Delta V})\mathbf{L}_0\mathbf{f}_0 + \mathbf{V}_1(\mathbf{\Delta L})\bar{\mathbf{f}} + \mathbf{V}_1\bar{\mathbf{L}}(\mathbf{\Delta f}) && (13.5)\\
&= (\mathbf{\Delta V})\mathbf{L}_0\mathbf{f}_1 + \mathbf{V}_1(\mathbf{\Delta L})\mathbf{f}_1 + \mathbf{V}_0\mathbf{L}_0(\mathbf{\Delta f}) && (13.6)
\end{aligned}
$$

$$= (\Delta\mathbf{V})\mathbf{L}_1\mathbf{f}_1 + \mathbf{V}_0(\Delta\mathbf{L})\mathbf{f}_1 + \mathbf{V}_0\mathbf{L}_0(\Delta\mathbf{f}) \quad (13.7)$$
$$= (\Delta\mathbf{V})\bar{\mathbf{L}}\mathbf{f}_1 + \bar{\mathbf{V}}(\Delta\mathbf{L})\mathbf{f}_1 + \mathbf{V}_0\mathbf{L}_0(\Delta\mathbf{f}) \quad (13.8)$$
$$= (\Delta\mathbf{V})\mathbf{L}_1\mathbf{f}_1 + \mathbf{V}_0(\Delta\mathbf{L})f_0 + \mathbf{V}_0\mathbf{L}_1(\Delta\mathbf{f}) \quad (13.9)$$
$$= (\Delta\mathbf{V})\mathbf{L}_1\mathbf{f}_1 + \mathbf{V}_0(\Delta\mathbf{L})\mathbf{f}_1 + \mathbf{V}_0\mathbf{L}_0(\Delta\mathbf{f}) \quad \text{[which equals (13.7)]}$$
$$= (\Delta\mathbf{V})\mathbf{L}_1\mathbf{f}_1 + \mathbf{V}_0(\Delta\mathbf{L})\bar{\mathbf{f}} + \mathbf{V}_0\bar{\mathbf{L}}(\Delta\mathbf{f}) \quad (13.10)$$
$$= (\Delta\mathbf{V})\mathbf{L}_0\bar{\mathbf{f}} + \mathbf{V}_1(\Delta\mathbf{L})\bar{\mathbf{f}} + \overline{\mathbf{VL}}(\Delta\mathbf{f}) \quad (13.11)$$
$$= (\Delta\mathbf{V})\mathbf{L}_1\bar{\mathbf{f}} + \mathbf{V}_0(\Delta\mathbf{L})\bar{\mathbf{f}} + \overline{\mathbf{VL}}(\Delta\mathbf{f}) \quad (13.12)$$
$$= (\Delta\mathbf{V})\bar{\mathbf{L}}\bar{\mathbf{f}} + \bar{\mathbf{V}}(\Delta\mathbf{L})\bar{\mathbf{f}} + \overline{\mathbf{VL}}(\Delta\mathbf{f}) \quad (13.13)$$
$$= (\Delta\mathbf{V})\overline{\mathbf{Lf}} + \bar{\mathbf{V}}(\Delta\mathbf{L})\mathbf{f}_0 + \bar{\mathbf{V}}\mathbf{L}_1(\Delta\mathbf{f}) \quad (13.14)$$
$$= (\Delta\mathbf{V})\overline{\mathbf{Lf}} + \bar{\mathbf{V}}(\Delta\mathbf{L})\mathbf{f}_1 + \bar{\mathbf{V}}\mathbf{L}_0(\Delta\mathbf{f}) \quad (13.15)$$
$$= (\Delta\mathbf{V})\overline{\mathbf{Lf}} + \bar{\mathbf{V}}(\Delta\mathbf{L})\bar{\mathbf{f}} + \bar{\mathbf{V}}\bar{\mathbf{L}}(\Delta\mathbf{f}) \quad (13.16)$$

Observe that equations (13.13) and (13.16) are different from each other since $\overline{\mathbf{Lf}} \neq \bar{\mathbf{L}}\bar{\mathbf{f}}$ and $\overline{\mathbf{VL}} \neq \bar{\mathbf{V}}\bar{\mathbf{L}}$, in general.

In each of the sixteen equations above the first term indicates the effect of changes in the value added coefficients, the second term that of changes in the Leontief inverse, and the last term that of changes in the final demand. Write each of the expressions in (13) as

$$\Delta\mathbf{a} = \mathbf{VAC}^{(k)} + \mathbf{LI}^{(k)} + \mathbf{FD}^{(k)}, \quad \text{with } k = 1, \ldots, 16$$

For the typical element corresponding to sector i,

$$\Delta a_i = VAC_i^{(k)} + LI_i^{(k)} + FD_i^{(k)}, \quad \text{with } k = 1, \ldots, 16 \text{ and } i = 1, \ldots, n$$

and for the total value added

$$\Delta a = \sum_{i=1}^{n} \Delta a_i = \sum_{i=1}^{n} VAC_i^{(k)} + \sum_{i=1}^{n} LI_i^{(k)} + \sum_{i=1}^{n} FD_i^{(k)}$$

6.6 CHANGES IN THE VALUE ADDED: EMPIRICAL RESULTS

In this section we present the results for the decomposition of the value added. Table 6.6 gives the results for the period 1976–7. For the effects of changes in the value added, for example, the percentage contribution was calculated for each of the 16 decompositions. That is $100VAC_i^{(k)}/\Delta a_i$ for each sector i and $\Sigma_i 100VAC_i^{(k)}/\Sigma_i\Delta a_i$ for the total. Next the average percentage contribution $\mu(VAC)_i$ and the standard deviation $\sigma(VAC)_i$ were obtained as

$$\mu(VAC)_i = \frac{1}{16}\sum_{k=1}^{16} 100VAC_i^{(k)}/\Delta a_i$$

$$\sigma(VAC)_i = \sqrt{\nu(VAC)_i}, \text{ with}$$

$$\nu(VAC)_i = \frac{1}{16}\sum_{k=1}^{16}[(100VAC_i^{(k)}/\Delta a_i) - \mu(VAC)_i]^2.$$

For the total this yields

$$\bar{\mu}(VAC) = \frac{1}{16}\sum_{k=1}^{16}\sum_{i=1}^{n} 100VAC_i^{(k)}/\sum_{i=1}^{n}\Delta a_i = \sum_{i=1}^{n}\Delta a_i\mu(VAC)_i/\sum_{i=1}^{n}\Delta a_i$$

$$\bar{\sigma}(VAC) = \sqrt{\nu(VAC)}, \text{ with}$$

$$\nu(VAC) = \frac{1}{16}\sum_{k=1}^{16}[(\textstyle\sum_i 100VAC_i^{(k)}/\sum_i \Delta a_i) - \bar{\mu}(VAC)]^2$$

Table 6.6 Value added decomposition, 1976–7

Sector *i*	$\mu(VAC)_i$	$\sigma(VAC)_i$	$\mu(LI)_i$	$\sigma(LI)_i$	$\mu(FD)_i$	$\sigma(FD)_i$
1	8.01	0.20	86.27	1.24	5.72	1.26
2	52.40	0.69	–38.84	0.77	86.44	0.76
3	887.51	41.82	759.70	40.06	–1547.21	69.91
4	–9.14	0.22	–6.77	6.12	115.91	6.04
5	438.83	16.60	317.43	13.97	–656.26	16.67
6	22.36	2.32	245.18	3.21	–167.55	3.64
7	–52.04	1.40	–161.27	20.78	313.31	20.06
8	12.84	0.22	–45.83	0.48	132.99	0.63
9	8.07	0.28	–0.64	2.69	92.57	2.81
10	–69.05	2.67	–30.09	0.61	199.14	2.69
11	–238.57	13.73	91.94	7.05	246.63	10.68
12	–12.72	0.27	16.89	1.48	95.83	1.40
Total	$\bar{\mu}(VAC)$	$\bar{\sigma}(VAC)$	$\bar{\mu}(LI)$	$\bar{\sigma}(LI)$	$\bar{\mu}(FD)$	$\bar{\sigma}(FD)$
	–47.22	2.63	22.57	1.46	124.64	2.73

The results in Table 6.6 show that the average percentage contributions $\mu(..)_i$ exhibit very large differences between the sectors. The variation between the methods, on the other hand, is rather small as indicated by the standard deviations $\sigma(..)_i$. Other calculations for a one-year lag confirmed this finding of large differences between the sectors and small differences between the methods. Note that Table 6.6 records several extremely large values. This finding was also frequently observed for decompositions of other one-year periods.

For the decomposition of changes in the Leontief inverse (in Sections 6.3 and 6.4), the large outcomes in Table 6.1 were caused by a denominator which was close to zero. This is not the case for the present decomposition. For example, for sectors 3, 5 and 11 the absolute change in the value added, in million Drachmes, amounts to 197.19, 294.77 and 491.68, respectively. Although these three values are the smallest, they are not spectacularly smaller than the average of the absolute changes (which equals 1629.96).

Expansion of the time lag reveals a tendency for the standard deviation to increase, indicating that the differences between the methods become larger. On the other hand, the variation of the average percentage contributions between the sectors seems to decrease while extremely large values are observed less frequently.

Table 6.7 presents the results for $\bar{\mu}(..)$ and $\bar{\sigma}(..)$. The reported values for $\bar{\mu}(..)$ indicate that the differences between the computations for different years decrease, when the time lag increases. That is, the variation of $\bar{\mu}(..)$ within a column decreases when the time lag is expanded. The average contributions $\bar{\mu}(..)$ for the decompositions of a ten-year period even seem to be rather stable. In part, this is due to the fact that extreme values (positive or negative) for individual sectors are typically observed for the shorter periods.

The values for the standard deviations $\bar{\sigma}(..)$ in Table 6.7 are invariably very modest and do not reveal a clearcut pattern. The detailed results (which are not reported here) for the standard deviations per sector, i.e. $\sigma(..)_i$, show that the differences between the methods may become substantial for individual sectors. That is, for example, the values $100VAC_i^{(k)}/\Delta a_i$ may vary widely over the methods k, but the overall value $\Sigma_i 100VAC_i^{(k)}/\Sigma_i \Delta a_i$ does not. Apparently, the variations cancel each other out when the sectoral values are summarized by an overall value.

In order to visualize our earlier observation that the values $\sigma(..)_i$ increase when the time lag is expanded, we have calculated the weighted average of the standard deviations (see Table 6.8). Recall that, for example, $\bar{\mu}(VAC)$ gives the average percentage of the value added coefficients in the total value added. $\bar{\mu}(VAC)$ could be rewritten as the weighted average of the values $\mu(VAC)_i$ using Δa_i as weights. Therefore it would seem appropriate to use

Table 6.7 Results for $\bar{\mu}$ and $\bar{\sigma}$ for a varying time lag

	time lag (in years)							
	1	2	5	10	1	2	5	10
year	$\bar{\mu}(VAC)$				$\bar{\sigma}(VAC)$			
1977	–47.22	–8.99	0.12	3.67	2.63	1.78	3.18	1.44
1976	8.53	–14.88	32.74	5.70	0.13	1.48	0.60	0.37
1975	–48.79	68.17	6.14	5.85	1.83	2.20	0.93	0.13
1974	–205.35	45.86	17.10	8.52	5.29	0.05	0.67	1.27
1973	–10.65	37.97	4.22	1.75	0.68	1.10	0.33	0.37
1972	83.23	6.51	6.91	1.64	1.17	0.29	0.92	0.36
1971	–81.20	–30.77	–14.09	–11.52	4.66	2.76	2.45	3.17
1970	18.08	9.02	6.38	–1.60	0.50	0.54	0.80	0.73
1969	1.16	1.43	1.47	–5.31	0.09	0.37	0.23	1.74
1968	2.17	0.75	–1.08	–3.99	0.73	0.15	0.27	1.25
year	$\bar{\mu}(LI)$				$\bar{\sigma}(LI)$			
1977	22.57	13.52	4.30	–4.57	1.46	1.23	1.40	0.67
1976	9.34	7.60	–21.16	–6.90	0.36	0.77	0.46	0.35
1975	4.64	31.86	–4.16	–7.42	0.45	1.92	0.72	0.62
1974	–32.77	–12.31	–6.22	–7.43	1.23	0.51	0.27	1.01
1973	–17.45	–41.32	–9.35	–7.39	0.67	2.03	1.22	1.52
1972	–63.47	–3.60	–9.36	–5.34	1.36	0.07	1.20	1.09
1971	64.88	26.99	3.25	1.25	2.94	2.05	1.03	0.71
1970	–9.29	–11.20	–10.71	–5.88	0.19	0.70	1.10	1.31
1969	–12.77	–15.61	–8.94	–7.36	0.52	0.99	0.94	1.79
1968	–19.79	–20.12	–4.62	–5.71	0.55	0.75	0.35	1.28
year	$\bar{\mu}(FD)$				$\bar{\sigma}(FD)$			
1977	124.64	95.47	95.58	100.90	2.73	1.78	3.12	1.48
1976	82.14	107.29	88.42	101.20	0.29	1.30	0.38	0.63
1975	144.16	–0.03	98.02	101.57	1.57	2.31	0.90	0.63
1974	338.12	66.45	89.11	98.92	5.79	0.54	0.72	1.22
1973	128.09	103.35	105.13	105.64	1.17	1.62	1.13	1.44

Table 6.7 Continued

	time lag (in years)							
	1	2	5	10	1	2	5	10
year	$\bar{\mu}(FD)$				$\bar{\sigma}(FD)$			
1972	80.23	97.09	102.46	103.70	0.58	0.29	1.18	1.02
1971	116.32	103.78	110.84	110.27	4.22	2.74	2.48	3.15
1970	91.21	102.18	104.34	107.48	0.43	0.69	1.04	1.71
1969	111.60	114.18	107.47	112.67	0.50	0.94	0.91	2.96
1968	117.62	119.37	105.69	109.70	0.50	0.79	0.50	2.16

$\Sigma_i \Delta a_i \sigma(VAC)_i / \Sigma_i \Delta a_i$ for the average standard deviation. It turns out, however, that for some sectors Δa_i is negative, in particular for the 1- and 2-year lags. As a consequence, such an average standard deviation summarizes the underlying standard deviations insufficiently. Instead we have calculated the following average standard deviations $\bar{\bar{\sigma}}$ (..), using the absolute values $|\Delta a_i|$ as weights. For example,

$$\bar{\bar{\sigma}}(VAC) = \sum_{i=1}^{n} |\Delta a_i| \sigma(VAC)_i \Big/ \sum_{i=1}^{n} |\Delta a_i|$$

The observation that the values of $\mu(..)_i$ vary less between the sectors when the time lag becomes longer, is explicated by the following results. For each of the ten years and for each of the four time lags we have counted the number of sectors i for which $\mu(..)_i$ falls within the interval $\bar{\mu}(..) \pm 50.00$. For example, *FREQ(VAC)* denotes the number of sectors i for which

$$\bar{\mu}(VAC) - 50.00 \leq \mu(VAC)_i < \bar{\mu}(VAC) + 50.00$$

The results for $\bar{\bar{\sigma}}$(..) and for *FREQ*(..) are presented in Table 6.8. Summing the frequencies over the years yields for *FREQ(VAC)* 67, 86, 102 and 111 for time lags of one, two, five and ten years, respectively. For the sum of *FREQ(LI)* we find 69, 82, 91 and 104, and for *FREQ(FD)* 50, 62, 85, 97.

Table 6.8 Results for $\bar{\bar{\sigma}}$ and *FREQ* for a varying time lag

	time lag (in years)							
	1	2	5	10	1	2	5	10
year	$\bar{\bar{\sigma}}$(*VAC*)				*FREQ*(*VAC*)			
1977	1.85	2.38	5.41	5.56	4	8	8	10
1976	0.80	2.04	5.27	4.42	11	9	9	9
1975	1.86	1.19	2.81	3.84	5	2	9	9
1974	1.76	1.25	2.53	3.39	0	6	9	11
1973	1.41	2.42	3.10	4.39	8	7	11	12
1972	1.90	1.14	2.42	3.19	4	12	11	12
1971	5.12	3.55	4.34	4.50	4	10	11	12
1970	0.67	1.20	1.87	2.34	9	11	12	12
1969	0.82	1.31	1.66	2.50	11	10	12	12
1968	0.92	1.07	1.74	2.06	11	11	10	12
year	$\bar{\bar{\sigma}}$(*LI*)				*FREQ*(*LI*)			
1977	2.70	4.22	14.32	13.49	3	6	7	9
1976	1.74	3.37	9.94	12.14	8	9	8	9
1975	1.75	5.15	6.69	10.47	8	4	9	10
1974	4.03	4.76	6.82	8.57	6	9	9	10
1973	1.38	3.33	5.66	7.04	9	10	10	11
1972	3.01	1.70	5.21	5.32	4	9	9	11
1971	3.64	4.10	6.56	7.17	6	8	9	11
1970	1.83	2.79	4.86	3.78	8	10	9	11
1969	1.30	2.31	3.54	3.66	10	10	10	11
1968	0.80	1.70	2.85	3.02	7	7	11	11
year	$\bar{\bar{\sigma}}$(*FD*)				*FREQ*(*FD*)			
1977	3.38	5.01	16.40	15.13	5	6	7	9
1976	2.00	4.11	11.48	13.67	7	7	5	7
1975	2.58	5.25	7.87	12.07	4	3	8	8
1974	4.55	5.26	7.88	10.18	1	6	10	9
1973	2.34	3.90	7.36	9.60	7	5	11	11

Table 6.8 Continued

	time lag (in years)							
	1	2	5	10	1	2	5	10
year		$\bar{\bar{\sigma}}$*(FD)*				*FREQ(FD)*		
1972	2.60	2.48	6.79	7.27	3	9	9	11
1971	6.02	5.22	8.41	8.79	4	6	6	9
1970	1.99	3.22	5.84	5.06	6	6	10	11
1969	1.76	3.09	4.40	5.24	6	8	10	11
1968	1.26	2.30	3.68	4.31	7	6	9	11

A last exercise we would like to report is the decomposition over the entire period 1958–77. Table 6.9 presents for each sector i the minimum and the maximum value of, for example, $100VAC_i^{(k)}/\Delta a_i$. The row '*Total*' gives the minimum and the maximum value of, for example, $\Sigma_i 100VAC_i^{(k)}/\Sigma_i \Delta a_i$.

It is clear from Table 6.9 that the results may vary largely between the different methods. Again, the computations for the aggregate measure $\Sigma_i 100VAC_i^{(k)}/\Sigma_i \Delta a_i$, as reported in the row '*Total*', show only little variation between the methods.

Consider the different decomposition formulae (13.1)–(13.16) again. Each of them is, essentially, obtained by applying the expressions (2.3)–(2.5) twice. One could argue that it is somewhat artificial to apply, for instance, (2.5) after (2.3). That is, one would probably favour those expressions which are constructed in a 'consistent' way. This implies that formulae (13.1), (13.7), and (13.13) or (13.16) are the most plausible ones. Indeed, (13.1) and (13.7) are the alternatives which are used most frequently in the literature. Therefore it is interesting to mention that out of the 72 extreme values in the upper part of Table 6.9, 40 correspond to the expressions (13.1) and (13.7).

Comparing the results for these two expressions with each other it turns out that the following observation holds for each sector. The percentage contribution of the changes in the value added coefficients, i.e. $100VAC_i^{(k)}/\Delta a_i$, is larger for (13.7) than for (13.1) when it is positive, and smaller when it is negative. The same observation holds for $100LI_i^{(k)}/\Delta a_i$, for most (but not all) sectors, while the opposite result holds for $100FD_i^{(k)}/\Delta a_i$, again for

Table 6.9 Value added decomposition, 1958–77

Sector	*VAC*		*LI*		*FD*	
i	*min*	*max*	*min*	*max*	*min*	*max*
1	–8.55	–1.15	–251.19	–82.18	184.73	355.50
2	25.09	60.77	–10.94	–2.18	45.85	84.37
3	–16.53	–2.60	–24.85	–5.15	108.30	138.99
4	5.43	28.85	3.49	26.12	51.49	89.93
5	–4.94	–0.82	–0.26	12.88	88.45	105.19
6	8.37	23.81	22.15	59.86	26.42	65.00
7	2.27	8.18	–0.13	17.73	75.16	97.85
8	3.64	12.22	–2.05	1.04	86.83	98.23
9	3.95	29.93	8.98	53.11	31.32	83.73
10	–50.56	–7.84	–2.28	0.10	109.26	152.84
11	–143.46	–16.91	17.12	156.67	41.68	207.81
12	–3.38	–1.18	3.51	18.21	83.36	99.79
Total	–2.98	0.88	–4.94	–3.05	102.33	107.48
$\bar{\mu}(..)$	–1.05		–3.94		104.99	
$\underline{\bar{\sigma}}(..)$	1.43		0.65		1.76	
$\bar{\bar{\sigma}}(..)$	6.12		11.68		14.66	
FREQ	11		10		10	

most (but not all) sectors. Further, it appears that the results for the expressions (13.13) and (13.16) are always remarkably close to the average contribution $\bar{\mu}(..)$.

6.7 SUMMARY AND CONCLUSIONS

In this paper we have considered structural decomposition analyses. Typically, the change between two points in time in one variable (a scalar, a vector or a matrix) is additively decomposed into the changes in key determinants. As is well known, such a decomposition is not unique. Moreover, when the number of key determinants increases, the number of alternative decomposition formulae also increases. Therefore we have examined whether the results are influenced by the specific decomposition formula that is used. In doing so, we have taken into account that the answer to this question might be affected by the length of the time period.

In this study we have focused on two examples of a decomposition analysis. First, the decomposition of changes in the Leontief inverse into technological changes and product-mix changes. Second, the decomposition of changes in the sectoral value added into changes in the value added coefficients, changes in the Leontief inverse and changes in the final demands. Our analysis has been applied empirically to the Greek economy for which annual input–output tables in constant prices were available for the period 1958–77.

In evaluating the results, a distinction is made between the results at a detailed level and those at the aggregate level. Results at a detailed level consider the changes in individual elements of the Leontief inverse or in the value added of individual sectors. At the aggregate level, we consider a summary measure of the changes in all elements of the Leontief inverse or the changes in the total value added as obtained by summing over all the sectors.

At the detailed level, the calculations show that the results may vary largely between the different decomposition formulae. The variation increases when the time period is expanded. At the aggregate level, the results are remarkably invariant between the different decomposition formulae. The differences between the computational alternatives apparently cancel each other out when the results are consolidated into an 'overall' scalar. Moreover, this observed invariance at the aggregate level seems to be independent of the length of the time period.

In conclusion, we would like to add some remarks to our findings. First, it should be emphasized that the decomposition formulae in this study have been chosen on the basis of their arithmetical equivalence. As indicated before, it is likely that some of these formulae may be preferred to others. For example, because some are constructed in a more 'consistent' way than others. For certain types of a structural decomposition analysis it may further be the case that some formula are singled out on theoretical grounds. This, however, does not affect our major conclusion that the results *may* vary largely.

Second, in this study we have considered only two specific examples of a structural decomposition analysis which have been applied to a single data set. Therefore it seems interesting to investigate whether our major findings carry over to other types of structural decomposition analyses and to other countries.

Third, our experiments have indicated that the contribution of one determinant to the change in the variable under consideration may crucially depend upon the way this contribution is measured. The economic significance of the results of a structural decomposition analysis can only be judged appropriately, if some insight is available with respect to the variability of the results across alternative methods of measurement. We would like to advocate that in empirical work more attention is paid to a sensitivity analysis of the computations and that the results also include information with regard to the dispersion of the outcomes.

NOTES

1. Obviously, any weighted average may be chosen. That is $\Delta v = (\Delta p)[\alpha q(0) + (1-\alpha)q(1)] + [(1-\alpha)p(0) + \alpha p(1)](\Delta q)$ for equations (2.3) and (2.4). Note that a weighted average of equations (2.1) and (2.2), however, does not remove the interaction term, unless the weights are $\frac{1}{2}$.
2. Fromm (1968) gives a lucid discussion of the index number problem.

REFERENCES

AFRASIABI, A. and S. D. CASLER (1991), 'Product-Mix and Technological Change within the Leontief Inverse', *Journal of Regional Science*, vol. 31, no. 2, pp. 147–60.

BARKER, T. (1990), 'Sources of Structural Change for the UK Service Industries 1979–84, *Economic Systems Research*, vol. 2, no. 2, pp. 173–83.

BLAIR, P. D. and A. W. WYCKOFF (1989) 'The Changing Structure of the U.S. Economy: An Input–Output Analysis', in R. E. Miller, K. R. Polenske and A. Z. Rose (eds), *Frontiers of Input–Output Analysis* (New York: Oxford University Press), pp. 293–307.

CARTER, A. P. (1970) *Structural Change in the American Economy* (Cambridge, MA: Harvard University Press).

CHENERY, H. B., S. SHISHIDO and T. WATANABE (1962) 'The Pattern of Japanese Growth, 1914–1954', *Econometrica*, vol. 30, no. 1, pp. 98–139.

DEWHURST, J. H. L. (1993) 'Decomposition in Input–Output Tables', *Economic Systems Research*, vol. 5, no. 1, pp. 41–53.

DIETZENBACHER, E. (1992) 'Aggregation in Multisector Models: Using the Perron Vector', *Economic Systems Research*, vol. 4, no. 1, pp. 3–24.

FELDMAN, S. J., D. MCCLAIN and K. PALMER (1987) 'Sources of Structural Change in the United States, 1963–1978: An Input–Output Perspective', *Review of Economics and Statistics*, vol. 69, no. 3, pp. 503–10.

FORSSELL, O. (1985) 'Changes in the Structure of the Finnish Economy, 1970–1980', in A. Smyshlyaev (ed.), *Input–Output Modeling* (Berlin: Springer-Verlag), pp. 61–71.

FORSSELL, O. (1988) 'Growth and Changes in the Structure of the Finnish Economy in the 1960s and the 1970s', in M. Ciaschini (ed.), *Input–Output Analysis: Current Developments* (London: Chapman & Hall), pp. 287–302.

FORSSELL, O. (1989) 'The Input–Output Framework for Analysing Transmission of Technical Progress between Industries', *Economic Systems Research*, vol. 1, no. 4, pp. 429–45.

FORSSELL, O. (1990) 'The Input–Output Framework for Analysing Changes in the Use of Labour by Education Levels', *Economic Systems Research*, vol. 2, no. 4, pp. 363–76.

FROMM, G. (1968) 'Comment on Vaccara and Simon', in J. W. Kendrick (ed.), *The Industrial Composition of Income and Product* (New York: Columbia University Press), pp. 59–66.

FUJIMAGARI, D. (1989) 'The Sources of Change in Canadian Industry Output', *Economic Systems Research*, vol. 1, no. 2, pp. 187–201.

FUJITA N. and W. E. JAMES (1991) 'Growth Patterns of the Japanese Economy in the 1980s: Before and After the Appreciation of the Yen', *Economic Systems Research*, vol. 3, no. 4, pp. 399–412.

KANEMITSU, H. and H. OHNISHI (1989) 'An Input–Output Analysis of Technological Changes in the Japanese Economy: 1970–1980', in R. E. Miller, K. R. Polenske and A. Z. Rose (eds), *Frontiers of Input–Output Analysis* (New York: Oxford University Press), pp. 308–23.

KARASZ, P. (1992) 'Influence of Interindustrial Relationships on Prices in Czechoslovakia', *Economic Systems Research*, vol. 4, no. 4, pp. 377–84.

LEE, C. (1990) 'Growth and Changes in the Structure of the US Agricultural Economy, 1972–82: An Input–Output Perspective', *Economic Systems Research*, vol. 2, no. 3, pp. 303–11.

LIN, X. and K. R. POLENSKE (1993) 'Input–Output Anatomy of China's Energy-Demand Change, 1981–1987', Paper presented at the Tenth International Conference on Input–Output Techniques, Seville, Spain.

ROSE, A. and W. MIERNYK (1989) 'Input–Output Analysis: The First Fifty Years', *Economic Systems Research*, vol. 1, no. 2, pp. 229–71.

SAWYER, J. A. (1992) 'Forecasting with Input–Output Matrices: Are the Coefficients Stationary?', *Economic Systems Research*, vol. 4, no. 4, pp. 325–48.

SCHUMANN, J. (1993) 'Does It Make Sense to Apply the Static Open Input–Output Model for Imputation and Structural Decomposition?', Paper presented at the Tenth International Conference on Input–Output Techniques, Seville, Spain.

SKOLKA, J. (1989) 'Input–Output Structural Decomposition Analysis for Austria', *Journal of Policy Modeling*, vol. 11, no. 1, pp. 45–66.

SKOUNTZOS, Th. A. and G. S. MATTHEOS (1980) *Input–Output Tables of the Greek Economy 1958–1977* (Athens: Center of Planning and Economic Research).

STÄGLIN, R. and H. WESSELS (1972) 'Intertemporal Analysis of Structural Change in the German Economy,' in A. Bródy and A. P. Carter (eds), *Input–Output Techniques* (Amsterdam: North-Holland), pp. 370–92.

VACCARA, B. N. and N. W. SIMON (1968) 'Factors Affecting Postwar Industrial Composition of Real Product', in J. W. Kendrick (ed.), *The Industrial Composition of Income and Product* (New York: Columbia University Press), pp. 19–58.

VAN DER LINDEN, J. A. and J. OOSTERHAVEN (1993) 'Intercountry EC Input–Output Relations: An Income Growth Decomposition for 1970–1980', Paper presented at the 33rd European Regional Science Association Congress, Moscow.

7 Measuring the Productivity of Nations

Pirkko Aulin-Ahmavaara

7.1 THE BACKGROUND

The importance of the reproduction of manpower as a vital part of the overall production system was emphasized by Andrew Bródy already in his book *Proportions, Prices and Planning* (1970). As an illustration he refers to the circumstances in the developing countries. How time consuming a process it indeed is to build a system of education for training teachers to teach engineers, who can teach technicians to train skilled workers. In a developed system of education these tasks are performed simultaneously, but still all of them have to be performed. All this affects both output proportions and prices and accordingly has to be taken into account in any complete representation of the overall production system. Thinking of the quantities of the funds fixed in reproducing manpower it becomes obvious that these effects can be quite remarkable. According to the estimates cited by Andrew Bródy the resources tied up in reproducing manpower are about 5–10 years' national income, while the total physical wealth of a society seldom exceeds 3–4 years' income.

In his later book *Slowdown: Global Economic Maladies*, Bródy (1985) amplifies his criticism of the narrow concept of production in national accounting. He suggests that we try (pp. 45–6):

> at least a mental analysis of growth not of bare national income but, more comprehensively, of the total metabolism of society: the full range of economic activities.

He finds the results of this mental exercise shocking:

> All that is recorded in the national accounts reflects only a very narrow segment and scanty fraction of the real activities of a society while it conceals an enormous and decisive part of it.

He estimates that of the total available time-bill of active population only 14 per cent is used in the production of national income. In the less developed countries this percentage might be even smaller. Yet even sleeping is productive because it is indispensable for the daily recreation of the workforce. The productive quality of such activities as household work as well as of nursing, rearing and schooling children and youth is even more obvious.

All these items have been listed, although not usually all of them at the same time, also by others who have been suggesting extensions and revisions to national income and product accounts (for a complete list, see Eisner, 1989, p. 120). Usually these suggestions have as the starting point the wish to measure the welfare contribution of economic activity. The problem however is that all the activities of human beings contribute to their welfare in one way or other. And what is the meaning of the word 'economic' unless it is a synomym of market? What is original, and interesting, in Andrew Bródy's reasoning is not actually the set of activities he thinks has to be included but why he suggests that they should be included. His starting point is the use of the total available time-bill of active population. The reason for including different activities is that they are productive in the sense that they are indispensable for the production process.

This paper is about developing this idea further; defining the complete production process starting from the total time-bill of the active population; representing this production process by means of the dynamic input–output model; and, finally, measuring the productivity of this process, i.e. the productivity of nations in using their time.

7.2 DEFINING PRODUCTION

The time available for active population is in this paper called active human time.

> *Active human time* is any use of time by human beings who have passed their basic education and have not become unable to work.

Production can then be defined as a circular process in which human time is involved and in which commodities are produced by means of commodities.

> *Production* is direct or undirect utilization of active human time to bring about something that can be used up or transformed into another form in a process utilizing active human time directly or indirectly.

And finally a product has to be distinguished from its intermediate phases:

> *A product* is a result of the production process that is used either outside the unit that has produced it or outside the time unit during which it has been produced or to produce another unit of similar product.

From these definitions it is obvious that active human time is also a product. Production of active human time evidently requires active human time both directly (household work and leisure) and indirectly (goods and services and human capital). Active human time can also be transformed into another form in the production of other products. The time of persons in retirement because of incapability of work has to be excluded since it cannot be used elsewhere in the production process. (In actual practice also those in retirement because of age – however capable of working they may still be – have to be excluded, since their working capabilities are not registered in national statistics.) The time of children and young people in compulsary basic education has to be excluded for the same reason. As to the time of the rest of the population it is a product no matter in which way it is used. Labour and leisure are only different uses of the same product, viz. active human time.

It follows from the definition of production that also that part of human capital which is created by raising children or by participating in education, has to be regarded as a product. It is fixed in human beings and passes away with them, which means that it is used up in the production of active human time. Also the intermediate phases of that part of human capital are products because they are moved over to the next time period in order to be used in the production of subsequent phases of human capital of the same type.

Let it be emphasized that production, as defined above, does not include the creation of new human knowledge, although it includes the transmission of knowledge and skills called education and training. New knowledge (e.g. in science) of course is indispensable to the production process and especially to its technical progress. It is created by utilizing products but the result is something more than a product. It outlives the individual who has created it and accordingly it cannot be used up in the production process. Its task in the production process is different from that of products. It is used to change the process not to be used up in it. On the other hand part of the research and development activities of the firms no doubt are directly linked to the production processes that are utilized or will be utilized in the firms. The results of these activities have to be regarded as products that will be used up when production process changes.

There is still another part of human capital that cannot be produced in the normal production process, viz. the human beings themselves and their natural talents and characteristics. This part of human capital is comparable to the natural resources.

It follows from the definition of a product above that different kinds of human capital and of active human time are the only output of the households they can use themselves. All the consumption of goods and services by households is used directly as an input in this production and not for instance as an input in the production of meals, or cleaning services or child care services for themselves. The latter types of services, when produced by the households for themselves, are not products because they are not used either outside the producing household or during the subsequent time units by the producing household itself. Neither are they used to produce another unit of similar services. On the other hand active human time and human capital produced within the households always meet at least one of these three conditions. In addition to this households, naturally, can also produce goods and services to be used by other production units.

7.3 REPRESENTING THE COMPLETE PRODUCTION PROCESS BY MEANS OF THE DYNAMIC INPUT–OUTPUT MODEL

The open static input–output model is the natural way of representing the overall production process, if we wish to measure the performance of a production system by its contribution to the present and future welfare in the form of gross national product. If, on the other hand, we wish to measure the performance of an economy in the utilization of the total time-bill of its active population the natural way of representing the production process is the dynamic input–output model. It allows us to trace the progress, through the production system, of the active human time and of other products made utilizing it. The flow coefficients ensure that quantities of every type of inputs large enough to cover the outflow of these inputs during a basic interval of time, are transferred to every sector during the same basic interval. Stock coefficients again take care that the stocks are during each basic interval of time raised to the level needed for the output during the next basic interval (for a more detailed discussion, see Aulin-Ahmavaara, 1990).

In order to represent the complete production process the dynamic input–output model has to be extended to include the production processes of human capital and active human time. Andrew Bródy (1970) takes the first step in this direction by augmenting both the matrix of flow coefficients as well as the matrix of stock coefficients by a row and a column for the sector producing labour or manpower.

There are however different categories of manpower and the resources needed to produce them are also different. It takes more time and resources to graduate from a university than to complete a vocational schooling. Besides the definition of product used in this paper requires that the production process of human capital is separated from the production process of active human time itself. Units of human capital produced during a year are used as capital equipment in the production of active human time during the subsequent years, ie. ouside the time unit during which they are produced. The gestation of a unit of human capital usually also takes several years. This means that the intermediate phases of a unit of human capital are actually used as inputs in the next phases of this same unit during the next year. Therefore our definition of product also requires that different phases of human capital are treated as separate products.

A fuller representation of the production processes of human capital and active human time can of course also in principle be introduced in the dynamic input–output model by means of the simple device of augmenting new rows and columns to the matrices of coefficients. Its main features will be explained here. For more details see Aulin-Ahmavaara (1987, 1989, 1990, 1991, 1992) and Aulin-Ahmavaara and Aulin (1992).

When the production of human capital and active human time are included there are three categories of sectors involved in the production process:

G = the totality of sectors producing market or non-market goods and services outside the households. It includes also a sector producing foreign goods and services.

E = the totality of sectors producing different types of human capital. Every person first produces a unit of simple human capital during his basic education $1E$. He has this unit of simple human capital fixed to himself until his retirement or death. Having completed his basic education he can participate in some other education, say, iE. When he has finished this education iE he has produced a unit of human capital of type i and has also this unit of human capital in his possession for the rest of his productive life, and so on.

T = the totality of sectors producing different types of active human time. Every person who has finished his basic education and has not retired produces human time of the type which matches his latest education. In this production all the units of human capital produced by him are used as capital equipment. He can use this active human time produced by him either in the production of goods and services, in the production of human capital of type $1E$ by taking care of children, in the production of human capital of some type jE he does not possess as yet by participating in education of the type j, or in the production of active human time in the form of household work or leisure.

The representation of the production process is complicated by the facts that both gestation periods and productive periods of the units of both human and physical capital often exceed the basic time unit of the model (about the definitions of these periods in the context of the model discussed here, see Aulin-Ahmavaara, 1990). In the case of human capital these problems accentuate because partly used units of human capital have to be moved from the production of one type of active human time to the production of another type of human time whenever an educated person completes a new education. Furthermore units of human capital often outlive their productive time and the consumption of persons in retirement has to be produced by the active population. And finally there might be different routes to the same education and the durations of the gestation periods S_j, productive periods P_{ij} and periods of retirement R_i can vary both between and within different categories of human capital.

All these facts mean that some of the coefficients depend on the earlier states of the production system. In the case of balanced growth this dependence can represented by means of a set of auxiliary coefficients depending on the rate of growth λ. A detailed derivation of these coefficients in different cases can be found in Aulin-Ahmavaara (1991). Here only the most straightforward cases will be shortly referred to when the structure of the matrices is explained below.

Both the matrix A of input coefficients and the matrix B of stock coefficients now have the following structure:

$$\left(\begin{array}{c|c|c} GG & GE & GT \\ \hline 0 & EE & ET \\ \hline TG & TE & TT \end{array}\right) \tag{1}$$

Here for example the blocks GE in the matrices A and B respectively represent input coefficients and stock coefficients originating from the sectors in the category G to the sectors in the category E and so on.

Accordingly the blocks GG of the matrices A and B respectively represent input coefficients and stock coefficients of goods and services in the production of goods and services. Besides the coefficients of intermediate inputs the matrix A includes also the coefficients of replacement of fixed capital. Besides the coefficients of fixed capital the matrix B includes also the coefficients of inventories. Replacement requirements of fixed capital depend on earlier investment. On the simplifying assumption of fixed production periods the replacement coefficients from a sector i in the category G to a sector j in the same category are in the case of balanced growth of the following form:

$$a^*_{iGjG} = v_{iGjG} b_{iGjG} \tag{2}$$

with

$$v_{iGjG} = \frac{\lambda}{(1+\lambda)^{P_{iGjG}} - 1} \tag{3}$$

where P_{iGjG} is the productive period of physical capital produced in sector i of the category G and utilized in sector j of the same category.

The block EG of both of the matrices is empty because human capital is not directly involved in the production of goods and services. Human capital is utilized in the production of active human time, which again can be used as an input in the production of goods and services. The latter coefficients are covered by the block TG of the matrices.

The block GE represents all the consumption of goods and services in the production of simple human capital by children who have not completed their basic education. It also includes the consumption of educational services in the production of educated human capital by persons who have completed their basic education.

The active human time used in nursing and rearing children within the households is taken into account in the coefficients to the production of simple human capital in the block TE of the matrices. The block TE also includes the time used in regular education after basic education. The time used in the basic education by children under active age is excluded for the simple reason that they do not produce active human time as yet. The participation in education may take place immediately after the basic education or later in life.

The block EE represents the inputs from one phase of gestation of human capital to the next phase in the gestation of human capital of the same type. In this block the stock coefficients are identical with the respective flow coefficients. Each phase of human capital is involved in the production of the next phase of the same category of human capital for the entire year, provided of course that there is a next phase. The magnitude of the coefficients is either unity or somewhat above it depending on the death rates, drop-outs, failures to pass to the next form etc.

While the consumption of regular educational services by the population in active age is included in the block TE, the rest of consumption of goods and services by them is covered by the block GT. The consumption of persons in retirement belonging to different educational categories is taken into account in the coefficients to the production of active human time in the respective category. In the simplest case these coefficients have, assuming balanced growth, following form:

$$a^*_{iGjT} = a_{iGjT} + u_j a_{iGjR} \tag{4}$$

$$b^*_{iGjT} = b_{iGjT} + u_j b_{iGjR} \tag{5}$$

where a_{iGjT}, a_{iGjR} indicate consumption of goods and services per person in active age and per person in retirement, respectively, and b_{iGjT}, b_{iGjR} are the corresponding stocks. Furthermore

$$u_1 = \frac{(1+\lambda)^{-P_1} - (1+\lambda)^{-P_1-R_1}}{1-(1+\lambda)^{-P_1}} \tag{6}$$

and

$$u_i = u_1 \text{ for } P_i + S_i = P_1 \text{ and } R_i = R_1 \tag{7}$$

The replacement and capital coefficients of human capital in the production of active human time form the blocks *ET* of the matrices *A* and *B* respectively. In the simplest case the replacement coefficients of human capital in the production of active human time are, in the balanced growth situation, of the type given in equations (2) and (3). Every person who is producing active human time has in his posession a unit of simple human capital and a unit of educated human capital corresponding to every type of education he has completed during his life. This means that when a person is producing educated human time belonging to some educational category it is not only a unit of human capital of the same educational category but also a unit of simple human capital and units of educated human capital corresponding to each of his previous educational attainments that are involved. The formulas for these replacement coefficients v, as well as for the coefficients v above, get more complicated when the variation in the lengths of active periods, the possibility of multiple education on the one hand and of several routes to the same educational attainment on the other are taken into account. (See Aulin-Ahmavaara, 1991.)

The block *TT* consists of the inputs of human time in the production of human time i.e. of the leisure time of active population as well as of the household work performed for it. In this system household work and leisure are different uses of the same product (human time), not different products. The household work performed for the children under active age was taken into account in the coefficients to the production of simple human capital (block *TE*).

In this representation of the production of human capital and active human time it is assumed that a unit of human capital a person acquires in initial education lasts throughout the person's active life. The fact is of course that part of this knowledge and of these skills become obsolete much earlier than his active life ends. However large part of them, such as for instance mathematical and linguistic skills, not to speak about such basic skills as literacy and numeracy, last throughout a person's life. And even outdated knowledge in some area, for instance in economics, makes it easier to absorb new knowledge in this same field. Therefore it is assumed here that any regular education once acquired lasts throughout a person's active life. The fact that a person can later in his life, after a spell at work, participate in education and training and thus acquire an additional unit of educated human capital, can be taken into account in this representation of the production process.

But the fact is of course that practically every work continuously requires learning new things. This continuous learning could in principle be taken into account as an addition to the human capital fixed to a person. But partly it only compensates his outdated knowledge and skills. It is very hard to know how large a share is needed for this purpose. The results of this continuous learning, if it is performed during the time paid by the employer, are not owned by the employee. They are not actually owned by the employer either because they are embodied in the employee. They can also be firm specific to such an extent that they are of little or no value outside the firm within which they have been produced.

Another possiblity could be to treat active human time and educational services consumed in on-the-job learning as inputs in the production of active human time itself. In this case they would be identified with the maintenance costs of fixed capital in the production of ordinary goods and services. The problem is that it is mostly not possible distinguish the time used in learning from the time used when performing other duties. On-the-job-training can take place either in the form of short courses or having instructors on the 'shop floor'. In the former case it is easier to count the number of hours used in training. But the number of hours used in training is not equal to that used in learning. It seems to me that it is useless to try find out which part of working time is used in learning. Learning is nowadays an integral and ever increasing part of practically every job. This is an inherent feature of the present-day production technology.

Finally, it should be noted that in this representation of the complete production process every row and every column of the matrix B contains at least one strictly positive element. This is because the matrix B consists, in addition to the coefficients of fixed capital, also of the coefficients of inventory. When the coefficients of inventory are calculated it is necessary, in order to be able to follow accurately the circulation of products in the production system, to take into account also the inventories of semifinished products and finished products hold by the producers. These inventories include also the inputs of services and of human time needed to produce them. Also the 'inventories' of semifinished phases of human capital contain services and active human time as their constituents. It is hard to think of any category of services or of active human time that wouldn't be used as an input in the production of some kind of material products or consumed by households. If it is consumed by households it is also used as an input in the production of simple human capital. Obviously services and active human time can be stored only as constituents of material products. Therefore there cannot be any inventories of semifinished products in the production of services and of active human time. However, a least one unit of human capital is always involved in the production of active human time. And it is hard to think of any kind of services, not at least within the classifications of services normally used, that could be produced entirely without any physical goods. The fact that also the coefficients of inventories are included in the stock coefficients makes also a very close resemblance between different columns of the matrix B unlikely. Thus the singularity of the matrix of stock coefficients is excluded. Other aspects of the existence and uniqueness of the balanced growth path of the model discussed here are treated in Aulin-Ahmavaara (1987, 1990, 1991).

7.4 MEASURING THE PRODUCTIVITY OF NATIONS

The rate of balanced growth λ associated with the empirical matrices of the dynamic input–output model gives a measure of the growth potential of an economy utilizing the production technology represented by these matrices. This property of the dynamic input–output model has been utilized, e.g. by Carter (1974) when studying the effects of the changes in the technical coefficients on the growth potential of the US economy.

When the rate of balanced growth is calculated from the dynamic input–output model augmented to include the production of human capital and active human time it can be called the productivity of a nation. It represents the efficiency of the nation in the utilization of the total time-bill of its active population. It is a generalization of the concept of total factor productivity to the complete production system that includes the production of human capital and human time. This can be shown by comparing the measure of the rate of productivity change $d\lambda/\lambda$ with the more traditional measures of overall rate of total factor productivity change.

By multiplying both sides of the fundamental equation of the closed dynamic input–output model

$$(I - A)\bar{x} = \lambda B\bar{x} \tag{8}$$

with $\bar{x}$ representing the vector of balanced growth output proportions, by the equilibrium price vector $\bar{p}$ we get:

$$\lambda = \frac{\bar{p}(I - A)\bar{x}}{\bar{p}B\bar{x}} \tag{9}$$

It can be proved (Bródy, 1970, and Johansen, 1978,) that we have, in the first approximation:

$$d\lambda = -\bar{p}(dA + \lambda dB)\bar{x}/\bar{p}B\bar{x} \tag{10}$$

From (9) and (10) we have:

$$d\lambda/\lambda = \tilde{\rho} = \frac{-\bar{p}(dA + \lambda dB)\bar{x}}{\bar{p}(I - A)\bar{x}} = -\bar{p}(dA + \lambda dB)\bar{x}/\bar{y} \tag{11}$$

where $\bar{y}$ is the value of the final output that would be produced, if an economy applying the production technology represented by the matrices A and B were in the state of balanced growth.

On the other hand the standard overall measure of the rate of productivity growth can be expressed as follows (see Wolff, 1985):

$$\rho = -(pdA + wdl + rdk)X/y \tag{12}$$

where X is the gross output vector by sector, l and k the vectors of labour and capital stock coefficients, respectively, w is the uniform wage rate and r the uniform rate of profit and p the equilibrium price vector computed from

$$p = (wl + rk)(I - A)^{-1}$$

The overall measure of total factor productivity growth in (12) is actually based on the assumption that the economy is in a competitive equilibrium, while the overall measure suggested in (11) is calculated on the basis of the output and price proportions, which the economy utilizing the production technology given by the matrices A and B would have, if it were on the balanced growth path. The formal similarity between the two measures is obvious. The definition of production is however, more comprehensive in the measure suggested here. It includes, as is evident from the previous section, the production of active human time and human capital as well. Also the scope of the definition of intermediate inputs is wider in the measure suggested here. It includes the replacement of fixed physical and of human capital as well. Then the final output consists solely of that part of the total output that can be used to enhance production.

The rate of balanced growth calculated from the representation of the complete production system by means of the dynamic input–output model tells how much the economy could grow provided that its production technology remained unchanged and all the losses in the productive capacity of both physical and human capital were replaced. The scope of the concept of production technology is very extensive here. It covers besides the production technology of goods and services also such items as per capita consumption of different types of goods and services and of leisure, the durations of different types of education, the lengths of the periods of retirement.

In reality the production technology is, of course, continuously changing. Normally the quantities of inputs and stocks needed per unit of output in the production of ordinary goods and services are, at least taken as a whole, decreasing. On the other hand more and more inputs and stocks are needed per unit of output in the production of human capital and active human time, when the per capita consumption of goods and services and leisure are increasing, the average educational attainment of the active population gets higher and perhaps also the time needed to acquire given educational qualifications gets longer.

A change in the growth potential of the complete production system, i.e. in the productivity of the nation can then roughly speaking be interpreted in the following way. Increasing per capita consumption of goods and services, especially of educational services, as well as increasing per capita quantities of active human time spent in education and leisure normally leads to higher productivity in the sectors producing ordinary goods and services. The higher productivity in the production of goods and services and the increased labour force participation lead to an increase in the production goods and services. The productivity of the nation grows if this latter flow of goods and services is larger than the one that has induced it.

It should, however, be remembered that the productivity of the nation is calculated as the rate of balanced growth that could be possible for an economy that is utilizing the production technology represented by the matrices of technological coefficients. This means that the flows of goods and services and of active human time we are talking about here are the ones that would take place in a balanced growth situation, not the actual ones. Therefore also the quantities of educational services and the quantities of active human time spent in education are the ones that would be needed to maintain the average educational level of the active population in its different uses and not the actual ones. The flows of educational services and of active human time needed to raise the future educational level of active population are not included.

The causes of the overall productivity change can be analysed further by calculating on the basis of the equilibrium price proportions of the dynamic input–output model the changes in the complete unit production costs of the different sectors. For this the unit prices have to be expressed in terms of some common standard, which can be the unit price, i.e. the unit production costs, of simple human time. Then a change in the price of a product

$$\breve{\pi}_j^* = \frac{-d\bar{p}_i}{\bar{p}_j} \tag{13}$$

can be interpreted as a change in total factor requirements per unit of this product measured in the factor requirements of a unit of simple human time. Moreover it can be interpreted as a measure of technical change for a composite sector j, in which all the sectors contributing directly or indirectly to the final output of sector j are vertically integrated to it (see Aulin-Ahmavaara, 1992, 1993). It is a generalization to the complete production system of the measures of the rate of productivity changes for vertically integrated sectors suggested by Peterson (1979) and Wolff (1985).

The aggregation of this sectoral measures gives

$$\breve{\pi}^*\hat{\bar{p}}Y/\bar{y} = -d\bar{p}Y/\bar{y} \tag{14}$$

where $\hat{\bar{p}}$ is a matrix whose diagonal is equal to the vector $\bar{p}$ and all the other elements are zero. Obviously $-d\bar{p}Y = \bar{p}dY$ represents the value of the final product, measured in the unit production costs of simple human time, that can be produced by means of the changes in sectoral productivity.

Accordingly,

$$\breve{\pi}^*\hat{\bar{p}}Y/y = \bar{p}dY/y = d\lambda/\lambda \tag{15}$$

To calculate the values of the sectoral measures in (13), we should actually be able to express the production prices of the year of comparison in terms of the production price of a unit simple human time in the base year. A method of establishing the link between the prices of two different years would be to utilize the formula (15). On the other hand, comparisons between the rest of the sectors, with respect to the development of their productivity can be simply performed on the basis of the prices measured in terms of the current year production costs of simple human time. A change in the price of a unit of simple human time only means a uniform relative change in the prices of the rest of the sectors.

7.5 THE FALLING PRODUCTIVITY OF A NATION IN WELFARE ECONOMIES

The application of the model to the Finnish data shows that the overall productivity of the complete production system in Finland has fallen in the 70s and that this fall has accelerated during the first half of the 1980s (Aulin-Ahmavaara, 1992, 1993). These results, though they concern only Finland, may however be indicative of the developments in the other welfare economies as well. They indicate that the higher per capita consumption of goods and services and the increased quantities of the active human time used to raise the educational level of active population have not been able to induce such an improvement in the productivity of labour that would have been large enough to compensate this additional consumption. It is also possible that some of the services transferred to the public sector, as a consequence of the higher labour force participation of the women, were earlier produced in a more efficient way within the households.

The causes of the declining growth potential can be further analysed on the basis of the sectoral measures of productivity change. The results of the calculations made with the Finnish data indicate for the sectors producing educated human capital a productivity development by far inferior to that in the sectors producing ordinary goods and services. Especially the total costs of producing educated human capital involved in the production of active human time with vocational education have been increasing at an accelerating speed. The same development has, to a somewhat lesser extent, taken place also in the total production costs of human capital involved in the production of active human time with university education. These increases in the ultimate production costs of educated human capital are partly due to multiple education and partly to the fact that the time needed to accomplish a given type of education has in many cases become longer. Whether or not the latter has brought about an improvement in the quality of human capital is an open question.

An important factor in improving productivity is the cost-consciousness among the users of the products. The economy will work more efficiently if the one who causes the expenditures also pays for them and if on the other hand it is not necessary to pay for products more than their complete production costs. The equilibrium price proportions calculated from the balanced growth solution allow us to compare the complete production costs of the products with their actual prices.

Comparisons based on the Finnish data seem to indicate, among other things, that active human time with secondary education is to some extent undercharged while active human time with higher education is overcharged when compared with the price of active human time with basic education. Here, I know Andrew Bródy does not quite agree with my results. He doubts that the relative production costs of human time with higher education shown by my empirical results might be too low and that the reason for this would be that my empirical applications do not properly take into account the fact that the knowledge and skills a person has acquired during his initial education have to be renewed during his working life.

However, all the education and training provided by the educational system, multiple education included, has been taken into as far as it is possible to trace it from the statistics. What is not possible to trace from the statitics is whether a person gets all his education at the beginning of his active life or whether he acquires part of it only later during his active life. Therefore it is assumed that he gets all of it at the beginning of his active life. This does not in any way diminish the total amount of investment in human capital embodied in a person during his lifetime. Neither does it have any effects on the quantity of human capital that has to be replaced during a person's active life. It does have some effect on the timing of both investment and replacement. But there is no reason to expect that this would diminish the average costs of producing active human time during a person's active life.

As to the learning connected with a job and done, at least in principle, during the working hours and paid for by the employer, it has not been taken into account. The reason for this is that, in my view, constant learning is nowadays an ever increasing and integral part of practically every job. It is a part of what the employee is paid for when he is paid for work. Mostly it is not even possible to tell which part of working hours have been used in learning. Even if hours used in on-the-job learning could and would be treated as inputs in labour production then they should also be subtracted from the denominator when the remuneration per hour is calculated and accordingly the results of the comparison would not change.

The fact of employers paying too much for labour with higher education does by no means rule out the possibility of the employees with higher education receiving too little, after progressive taxation and means tested benefits. My results seem to indicate that while the remuneration for work received by people with higher education probably is too small after progressive taxation and means tested benefits, the costs of this kind of work to the employers might be too high. There are problems in counting what the employees in different educational categories are actually paid for their work after taxation and benefits, because these both depend on the structure of households and their other incomes. One of the possible consequencies of this situation in any case is that people with higher education might be underrepresented in the work force, which again can have adverse consequencies to the growth of productivity.

The unit production costs counted from the dynamic input–output model are based on an unchanging production technology. When the actual remuneration for different types work is determined it no doubt will be in the interest of the society to pay more than the complete production costs of any kind of work that can contribute to productivity growth.

A central role in the productivity growth is played by the development of human knowledge, i.e. of science, by the efficiency in its transmission through the educational system and by the ability of the nation in utilizing this knowledge in production, e.g. in organizing its industries and firms. In his book *Slowdown: Global Economic Maladies*, Andrew Bródy warns of the severe consequencies on productivity and growth that the current weakening position, and condition, of science and education might have (p. 103):

> Perhaps it is not *only* the quality and the results of research and educational work that are found to be lacking and not *only* the selection, motivation, remuneration and public appreciation of research work and teachers that matters – but they do matter is certain. If we fail to rectify the current state of affairs, the efficiency of economic process will not develop at the old rate and might even fall into stagnation.

REFERENCES

AULIN-AHMAVAARA, P. (1987) *A Dynamic Input–Output Model with Nonhomogeneous Labour for Evaluation of Technical Change*, Annales Academiae Scientiarum Fennicae, ser. B., no. 242 (Helsinki: The Finnish Academy of Science and Letters).

AULIN-AHMAVAARA, P. (1989) 'A Complete Dynamic Input–Output Model Including the Production of Human Capital and Labour', *Economic Systems Research*, vol. 1, no. 1, pp. 121–9.

AULIN-AHMAVAARA, P. (1990) 'Dynamic Input–Output and Time', *Economic Systems Research*, vol. 2, no. 4, pp. 329–44.

AULIN-AHMAVAARA, P. (1991) 'Production Prices of Human Capital and of Human Time', *Economic Systems Research*, vol. 3, no. 4, pp. 345–65.

AULIN-AHMAVAARA, P. (1992) *The Productivity of a Nation. Measurement of Technical Change in the Total Production System. Example Finland 1970–1985*, Studies 195 (Helsinki: Statistics Finland).

AULIN-AHMAVAARA, P. (1993) 'Measurement of Technical Change in the Total Production System', Tenth International Conference on Input–Output Techniques, papers for the plenary session.

AULIN-AHMAVAARA, P. and A. AULIN (1992) 'Extended Input–Output Dynamics and the Concept of National Economy', in Arvid Aulin, *Foundations of Economic Development* (Berlin–Heidelberg: Springer Verlag).

BRÓDY, A. (1970) *Proportions, Prices and Planning: A Mathematical Restatement of the Labour Theory of Value* (Budapest – Amsterdam: Akadémiai Kiadó – North-Holland).

BRÓDY, A. (1985) *Slowdown: Global Economic Maladies* (Beverly Hills, California: Sage).

CARTER, A. P. (1974) 'Energy, Environment and Economic growth' *Bell J. of Econ. Manage. Sci.*, vol. 5, pp. 578–92.

EISNER, R. (1989) *The Total Incomes System of Accounts* (Chicago: University of Chicago Press).

JOHANSEN, L. (1978) 'On the Theory of Dynamic Input–Output Models with Different Time Profiles of Capital Construction and Finite Life-Time of Capital Equipment', *Journal of Economic Theory*, vol. 19, pp. 513–33.

PETERSON, W. (1979) 'Total Factor Productivity in the UK: A Disaggregated Analysis', in K. D. Patterson and Kerry Schott (eds) *The Measurement of Capital: Theory and Practice* (London: Macmillan).

WOLFF, E. N. (1985) 'Industrial Composition, Interindustry Effects and the US Productivity Slowdown', *Review of Economics and Statistics*, vol. 67, pp. 268–77.

8 Equilibrium and Disequilibrium in a Disaggregated Classical Model

László Halpern and György Molnár

8.1 INTRODUCTION

Between 1985 and 1989 we made an extensive investigation (Halpern and Molnár, 1985, 1989) of Bródy's well-known stationary model.[1] Our aim was to analyze the structural relations of the Hungarian economy and to reveal the interindustry aspects of the development preferences of economic policy. We modelled the structural relations of the economy in such a way that the structure of equilibrium was simultaneously determined from the production-accumulation side and the price-income side, taking into account the most important consistency relations between these two sides. As a matter of fact, with the help of the flow and stock input matrices of interindustry relations we first determined the model's equilibrium structure of prices and outputs. This ensured uniform accumulation to a fixed asset ratio, growth rate and profit rate by industries.

We have calculated the equilibrium solution for every year of the analysis and drew conclusions from the dynamics of the deviation of the actual path from the equilibrium path. These deviations in prices as well as in outputs were persistent and very characteristic. On this basis we were able to identify the consequences of the forced industrialization on the economic structure and we revealed the most important relations of their reproduction.

The model applied, however, was not fully appropriate to fulfil the objectives of the study. Because of the static character of the model it was not possible to examine the effects of disequilibria, and – partly as a consequence – we could not take into account the role of economic policy. First we tried to answer the original questions on the basis of information outside of the model (Halpern and Molnár, 1986). Thus – distinguishing the structure of fixed assets as machines and buildings – we extended the analysis to the ratio of investments to fixed assets, the ratio of net and gross values of the fixed assets and the proportions of income redistribution among branches. We defined the income redistribution as the difference between the produced and consumed income used for investment purposes by the branches.

With the help of 'auxiliary' information we were able to underline certain causes of the persistent and one-directional disequilibrium. At the same time, the analysis of the conditions of reaching equilibrium presupposes a dynamic model. To have a dynamic model became especially important, because the following obvious question was suggested by our analysis: can the persistence of disequilibria be described in a dynamic model?

Working with a dynamic model accentuates the questions concerning the role of economic policy. We must decide what role economic policy plays in reality and how it can be modelled. To consider economic policy as an exogenous factor raises numerous problems on the one hand, and its endogenous description in the model is decided at the determination of basic properties of the model, on the other hand.

Having studied the models of Duménil and Lévy (1987, 1989 and 1991),[2] we were able to return to our original aims. We used their framework in forming the present model, satisfying the ideas expressed above. We were able to apply such equations for price regulation, which approximated the functioning of the socialist economic system better than before. With respect to the original model, we modified the method of profit calculation, improving the coherence with the other relations of the model. Finally, with the help of the new model, we could explain the persistence of disequilibrium. More precisely, we obtained a model, in which, in addition to the usual equilibrium path, there exist infinitely many equilibrium paths with different growth rates. The model provides alternatives whether the investment decisions (connected to the capital) are described with a centralized or a decentralized mechanism. In the first case the prices are set centrally, in the second case the price mechanism is similar to the monopolist price setting.

Below we first present our new model, then interpret the results obtained with it and depict those differences which distinguish it from Duménil and Lévy's model.[3]

8.2 NOTATIONS

General Notations

Matrices and vectors are denoted by bold upper and lower-case letters, respectively. Vectors are column vectors, their entries are denoted by a superscript. The time index is denoted by a subscript.

$\langle \mathbf{v} \rangle$: the diagonal matrix formed from vector **v**.
$\mathbf{v}'$: the transpose of **v**.
e : summation vector comprising unit entries.
E : identity matrix.
$\mathbf{w} > \mathbf{v}$: for all $i w^i \geq v^i$ *and at least for one i the relation > holds.*

Time-invariant Parameters

A = the matrix of input–output coefficients. It contains the coefficients concerning the reproduction of labour power. (More precisely: Let **l** denote the vector of relative labour inputs of firms, **c** the vector of structure of consumption and ω the real wages (scalar). We assume that **A** contains the dyadic matrix $\omega \mathbf{c}\mathbf{l}'$, i.e. $\omega c^i l^j$ is added to the entry (i, j) of the (original) matrix.)
B = the technological matrix of fixed assets used for unit output (i.e. defined for maximal capacity utilization).
$\hat{\mathbf{D}}$ = the matrix of amortization coefficients. We assume that the amortization and the actual wear and tear are equal to each other.
D = $\hat{\mathbf{D}} \otimes \mathbf{B}$, where $\otimes$ denotes matrix multiplication by entries.
$\bar{\mathbf{u}}$ = vector of normal capacity utilization $(0 \leq \bar{u}^i \leq 1)$.
$\bar{\mathbf{s}}$ = vector of relative normal output stocks.
$\bar{\mathbf{m}}$ = vector of normal amount of money held by the firms.

Variables (their values are given at t_0)

$\mathbf{K}_t$ = matrix of fixed assets of firms.
$\mathbf{u}_t$ = vector of capacity utilization.
$\mathbf{x}_t$ = output vector.
$\mathbf{z}_t$ = vector of output stocks.
$\mathbf{s}_t$ = vector of relative output stocks $(s_t^i = z_t^i / x_t^i)$.
$\mathbf{p}_t$ = vector of price indices.
$\mathbf{m}_t$ = money stock of firms.

8.3 THE FRAMEWORK OF THE MODEL

The model is built on the following basic assumptions:

A1. The economic processes take place in real time. Time is a discrete variable. Production in period t is followed by market transactions which in turn are followed by production in period $t + 1$, etc. During the production process in period t the following quantities are known: the fixed asset stocks, the capacity utilization, the output and output stock and the prices at the market to be arranged at the end of period *t*. These variables as well as the results of the market transactions determine the corresponding variables of the following period.

A2. A standard Leontief model is assumed. There is a one-to-one correspondence between the firms and the products; the technology is time-invariant; there are no alternative technologies. The length of the production cycle of every firm is equal to one period.

A3. The labour supply does not constrain the production decisions. The real wages are given, time-invariant and uniform across firms. The structure of consumption is also fixed.

A4. A centre for allocation of fixed assets decides on investments, the firms decide on outputs and prices, independently of each other.

According to the assumption on the time-invariance of technology, each column of the fixed assets matrix $\mathbf{K_t}$ is equal to the corresponding column of matrix $\mathbf{B}$ multiplied by a scalar. Thus we have by definition the following relation among the fixed assets, capacity utilization and output:

$$\mathbf{K_t}\langle\mathbf{u_t}\rangle = \mathbf{B}\langle\mathbf{x_t}\rangle \tag{1}$$

To preserve the proportions among the columns of $\mathbf{K_t}$, we assume that each firm replaces the amortized fixed assets by the next period. (An alternative assumption may be that the relative amortization is uniform across branches and types of fixed assets. In this latter case the assumption of invariant replacement is superfluous.)

The output in the next period is determined by the stock of fixed assets and capacity utilization. According to our basic assumptions, the net investment is proportional to the stock of fixed assets. At this point we leave the specific form of net investment open. Denoting by $\mathbf{f_t}$ and $\mathbf{J_t}$ the vector of proportionality coefficients for investment and the matrix of net investments, respectively, the matrix of gross investments is given by

$$\mathbf{I_{t+1}} = \hat{\mathbf{D}} \otimes \mathbf{K_t} + \mathbf{J_{t+1}} = \hat{\mathbf{D}} \otimes \mathbf{K_t} + \mathbf{K_t}\langle\mathbf{f_t}\rangle \tag{2}$$

Therefore the stock of fixed assets in the next period is as follows:

$$\mathbf{K_{t+1}} = \mathbf{K_t} - \hat{\mathbf{D}} \otimes \mathbf{K_t} + \mathbf{I_{t+1}} = \mathbf{K_t}(\mathbf{E} + \langle\mathbf{f_t}\rangle) \tag{3}$$

The firms determine their capacity utilization in the next period on the basis of their capacity utilization and relative output stocks in the present period. If the output stock of a firm is higher (lower) than normal, the firm sets its capacity utilization below (above) the norm. At the same time, by our assumption there is some inertia in capacity utilization. Thus if the normal capacity utilization of a firm is higher (lower) than normal, there is a tendency to preserve it above (below) the norm in the next period. For the sake of simplicity these two rules are formulated as a linear feedback rule:

$$\mathbf{u}_{t+1} = \bar{\mathbf{u}} + \langle \boldsymbol{\sigma} \rangle (\mathbf{u}_t - \bar{\mathbf{u}}) + \langle \boldsymbol{\epsilon} \rangle (\bar{\mathbf{s}} - \mathbf{s}_t) \tag{4}$$

where $0 \leq \sigma^i < 1$ and $0 < \varepsilon^i$.

Knowing the fixed asset stock and output in period $t + 1$, on the basis of (1) output is determined as follows:

$$\mathbf{x}_{t+1} = (\mathbf{E} + \langle \mathbf{f}_t \rangle) \langle \mathbf{u}_t \rangle^{-1} \langle \mathbf{u}_{t+1} \rangle \mathbf{x}_t \tag{5}$$

Knowing the investment and output in period $t + 1$, and substituting (2) into (5), the demand appearing at the market at the end of period t is determined as follows:

$$\mathbf{h}_{t+1} = \mathbf{I}_{t+1}\mathbf{e} + \mathbf{A}\mathbf{x}_{t+1} = (\mathbf{D} + \mathbf{B}\langle \mathbf{f}_t \rangle + \mathbf{A}(\mathbf{E} + \langle \mathbf{f}_t \rangle)\langle \mathbf{u}_{t+1} \rangle)\langle \mathbf{u}_t \rangle^{-1} \mathbf{x}_t \tag{6}$$

A basic assumption of the model is that the demand determined in (6) is satisfied at the listed prices. Insufficient (excess) demand shows up in the increase (decrease) in output stocks. As a simple balance equation, the dynamics of output stocks and money stocks can be described:

$$\mathbf{z}_{t+1} = \mathbf{z}_t + \mathbf{x}_t - \mathbf{h}_{t+1} \tag{7}$$

and

$$\mathbf{m}'_{t+1} = \mathbf{m}'_t + \mathbf{p}'_t \langle \mathbf{h}_{t+1} \rangle - \mathbf{p}'_t (\mathbf{I}_{t+1} + \mathbf{A} \langle \mathbf{x}_{t+1} \rangle) \tag{8}$$

At this point we introduce the notation for the relative matrix of fixed assets per output $\mathbf{C}_t$ in period t:

$$\mathbf{C}_t = \mathbf{B} \langle \mathbf{u}_t \rangle^{-1} + \langle \mathbf{s}_t \rangle + \mathbf{A} \tag{9}$$

(Since the length of the production cycle is equal to one period, the matrix of current assets per output is equal to **A**.)

After executing the suitable substitutions and arrangements, with the help of notation (9) equations (7) and (8) are transformed into

$$\begin{aligned}(\langle \mathbf{s}_{t+1} \rangle \langle \mathbf{u}_{t+1} \rangle \langle \mathbf{u}_t \rangle^{-1} - \langle \mathbf{s}_t \rangle)\mathbf{x}_t &= \\ = (\mathbf{E} - \mathbf{A}\langle \mathbf{u}_{t+1} \rangle \langle \mathbf{u}_t \rangle^{-1} - \mathbf{D}\langle \mathbf{u}_t \rangle^{-1} - \mathbf{C}_{t+1}\langle \mathbf{f}_t \rangle \langle \mathbf{u}_{t+1} \rangle \langle \mathbf{u}_t \rangle^{-1})\mathbf{x}_t\end{aligned} \tag{10}$$

and

$$\mathbf{m}'_{t+1} - \mathbf{m}'_t + \mathbf{p}'_t(\langle \mathbf{s}_{t+1}\rangle\langle \mathbf{u}_{t+1}\rangle\langle \mathbf{u}_t\rangle^{-1} - \langle \mathbf{s}_t\rangle)\langle \mathbf{x}_t\rangle =$$
$$= \mathbf{p}'_t(\mathbf{E} - \mathbf{A}\langle \mathbf{u}_{t+1}\rangle\langle \mathbf{u}_t\rangle^{-1} - \mathbf{D}\langle \mathbf{u}_t\rangle^{-1} - \mathbf{C}_{t+1}\langle \mathbf{f}_t\rangle\langle \mathbf{u}_{t+1}\rangle\langle \mathbf{u}_t\rangle^{-1})\langle \mathbf{x}_t\rangle \tag{11}$$

Thus we have completed the description of the model framework, which consists of equations (4), (5), (10) and (11). For the time being we can only speak of a model framework, since the price equations as well as the vector of investment coefficients $\mathbf{f}_t$ are not yet given.

8.4 THE FRAMEWORK OF THE EQUILIBRIUM SOLUTION

First we shall use a very wide concept of the equilibrium path: the capacity utilization and the relative output stocks are time-invariant. We shall denote the time-invariant variables with the corresponding values in period 0. Under the equilibrium conditions, the equations (4), (5) and (10) – after some manipulation and use of notation (9) in the last equation – appear as follows:

$$\mathbf{u}_0 = \bar{\mathbf{u}} + \langle \boldsymbol{\epsilon}\rangle\langle \mathbf{e} - \boldsymbol{\sigma}\rangle^{-1}(\bar{\mathbf{s}} - \mathbf{s}_0) \tag{12}$$

$$\mathbf{x}_{t+1} = (\mathbf{E} + \langle \mathbf{f}_t\rangle)\mathbf{x}_t \tag{13}$$

$$(\mathbf{E} - \mathbf{A} - \mathbf{D}\langle \mathbf{u}_0\rangle^{-1})\mathbf{x}_t = \mathbf{C}_0\langle \mathbf{f}_t\rangle\mathbf{x}_t \tag{14}$$

Already with this wide concept of equilibrium we can analyze the case of exogenous preferences, when – relying on some consideration – the centre fixes the investment proportions for several periods in advance. In a formal language, this means that $\mathbf{f}_t = \mu_t\mathbf{f}$, where μ_t is a scalar and $\mathbf{f}$ is a fixed vector.

By plugging the relative investment vector $\mathbf{f}_t$ in (13) and (14), it is easy to see that for vector $\mathbf{f}$ of a general form, we get a contradiction. The two equations have only a solution in $\mathbf{x}_t$, if $\mathbf{f}_t = \mu_t\mathbf{e}$, i.e. the output increases uniformly across firms, i.e. there are no genuine preferences. We shall return to the issue of uniform growth below, but now we underline that for genuine preferences equilibrium is infeasible even in this wide sense.

We shall need the simplified form of the monetary balance equation of the model framework. Suppose that for time-invariant capacity utilization and relative output stocks the money stock of a firm is also time-invariant. Substituting these assumptions into (11), after rearrangements and dividing by $\langle \mathbf{x}_t\rangle$, we obtain the following equation:

$$\mathbf{p}'_t(\mathbf{E} - \mathbf{A} - \mathbf{D}\langle \mathbf{u}_0\rangle^{-1}) = \mathbf{p}'_t\mathbf{C}_0\langle \mathbf{f}_t\rangle \tag{15}$$

Now we turn to the discussion of those relations which complete the model.

8.5 DECISIONS ON PRICES AND INVESTMENTS

In our model the prices are not determined directly by the relation of market demand and supply. At the same time, the prices are not rigid, at least not rigid upward. We assume that in the closed economy the monopolist (or the Price Board) regulates prices in a passive way, i.e. to minimize the difficulties in the working of firms, i.e. to avoid shortage in money stocks. The monopolist firm passes over the consequences of its investment and production decisions to the users of its products, i.e. it raises prices if it is necessary to finance its working. At the same time the prices are rigid downward; they are never decreased. We believe that this mechanism is a good approximation to the collaboration of the traditional state-owned big firm and the centre in setting prices.

According to our assumptions, each firm raises its price, if after market transactions its money stock falls below its norm, but if its money stock jumps (remains) above the norm, it does not change its price[4]:

$$\mathbf{p}'_{t+1} = \mathbf{p}'_t + \max(0, \mathbf{p}'_t\langle\boldsymbol{\beta}\rangle\langle\overline{\mathbf{m}} - \mathbf{m}_{t+1}\rangle) \tag{16}$$

where $\beta^i > 0$.

The decision on net investment consists of two parts: determination of (i) the total value of investment, and (ii) the proportions of investments. The centre makes decisions on the basis of profit expectations. It supposes that the total current output will be sold in the market to be held at the end of the period. The values of current and fixed inputs are taken into account at the prices of reproduction (i.e. at the prices of period *t*). Thus the vector of expected profits is given by

$$\boldsymbol{\pi}'_t = \mathbf{p}'_t(\mathbf{E} - \mathbf{A})\langle\mathbf{x}_t\rangle - \mathbf{p}'_t\hat{\mathbf{D}} \otimes \mathbf{K}_t = \mathbf{p}'_t(\mathbf{E} - \mathbf{A} - \mathbf{D}\langle\mathbf{u}_t\rangle^{-1})\langle\mathbf{x}_t\rangle \tag{17}$$

The value of the fixed capital (via equation (9)) is

$$\mathbf{v}'_t = \mathbf{p}'_t\mathbf{C}_t\langle\mathbf{x}_t\rangle \tag{18}$$

The vector of expected profit rates is as follows:

$$\mathbf{r}'_t = \boldsymbol{\pi}'_t\langle\mathbf{v}_t\rangle^{-1} = \mathbf{p}'_t(\mathbf{E} - \mathbf{A} - \mathbf{D}\langle\mathbf{u}_t\rangle^{-1})\langle\mathbf{p}'_t\mathbf{C}_t\rangle^{-1} \tag{19}$$

Hence the average profit rate is equal to

$$\boldsymbol{\rho}_t = \frac{\boldsymbol{\pi}'_t \mathbf{e}}{\mathbf{v}'_t \mathbf{e}} = \frac{\mathbf{p}'_t(\mathbf{E} - \mathbf{A} - \mathbf{D}\langle \mathbf{u}_t \rangle^{-1})\mathbf{x}_t}{\mathbf{p}'_t \mathbf{C}_t \mathbf{x}_t} \tag{20}$$

The firms' investment proportions are determined on the basis of the firms' profit rates, using a strictly increasing scalar function $f > 0$. The function f is the same for every firm, since the investment centre is only interested in the value of profitability, independently of which firm is concerned. Denoting the diagonal matrix with entries $f(r_t^i)$ by $\langle \mathbf{f}(\mathbf{r}_t) \rangle$, the matrix of net investment is given by

$$\mathbf{J}_{t+1} = \boldsymbol{\mu}_t \mathbf{K}_t \langle \mathbf{f}(\mathbf{r}_t) \rangle \tag{21}$$

According to our assumption, the investment centre adjusts the growth of investments to the expected growth in the total value of capital, thus the ratio of total value of net investment to that of fixed assets is equal to the expected profit rate:

$$\boldsymbol{\rho}_t = \frac{\mathbf{p}'_t \mathbf{J}_{t+1} \mathbf{e}}{\mathbf{p}'_t \mathbf{K}_t \mathbf{e}} \tag{22}$$

Hence – also using (1) and (21) – the scalar μ_t is as follows:

$$\boldsymbol{\mu}_t = \frac{\boldsymbol{\rho}_t \mathbf{p}'_t \mathbf{B}\langle \mathbf{u}_t \rangle^{-1} \mathbf{x}_t}{\mathbf{p}'_t \mathbf{B}\langle \mathbf{f}(\mathbf{r}_t) \rangle \langle \mathbf{u}_t \rangle^{-1} \mathbf{x}_t} \tag{23}$$

The diagonal matrix of the investment decision is

$$\langle \mathbf{f}_t \rangle = \boldsymbol{\mu}_t \langle \mathbf{f}(\mathbf{r}_t) \rangle \tag{24}$$

where $\mathbf{r}_t$ and $\boldsymbol{\mu}_t$ are defined in (19) and (23), respectively.

8.6 THE MODEL

The complete model consists of the equations (4), (5), (10), (11) forming the model framework, and of the price equation (16), and the investment equations (19), (20), (23) and (24). The listed equations determine a *recursive system*: from the variables of period t ($\mathbf{u}_t, \mathbf{s}_t, \mathbf{x}_t, \mathbf{p}_t$ and $\mathbf{m}_t$ the corresponding variables can uniquely be determined for period $t + 1$.

A special case of the investment decision when $\mathbf{f}(\mathbf{r}_t) = \mathbf{r}_t$. This corresponds to a complete decentralization of investments (there is no investment centre, and each firm spends its profit on its own accumulation).

8.7 THE EQUILIBRIUM SOLUTION

Considering our equilibrium, we assumed that the capacity utilization, the relative output stocks and the money stocks are time-invariant. In addition, at an equilibrium path the growth rate of output and the rate of profit are uniform across firms and periods, moreover, prices are time-invariant.

On the basis of (12)–(14) the equilibrium solution(s) – as there are infinitely many of them – can easily be obtained.

Let $\mathbf{s}_0$ be an arbitrarily given vector, and $\mathbf{u}_0$ corresponding to (12). Consider the following characteristic root – characteristic vector problem:[5]

$$(\mathbf{E} - \mathbf{A} - \mathbf{D}\langle \mathbf{u}_0 \rangle^{-1})\mathbf{x} = \lambda \mathbf{C}_0 \mathbf{x} \tag{24}$$

$$\mathbf{p}'(\mathbf{E} - \mathbf{A} - \mathbf{D}\langle \mathbf{u}_0 \rangle^{-1}) = \lambda \mathbf{p}'\mathbf{C}_0 \tag{25}$$

Under the customary suitable assumptions, there exists a unique solution $\bar{\lambda} > 0$, $\mathbf{x}_0 > \mathbf{0}$, $\mathbf{p}_0 > \mathbf{0}$ to this pair of equations.[6] Let $\mathbf{m}_0 \geq \overline{\mathbf{m}}$ arbitrary.[7] Then we have

Proposition 1. $\mathbf{s}_t = \mathbf{s}_0$, $\mathbf{u}_t = \mathbf{u}_0$, $\mathbf{m}_t = \mathbf{m}_0$, $\mathbf{p}_t = \mathbf{p}_0$, $\mathbf{x}_t = (1 + \lambda)^t \mathbf{x}_0$ is a solution to the recursive system.

Proof. $\mathbf{s}_t = \mathbf{s}_0$, $\mathbf{u}_t = \mathbf{u}_0$, $\mathbf{m}_t, = \mathbf{m}_0$ imply (12)–(15) (derived above). Plugging $\mathbf{p}_0$, $\mathbf{u}_0$ and $\mathbf{s}_0$ in (19) (using also (9), the definition of $\mathbf{C}_t$), the relation $\mathbf{r}_t = \bar{\lambda}\mathbf{e}$ is obtained, i.e. $\langle \mathbf{f}(\mathbf{r}_t) \rangle = f(\bar{\lambda})\mathbf{E}$. Hence $\rho_t = \bar{\lambda}$. After substituting into (23), $\mu_t = \bar{\lambda}/f(\bar{\lambda})$, i.e. $\langle \mathbf{f}_t \rangle = \mu_t \langle \mathbf{f}(\mathbf{r}_t) \rangle = \bar{\lambda}\mathbf{E}$. Plugging this in (13)–(15), $\mathbf{x}_t$ in (13), (14); $\mathbf{p}_0$ in (14), (15); $\mathbf{m}_0$ in (16), using also the inequality $\mathbf{m}_0 \geq \overline{\mathbf{m}}$, we see that all equalities hold, proving the proposition.

For any initial value $\mathbf{s}_0$ (and for any $\mathbf{m}_0 \geq \overline{\mathbf{m}}$) there exists a unique equilibrium solution. In the following proposition we investigate the dependence of equilibrium growth rate in the function of the initial value of the output stock.

Proposition 2. Let $\hat{\mathbf{s}} > \tilde{\mathbf{s}}$ be two different initial values of the relative output stock. Then $\bar{\lambda}(\hat{\mathbf{s}}) < \bar{\lambda}(\tilde{\mathbf{s}})$, i.e. entry-wise larger relative output stock vector yields a smaller equilibrium growth rate.[8]

8.8 INTERPRETATION OF THE RESULTS

We have already mentioned in the Introduction that in creating our model, we have strongly relied on Duménil and Lévy's models. It is worthwhile comparing our model with a member of their model family (Duménil and Lévy, 1987). The fundamental objective of Duménil and Lévy's (for short: DL) model is to model the processes of the capitalist economy along the line of classical economists. Our model intends to describe some characteristics of a reformed planned economy, sometimes referring to the problems of transition. As a result, there are two decisive differences in the control mechanisms of the two papers.

In the DL model the changes in prices are controlled by the deviation of the output stocks from their norms. In our model the same role is played by the deviation of the money stocks from their norms, however the output stocks and other variables affect the outcome indirectly. This approach – within the limits of the model – means that the Price Board or the monopolist firm is capable to set a price which fits its aims. If after the market transaction the money stock of a firm is lower than normal, because it has low profits or excessive investment cost, to give two examples, then it can raise its price or – what is the same in the model – the centre authorizes the price increase.

We have already mentioned a special version of our model without a centre for investment decisions. This means that the economy is fully decentralized and that there is no asset transfer among firms. Then the price regulation can be interpreted as a monopolistic one. It reflects certain characteristics of the transforming Hungarian economy.

Another difference between the two models lies in the method of evaluation of the fixed assets and, indirectly, of the profitability. The DL model calculates with actual fixed assets and normative current assets and stock, while we always work with actual values. This difference is decisive in that we have infinitely many solutions.[9]

In this way we succeeded in modelling the phenomenon of the reformed Hungarian economy that it moves 'parallel' to the equilibrium path. For an unfavourable initial condition such a path produces a lower growth rate than if the economy were in an equilibrium corresponding to the norms. There is a decisive difference from the reality in that we modelled a closed economy. And the economy working with persistently relative low growth rate goes bankrupt just through the foreign trade.

It is an important feature of our model that the *incoming and outgoing norms* are different. The normal values of capacity utilization, of stocks of output and money ($\bar{\mathbf{u}}$, $\bar{\mathbf{s}}$ and $\bar{\mathbf{m}}$) are given from outside. These are called incoming norms. At the same time $\mathbf{u}_0$ and $\mathbf{s}_0$ may be taken as norms (to be called outgoing norms) since the corresponding variables persistently take up these values. As a consequence, we have a special situation where the actors of the economy control their behaviour according to certain norms (e.g. on the basis of former experience or emulating other economies). At the same time, the other variables of the economy (prices and outputs) are inconsistent with these norms. If the actors still follow the incoming norms, then they can preserve a path yielding a lower than equilibrium growth rate.

NOTES

1. A detailed description of the model is to be found in Bródy (1970).
2. We thank A. Simonovits for his calling our attention to the first model.
3. Our model, similarly to Duménil and Lévy's, differs from Leontief and Bródy in the application of truly (non-stationary) dynamic relations.
4. From the point of view of further developments an equivalent regulation of prices would be given by equation

$$\mathbf{p}'_{t+1} = \mathbf{p}'_t + \mathbf{p}'_t\langle\boldsymbol{\beta}\rangle\langle\bar{\mathbf{m}} - \mathbf{m}_{t+1}\rangle \qquad (16a)$$

where if the firm's money stock is above the norms, it diminishes its price. In certain cases this type of price regulation is also conceivable, but (16) is more realistic. This version is very similar to one model of Bródy (1981) where prices are depending on the change in profits.

5. These equations are the analog of $(\mathbf{E} - \mathbf{A})\mathbf{x} = \lambda\mathbf{B}\mathbf{x}$ and $\mathbf{p}'(\mathbf{E} - \mathbf{A}) = \lambda\mathbf{p}'\mathbf{B}$ from Bródy (1970). The deviation stems from two factors: (i) we take into account amortization, and more important, (ii) the relative capital stock matrix, in addition to the fixed assets, explicitly contains the current assets and the output stocks.
6. We assume that the dominant characteristic root of matrix $\mathbf{A} + \mathbf{D}\langle\mathbf{u}_0\rangle^{-1}$ is less than 1. (This assumption ensures that the system is capable for extended reproduction.) Then there exists a positive matrix $\mathbf{Q}_0 = (\mathbf{E} - \mathbf{A} - \mathbf{D}\langle\mathbf{u}_0\rangle^{-1})^{-1}$. We assume that $\mathbf{Q}_0\mathbf{C}_0$ is irreducible. $\bar{\lambda}$ is the reciprocal of the dominant characteristic root of matrix $\mathbf{Q}_0\mathbf{C}_0$, $\mathbf{x}_0$ is the corresponding right hand side characteristic vector, $\mathbf{p}_0$ is the corresponding left hand side characteristic vector of $\mathbf{C}_0\mathbf{Q}_0$. These matrices have no other characteristic vectors with non-negative entries.
7. In case of price regulation described in Note 4 the inequality should be replaced by equality $\mathbf{m}_t = \bar{\mathbf{m}}$.
8. **Proof.** The proposition is quite evident, therefore we only outline the proof. Denoting the functional connection, as defined by (12), between the initial relative output stock and the capacity utilization $\mathbf{u}(\mathbf{s})$, we can easily demonstrate that $\mathbf{u}(\hat{\mathbf{s}}) < \mathbf{u}(\bar{\mathbf{s}})$. Using an analogous notation for matrices, hence $\mathbf{Q}(\hat{\mathbf{s}}) > \mathbf{Q}(\bar{\mathbf{s}})$ and $\mathbf{C}(\hat{\mathbf{s}}) > \mathbf{C}(\bar{\mathbf{s}})$. Larger matrix has larger dominant root, thus, $\bar{\lambda}$ being the reciprocal of the dominant characteristic root, the proposition is proved. In a non-price model based on stock signals Kornai and Simonovits (1981) have proved analogous statement on the trade-off between growth and stock norms.
9. Another important difference, which does not concern the interpretation, is as follows. Using a special system of notations, the DL model describes a rather special economy, which only consists of three firms. The first only produces fixed assets, the second only current assets and the third only consumer goods. On the other hand, for a certain system of parameter values they were able to prove the local stability of the equilibrium solution.

REFERENCES

BRÓDY, A. (1970) *Proportions, Prices and Planning*, Amsterdam, North-Holland.

BRÓDY, A. (1981) 'An Economy Controlled by Stocks and Profits', in Kornai and Martos (1981), pp. 149–62.

DUMÉNIL, G. and D. LÉVY (1987) 'The Dynamics of Competition: A Restoration of the Classical Analysis', *Cambridge Journal of Economics*, vol. 11, no. 1., pp. 133–64.

DUMÉNIL, G. and D. LÉVY (1989) 'The Competitive Process in a Fixed Capital Environment: A Classical View', *The Manchester School of Economic and Social Studies*, vol. LVII, no. 1, pp. 34–57.

DUMÉNIL, G. and D. LÉVY (1991): 'Micro Adjustment Toward Long-Term Equilibrium', *Journal of Economic Theory*, vol. 53, pp. 369–95.

HALPERN, L. and G. MOLNÁR (1985) 'Income Formation, Accumulation and Price Trends in Hungary in the 1970s', *Acta Oeconomica*, vol. 35, no. 1–2, pp. 105–32.

HALPERN, L. and G. MOLNÁR (1986) *The Structures of Income, Investment and Prices in Hungary during the 70s*, Studies No. 30, Institute of Economics, Budapest, pp. 120.

HALPERN, L. and G. MOLNÁR (1989) 'Macro Features of the Hungarian Economy since 1970', *Economic Systems Research*, vol. 1, no. 1, pp. 111–20.

KORNAI, J. and B. MARTOS (eds) (1981) *Non-Price Control, Budapest*, Akadémiai Kiadó, pp. 334.

KORNAI, J. and A. SIMONOVITS (1981) 'Stock-Signal Model Regulated from a Normal Path', in Kornai and Martos (1981), pp. 223–46.

9 Structural Economic Dynamics: Catching-Up and the Global Deflationary Bias

Michael A. Landesmann,
Richard M. Goodwin and Robert Stehrer

9.1 INTRODUCTION

András Bródy has had, just as one of the co-authors of this paper (Richard Goodwin), a life-long interest in the relationship between dynamics and structure. Formally, it is difficult to bring these two elements together since sensible dynamic economic models should be non-linearly specified, but models which introduce many dimensions (to represent 'structure') are not well understood analytically if they contain non-linearities. Nonetheless, both Bródy and Goodwin have always pointed out that to study dynamics in capitalist economies as well as in formerly planned economies properly, structure and structural change cannot be abstracted from; furthermore, they were keenly aware of the importance of using the advances made in non-linear dynamics for modern business cycle analysis (for examples in Bródy's work of both concerns see Bródy, 1983, 1989, 1990, 1992). Bridging the gap between the detailed analysis of changing structure and macrodynamics remains a challenge to the students of both Bródy and Goodwin.

In this paper we shall extend work we have done recently (see Landesmann and Goodwin, 1994) on the relationship between structural adjustment in capitalist economies and potential demand failures. The previous paper discussed, in the context of a closed-economy model, the potential conflict between rapid structural change and counteracting the potential for effective demand failures in capitalist economies. In this paper we analyze the process of uneven growth and the dynamics of industrial specialization in an open economy framework. The model is extended to deal with the dynamics of industrial specialization of two economies (an advanced economy and a catching-up economy) and the difficulties which are encountered at the global level to sustain high and stable levels of aggregate demand in the face of the requirements for structural adjustment.

The open economy case, in which mature economies operating at higher *levels* of productivity face catching-up economies which attain higher *rates* of productivity growth, explicitly brings into focus the impact which changes in the international division of labour can have upon aggregate production and employment levels in mature economies.

From the point of view of global aggregate demand and employment levels there are a variety of dilemmas which the (technologically) advanced and catching-up economies face respectively:

For the *catching-up economy* it is the issue of deciding how to distribute the gains from rapid technological and productivity advance. A catching-up economy is normally characterized by a situation in which real wage growth (though often rapid) is lagging behind productivity growth. This leads to high savings and investment rates and hence to the possibility of rather rapid capital accumulation. Rapid accumulation (in both physical and human assets) is the driving force behind the catching-up process itself. However, at some point, the success of catching-up economies leads to high positive trade balances and, after some time, this requires adjustment. There are various forms of adjustment: capital exports are one form, exchange rate adjustment is another and higher real wage growth (and hence a catching-up of domestic consumption) is a third. All these forms of adjustment have implications on the speed of further structural change and the dynamics of international specialization and on the weights of different markets in global demand, as well as on the distribution of the gains from fast technological and structural change.

The (technologically) *advanced economy* is usually characterized by lower savings and investment rates, by a more balanced growth pattern of real wages and productivity and by a production pattern directed towards either domestic demand or demand in markets which are similar to their own. Pressures from international catching-up imply that industrial structural adjustment is required which is no longer dominated by the evolution of domestic demand patterns but results from the pattern of import penetration initiated by the dynamics of industrial specialisation of catching-up economies. Important distributional issues arise here as well as the question is posed whether high levels of employment and economic activity can be maintained in the wake of the need for structural adjustment.

We shall attempt to show that processes of catching-up and the reaction of advanced economies lead, in most likelihood, to – what has been coined – an inbuilt *global deflationary bias*. The reason for such a deflationary bias results from the incentives of catching-up economies to continue to proceed with rapid structural change, requiring high rates of investment and hence a continued lagging of domestic consumption behind production potential. It also results from the impact which structural adjustment has in advanced economies through the necessity to shift towards higher investment levels (both in physical and human asssets) by re-establishing higher profit margins as well as to shift investible resources into sectors with high productivity growth. These developments lead to an increase in the potential for effective demand failures at the global level analogous to the one discussed in the closed-economy version of the model (see Landesmann and Goodwin, 1994). However, we shall see that the instruments which could be used in the closed-economy situation to alleviate the potential for effective demand failures are much less likely to be used in the open economy situation.

The paper will consider a model of the global economy consisting of two economies and two industries: the more advanced economy is characterised by higher productivity levels while the catching-up economy has a higher potential for productivity growth. Across industries there is also a differential potential for productivity growth and this – together with a sluggish adjustment of prices to units costs – gives rise to industry-specific *technological* (or Schumpeterian) *rents*. Parts of these technological rents will be recouped in the form of higher wage rate growth, but the remainder will be used to achieve higher endogenous investment rates in the higher productivity growth industry with further possible repercussions on (endogenous) productivity growth. Depending upon the relationship between productivity and wage rate growth and the adjustment of prices to unit costs, differential productivity growth will affect relative price structures leading to substitution effects on the demand side.

In our model, the catching-up economy, although it has faster productivity growth in both industries, does more catching-up in the more labour-intensive industry. Hence its advantages in relative price competitiveness will be particularly felt in the more labour-intensive industry and it will gain export markets there in particular. International trade patterns reflect the dynamics of catching-up, so that the strongest market share gains will be obtained by the catching-up economy in the relatively more labour-intensive industry which (by assumption) experiences higher rates of (labour) productivity growth in both advanced and catching-up economies.

Given the pressure of international competition from catching-up economies, the advanced economy has three options: (i) keep relative wage structures rigid which will lead to increasing loss of competitiveness in the industry with the faster productivity growth or (ii) allow adjustments in the relative wage structure or (iii) change techniques could make the industry less dependent on the high wage costs.

In the model (iii) does not take place automatically but depends upon high investment rates from earned profits and is thus linked to the issue of whether wage rate growth and price adjustment leave sufficient room for retained profits. Rigid wage structures, in the face of strong competitive pressure in the industry which faces the faster catching-up, leads to structural employment losses in that industry (the labour-intensive industry) with implications for the structure and level of domestic demand.

Section 2 will introduce the basic structure of our model; section 3 will report the main results concerning the differences of facing structural adjustment in the context of a closed or open economy respectively; section 4 will discuss the developmental options of both advanced and catching-up economies by showing the impact of changes in various behavioural parameters of the model and in section 5 some conclusions will be drawn.

9.2 THE STRUCTURE OF THE MODEL

Just as in the closed economy version of the model (see Landesmann and Goodwin, 1994), productivity growth is driven in this model by a logistic function which characterises the evolution of an economy's *innovative potential* (Figure 9.1). The two industries' productivity growth feeds on the

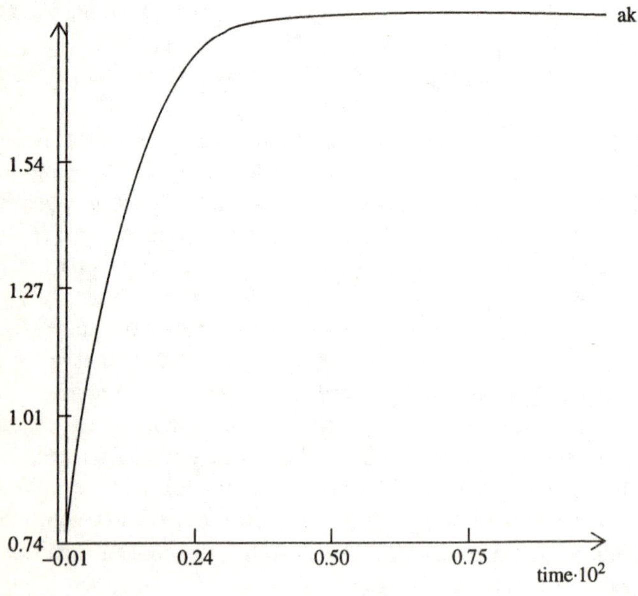

Figure 9.1 Development of the innovative potential

economy's innovative potential to different degrees, so that there are faster and slower productivity growth industries (Figure 9.2). In the open economy case in which we consider two economies (a more advanced economy A and a catching-up economy B), the economies' innovative potential differs (since there is more scope for a catching-up economy to upgrade its technology compared to the more mature economy) and hence there is scope for faster productivity growth in economy *B* than in economy *A*. Figure 9.2 also shows that the scope for faster (labour) productivity growth is greater in industry 2 (the more labour-intensive industry), than in industry 1 and it is in this industry that we would expect the fastest catching-up to take place.

Equations (1), (2) in Table 9.1 give the formulation of the two economies' logistic functions as well as the development of the labour input coefficients (the inverse of labour productivity) as a function of the logistic. We have omitted country-specific superscripts which could be added throughout; these have only been included when reference had to be made to both countries' variables (and parameters) within the same equation (such as in the export equations (5a) and (5c).

Next we come to the *evolution of costs, prices and rents*: Equations (3) in Table 9.1 present the price equations for the two industries (i = 1,2) which follow the general formula that prices adjust to unit costs (plus a mark-up) but

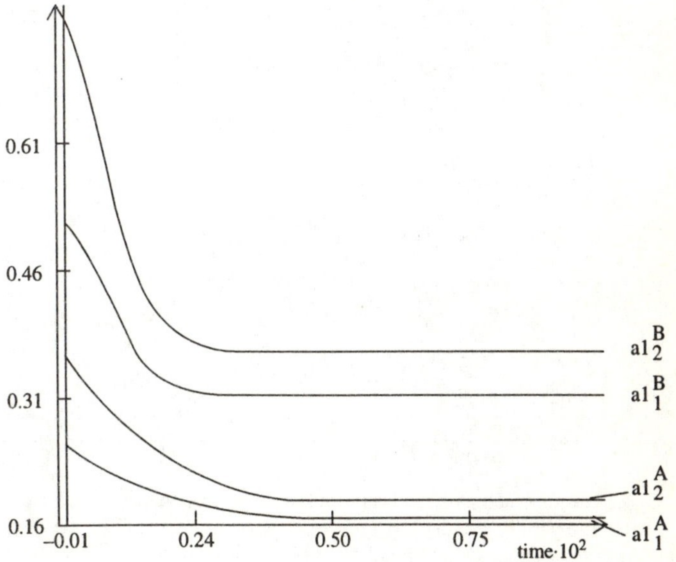

Figure 9.2 Development of the labour input coefficients

Table 9.1 Structure of the model

countries A,B industries $i,j = 1,2$

(1) $$\dot{k} = g_1 + (g_2 + (1 + g_4 \sum_j I_j^\beta) k(1 - k/g_3)$$

(2) $$\dot{a}_{Lj} = -d_{1j}\dot{k} - d_{2j}(1 - h_j - j_j) r_j$$

(3) $$\dot{p}_j = f_j(1 + m_j)(\sum_i p_i a_{ij} + w_j a_{Lj} + b_j) - p_j)$$

(4a) $$\dot{q}_1^d = e_1(\sum_i a_{1i} q_i^d + WL.s_1 s_1^A/p_1 + (si_1 a_1 \dot{k} + (1 - si_2) a_2 \dot{k})/ p_1 + si_1 |_1^\beta/p_1 + c_1 - q_1^d$$

(4b) $$\dot{q}_2^d = e_2(\sum_i a_{2i} q_i^d + WL(1 - s_1) s_2^A/p_2 + (si_2 a_2 \dot{k} + (1 - si_2) a_1 \dot{k})/ p_2 + (1 - si_1) I_2^\beta/p_2 + c_2 - q_2^d)$$

(5a) $$\dot{x}_1^A = e_1(\sum_i a_{1i} x_i + WL^B s_1^B(1 - s_1^B).ex/p_1 + I_{B1}^\beta(1 - si_1^B).ex/p_1 - x_1^A)$$

(5c) $$\dot{x}_1^B = e_1(\sum_i a_{1i} x_i + WL^A s_1^A(1 - s_1^A)ex/p_1 + I_{A1}^\beta(1 - si_1^A)ex/p_1 - x_1^B)$$

(6) $$\dot{w}_j = f_3 \mathrm{UN} + h_j r_j / a_{Lj}$$

Definitions:

$$si_j = p_j.a_{jj} / \sum_i p_i a_{ij}$$

$$I_1^\beta = si_1(1 - h_1 - j_1) r_1 (q_1^d + x_1) + (1 - si_2)(1 - h_2 - j_2) r_2 (q_2^d + x_2)$$

$$I_2^\beta = si_2(1 - h_2 - j_2) r_2 (q_2^d + x_2) + (1 - si_1)(1 - h_1 - j_1) r_1 (q_1^d + x_1)$$

$$r_j = p_j - (\sum_i p_i a_{ij} + w_j a_{Lj})$$

$$\mathrm{UN} = (L^d - L)/L \quad \text{where} \quad L^d = \sum_j a_{Lj}(q_j^d + x_j)$$

$$WL = \sum_j w_j.a_{Lj}(q_j^d + x_j)$$

Notes:
Country-specific superscripts have been omitted from all parameters and variables except when the partner country's parameters (and variables) entered the other country's equation (such as the export equations). The above table only shows the general form of the equations which are specified in the model for each industry and each country.

with adjustment parameters f_i < I so that falls in unit costs open up the possibility of *innovational rents* above normal mark-ups (we use r_i to denote these rents). The parameters f_i reflect the pricing strategies of firms in fast and slow productivity growth[1] industries which depend upon the market structure (such as the nature and degree of competition among alternative innovators and among innovators and imitators).[2] As we know there is a trade-off between fast expansion of market shares by the technological leaders in an industry by passing on quickly the results from higher productivity growth in the form of lower prices (high f_is) as against the possibility of utilising the cost advantages to reap above normal profits by maintaining price levels (low f_is). However, the possibility in high productivity industries to reap high (per unit) profits depends not only on the degree of competition on the product markets but also on the *behaviour of wage rates*. Equations (6) show that there are two factors influencing the evolution of the wage rate: one factor is *economy-wide* (i.e. the rate of economy-wide unemployment), the other is *industry-specific* (i.e. the degree to which different rates of (labour) productivity growth in different industries open up the possibility to attain different increases in wage rates; this would lead to a change in the structure of relative wage rates across different industrial branches). The second, industry-specific factor will be our main concern in this paper and here parameters h_i represent the shares of (per-unit) technological rents r_i which are appropriated by the workers in an industry in the form of higher wage rates; $(1-h_i)r_i$ are then the profit residuals of the innovational rents, in other words, the Schumpeterian profits.

Next we come to *quantities*: Equations (4) and (5) give output level changes as a function of sales in domestic (equs. 4a and 4b) and export markets (equs. 5a and 5c) respectively. We can see that international competition plays a symmetric role in both the two countries' domestic and export markets. Both in consumption expenditure (spending out of wages) as well as in investment expenditure we have specified constant nominal shares (s_i^A, si_i^A and s_i^B, si_i^B) which are supplied by domestic producers respectively (and, correspondingly, $1-s_i^A$ and $1-s_i^B$, etc. which refer to the nominal shares supplied by importers). This constant nominal shares specification allows a change in the quantities supplied by importers and domestic suppliers respectively if their relative supply prices change.[3] As in the closed economy version, we include two components of investment expenditure, one (called I^α) which is directly linked to the economy's evolution of its innovative potential ($a_i\dot{k}_i$), the other (called I^β) refers to endogenous investment expenditure due to the appearance of Schumpeterian profits; of these Schumpeterian per-unit profits certain proportions $(1-j_i-h_i)$ are invested (we call j_i the 'whimp' factor).[4] Endogenous investment expenditures (I^β), which channel investible funds to those industries with the highest Schumpeterian profits have played an important role in the closed economy version of our model since they were the basis for our analysis of a potential conflict between alleviating potential demand failures and the speed of structural change in a capitalist economy. In the current context of an open economy, endogenous investment expenditure plays similarly an important role in determining the speed by which changes in international specialisation and hence in trade patterns takes place between mature and catching-up economies. We will return to this issue extensively when discussing the results from our simulations in section 9.4 of the paper.

9.3 CATCHING-UP AND GLOBAL EFFECTIVE DEMAND

Figures 9.3a and 9.3b show the great boost which trade gives to catching-up economies. We can see that in the *scenario without trade* there is some catching-up by economy B due to its faster productivity growth which leads to faster domestic demand growth than in economy *A*; but, given that output growth is entirely dependent upon the evolution of domestic demand, the catching-up process proceeds at a very slow pace. *The opening-up of trade* (in this scenario we assumed nominal import shares of each country in the other's final demand market of 25 per cent) speeds up the catching-up process dramatically; it is complete after about 30 years.[5]

The mechanism through which this dramatic expansion takes place is the relative rate of growth in the volume of exports (see Figure 9.4a); the catching-up economy gains rapidly market shares in volume terms as a result of its superior unit-cost performance (faster productivity growth is not fully compensated by wage rate increases, although the wage catch-up parameters h_i are assumed to be the same in the two economies). The results are dramatic deficits in the trade balance by country *A* (see Figure 9.4b where the volume movements of aggregate exports are shown). Over time, however, the catching-up economy's price competitiveness gets eroded as wage rates catch up with productivity growth and/or exchange rates adjust[6] and no further longer-term differential in the productivity growth of the two economies is assumed (after catching-up has been accomplished). It is then that both economies converge to the same growth trend with stable shares in each other's markets.

As regards the global levels of activity and global unemployment, the basic pattern is the one encountered in the closed economy version of the model: the impact of a 'productivity shock' gives rise to the possibility of higher potential output growth, but whether and to what extent higher

Figure 9.3a Without trade

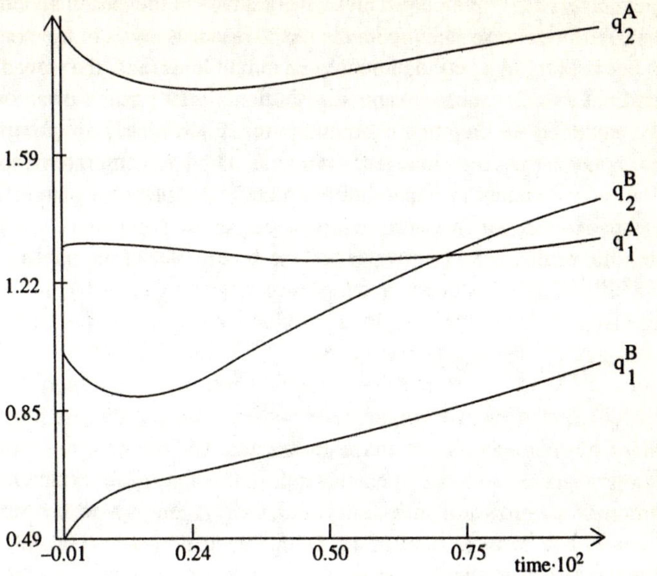

Figure 9.3b With trade

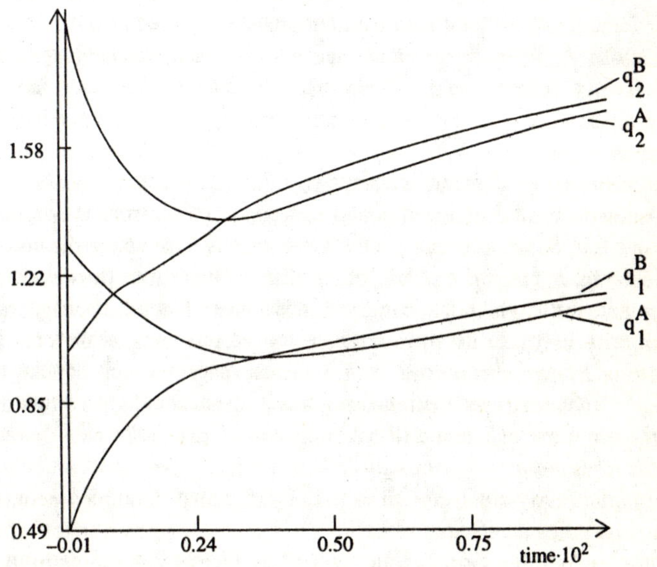

Figure 9.3 Output movements of A's and B's industries without (Fig. 9.3a) and with (Fig. 9.3b) trade

activity and employment levels are actually attained depends upon the impact which the redistribution of income (lower wage share, higher Schumpeterian profit share) has upon expenditure levels. As was discussed in our previous paper, the possibility of a period of depressed output level in which structural adjustment (of both production and distributional structures) takes place cannot be excluded. In the open economy case, structural adjustment does not only involve national expenditure to potential output matching but also to international adjustments in expenditure structures. Figures 9.4a and 9.4b refer to a scenario in which global levels of output are following a similar path with and without trade; however, in the trade case, there has been a major redistribution of production activity from the mature to the catching-up economy. This redistribution of global production activity has a positive impact on global unemployment (compare Figures 9.5a and 9.5b) as productivity levels are lower in the catching-up economy *B* (even though its rates of productivity growth are higher) and hence the same global output can be produced by more people; furthermore, because of the improving price-competitiveness of the labour-intensive industry (industry 2 experiences higher productivity growth than industry 1 globally) there is also a positive substitution effect towards the more labour-intensive industry. At the national level, however, the reallocation of production (and, as we will see later on, the increasing specialization of country *A* towards the less labour-intensive industry 1) leads to a terrible *jobs crisis in country A* which exceeds the closed-economy 'structural adjustment crisis' discussed in our previous paper. Country *B*, on the other hand, can rely on a fast expansion of world demand for its products and a specialisation towards the more labour-intensive sector which alleviates the unemployment problem compared to the closed-economy case.

Let us sum up the comparison between the closed- and open-economy situations: Already in the closed economy version of our model, we have pointed out that Schumpeterian profits are a means to speed up structural change; they lead to the direct allocation of investible funds towards those industries and firms which achieve the fastest rates of productivity growth (and commercially successful product developmens); however, the emergence of Schumpeterian profits and the uneveness of their appearance across the different parts of the industrial landscape also causes a change in the overall structure of income distribution and of expenditures. We have pointed out that these changes might lead to a shortfall between actual and potential output and output growth in periods in which rapid technological and industrial adjustment takes place.

This issue gets further complicated when the international dimension of uneven productivity growth is considered: In this case, economies not only

Figure 9.4a Total exports

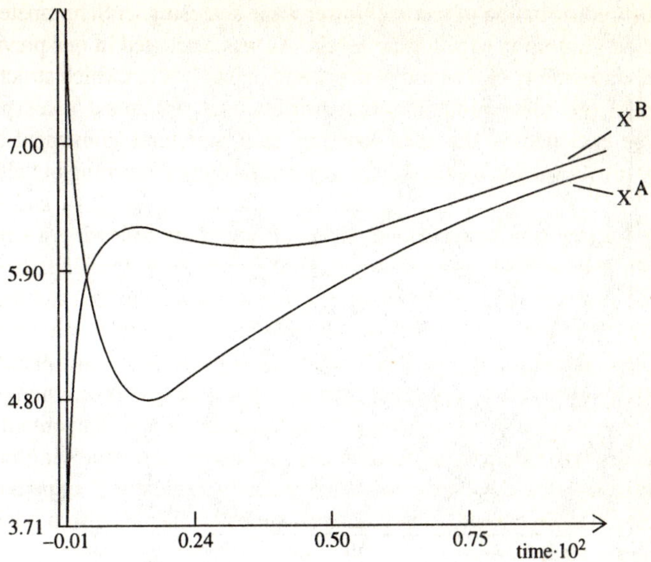

Figure 9.4b Industry exports

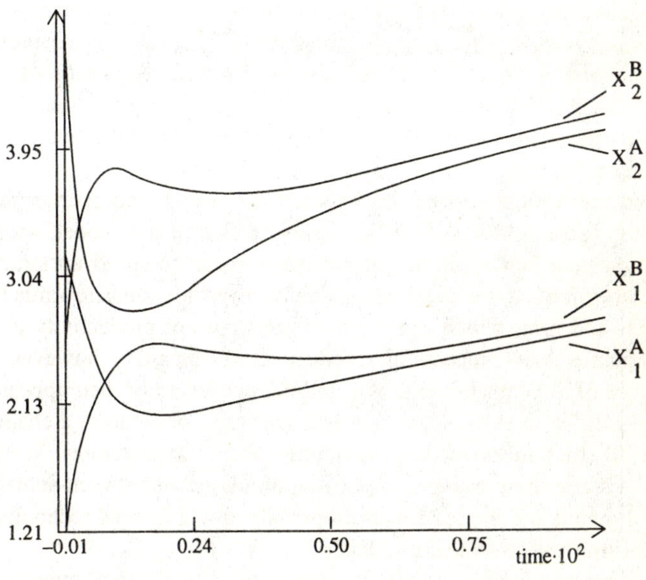

Figure 9.4 Export (volume) movements in countries A and B

Figure 9.5a Without trade

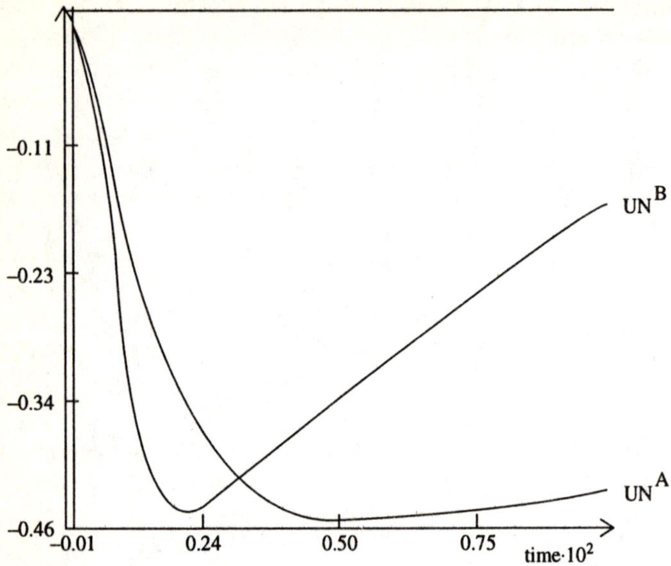

Figure 9.5b With trade

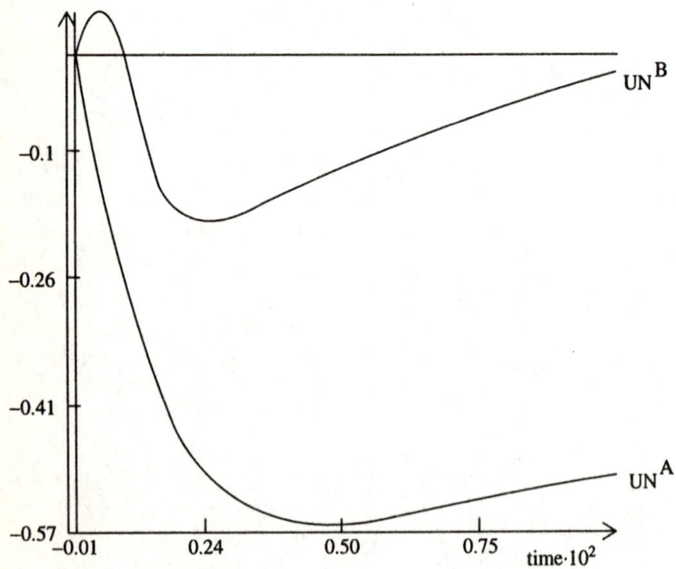

Figure 9.5 Unemployment rates in countries A and B without (Fig. 5a) and with (Fig. 5b) trade

have to consider the potential mismatch between the structure of domestic potential output and domestic expenditure, but activity and employment levels become dependent upon global expenditure patterns. The fact that catching-up takes place for a group of developing economies, means that shares in global production will shift to these economies. It will, furthermore, shift differentially depending upon the evolution of dynamic comparative advantage. The dynamics of comparative advantage (as has – realistically, we believe – been assumed in this paper) is such that productivity gaps will be closed more easily – at first – in the more labour-intensive industries, which (by assumption) are also the industries in which the rates of labour productivity growth are the highest. Mature economies are thus under a double pressure of structural adjustment: from the impact of the productivity-enhancing logistic internally and from the pressure which international competition from catching-up economies exerts upon the more labour-intensive branches.

Another important difference between the closed and open economy cases lies in the efficacy (and thus likelihood of use) of the different control variables which helped, in the closed economy case, to regain a new long-run equilibrium in the potential output and expenditure patterns. In the closed economy case we saw that

(i) an increase in the wage catch-up parameters h_i;
(ii) a reduction in the whimp factor j_i and hence a fuller utilization of Schumpeterian profits for industry-specific investment; and
(iii) a faster adjustment of prices to unit costs through an increase in f_i

all assisted in reducing the potential for an effective demand failure. However, we also saw that using control variables (i) and (iii) reduced the speed of structural adjustment towards the higher productivity sectors.

In the open economy case, the issue is more complicated: There are two sets of parameters, those of country *A* and those of country *B* and the use of these two sets of control variables will have a different impact on levels of activity and employment in countries *A* and *B* respectively. In the next section we will explore this issue in detail.

9.4 THE GLOBAL DEFLATIONARY BIAS AND REASONS FOR NON-COOPERATION

From a global perspective we have shown, in section 9.2 (para. 3), that trade can improve the global growth and employment prospects. In this section we shall show, *firstly*, that the joint use of control variables (i), (ii) and (iii) (see above) by both sets of countries would alleviate the danger for potential effective demand failure at a global level just as it did in the closed economy case for the single economy. However, we shall also, *secondly*, show that in the open-economy case there will not be the same incentive to use the different control variables at the national level in the same way as in the closed-economy case. *Thirdly*, there might, from a national development perspective also be an incentive to resist the coordinated use of the control variables in a way which would alleviate the danger of global deflation. We shall address these issues by reporting the results of sensitivity exercises with respect to the independent use of the control variables h_i^c, j_i^c, f_i^c (where superscript C refers to the country index $C = A,B$).

Let us address the *first issue* above: The joint use (by the mature and catching-up economies) of instruments (i) to (iii) does indeed, as in the closed economy case, have the impact of alleviating the dangers of effective demand failures. Figures 9.6a–c show the impact of joint proportionate increase of control variables h_i (the wage catch-up parameters), of reductions in the 'whimp factors' j_i (or, correspondingly, an increase in $1-j_i$, the propensities to invest out of Schumpeterian profits), and of increases in the price adjustment parameters f_i (which lead to a quicker passing on of the benefits

Figure 9.6a Increase in wage catch-up parameters f_i^c

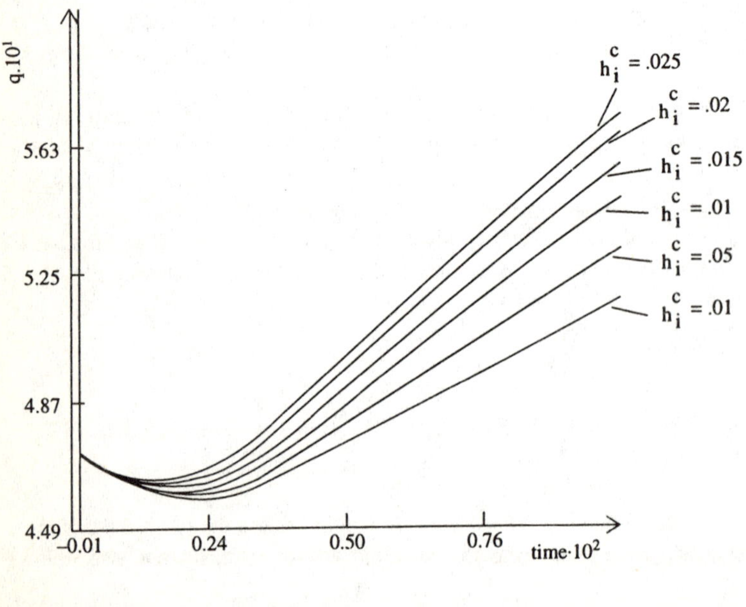

Figure 9.6b Reductions in 'whimp' factor j_i^c

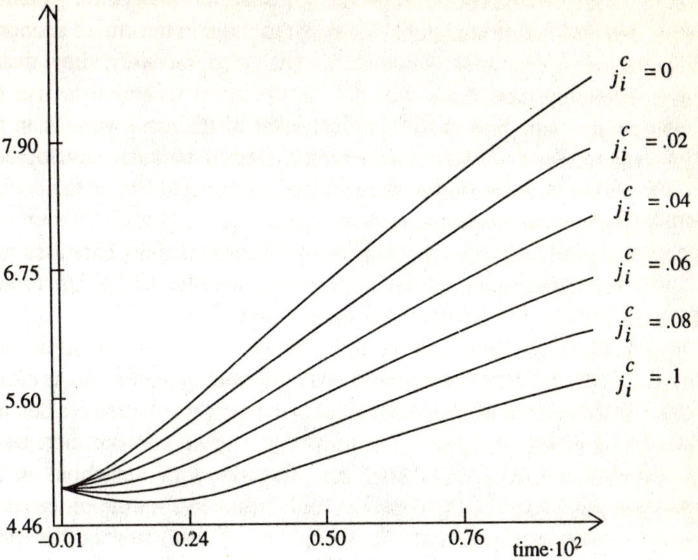

Figure 9.6c Increase in price-unit cost adjustment f_i^c

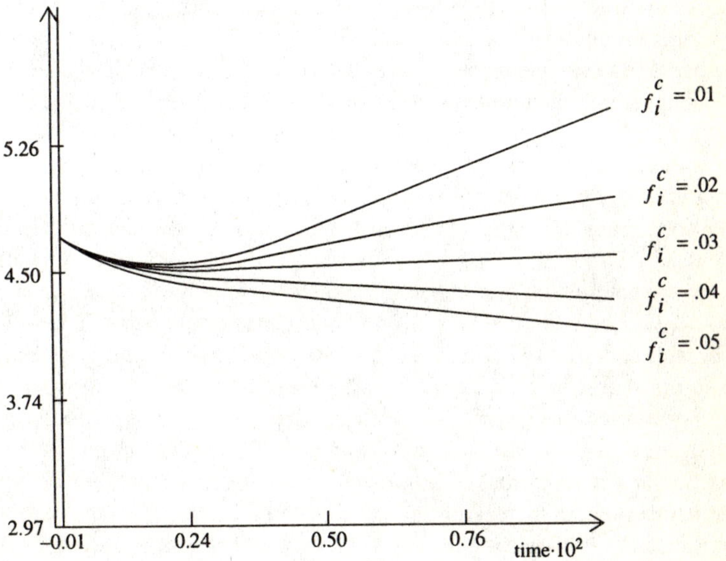

Figure 9.6 Joint changes in control parameters – impact on global output (q)

of productivity advances to consumers). We can see that the joint use by both sets of countries of these control variables has a beneficial effect on global output q, just as they did in the closed-economy case. The structural impact of the joint use of these instruments will be discussed below, when addressing issue three above.

Concerning *issue two* above, which refers to the two countries' independent use of the instruments, we would like to first recapitulate what the principal cause was of the potential effective demand failure in the closed-economy case, following the impact of a logistic pattern of differential (labour) productivity growth. There we argued that fast productivity growth will go along with the appearance of Schumpeterian profits and hence with a redistribution of national income from wages to profits. This *redistribution has a negative and a positive implication*: positive is that it allows a faster targeting of demand structures towards the high productivity growth industries since Schumpeterian profits arise particularly in those industries in which productivity growth is highest; these Schumpeterian profits can then feed directly into industry-specific investments which could then lead to further (endogenous) productivity growth and product development. Spending out of wages, on the other hand, will only gradually be redirected towards higher productivity growth industries depending on the evolution of relative prices and the strength of substitution effects. The negative side of macroeconomic distribution towards profits is that spending out of profits is (in a Keynesian fashion) a rather unstable component of overall spending; we have introduced the 'whimp' factor into our investment equations to account for this. Thus while redistribution of income might have no impact on the aggregate level of economic activity if the whimp factor were very low, one cannot automatically count on it. The redistribution of income which accompanies the appearance of Schumpeterian profits thus bears a 'potential' for effective demand failures.[7]

In the open-economy scenario, the direct link between domestic levels of activity and the use of policy instruments to alleviate the effective demand constraint is somewhat broken since not only the level of but also the shares in global demand which different national producers are able to attract are relevant. These shares depend upon competitiveness in cost, but also in product development. The contribution which a particular economy makes to alleviate the potential instability of gobal demand, such as increasing the control variables h_i (the wage catch-up parameters) or increasing the speed of price adjustment by increasing the f_i, might – as we will show – have a detrimental effect on the country's overall competitiveness and/or might have undesirable consequences for the country's speed of industrial specialisation. Only reductions in the control variables j_i do not conflict with either competitiveness or targets for industrial specialization (towards the high productivity growth industry); however, the possibility that the behavioural parameter j_i would be greater than zero was at the basis of potential demand failures in the first place.

Figures 9.7a, b and 9.8a, b show respectively the impact of the asymmetric use of control variables h_i^c, j_i^c ($c = A,B$) in countries A and B upon the activity levels in both countries. The impact of the independent use of control variables f_i^c will be discussed in terms of the impact this has on industrial specialization patterns when addressing issue three above.

We can see that the asymmetric increase of the wage catch-up parameters h_i uniformly benefits the other country's economy and is detrimental to one's own country (here the size of the countries is important in the initial phase; see n. 5). An increase in the propensity to invest out of Schumpeterian profits benefits the own economy both structurally and in terms of the overall level of activity. This would, of course, indicate that it would be a good policy, from an individual country's point-of view, not to allow Schumpeterian profits to be dwindled away through fast price adjustments or quick wage catch-up.

Finally, we want to address *issue three* whether the joint or independent use of contral variables h_i^c, j_i^c, f_i^c ($c = A,B$) has desirable or undesirable consequences for the pattern for industrial specialisation. We shall discuss this question without overloading the paper with further graphs and will just report the rather robust results from sensitivity analyses. We shall also address the issue of desirable or undesirable effects on industrial specialisation from the point of view of only one economy, the catching-up economy, since if it is possible to show that cooperation is of no interest to one of the partners, then overall coordination becomes very difficult. The results of the analysis of the impact of variations of control parameters h_i^c, j_i^c, f_i^c ($c = A,B$) on industrial specialization are summarized in Table 9.2.

We can see that the independent increase of the wage catch-up parameter h_i^B by country B is detrimental for the speed of its catch-up in the high-productivity growth industry, and the same is true for an increase of the price-cost adjustment parameter f_i^B. The reason is, of, course that both of these two factors diminish the possibility of country B to reap high Schumpeterian profits in the high productivity growth industry. What is even more interesting is that even the joint increase in parameters h_i^c in both countries ($c = A$ and B) has the same effect. The reason for this is that country B, being the country with the higher overall productivity growth would loose out more on Schumpeterian profits than country *A* and hence on the contribution which these profits make to channelling investments speedily into the fast productivity growth industry. Hence country *B* has, relative to country *A*, more to loose if it either agrees on a joint faster distribution of technological rents to the employees or to the international consumers by quickly adjusting prices to unit costs. An increase in the propensities to invest $(1 - j_i^c)$ in both countries would be of benefit for *B's* fast catching-up in the high productivity growth industry since it attains higher rents in the first place and hence a greater targeted spending out of these rents will benefit the speedy upward mobility of country B in the international division of labour.

Figure 9.7a In country A

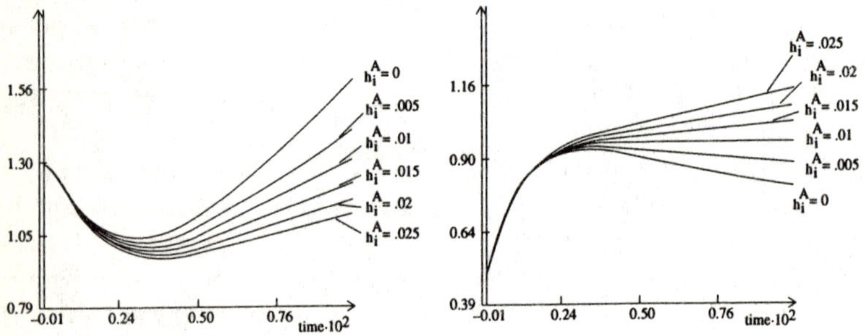

Figure 9.7b In country B

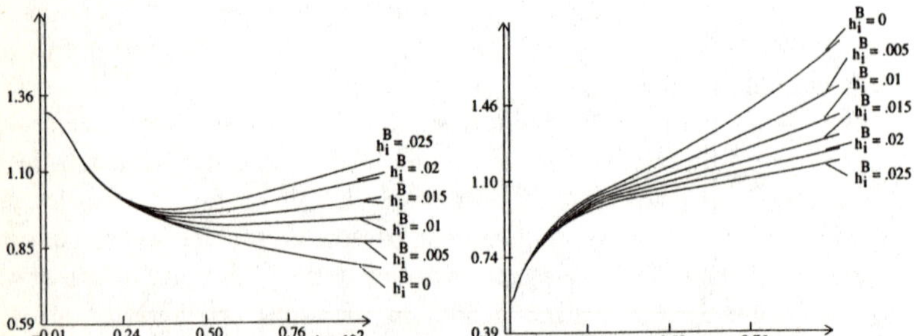

Figure 9.7 Asymmetric increase of wage catch-up parameter h_i^c

Figure 9.8a Reduction of j_i^A

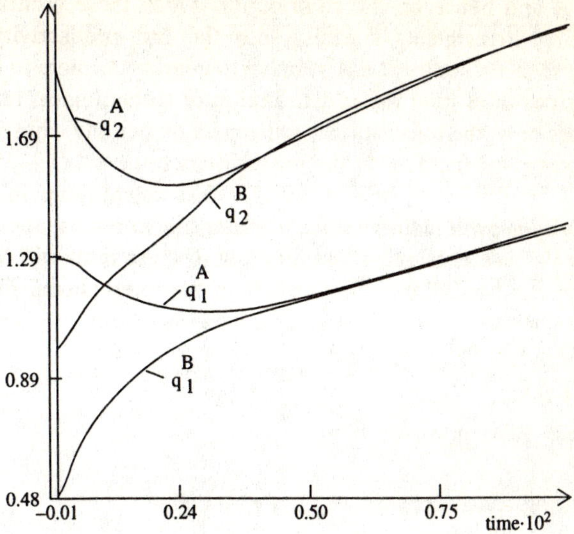

Figure 9.8b Reduction of j_i^B

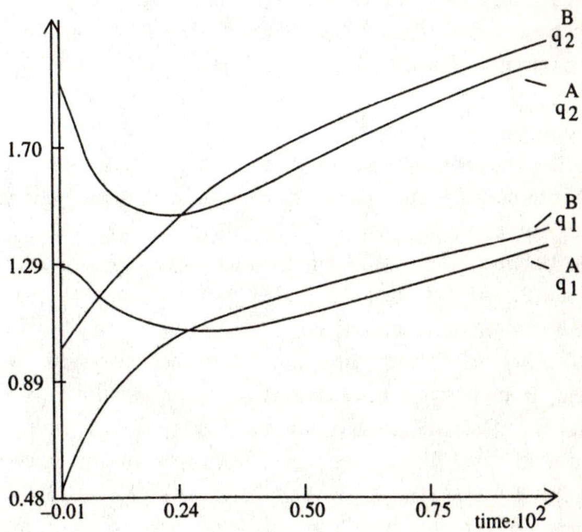

Figure 9.8 Asymmetric reductions (to zero) of 'whimp' factors j_i^c on A's and B's industrial output

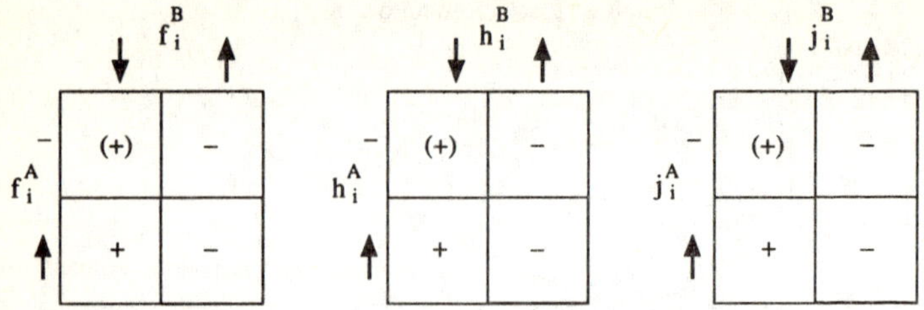

Figure 9.9 Impact of independent or joint use of control parameters h_i^c, j_i^c, f_i^c $(c = A, B)$ on the speed of country *B's* catch-up/specialization in the high productivity-growth industry

Notes: ↑ ↓ – means, respectively, an increase, decrease, no change in the control parameter; + (–) indicates a faster (lower) speed in country B's catch-up/specialization in the high productivity growth industry.

9.5 CONCLUSIONS

The following conclusions can be drawn from Figure 9.9:

The numerical analysis of a model which distinguishes two countries (a catching-up economy *B* and a mature economy *A*) has shown that the results concerning the impact of a productivity-enhancing logistic on the macro- and structural dynamics of an economy are substantially affected by whether we are considering the case of a closed or open economy. The central theme of a trade-off between the speed of structural change vs. various means to alleviate the potential for effective demand failures which emerged from our previous analysis of the closed economy case (Landesmann and Goodwin, 1994) reappears in a modified form at the international level:

Here it is the speed by which redistribution of production activity and new patterns of international specialisation takes place between the mature and the catching-up economy which takes the place of national structural reallocation between low- and high-productivity growth industries in the closed economy context. Just as in the closed economy case, structural adjustment leads to the emergence of Schumpeterian profits which, on the one hand, allow a faster targeting of higher productivity (product development) branches but, on the other hand, bring with it an increase in the potential for effective demand failures. This potential could be reduced by rather quickly distributing the gains from fast productivity growth to consumers (high f_i s) and/or to workers (high h_i s). In the closed economy context, these instruments would not only be effective but could also be beneficial for raising the national level of economic activity and employment. In the international context, our analysis showed that the use of these instruments, while being effective to reduce the danger of effective demand failures at the (aggregate) global level, they could be counterproductive from a national economic development point of view.

In the first instance, this would be the case for the catching-up economy (being a smaller economy initially) which depends to a large extent upon the world market for the demand of its products and hence benefits more from a fast expansion of its market shares in international markets (the markets of the mature economies) than from assuring that real income growth keeps immediate pace with potential output growth domestically. Furthermore, country B has an interest to move rather quickly towards a higher overall productivity growth trajectory by speeding up the process of change in the international division of labour and accounting for a higher share of world output in the high-productivity growth industries. This requires high Schumpeterian profits and the targeted investment of these profits in the high productivity (and product development) industries. The use of the instruments of faster wage catch-up or quick adjustment of prices to unit costs which, in the closed-economy context, were working towards alleviating the dangers of effective demand failures, would thus be counter-productive from country *B*'s development point-of-view even if it was done in a coordinated manner at the global level (see the discussion in the last part of section 9.4).

In response, also the mature economies (country *A*) have to pursue a similar strategy in order to avoid losing rapidly market shares in high productivity growth areas both in domestic and export markets and this, similarly, requires targeted investment out of Schumpeterian rents and hence the maintenance of Schumpeterian profits (low h_i s and f_i s). The outcome from the non-cooperative situation is a bias in both types of economies towards high speed of structural change in the trade-off discussed above; the result of this is a *global deflationary bias*.

Over time, just as in the case of the closed economy, there are a number of reasons why that bias will disappear:

- the global logistic peters out which caused the emergence of Schumpeterian profits and the uneven productivity growth within and across the countries leading to the requirement of adjustment in patterns patterns both globally and nationally;
- the productivity gap between country A and country B will be closed and, allowing for a full long-run recouping of productivity growth by wages, no further changes in price competitiveness will take place; and, consequently, no further changes in volume shares of international production;

– whatever has not been recouped in higher wages will lead to exchange rate adjustments.

NOTES

1. Henceforth, we shall refer to productivity growth as a short-hand to include both productivity (process technology) growth and product development.
2. A large literature has developed around the issue of technological competition and the emergence of technological rents (see, e.g. Dasgupta and Stiglitz, 1980, Katz and Shapiro, 1986, Aghion and Howitt, 1992).
3. As András Simonovits pointed out to us, the implied substitution elasticities in this constant nominal shares specification are the ones which would be obtained from a Cobb–Douglas formulation of expenditure decisions.
4. The analysis in this paper will focus on investment expenditure out of Schumpeterian profits (component I^{β}), neglecting for the most part the autonomous (or *ex ante*) innovational investment expenditure (component I^{α}). The latter, however, is important in an analysis of the role which forward financing either by banks or the government can play in a development process.

   At this point we might also mention that the interindustry intermediate demand is, for the sake of simplification, assumed to be entirely satisfied from domestic sources.
5. We have undertaken a variety of sensitivity analyses concerning the influence which the relative size of the countries has upon the catching-up process; for shortage of space we will not report these results; they are available upon request from the authors.
6. We have also used the model to analyse exchange rate adjustments in the wake of uneven global growth. Because of shortage of space, we are again unable here to report on the results from the endogenous exchange rate simulations.
7. In our previous paper we mentioned that the original empirical motivation behind the setting-up of the model was to try to account for the experience in OECD economies in the 1980s when there was, by many accounts, a strong expansion of technological opportunities and, nonetheless, the levels of overall economic activity and, of course, employment levels were rather depressed.

REFERENCES

AGHION, P. and P. HOWITT (1992) 'A Model of Growth through Creative Destruction', *Econometrica*, vol. 60, 323–51.

BRÓDY, A. (1983) 'About Investment Cycles and their Attenuation', *Acta Oeconomica*, vol. 31, 37–51.

BRÓDY, A. (1989) 'Growth Cycles in Economics', in J. Casti and A. Karlqvist (eds), *Newton to Aristotle, Towards a Theory of Models for Living Systems*, Springer-Verlag, New York.

BRÓDY, A. (1990) 'Observations Concerning the Growth Cycle', in K. Vellupillai (ed.), *Nonlinear and Multisectoral Macrodynamics*, Macmillan, London.

BRÓDY, A. (1992) 'On Measuring Growth', *Structural Change and Economic Dynamics*, vol. 3, 93–102.

DASGUPTA, P. and J. STIGLITZ (1980) 'Industrial Structure and the Nature of Innovative Activity', *Economic Journal*, vol. 90, 266–93

KATZ, M. and C. SHAPIRO (1986) 'Technology Adoption in the Presence of Network Externalities', *Journal of Political Economy*, vol. 94, 822–41.

LANDESMANN, M. and R. GOODWIN (1994) 'Productivity Growth, Structural Change and Macroeconomic Stability', in L. Pasinetti and R. Solow (eds), *Economic Growth and the Structure of Long-Term Development*, Macmillan, London.

ROSENBERG, N. (1976) 'On Technological Expectations', *Economic Journal*, vol. 86, 523–35.

WOOD, A. (1994) *North–South Trade, Employment and Inequality*, Clarendon Press, Oxford.

10 Complex Dynamics in Control Models with Bounds: A Review

András Simonovits

10.1 INTRODUCTION[1]

The present paper deals with one of Bródy's major topics: the question of growth cycles. Since he discovered cycles in the Hungarian economy (Bródy, 1969), he has used several models to describe them. Bródy (1992; original draft, 1972) was the first model which applied Frisch's (1993) simplified idea to the modelling of socialist investment cycles which was one of the building block of Bauer's (1978) theory. In 1973 he used a variant of Kornai and Martos's (1973) stock-signal control model (Bródy, 1981). Bródy (1983) returned to Bauer's theory and successfully popularized it. In Bródy and Farkas (1987) and Bródy (1989), Goodwin's (1967) ideas on Lotka and Volterra's cycles were developed. The reader will also meet his ideas in this paper but in modified forms.

The present paper reviews several discrete-time control models with bounded control: the state space equations and the planned feedback equations are linear (unbounded) but the plans are restricted by lower and upper control bounds. Such models were considered in different contexts by several authors. The main issue of those models was the following: What is the relation between the stability properties of the *free* and the *constrained* models?

Historically, it was Hicks (1950) who first compared free and constrained systems: he considered an unstable free system, describing a Keynesian investment cycle and imposed floor on investment and ceiling on employment. He claimed the existence of a *cycle*, to which the system jumps after the first meeting with any of the bounds. A special feature of this cycle is that it is independent of the initial conditions, i.e. it is a *limit cycle*. Hommes (1991, Chapter 4) and Hommes (1993) showed that, in addition to limit cycles, quasi-cyclic and chaotic systems occur in Hicks' model. In a witty paper Blatt (1978) showed how the usual econometric practice transforms this determinstic nonlinear model into a stochastic linear one.

The next comparison is due to Uzawa (1958), who examined the Walrasian price adjustment process with zero lower bound. He deduced the stability of the constrained system from the stability of the free system under the assumption of sufficiently weak feedbacks.[2]

I gave a more general formulation of the problem (Simonovits, 1981). General theorems on preserving and losing stability were proved and the terms *superstability* and *destabilizability* were introduced respectively. Two special cases illustrated the general definitions and theorems: (i) A stock-signal control (S) and (ii) an order-signal control (O), whose original versions were discussed by Kornai and Simonovits (1977, 1981a) and Kornai and Simonovits (1981b).[3] The S model is superstable for all weak and some (all?) strong reactions and the O model is destabilizable for certain (if not all) reactions.

A year before the publication of Simonovits (1981), Honkapohja and Ito (1980) considered a piecewise linear non-walrasian macro model with inventory dynamics and perfect foresight (rational expectations). In their one-dimensional E_1 model it was easy to prove that the introduction of nonlinearities does not destroy stability. Moreover, they did not ask: what happens globally if the system is locally stable (Hommes, 1991, Chapter 2B)?

Revising their model, I replaced perfect foresight by naive expectations (Note that Lovell, 1962, modelled both types of expectations in a related multi-sectoral model, foreshadowing also the models of Kornai and Martos (eds), 1981, and Simonovits, 1979.) I proved a special superstability theorem for the two-dimensional E_2 model (Simonovits, 1982): any stable free E_2 system yields stable constrained system (with constant bounds). I also risked the following conjecture: (almost) any unstable free E_2 system yields a *chaotic* constrained system (with constant bounds). Hommes and Nusse (1989), Hommes (1991, Chapter 2A) and (1992) discovered that the conjecture is *not* true: while chaos arises for a large set of parameter vectors, limit cycles (and quasi-cycles) develop for another large set of parameter vectors.

This refutation of my conjecture led me to consider a constrained version (I) of the linear model of socialist investment cycles (Simonovits, 1991a). (That model is a simplification of Kornai, 1982, and Lackó, 1980, see also Bauer, 1978, and Bródy, 1983.) Choosing the most important special case, it was possible to determine the characteristics of a four-phase limit cycle for a set of parameter vectors (Simonovits, 1991b). Further, Hommes, et al. (1995) showed that the model can also produce quasi-cycles and chaotic paths, moreover, co-existence of different attractors also occurs.

Table 10.1 Stability and other relations in five models

Free system	Constrained system: Stable	Constrained system: Unstable (cyclic = P, quasi-cyclic = QP, chaotic = C)
Stable	Uzawa	
	S	O: C
	E_2	I: C
	H	
Unstable		H: P, QP, (C)
		E_2: P, QP, C
		I: P, QP, C

Table 10.1 displays the relation of stability for the foregoing models.

Some words on related studies will be helpful. Issues of piecewise linear systems in continuous time were studied by different authors: Kondor (1981) demonstrated that a mild restriction on the demand function guarantees that a locally stable free system yields locally stable constrained system. Honkapohja and Ito (1983) showed that the 'union' of two stable linear systems may yield an unstable system.

With the emergence of the Theory of Chaos (e.g. Li and Yorke, 1975) limit cycles with discrete time have come to the fore. We list some papers: Cugno and Montrucchio (1984) analyzing the business cycle model of Goodwin (1967), Grandmont (1985) studying an optimization model of overlapping generations, Boldrin and Woodford (1990) reviewing optimal growth models.

The paper is a review, therefore the explanations are sketchy. (For a more detailed review with many figures, see Simonovits, 1992.) I still hope that the paper is self-contained, but consultation of the reviewed papers will undoubtedly much help the reader. Similarly to many old-fashioned macromodels, none of the reviewed models is based on optimization. Orthodox economists may not like these models, but it would be premature to reject them out-of-hand.

The order of presentation is based on logic rather than on history. Section 10.2 presents the *family* of models with bounded controls. Section 10.3 discusses *regular* models: stock-signal control, order-signal control and investment limit cycles and chaos in a socialist economy. Section 10.4 analyzes *irregular* models: Hicks' trade cycle model and a disequilibrium model of inventory control with expectation. Section 10.5 contains the *conclusions*.

10.2 A FAMILY OF CONTROL MODELS

In this paper a family of control models will be considered.

Notations

Time is discrete. Time index t is generally suppressed, lagged variable $x(t-1)$ is denoted by x_{-1}. A time series $x(1)$, $x(2)$, ... is denoted by $x_{(1)}, x_{(2)}, \ldots$

The arrays of an N-vector x are denoted by $x_1, \ldots, x_N$.
x = N-vector of state variables,
u = N-vector of control variables,
$\langle q \rangle$ = time-invariant diagonal matrix of order N,
R = time-invariant non-singular $N \times N$ matrix,
h = time-invariant N-vector,
u^m = N-vector of lower bounds on control variables,
u^M = n-vector of upper bounds on control variables.
The bounds may be time-invariant as well as time-variant.

Equations

State space equations

$$x = \langle q \rangle x_{-1} + Ru + h$$

our system of state spaca equations is simpler than usual, since for our purposes we can restrict the analysis to diagonal qs and *sguare Rs*

Planned control

$$u^p = u^* - Fx_{-1} \qquad (2.2p)$$

where u^* is the *maximal control* belonging to $x_{-1} = 0$ and F is the feedback-matrix.

Actual control

$$u_j = \begin{cases} u_j^m \text{ if } u_j^p < u_j^m \\ u_j^p \text{ if } u_j^m \leq u_j^p \leq u_j^M \\ u_j^M \text{ if } u_j^p > u_j^M \end{cases} \qquad j = 1, \ldots, N \qquad (2.2a)$$

In words: if the planned value of the jth control variable is below (above) the jth lower (upper) bound, then the jth actual control will be equal to the corresponding bound. If the planned value of the jth control variable is between the jth lower and upper bounds, then the jth actual control will be equal to the planned value.

Basic equations

Substituting (2.2) into (2.1) we get a more concise system of equations, to be called *basic equations.*

$$x = f(x_{-1}) \tag{2.3}$$

where $f(x_{-1}) = \langle q \rangle x_{-1} + Ru(x_{-1}) + h$ and $u(x_{-1})$ is a piecewise linear function in (2.2).

Equilibrium (or Normal) Path[4]

In any dynamical system the equilibrium path plays a distinguished role.

Definition. *An equilibrium (or normal) path* (steady state) of (2.1) – (2.2) is a point which reproduces itself:

$$\text{If} \quad (x_{(-1)}, u_{(-1)}) = (x^0, u^0), \text{ then } (x, u) = (x^0, u^0) \tag{2.4}$$

To avoid degenerate cases[5] we shall apply the following *assumption:* $u^m < u^0 < u^M$.

Remark. It is easy to see that this assumption ensures that (x^0, u^0) is also an equilibrium path of the linear system (2.1) – (2.2p). It is given by

$$x^0 = (I - \langle q \rangle + RF)^{-1}(Ru^* + h) \quad \text{and} \quad u^0 = u^* - Fx^0 \tag{2.5}$$

Stability, Cycles and Chaos

To consider the relation of the stability properties of free and constrained systems, we shall need some lemmas and definitions, (for details, see Devaney, 1989).

The qualitative behaviour of the free system (or what is the same, the local behaviour of the constrained system) is determined by the characteristic polynomial $\langle q \rangle - RF$. Defining the spectral radius of a square matrix as the maximum of moduli of all characteristic roots, we have

Lemma 2.1. *(i) The free system is stable if and only if the spectral radius of* $I - \langle q \rangle + RF$ *islessthanunity.*

(ii) The free system oscillates if its characteristic polynomial has a pair of complex roots.

Definitions. 1. A linear stable system (2.1) – (2.2p) is *superstable* if after the imposition of any control bounds (u^m, u^M) the non-linear system (2.1)–(2.2) remains stable.

2. A linear stable system (2.1) – (2.2p) can be *destabilized* if after the imposition of certain control bounds (u^m, u^M) the non-linear system (2.1) – (2.2) becomes unstable (i.e. it is not superstable).

The following definition captures the *return* property of a cyclic path:

Definition. Let $x \epsilon R^n$ and $x = f(x_{-1})$. The system *f has a cycle* $x_{(1)}, x_{(2)}, ..., x_{(T)}$ with *period T*, if $x_{(t+1)} = f(x_{(t)}), t = 1, 2, ..., T$, and $x_{(T+1)} = x_{(1)}$.

Remarks. 1. In case of several periods, we shall only consider the minimal period. Then $x_{(q)}/x_{(r)}$ for $1 \leq q < r \leq T$.

2. The mathematical definition of the cycle is much narrower than is usual in verbal economics. We shall return to this problem at the end of this section.

3. As was mentioned in the Introduction, the issue of stability (or instability) of the cycle is more important than that of existence. This is addressed in the following

Definition. The cycle $x_{(1)}, x_{(2)}, ..., x_{(T)}$ of the system $x = f(x_{-1})$ is a *limit cycle*, if any initial state $y_{(1)}$ close enough to $x_{(1)}$ generates a *y*-path, which converges to the cycle: $\lim_m y_{(mT+r)} = x_{(r)}$, where *m* and *r* are integers, $0 < r \leq T$.

Remarks. As usual, we defined a locally stable cycle. If we want to stress that any initial state (except for few initial states, like the stationary state) can be considered, we use the adjective *global.*

To obtain a criterion for the existence of a limit cycle, we introduce the following notations for the interations of the function f:

$$f^1(x) = f(x), \ldots, f^t(x) = f(f^{t-1}(x)), \quad t = 2, 3, \ldots.$$

It is easy to see that $x_{(1)}, x_{(2)}, ..., x_{(T)}$ is a cycle of $x = f(x_{-1})$ with period *T* if and only if $x_{(1)}$ is a fixed point of $z = f^T(z_{-1})$: $x_{(1)} = f^T(x_{(1)})$. Relying on the well-known local stability condition of a fixed point, one obtains

Lemma 2.2. *The cycle* $x_{(1)}, x_{(2)}, ..., x_{(T)}$ of the system $x = f(x_{-1})$ *is a limit cycle if*

$$H(Df^T(x_{(1)})) < 1$$

holds, where H is the spectral radius of the Jacobian Df^T.

Remarks. 1. Economists define cycles by the triple of recurrence, reinforcement and regularity. *Recurrence* means that the phases of expansion and contraction follow each other. *Reinforcement* means that each phase produces the conditions which usher in the next phase of the cycle'. *Regularity* means that 'successive cycles ought to resemble each other'. Note that *periodicity* (replication) cannot be required from real cycles (see further Ickes, 1986, p. 43).

2. Some cycles are unions of several 'smaller cycles', and the latter are similar, their 'periods' may differ only by unity. In these cases we shall speak of *composite cycles.*

3. Very often the path is *aperiodic*, i.e. it never returns to any earlier state. Aperiodic paths are diverse.

Definitions. 1. A *path* is *quasi-cyclic*, if it is similar[6] to a circle-rotation with an irrational rotation number.

2. A dynamic system f is *topologically chaotic* (in the sense of Li and Yorke, 1975) if (i) there exist infinitely many cycles with different periods, (ii) there exists an uncountable set of aperiodic paths and (iii) none of the aperiodic paths stay close to cycles for ever.

3. A dynamic system f is *ergodically chaotic* (in the sense of Guckenheimer, 1979) if it has *sensitive dependence on initial values* with a positive probability.

(a) A dynamic system displays *primitive chaos* if its attractor (determining its long run behavior) is connected.

(b) A dynamic system f displays *chaos of period p* if the p-iterated dynamic system f^p displays primitive chaos.

Remarks. 1. Note that a topologically chaotic system may have an *almost globally stable* limit cycle (i.e. with probability 1 the initial states generate one limit cycle). Note however, that with positive probability the initial states generate *transient chaos.*[7] It is the ergodically chaotic systems which behave really wildly. This means that Laplacian determinism (i.e. the initial state determines the entire path) does not apply to such a system, notwithstanding the extreme simplicity and the low degree of freedom of the system.

This strange behaviour is obvious for primitive chaos, but indeterminacy may be weaker for cyclic chaos, where it is at least known that the system jumps from the connected set A_q to another connected set A_{q+1} asymptotically, $q = 1,2, ..., p$, where $A_{p+1} = A_1$ (Hommes, 1992).

2. It is possible that the range of the variable is so narrow that the qualitatively erratic dynamics can quantitatively be conceived as an equilibrium position. In these cases the mathematical tools are too sharp to be used in economics.

Analysis of Complex Dynamics in the Plane

The analysis of complex dynamics is much more difficult than the stability analysis of equilibrium and cycle. Most of the economic papers on chaos simply rely on the well-known properties of the one-dimensional, unimodal smooth maps. The models or their simplest variants to be studied in this paper, however, have two basic variables ($N = 2$), therefore their analyses have to apply more sophisticated tools.

A basic analytical tool is the *return map* which can loosely be defined as follows: Consider for example those t , s where $u_{1(t)} = u^M{}_1$ and select two consecutive t s with that property: t' and t''. Denote J the range of $x_{2(t')}$ for all feasible initial states $x_{(-1)}$ and then $x_{2(t'')} = R[x_{2(t')}]$ is the return map. The behavior of f and R is related: both are chaotic (or cyclic) for the same parameter values (see Hommes, 1992, Corollary 1).

Computer simulations are widely used in this field. They help in deducing the properties of certain functions to be used in analytical studies and substitute the missing analysis. An additional advantage of computer simulations is that they highlight certain quantitative results.

A special tool of computer analysis is the so-called *bifurcation diagram.* It simultaneously depicts the asymptotic behavior of the system for many close parameter values, and highlights the qualitative changes. It can be described as follows.

Select an important parameter which can change in a relatively large interval. For example, let it be $f_{11} \epsilon (0, 4)$ and fix the other parameter values. Let f_{11} lie on the horizontal axis and $x_{1(t)}$ ($t = U, U + 1, ..., V$) on the vertical axis. Let U and V be so large that the behaviour in $t \epsilon [U, V]$ characterizes well the long run behaviour of the system. Let the division of the horizontal axis be sufficiently fine that an interesting value will not lie between two subsequent points: $f_{11}(1), f_{11}(2), ..., f_{11}(Z)$. The initial value $(X_{1(-1)}, X_{2(-1)}$ belonging to $f_{11}(Z)$ is generally given by the end value $(X_{1(v)}, X_{2(v)})$ of the path belonging to $f_{11}(z - 1)$, $z = 1,2, ..., Z$.

Having finished the general analysis, we turn to the special models.

10.3 REGULAR MODELS

In this section three models will be discussed, each of them being special a case of the model examined in Section 2.

The Stock-Signal Model (S)

The first model to be studied (a stock-signal control model) is due to Kornai and Simonovits (1977, 1981a), (see also Kornai and Martos (1973) and Martos (1990, Chapter 9).[8]

There are n industries, forming a Leontief economy. Industry j produces r_j units of good j and purchases y_{ij} units of good from industry i in year t. It has w_j units of output stocks and v_{ij} units of input stocks, $i = 1,2, ..., n$, at the end of the year. The control structure is totally decentralized and relies on stock-signalling: producer j reacts to signal w_j, input buyer (i, j) reacts to signal v_{ij}. To adhere to the framework of Section 10.2, we shall normalize the variables with exponential trends by dividing them by the cumulated growth factor Γ^t.

Apart from normalization, $x = (s, B)'$ and $u = (r, Y)'$. Without going into details, we note that the feedback matrix is diagonal, i.e. the control is decentralized (or uncoordinated). Its matrix R is of general structure.

$$q = f1, \quad R = \begin{bmatrix} 1 & -1 \\ -A & 1 \end{bmatrix}, \quad F = \langle f \rangle$$

$$\text{where } f = 1/\Gamma \text{ and } 0 < A < 1$$

The Order-Signal Model (O)

The second model to be studied (an order-signal control model) is a twin model of the first and is due to Kornai and Simonovits (1981b), see also Martos (1990, Chapter 10).

There are n industries, forming a Leontief economy. Industry j produces r_j units of good j and receives y_{ij} units of good from industry i in year t. It has no output stocks, but it accumulates unfilled orders k_{ij} and keeps v_{ij} units of input stocks, $i = 1,2, ..., n$, at the end of the year. The control structure is totally decentralized and relies on stock- and order signalling: producer j reacts to signal k_{ij}, input buyer (i, j) reacts to signal v_{ij}.

In this model

$$q = f1, \quad R = \begin{bmatrix} 1 & -1 \\ A-1 & 1 \end{bmatrix}, \quad F = \langle f \rangle$$

$$\text{where } 0 < A < 1$$

The Socialist Cycle Model (I)

The third model to be studied (investment cycles in a socialist economy) was analyzed by Hommes *et al.* (1995) and Simonovits (1991b). The model is a non-linear generalization of Simonovits (1991a), which in turn formalized Bauer (1978), relying on Lackó (1980) and Kornai (1982).

Investment outlays (for short: investment, I) is the total value of inputs used up for investment in a given year. A significant part of the investment projects which are in the pipeline in this year, were started in previous years. Consider the estimated total cost of those projects which are started in a given year, and refer to this variable as investment start (for short: start, *S*). In addition to estimated total costs, the estimated remaining costs of those projects, which are in the pipeline in a given year, also play a role. The second quantity is also referred to as investment commitment (for short: commitment, *K*).

We assume that the net import *B* is an inhomogeneous linear function of the investment: $I = -\beta + \beta_i$I. If there were no cost overrun, then *K* would be given by an identity: $K = K_{-2} + S -$ I. However, cost overruns $(\sigma_s - 1)S$ are to be added to the right hand side.

Having introduced ratios and tensions, we can formulate the control rules as well: We assume that the start ratio is smaller than the ratio of requests for start (σ) and is a decreasing function of previous internal and external tensions. The explanation of the investment ratio is similar: it is greater than the ratio of autonomous investment and is an increasing function of the previous internal tension.

In this model

$$q = \begin{bmatrix} f \\ 0 \end{bmatrix}, \quad R = \begin{bmatrix} \sigma_s & 1 \\ 0 & \beta_i \end{bmatrix}, \quad F = \begin{bmatrix} \sigma_e & \sigma_a \\ -i_e & 0 \end{bmatrix}$$

Remark. Note that *R* is reducible ($r_{21} = 0$) and *F* is not diagonal, i.e. there is some coordination between start and investment.

10.4 IRREGULAR MODELS

In this Section two models will be discussed which are related to the general model of Section 10.2, but are not special cases of it.

The H Model

The fourth model to be studied (the investment cycle model of a capitalistic economy) is due to Hicks (1950). He took Samuelson's (1939) linear trade cycle model, assumed its instability and truncated the explosive paths. It slightly transgresses the present general framework.

Bounds and actual controls follow Section 2 with the exception of the upper bounds which are not independent: $i + c \leq y_0^M$, where y_0^M is the normalized value of the full-employment GDP, and there are many possibilities to distribute the arising excess demand between investment and consumption. (The simplest solution would be a fixed-ratio or a lexicographic distribution.)

In this model $x = (y, v)'$, $u = (i, c)'$,

$$Q = \begin{bmatrix} 0 & 0 \\ -1 & 0 \end{bmatrix}, \quad R = \begin{bmatrix} 1 & 1 \\ 1 & 1 \end{bmatrix}, \quad F = f\begin{bmatrix} 0 & -\beta \\ -\tau & 0 \end{bmatrix}, \quad h = \begin{bmatrix} a_0 \\ \tau_0 \end{bmatrix}$$

Note that deviating from the general assumptions, here Q is not diagonal and R is singular.

Basic equations

$$y = f_1(y_{-1}, v_{-1}) = \min(\max[f\beta v_{-1} + a_0, i^m] + f\tau y_{-1} + \tau_0, y_0^M) \tag{4.1}$$

$$v = f_1(y_{-1}, v_{-1}) - fy_{-1} \tag{4.2}$$

Hicks' Model with Distributed Lags

Hicks (1950) already studied the non-elementary model, where consumption and investment are functions of incomes at least of two or three past periods. He noticed strange behaviour but paid little attention to it. Hommes (1991b, Chapter 4) establishes chaotic dynamics for several sets of parameter values (pp. 219–54).

The Inventory Model (E_2)

The basic idea of the fifth model to be studied (a simple non-walrasian inventory model) is due to Honkapohja and Ito (1980). Simonovits (1982), Hommes and Nusse (1989), Hommes (1989) and (1991, Chapter 2A) replaced naive expectations and derived exact results. Contrary to the preceding models, this model does not fit directly to the general framework, but with appropriate reinterpretations, it can be reduced to a more general case.

In disequilibrium theory supply and demand are always distinguished, further, actual transaction is equated to their minimum.

Let $x = I$, $u^p = L^{Dp}$, both scalar, $q = 1$, $R = \delta - b$, $h = -a$, $u^M = d$. If we want to regain the linearity of the state space equation, u^m should be defined as follows:

$$u^m = \frac{(a - I_{-1})_+}{\delta - b} = u^m(x_{-1}) \tag{4.3}$$

Note that here u^m depends on the state X_{-1} of the system. Furthermore, the general form of the *planned control* equation has to be modified as follows:

$$u^p = u^* - Fx_{-1} + Gu_{-1} \tag{2.2p*}$$

where the planned control depends on state as well as on past control.

Finally, introducing $z = (x, u)'$ as a generalized state vector, we obtain a formal generalization of the usual *basic equations*

$$z = f(z_{-1}) \tag{2.3*}$$

where $f(z_{-1})$ is a piecewise linear map of the plane into itself.

The *Tâtonnement* Model (P)

Finally, we turn to the discussion of the last model, namely that of the *tâtonnement* model. In continuous time, it was discussed by many authors, an excellent summary to be found in Arrow and Hahn (1971). We follow the discrete time formulation of Uzawa (1958). Let s be the n-dimensional price vector and e is the n-dimensional excess demand vector. The planned price change is proportional to the excess demand and excess demand is a linear function of (all previous) prices:

$$s^P = s_{-1} + \langle f \rangle e \tag{4.4}$$

$$e = As_{-1} + b \tag{4.5}$$

If we adhere to the idea that only control can be bounded, then e is the state-vector and s is the control variable. That is, $x = e$, $u = s$, $q = 0$, $R = A$, $h = b$ and (2.2p) should be modified as follows:

$$u^P = u_{-1} + Fx_{-1} \tag{2.2p*}$$

Of course, $u^m = 0$ and $u^M = \infty$.

10.5 CONCLUSIONS

In the preceding sections we have reviewed six different economic models with similar but not identical mathematical structures. Comparing these models it turned out that there are some qualitative similarities and differences among their behaviour. For example, in some models (S and H) local stability implies global stability (superstability), while in others (O, I and E_2) local stability may co-exist with global instability (destabilizability).

Realizing the similarities among particular models, we (Hommes, Nusse and myself) were able to use experiences gained with one model in the analysis of another model. For example, co-existence of limit cycles and chaos occurring in model E_2 warned us that similar co-existence may arise in model I. Or to give a negative example when an analogy was not used: Limit cycles occurring in model H should have warned me that limit cycles may also arise in model E_2, nevertheless, I conjectured almost universal chaos.

We are still very far from having a satisfactory theory of control systems with bounds. Nevertheless, I hope that summarizing the accumulated knowledge may help interested researchers to continue this promising path.

NOTES

1. This is a splendid occasion to acknowledge my debt to András Bródy who introduced me to Input–Output Analysis and the Theory of Cycles. I would also like to express my debt to Cars Hommes and Helena Nusse for acquainting me with the modern analysis of piecewise linear dynamic systems and for participating in a joint project reviewed in Section 10.3. I am also deeply indebted to János Kornai who initiated and co-authored two papers on autonomous control analyzed in Section 10.3. I express my gratitude to Daniel Friedman, who kindly read an earlier version and gave advice. The usual disclaimer applies.
2. In similar models with continuous time the distinction between weak or strong reactions has no meaning. Restricting our attention to discrete time models, we do not consider such models.
3. Bródy (1981) studied a third variant.
4. For the relation of equilibrium and normal path, see Kornai and Marlos (1981).
5. Hommes, *et al.* (1995) and Nusse and Yorke (1992) devoted much attention to the analysis of the excluded case.
6. Mathematically speaking, topologically similar.
7. In fact, even for one-dimensional maps the existence of period 3 may only yield topological chaos, when the set of initial values generating erratic paths is of zero measure. For example, this is the case for $f(x) = 3.839x(1 - x)$, where the unique cycle of period 3 is almost globally attracting (Devaney, 1989).
8. In fact, this and the next models slightly differ from the original ones in replacing exogenous norms with endogenous ones and introducing the maximal decisions. This process was justified for the I model in Simonovits (1991a) to be discussed below.

REFERENCES

ARROW, K. J., HURWICZ, L. and UZAWA, H. (1958) *Studies in Linear and Nonlinear Programming*, Stanford, Stanford University Press.

ARROW, K. J. and HAHN, F. (1971) *General Competitive Analysis*, San Francisco, Holden-Day.

BAUER, T. (1978) 'Investment Cycles in Centrally Planned Economies', *Acta Oeconomica 21*, pp. 243–60.

BLATT, J. M. (1978) 'On the Econometric Approach to Business Cycle Modeling', *Oxford Economic Papers 30*, pp. 292–300.

BOLDRIN, M. and WOODFORD, M. (1990) 'Equilibrium Models Displaying Endogenous Fluctuations and Chaos: A Survey', *Journal of Monetary Economics 25*, pp. 189–222.

BRÓDY, A. (1969) 'Hungarian Growth Rates 1924–1964', in Bronfenbrenner, M. (ed.), pp. 312–327.

BRÓDY, A. (1981) 'An Economy Controlled by Stocks and Profits', in Kornai and Martos (eds), pp. 149–61 (Hungarian original, 1973).

BRÓDY, A. (1983) 'About Investment Cycles and Their Attenuation', *Acta Oeconomica 31*, pp. 37–51.

BRÓDY, A. and FARKAS, M. (1987) 'Forms of Economic Motions', *Acta Oeconomica 38*, pp. 361–70.

BRÓDY, A. (1989) 'Growth Cycles in Economics', in Casti, J. and Karlqvist, A. (eds), pp. 227–44, (Hungarian original, 1980).

BRÓDY, A. (1992) 'Gestation Lags and the Explanation of Socialist Investment Cycles', in Hillinger, C. (ed.) (German manuscript, 1972).

BRONFENBRENNER, M. (ed.) (1969) *Is the Business Cycle Obsolete?*, New York, Wiley and Son.

CASTI, J. and KARLQVIST, A. (eds) (1989) *Newton to Aristotle. Towards a Theory of Models for Living Systems*, New York, Springer-Verlag

CUGNO, F. and MONTRUCCHIO, L. (1984) 'Some New Techniques for Modeling *Non-Linear Economic Fluctuations: A Brief Survey', in Goodwin, R. M., et al (eds), Non-Linear Model of Fluctuating Growth. Lecture Notes in Economics and Mathematical Systems* 228, Berlin, Springer. pp. 146–65.

DEVANEY, R. (1989) *An Introduction to Chaotic Dynamical Systems*, Second ed, Redwood City, Addison Wesley.

FEICHTINGER, G. (ed.) (1992) *Dynamic Economic Models and Optimal Control*, Amsterdam, North-Holland.

FEINSTEIN, G. H. (ed.) (1967) *Socialism, Capitalism, and Economic Growth*, Cambridge, Cambridge University Press.

FRISCH, R. (1933) 'Propagation Problems and Impulse Problems in Dynamic Economics', *Economic Essays in Honor of Gustav Cassel*, London, pp. 171-205

GOODWIN, R. M. (1967) 'A Growth Cycle', Feinstein, G. H. (ed.), pp. 54–8.

GOODWIN, R. M. KRÜGER, M. and VERCELLI, A. (eds) (1984) *Non-Linear Models of Fluctuating Growth. Lecture Notes in Economics and Mathematical Systems 228*, Berlin, Springer.

GRANDMONT, J.-M. (1985) 'On Endogenous Business Cycles', *Econometrica 45*, pp. 995–1045.

GUCKENHEIMER, J. (1979) 'Sensitive Dependence to Initial Conditions for One-dimensional Maps', *Communications of Mathematical Physics 70*, pp. 133–60.

HICKS, J. (1950) *A Contribution to the Theory of the Trade Cycle*, Oxford, Clarendon.

HILLINGER, C. ed. (1992) *Cyclical Growth in Market and Planned Economies*, Oxford, Clarendon.

HOMMES, C. H. (1991) *Chaotic Dynamics in Economic Models: Some Simple Case Studies*, Groningen Thesis in Economics, Management and Organization, Groningen, Wolters-Norodhoff.

HOMMES, C. H. (1992) 'Periodic, Quasi-Periodic and Chaotic Dynamics in a Simple Macro-Model with Hicksian Nonlinearities', in Feichtinger, G. (ed.), pp. 385–405.

HOMMES, C. H. (1993) 'Periodic, Almost-Periodic and Chaotic Behavior in Hicks Nonlinear Trade Cycle Model', *Economic Letters 41*, pp. 391–7.

HOMMES, C. H. and NUSSE, H. E. (1989) 'Does an Unstable Keynesian Unemployment Equilibrium in a Non-Walrasian Dynamic Macroeconomic Model Imply Chaos?', *Scandinavian Journal of Economics 91*, pp. 161–7.

HOMMES, C. H., NUSSE, H. E. and SIMONOVITS, A. (1995) 'Cycles and Chaos in a Socialist Economy', *Journal of Economic Dynamics and Control*, 19, pp. 155–79.

HONKAPOHJA, S. and ITO, T. (1980) 'Inventory Dynamics in a Simple Disequilibrium Macroeconomic Model', *Scandinavian Journal of Economics 82*, pp. 184–98.

HONKAPOHJA, S. and ITO, T. (1983) 'Stability with Switching Regimes', *Journal of Economic Theory 29*, pp. 22–48.

ICKES, B. W. (1986) 'Cyclical Fluctuations in Centrally Planned Economies', *Soviet Studies 38*, pp. 36–52.

KONDOR, G. (1981) 'On the Asymptotic Local Stability of Autonomous Systems with Nonnegative Conditions', *Journal of Economic Theory 25*, pp. 466–70.

KORNAI, J. (1982) *Growth, Shortage and Efficiency*, Oxford, Basil Blackwell.

KORNAI, J. and MARTOS, B. (1973) 'Autonomous Functioning of the Economic System', *Econometrica 41*, pp. 509–28.

KORNAI, J. and MARTOS, B. (eds) (1981) *Non-Price Control*, Amsterdam, North-Holland.

KORNAI, J. and SIMONOVITS, A. (1977) 'Decentralized Control Problems in Neumann-economies', *Journal of Economic Theory 14*, pp. 44–67.

KORNAI, J. and SIMONOVITS, A. (1981a) 'Stock-Signal Model Regulated from a Normal Path', in Kornai, J. and Martos, B. (eds), pp. 223–45.

KORNAI, J. and SIMONOVITS, A. (1981b) 'Control by Order-Signals', in Kornai, J. and Martos, B. (eds), 267–79.

LACKÓ, M. (1980) 'Cumulation and Easing of Tensions', *Acta Oeconomica 24*, pp. 357–78.

LI, J. A. and YORKE, J. A. (1975) 'Period Three Implies Chaos', *American Mathematical Monthly 82*, pp. 985–92.

MARTOS, B. (1990) *Economic Control Structures: A Non-Walrasian Approach*, Amsterdam, North-Holland.

LOVELL, M. C. (1962) 'Buffer Stocks, Sales Expectations and Stability: A Multi-sector Analysis of the Inventory Cycle', *Econometrica 30*, pp. 267–96.

NUSSE, H. E. and YORKE, J. A. (1990) 'Border-Collision Bifurcations Including 'Period Two to Period Three' for Piecewise Smooth Systems', *Physica D 57* 39–50.

SAMUELSON, P. A. (1939) 'Interactions between the Multiplier Analysis and the Principle of Acceleration', *Review of Economic Studies 21*, pp. 75–78.

SIMONOVITS, A. (1979) 'Expectations and Stability in a Decentralized Control Model', *CORE Discussion Papers 7923*, Université Catholique de Louvain, Louvain-La-Neuve.

SIMONOVITS, A. (1981) 'Constrained Control and Destabilization', Kornai, J. and Martos, B. (eds), 281–320.

SIMONOVITS, A. (1982) 'Buffer Stocks and Naive Expectations in a Non-Walrasian Dynamic Macrodynamic Model: Stability, Cyclicity and Chaos', *Scandinavian Journal of Economics 84*, pp. 571–81.

SIMONOVITS, A. (1991a) 'Investment, Starts and Cycles in a Socialist Economy', *Journal of Comparative Economics 15*, pp. 460–75.

SIMONOVITS, A. (1991b) 'Investment Limit Cycles in a Socialist Economy', *Economics of Planning 24*, pp. 27–46.

SIMONOVITS, A. (1992) 'Superstability, Limit Cycles and Chaos in Control Systems with Bounds', *Working Paper 4*, Institute of Economics, Budapest.

UZAWA, H. (1958) 'Gradient Method for Concave Programming, II: Global Stability in the Strictly Concave Case', in *Studies in Linear and Non-Linear Programming*, Arrow, K. J. *et al.* (eds), pp. 127–32, Stanford, Stanford University Press.

11 Proportions, Growth and Cycles between Constant and Non-Constant Returns to Scale[1]

Maurizio Ciaschini

11.1 BALANCED GROWTH PATHS, FIXED PROPORTIONS AND STEADY STATE OUTPUT

One of the main features which characterizes current production processes is that of non-constant returns to scale. While this feature is generally accepted in theoretical analysis, it fails to generate any effective applied instruments for multi-sectoral modelling. This fact may be due to the popularity of the constant returns to scale hypothesis, and in particular to the high reputation of the Leontief assumptions. In fact, these provide both an operational framework for production accounts and a clear-cut derivation of sectoral input requirements functions from actual data. Nevertheless, they also induce the erroneous view that a dynamic multisectoral model is explosive (i.e. highly unstable) outside its balanced growth path.

The implications of the Perron–Frobenius theorem for the dynamic Leontief model are, in fact, twofold. On the one hand, the multisectoral systems can grow at a constant rate, keeping constant all proportions among sectoral aggregates. This feature virtually reduces the multisectoral problem to a problem of scale, concentrating on those types of behaviour that do not imply any changes in the structure of macroeconomic variables. On the other hand, if the initial proportions are inconsistent with the balanced growth path, the system will exhibit highly unstable trajectories resulting in increasingly high negative or complex numbers in the solutions. If initial conditions are given according to the proportions established by the Perron–Frobenius[2] eigenvector u_F, all sectoral aggregates will remain positive and grow at a rate σ_F. Outside this path, all trajectories will be attracted by the dominant eigenvalue σ_D towards the proportions indicated by the associated eigenvector u_D, where some sectoral components become negative or complex after a few iterations.

The sectoral interaction implied by the traditional Leontief model, which we will call 'weak interaction', operates on the basis of the sectoral level through the determination of inputs according to constant technical coefficients.[3] The technical coefficient a represents the demand for materials per unit output, while the technical coefficient b gives the capital requirement per unit output. The dynamic Leontief system is given by:

$$x_{t+1} = \{1 + (1 - a)/b\}x_t - (1/b)f_t$$

Assuming final demand to be equal to zero, the system will allow for the origin as a steady state. The scalar $r = (1 - a)/b$ represents the unrestricted growth rate, since starting from initial conditions x_0, the system will grow by the factor $(1 + r)$ over every period.

Standard assumptions state that the capital coefficient is positive, i.e. $b > 0$, while the technical coefficient a lies between zero and one, so that the growth rate will be positive. Thus the system will be progressively repelled from the origin.

If we weaken the hypothesis of constant returns to scale by introducing a dependency of input requirements on the scale of activity, we can get a model of the Leontief type that is able to quantify the implications of the differentials in returns to scale among sectors. The unit input requirement will be given by:

$$m/x = a(x) = a \pm cx$$

In the case of diseconomies of scale, it will take the plus sign, while in the case of economies of scale, the minus sign is required. Clearly, in the case of non-constant returns, a further interaction is superimposed, which operates from the level of sectoral outputs to the technical coefficients. This type of interaction, which we shall call 'strong interaction', implies that there are two causal links: the first one between sectoral outputs and the corresponding input requirements, and the second one between outputs and technical coefficients (see further Lahiri, 1976 or Lahiri and Pyatt, 1980).

Let us concentrate now on diminishing returns. In this case, production can take place as far as the inputs required for production are lower than total output. However, it is to be expected that, as it approaches a certain output level x_S, which we shall define as 'sustainable output' or 'steady state output', production will become more difficult to obtain, given the increasing rate of inputs needed for production.

The output levels which can be maintained over time are those for which the implied input requirements m do not exceed total production x

$$m/x = a + cx \leq 1$$

which yields

$$x \leq (1 - a)/c$$

Defining

$$x_S = (1 - a)/c$$

we can write

$$x \leq x_S$$

Taking into consideration the new unit input requirements, the dynamic Leontief system with scale-dependent input requirements (SDIR) will be given by

$$x_{t+1} = [1 + (1 - a)/b]x_t - (c/b)x_t^2 \tag{2}$$

The cobweb diagram in Figure 11.1 shows the appearance of a second fixed point other than zero, which corresponds to the intersection of the parabola $x_{t+1} = [1 + (1 - a)/b]x_t - (c/b)x^2{}_t$ with the line $x_{t+1} = x_t$.

From Figure 11.1 we see that the cobweb diagram approaches x_{d2}, which is the level that we defined as sustainable output x_s. The cobweb moves towards the fixed point x_d which is attracting, as long as $f'(x_t) = -2(c/b)x_t + [1 + (1 - a)/b]$ is < 1 in each x_d.

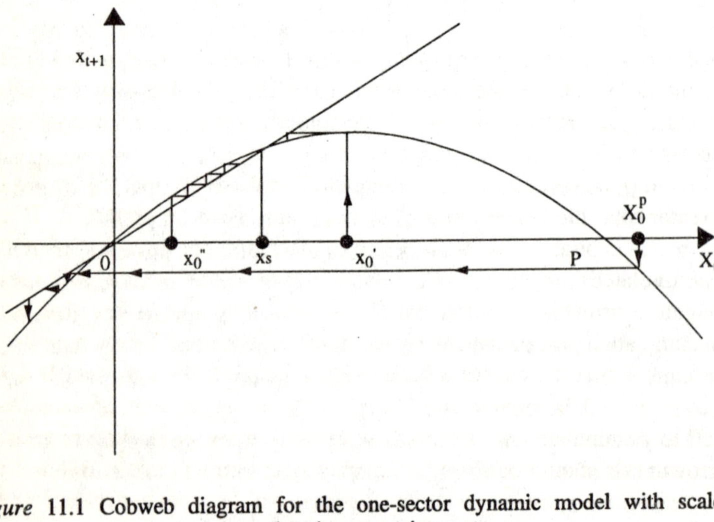

Figure 11.1 Cobweb diagram for the one-sector dynamic model with scale-dependent input requirements

Moreover, we may determine the basin of attraction of fixed point x_d, $D(x_d)$, as being the locus of points whose trajectories converge to x_d. This domain is the open interval bounded by the repelling fixed point $x_{d1} = 0$ and a second point P, which is given by the intersection of the parabola and the horizontal axis. Thus, $D(x_d) =]0,P[$. In fact, we immediately see that an initial condition outside that interval will have a trajectory approaching $-\infty$. An example with initial condition $x_0^P > P$ is shown in Figure 11.1. We then come to the general conclusion that the fixed point is attracting if $|f'(x_d)| < 1$, and repelling if $| f'(x_d)| > 1$; i.e., the system has an asymptotic output structure x_d, towards which it is attracted or from which it is repelled.

11.2 CYCLES, CHAOS AND THE ROLE OF FINAL DEMAND

If $| f'(x_d) | = 1$, some further analysis will be needed. This will provide us with the opportunity to detect some interesting behaviour of the system, which takes place if the parameters of the system are such that the fixed point becomes repelling. In this case, it is possible that the system is attracted by some other attractor, rather than being repelled towards infinity. We can interpret the changes caused by our SDIR-system using the concepts of unrestricted growth and of sustainable output. In fact, system (2) can be written as

$$x_{t+1} - x_t = r[1 - (x_t/x_s)]x_t \tag{3}$$

If our system exhibited decreasing returns to scale, the rate of growth of the economic system would be determined by the ratio between the share of resources not devoted to intermediate consumptions, $(1 - a)$, and the capital coefficient b.

If output exceeds x_s, diseconomies of scale imply that inputs become greater than the corresponding output which is to be produced. Thus, if $x_t > x_s$, capital stock will begin to decrease (or inventories will be decumulated), so that production can take place, which will mean a negative growth of output $(x_{t+1} - x_t) < 0$. If output is less than x_s, the accumulation process can take place, since there is room for the reproduction of capital after the materials were used in the production process. If $x_t < x_s$, $(x_{t+1} - x_t) > 0$. If output is small compared to x_s, i.e. if plenty of resources are left to accumulate after materials were used in the production process, the growth rate should be close to the unrestricted growth rate r. But as output increases, the growth rate diminishes and will become zero when $x_t = x_s$.

Fixed points of system (3) can be determined by considering that $x_{t+1} = x_t = x_d$:

$$x_d = (1+r)x_d - (r/x_s)x_d^2$$

Subtracting x_d from both sides and dividing by r, we obtain the equilibrium values $x_{d1} = 0$ and $x_{d2} = x_s$.

We can choose the size of our unit, defining one unit as x_s, in order to obtain $x_{d2} = 1$. By means of this procedure we standardize the SDIR-system in such a way that total output and final demand (which here is assumed to be equal to zero) will be expressed as a proportion of sustainable output. The one-sector SDIR-system then becomes:

$$x_{t+1} = (1+r)x_t - rx_t^2 \tag{4}$$

It is easy to see that $x_{d1} = 0$ and $x_{d2} = 1$ are the fixed points, with $f(x) = (1 + r)x - rx^2$ and $f'(x) = 1 + r - 2rx$. The fixed point in the origin, i.e. the Leontief fixed point $x_{d1} = 0$, will always be repelling, because for $0 \leq a < 1$ and $b > 0, f'(0) = 1 + r > 1$. The other fixed point $x_{d2} = 1$ will be attracting if $|f'(1)| = |1 - r| < 1$, that is if $0 < r < 2$. If $b = (1 - a)/2$, the unrestricted growth rate r becomes equal to 2, and the method based on the first derivative will become inconclusive, since $f'(1) = -1$.

In order to determine the stability of x_d, we need to define an iterated map. The resulting dynamic system $x_{t+2} \equiv g(x_t) = f(f(x_t))$ also has x_d as a fixed point. After some calculation we get $g'(x_d) = 1$, $g''(x_d) = 0$, and $g'''(x_d) = -48$. Since $g'(x_d) = 1$, $g''(x_d)$ and $g'''(x_d) < 0$, the cobweb diagram is such that the curve changes from concave up to concave down at the fixed point, so that x_d is attracting. If $r > 2$, the fixed point $x_d = 1$ is repelling, since $|f'(1)| = |1 + r - 2r| > 1$. If the initial value x_0 is chosen close to the fixed point $x_d = 1$, x_t moves away from it towards a 2-cycle, as shown in Fig. 11.2. The fixed point $x_d = 0$ is also unstable since $f'(0) = 1 + r > 1$. However, if a cobweb diagram is constructed starting from a small enough positive value, the solution would be repelled from $x_d = 0$, and would finally result in the same 2-cycle.

In order to show algebraically that a 2-cycle is stable, we refer to the iterated map:

$$x_{t+2} \equiv g(x_t) = f(f(x_t)) = f^{(2)}(x_t)$$

If for this iterated mapping both x_{c1} and x_{c2} are attracting fixed points, these points will constitute an attracting 2-cycle for $f(x_t)$. Let us now see for what values of r our system exhibits a 2-cycle and how that 2-cycle looks like. The

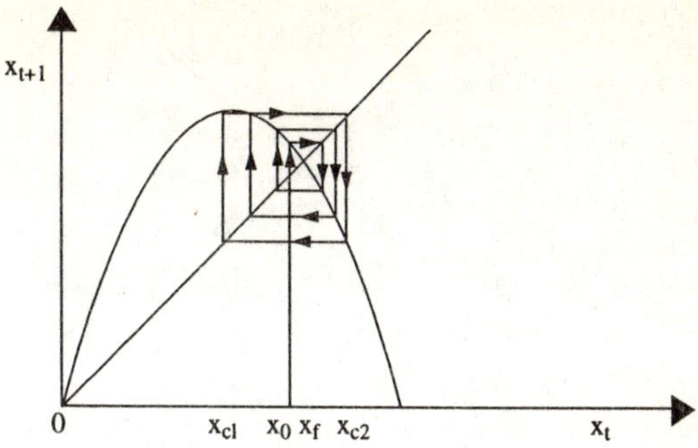

(a)

Figure 11.2 A repelling fixed point

fixed points that satisfy $x_d = f(f(x_d))$ with $f(x_d) = (1 + r)x_d - rx_d^2$ are

$$x_{c_{1,2}} = \frac{2 + r \pm \sqrt{r^2 - 4}}{2r}$$

These two numbers define our 2-cycle. Since $f'(x) = (1 + r) - 2rx$, $f'(x_{c1})f'(x_{c2}) =$

$$[1 + r - 2r\frac{2 + r + \sqrt{r^2 - 4}}{2r}][1 + r - 2r\frac{2 + r + \sqrt{r^2 - 4}}{2r}]$$
$$= 1 - r^2 + 4 = 5 - r^2.$$

If

$$-1 < 5 - r^2 < 1$$

or

$$2 < r < \sqrt{6}$$

the 2-cycle is attracting. If $r > \sqrt{6}$, the 2-cycle becomes repelling. While augmenting the value of r, the stable cycle doubles its period; we observe ‘period doubling’. Beyond a given value of r we enter a ‘chaotic regime’, which is characterized by a sensitivity to initial conditions and a periodic trajectories in bounded intervals.

Sensitivity to initial conditions means that two trajectories having nearby initial conditions x_0 and $(x_0 + \epsilon)$ for a small positive ϵ will show a completely

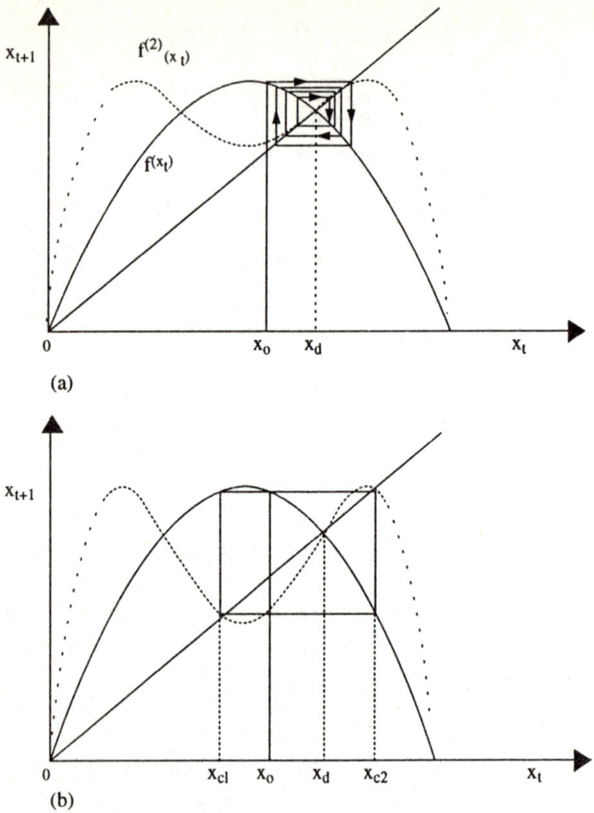

Figure 11.3 (a) Attracting fixed point, (b) Emergence of a 2-cycle

different dynamic behaviour. We can follow the first steps of the period doubling process with reference to Figure 11.3(a)–(b). In Figure 11.3(a) we have represented the iterated map $f^{(2)}(x_t)$ and the original function $f(x_t)$. The technology is given by the technical coefficients $a = 0.2$, and $b = 0.57$. The remaining technical coefficient c does not influence the features of the model in terms of its fixed points. The unrestricted growth rate will be equal to 1.4; the fixed point x_d is unique and attracting. As can be seen in the figure, $f(x_d)$ and $f^{(2)}(x_d)$ coincide, while $f'(x_d)$ and $f'^{(2)}(x_d)$ are less than one (see further Chiarella, 1988).

The emergence of a stable 2-cycle is depicted in Figure 11.3(b). The capital coefficient b has dropped from 0.57 to 0.33, and the unrestricted

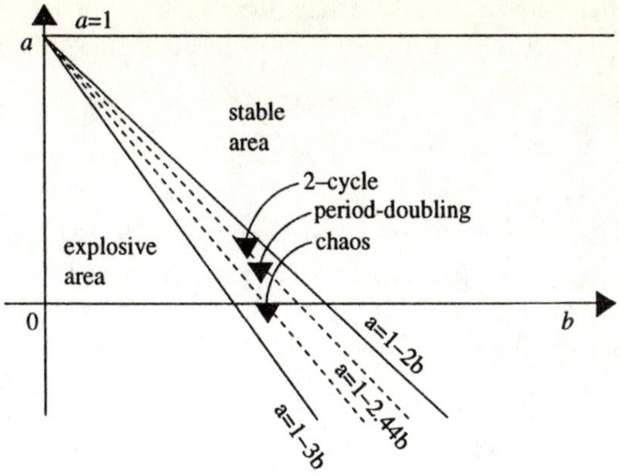

Figure 11.4 Critical values for technical coefficients

growth rate r has risen to 2.42. The fixed point x_d has become repelling, as is evident from the slope of the original function evaluated at the fixed point $| f(x_d) | >1$.A 2-cycle has appeared, constituted by the two fixed points on the iterated map, x_{c1} and x_{c2}. This 2-cycle is attracting, since the slope of the iterated map, $f^{(2)}(x_t)$, evaluated at the two points, is less than one, $|f'^{(2)}(x_{c1})| < 1$ and $|f'^{(2)}(x_{c2})| < 1$. Further substantial decrease in the value of b, via various intermediate stability cases, finally will lead to a chaotic regime (see also Lorenz, 1989, or Goodwin, 1990). The diagram in the (b,a)-plane, which summarizes the possible equilibrium configurations and the critical values for switching from one regime to another, is shown in Figure 11.4.

Above we have looked at stability from a theoretical point of view. However, our exercise may also be considered from an empirical point of view. For example, the capital coefficient b_{21} is defined as the quantity of the *i*th good invested in the *j*th industry needed to increase the output of that industry by one unit. This definition, however, leaves much room for operationalization. Bródy (1970), for example, revived the method based on turnover times. It will be obvious that, depending on the way we have estimated our flow coefficients and the corresponding turnover time, the capital coefficient b_{21} can vary widely, especially since the role of the full capacity assumption is still not very clear to us. Moreover, this is only one method out of several available, including a number of mixed ones. So it may be worthwhile to study the effects of variations in the coefficients in certain detail.

The explicit consideration of a time-invariant final demand vector, $f_t = f^*$ in the one-sector SDIR system (4), will result in the following dynamic system:

$$x_{t+1} = (1+r)x_t - rx_t^2 - (1/b)f^* \tag{5}$$

where variables again are measured with respect to x_s. The final demand vector operates on the parabola as a varying intercept. As the demand level increases, the parabola shifts downward until the two points coincide and the fixed points eventually disappear.

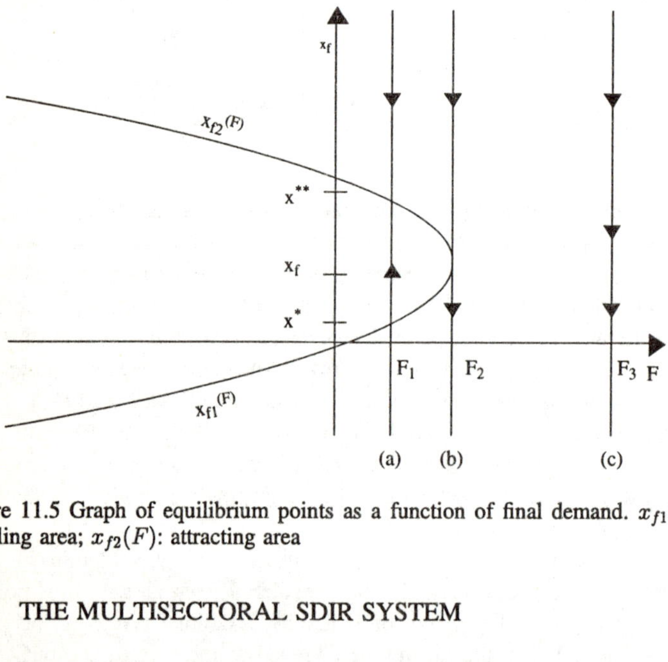

Figure 11.5 Graph of equilibrium points as a function of final demand. $x_{f1}(F)$: repelling area; $x_{f2}(F)$: attracting area

11.3 THE MULTISECTORAL SDIR SYSTEM

We are now familiar with the dynamic behaviour of the one-sector SDIR system, and the way it affects the dynamic equilibrium configuration. The extension to *n* sectors of the SDIR function is based on varying unit input requirements given by:

$$m_{ij}/x_j = a_{ij} \pm c_{ij}x_j$$

The coefficients a_{ij} and c_{ij} are the *n*-sector's extension of the coefficients *a* and *c*. A plus sign on the right-hand side denotes decreasing returns, while a minus sign will denote increasing returns.

We may write the sectoral intermediate demands in matrix form as follows:

$$m_t = Ax_t + C\hat{x}_t x_t$$

where $C = [c_{ij}]$ and $\hat{x}_t$ is a diagonal matrix, whose diagonal elements are given by the elements of vector x_t. The SDIR dynamic model now becomes:

$$x_{t+1} = [I + B^{-1}(I - A)]x_t - B^{-1}C\hat{x}_t x_t - B^{-1}f_t \tag{6}$$

As in the one-sector case, we may refer to a linearization of system (6) around the fixed point. After having calculated the fixed point, we obtain the matrix of first derivatives, the Jacobian matrix

$$\begin{aligned} J(x_d) = & \begin{bmatrix} f_{11}(x_{1d}, x_{2d}) & f_{12}(x_{1d}, x_{2d}) \\ f_{21}(x_{1d}, x_{2d}) & f_{22}(x_{1d}, x_{2d}) \end{bmatrix} = \\ = & \; [(I + B^{-1}(I - A)) - 2B^{-1}Cx_d] \end{aligned}$$

Locally, that is in a suitable domain containing the fixed point x_d, the trajectories of the dynamic system (6) are qualitatively the same as the ones present in the linear system

$$y_{t+1} = [(I + B^{-1}(I - A)) - 2B^{-1}Cx_d]y_t \tag{7}$$

where y_t (again) is measured with respect to x_d, i.e. $y_t = (x_t - x_d)$. This means that we may observe spiralling paths, depending on the type of eigenvalues of J (real or complex), converging towards x_d or resulting from x_d. For a discussion of the possible shape of the paths of the system, it will be convenient to assume that the system has already been transformed into a canonical form. The state-space diagram of the actual system may differ, because non-singular transformations generally will distort the diagram. Nevertheless, the transformation does not alter the character and the properties of these diagrams.[4] Let us give a brief survey of possible trajectories of the system. These depend on the nature of the fixed point itself: a node, a focus, a saddle or a centre.

If the fixed point is a node, the system's trajectory moves towards the fixed point, approaching it without any fluctuations. In this case, matrix J has two real and distinct eigenvalues, i.e. σ_1 and σ_2, and can be written as:

$$J = \begin{bmatrix} \sigma_1 & 0 \\ 0 & \sigma_2 \end{bmatrix}$$

We may then distinguish two cases:

(i) $|\sigma_1| < | \sigma_2 | < 1$, where the fixed point is a stable tangent node. If $x_{1,t=0} = x_{2,t=0} = 0$, we obtain the fixed point. If $x_{1,t=0} = 0$ and $x_{2,t=0} \neq 0$, we obtain the x_2-axis (with the fixed point deleted), and we may note that as $t \to \infty$, $x_2 \to 0$. In a similar way, if $x_{2,t=0} = 0$ and $x_{1,t=0} \neq 0$, we obtain the x_1-axis (with the fixed point deleted) and we note that as $t \to \infty$, $x_1 \to 0$. Generally speaking, the motion along an arbitrary trajectory consists of an asymptotic approach toward the origin. If $\sigma_1 < \sigma_2 < 1$, the trajectories would be tangent to the x_2-axis.

(ii) $1 < | \sigma_2 | < | \sigma_1 |$, where the fixed point is an unstable tangent node. This is similar to case (i), but the orientation of the trajectories is reversed.

If matrix J has a repeated real eigenvalue σ, but is not diagonal (which occurs when the multiplicity of the real eigenvalue is less than the state-space dimension, i.e. the case of the Jordan-block), it may be written as:

$$J = \begin{bmatrix} \sigma & 1 \\ 0 & \sigma \end{bmatrix}$$

In this case, if $\sigma < 1$, the fixed point is a stable improper node since x_1 and x_2 approach zero because $t \to \infty$. If $\sigma > 1$, the fixed point is an unstable improper node.

If the fixed point is a focus, the system's trajectories will move towards (or away from) the fixed point while oscillating. In this case, matrix J has complex eigenvalues and may be written as

$$J = \begin{bmatrix} \alpha & \mu \\ \mu & \alpha \end{bmatrix}$$

where α represents the real part and μ the imaginary part.

We may distinguish two cases: if $\alpha < 1$, the fixed point is a stable focus, if $\alpha > 1$, the fixed point is an unstable focus. A special case is the case where matrix J has a repeated real eigenvalue σ. This can be written as:

$$J = \begin{bmatrix} \sigma & 0 \\ 0 & \sigma \end{bmatrix}$$

We now obtain $x_{2,t}/x_{1,t} = x_{2,t=0}/x_{1,t=0}$ or $x_{2,t=0}$ $x_{2,t=0}/x_{1,t=0})x_{1,t}$. This means that we will get straight lines passing through the fixed point generated according to the initial conditions with ratios $(x_{2,t=0}/x_{1,t=0})$. If $\sigma < 1$, the phase point moves towards the fixed point and is a stable focus. If $\sigma > 1$, this motion is away from the fixed point; this fixed point is an unstable focus.

If the fixed point is a saddle, the trajectories initially move towards the fixed point, but when they are in its vicinity, they are repelled. If $\sigma_1 < 1 < \sigma_2$, the fixed point is a saddle point. If $x_{1,t=0} = 0$ and $x_{2,t=0} \neq 0$, we obtain the x_2-axis (with the fixed point deleted), and as $t \to \infty$, $x_2 \to \pm\infty$. The motion along the positive x_1-semi-axis is directed towards the fixed point, while the motion along the positive x_2-semi-axis is directed away from the fixed point. If $\sigma_2 < 1 < \sigma_1$, the orientation of the trajectories in the same figure would be reversed.

If the fixed point is a center, the system's trajectories neither approach the fixed point, nor move away from it. If matrix J has complex eigenvalues, it can be written as:

$$J = \begin{bmatrix} \alpha & \mu \\ \mu & \alpha \end{bmatrix}$$

where, as before, α represents the real part and μ the imaginary part. If $\alpha = 0$, the trajectories are circles centred around the origin. Furthermore, if $\mu > 0$, the arrows will point in clockwise direction, while if $\mu < 0$, the arrows will point in counterclockwise direction. In this case the fixed point is a centre.

Let us show the results of some numerical simulations. The first set of simulations shows a case of adjusting proportions towards those of the steady state, but it also shows endogenous oscillations near the initial positions.

The two-sector SDIR-system is given by:

$$A = \begin{bmatrix} 0.5660 & 0.1144 \\ 0.4027 & 0.4070 \end{bmatrix}, \quad C = \begin{bmatrix} 0.0284 & 0.0574 \\ 0.0175 & 0.0177 \end{bmatrix}$$

and (8)

$$B = \begin{bmatrix} 8 & 0.8 \\ 15 & 0.5 \end{bmatrix}$$

The system is characterized by slow diseconomies of scale and large differences in the magnitudes of capital coefficients through the investing sectors. The Jacobian matrix is given by

$$J = [(I + B^{-1}(I - A)) - 2B^{-1}Cx_d]$$

Numerical evaluation results in

$$J = \begin{bmatrix} .9327 & 0.0807 \\ .9094 & -0.5159 \end{bmatrix}$$

with eigenvalues $\sigma_1 = 0.9818$ and $\sigma_2 = -0.5649$. The fixed point (4.3038, 3.9375) will be an attracting node. As Figure 11.6(a) shows, from the initial endowment x_0 the system will reach the fixed point, adjusting the proportions towards the ones indicated by the eigenvector u_D associated with the dominant eigenvalue σ_D. We should note here that if all eigenvalues are less than unity in modulus, the system's dominant eigenvalue will be a function of the lowest of the two, which corresponds to the slowest dynamic pattern, in this case $\sigma_D = \sigma_2$. The motion will be characterized by an alternating pattern, and the system will eventually settle at the fixed point.

Figure 11.6(b) shows the behaviour of the system when the value of the capital coefficient b_{21} falls below 11.61. The system starts from the same endowment, approaches the proportions u_D, but does not settle at the fixed point x_D. Rather, remaining in the neighbourhood of the fixed point for a few periods, oscillating behaviour will lead to a 2-cycle. In this case eigenvalues of the Jacobian matrix become $\sigma_1 = .9778$ and $\sigma_2 = -1.143$. The fixed point $x_d = [4.3038, 3.9375]$ changes from attracting to repelling, and trajectories are repelled while showing an alternating pattern (due to the eigenvalue σ_1).

The second set of simulations will show certain stages of the period-doubling process for a two-sector system. The system will be characterized by the following matrices:

$$A = \begin{bmatrix} 0.00566 & 0.01144 \\ 0.00004 & 0.00407 \end{bmatrix} \qquad B = \begin{bmatrix} 9 & 0.8 \\ 29 & 0.5 \end{bmatrix}$$

and

$$C = \begin{bmatrix} 0.02841 & 0.05745 \\ 0.01759 & 0.01778 \end{bmatrix}$$

In the fixed point the Jacobian is given by

$$J = \begin{bmatrix} 0.9737 & 0.0612 \\ -0.0815 & -1.3978 \end{bmatrix}$$

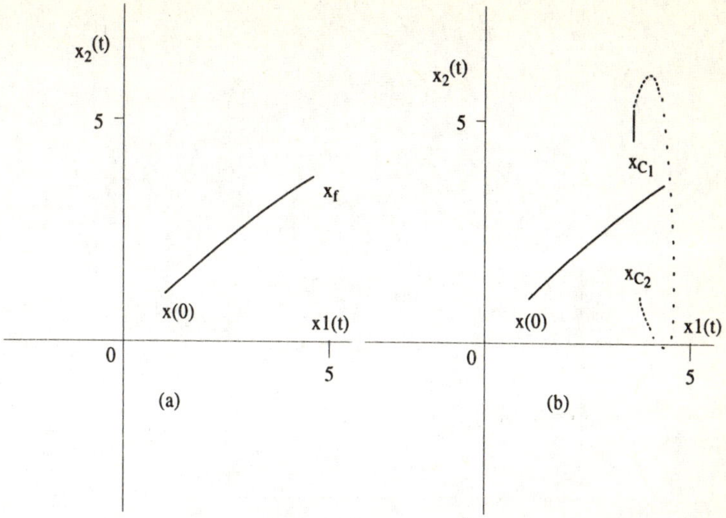

Figure 11.6 State space diagrams for system (8) for decreasing values of b_{21}

The eigenvalues of the Jacobian matrix, $\sigma 1 = 0.9716$ and $\sigma_2 = -1.3957$ show that the fixed point $x_d = [22.81, 11.8]$ is repelling while its trajectory settles on a 2-cycle in the long period, see Figure 11.7. As long as its capital coefficient decreases in value, the process doubles its period, eventually resulting in chaos. If the capital coefficient $b_{21} = 25$, the long-term cycle will become a 4-cycle. If this coefficient decreases further, the system will become highly unstable (explode), and show a dynamic pattern which is similar to the instability of the dynamic Leontief model.

It now becomes crucial to determine the basin, since we should expect that Leontief dynamic instability will govern the system's dynamic behaviour outside the basin of attraction of the attracting set. In fact, as Figure 11.1 already shows for the one-sector system, if initial conditions are set within the basin of attraction, the system's trajectory will be attracted by the fixed point (the attractor) which is necessarily included in the basin. If initial conditions are given outside the basin of attraction, the system's trajectory will be repelled towards infinity, analogously to what happens in the case of the standard dynamic Leontief model. If initial conditions are set at the border of the basin, the trajectory will be neither attracted not repelled by the fixed point, but will remain confined to the border of the basin.

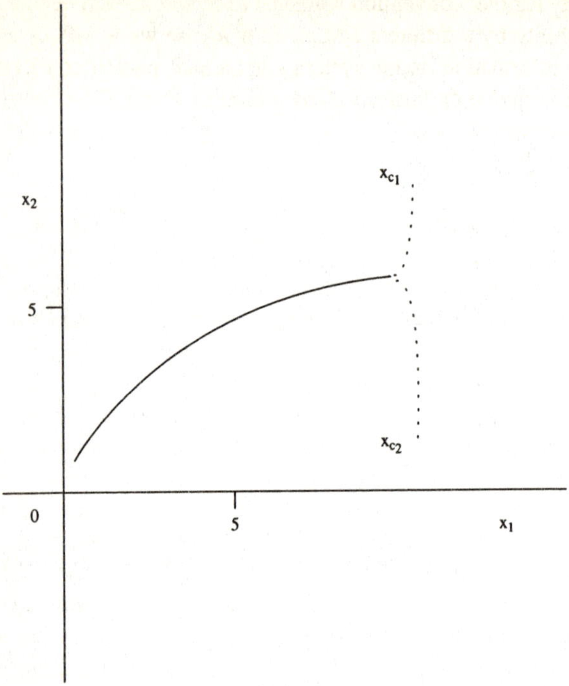

Figure 11.7 State-space diagrams for the multisectoral system

A numerical simulation enables us to determine the basins of attraction for the different attractors. Numerical measures of the degree of instability for each initial condition may be defined according to the following criterion: If the equilibrium configuration is a fixed point, the degree of stability will be given by the number of iterations required to reach the fixed point – according to a previously defined tolerance limit – starting from the initial conditions which were specified. The degree of instability will be measured on the basis of the number of iterations required by the system variables in order to reach infinity (see Gardini, 1992).

The remaining cases, i.e. those cases in which the system does not reach a fixed point or infinity, will indicate the system's convergence towards an *n*-cycle or a chaotic attractor. These results may be shown in a table in which all relevant initial conditions are represented by a number. Conventionally, non-negative numbers will represent degrees of stability; the figure zero will indicate non-divergence, while negatives represent the degre of instability.

A more 'legible' convention would be to represent each degree of stability and instability by a different colour. In that case we would be able to give complete information on the system's dynamics, particularly in those cases where the system is explosive for any initial condition. This, however, will be left for later work.

11.4 CONCLUSION

We have become used to the idea that multisectoral dynamics involves many types of instabilities. This characteristic essentially confines analysis to so-called 'equilibrium dynamics' (apart from certain heroic attempts to justify and use an unstable analytical instrument). However, equilibrium dynamics necessarily confines multisectoral analysis to those 'equilibrium' trajectories that imply constant growth rates with fixed proportions: virtually an aggregated framework with a multisectoral appearance (Ciaschini, 1980, 1993). More recently, the fact that a distinction is made between proportional and structural dynamics (Pasinetti, 1993) seems to imply the acknowledgement of this 'artificial' role of equilibrium dynamics.

This set of concepts and pre-concepts is the paradigm of dynamic multisectoral analysis, which we have tried to question by introducing the concept of economies of scale. Nevertheless, non-constant returns appear to compromise the applicability of dynamic multisectoral analysis, since we are unable to obtain explicit qualitative solutions and link their features to the parametric structure of the system. Dynamic patterns tend to remain hidden; they can be revealed in full detail only by means of numerical simulation.

Numerical simulation enables us to reveal certain fatures of a specific system, which may be extended to other systems by analogy. In many cases, the system admits a steady-state vector which determines its long-term proportions. The growth path which leads to this steady-state output may assume different configurations, depending on whether this equilibrium output vector is a node, a focus, a saddle or a centre.

Leontief dynamic instability does not completely disappear, however. In fact, in our scale-dependent framework stability is not a property which is determined by the system's parameters once and for all. The structure and magnitude of both initial conditions and final demand shocks play a major role, together with the system's parameters, in determining the dynamic features of the system's trajectories. If certain parameters of the system are forced to change, fixed points will degenerate into cycles, and chaotic attractors will emerge just before the onset of instability, serving to indicate the approach of Leontief instability.

Of all the possible changes in parameters, the ones that result in bifurcations are extremely relevant, since they produce changes in the system's overall qualitative reply. The actual determination of the fixed points and their associated basins of attraction enables us to follow the system's trajectory towards the equilibrium configurations before the trajectory has definitely left the vicinity of the fixed point.

Thus, the introduction of non-constant returns opens new frontiers in multisectoral analysis. Common places of traditional analysis such as the 'balanced growth path' and 'equilibrium dynamics' now appear too rigid and somewhat obsolete. A paradigm emerges where proportions, growth and cycles have a deeply interactive and consistent role to play. Initial conditions and exogenous outputs can either lead to a system being in equilibrium, or disrupt this equilibrium. So, on methodological grounds, a new attitude emerges where numerical simulations play a major role both in the quantitive and in the qualititative analysis of multisectoral dynamics. This deep integration between theory and numerical simulation opens up many interesting possibilities for multisectoral analysis. This new trend appears not to be limited by a lack of numerical methods or instruments.

NOTES

1. This paper reports on results of a research project at the University of Macerata, which was partly funded by the CNR (National Council for Researches) in Rome. I wish to thank Laura Gardini for some fruitful discussions on the subject and Laerte Sorini for his assistance with the programming work. This version of the paper has also benefited from the comments of both editors and Gerhard Meinen, which are hereby gratefully acknowledged.
2. Given A as the $n \times n$ technical coefficient matrix and B as the $n \times n$ capital coefficient matrix, the dynamic Leontief model is formulated as:

$$x_{t+1} = [\mathrm{I} + B^{-1}(\mathrm{I} - A)]x_t + B^{-1}f_t$$

Since matrix $(I - A)^{-1}B$ has a dominant eigenvalue σ_F with associated eigenvector u_F, all of whose elements are positive, the dynamic Leontief model can exhibit and maintain positive solutions only if initial conditions are given according to the proportions established by u_F. Its constant growth factor will be given by $1 + 1/\sigma_F$ and the growth path will usually be unstable, since the eigenvalue $1 + 1/\sigma_F$ is usually the lowest eigenvalue of matrix $[I + B^{-1}\ (I - A)]$.
3. In order to confine this exposition to the essentials, we will reduce the number of industries to one whenever possible.
4. The transformation U amounts to a rotation around the origin or a reflection in a line through the origin; see Brock and Malliaris (1989).

REFERENCES

BROCK, W. A. and A. G. MALLIARIS (1989) *Differential Equations, Stability and Chaos in Dynamic Economics*, North-Holland, Amsterdam.

BRÓDY, A. (1970) *Proportions, Prices and Planning*, North-Holland, Amsterdam.

CHIARELLA, C. (1988) 'The Cobweb Model: Its Instability and the Onset of Chaos', *Economic Modelling*, vol. 5, no. 4, October.

CIASCHINI, M. (1980) 'L'approccio sistemistico ai modelli multisettoriali con capitale fisso', Quaderni dell'Istituto Matematico 'G. Castelnuovo', Università di Roma La Sapienza.

CIASCHINI, M. (1993) *Modelling the Structure of the Economy*, Chapman & Hall, London.

GARDINI, L. (1992) 'Absorbing Areas and Their Bifurcations', Quaderni dell'Istituto di Scienze Economiche, no. 16, Università di Urbino.

GOODWIN, R. M. (1990) *Chaotic Income Dynamics*, The Clarendon Press, Oxford.

LAHIRI, S. (1976). 'Input–Output Analysis with Scale Dependent Coefficients', *Econometrica*, September, pp. 947–961.

LAHIRI, S. and G. PYATT (1980) 'On the Solution of Scale Dependent Input–Output Models', *Econometrica*, November, pp. 1827–1830.

LORENZ, H. W. (1989) 'Non-Linear Dynamical Economics and Chaotic Motion', Springer-Verlag, New York.

PASINETTI, L. (1993) *Dinamica Economica Strutturale*, Il Mulino, Bologna.

12 Bródy's Capital

Thijs ten Raa

12.1 INTRODUCTION

The dynamic input–output model reads (Leontief, 1970)

$$x = Ax + B\dot{x} + y \quad (1)$$

The left-hand side features the state variable of the economy, the vector of sectoral capacities, as measured by the output levels. The right-hand side lists the material inputs, investment, and household demand, respectively. The structure of the economy is given by two matrices of technical coefficients. A is the matrix of input flow coefficients and B is the matrix of input stock coefficients. Input flows, for example electricity, are fully consumed, but input stocks, like housing, carry over. Material inputs are, therefore, proportional to the output levels, but investment is proportional to the new capacity, $\dot{x}$, where the dot denotes the time derivative. Output x and household demand y are functions of time, but the technical coefficients are constant in the absence of structural change. Implicit in the dynamic input–output model is the assumption that productive activity is instantaneous. If you have the commodity vectors $a_{\cdot 1}$ and $b_{\cdot 1}$ (the first columns of technical coefficients matrices A and B), then you get instantaneously the commodity vectors e_1 and $b_{\cdot 1}$, where e_1 is the first unit vector, representing the output flow, and $b_{\cdot 1}$ is the carry-over stock. In ten Raa (1986a) I have dropped this assumption, redefining an input flow coefficient as a time profile on the past. Thus, to produce one unit of output 1 at time zero, you need inputs $\alpha_{\cdot 1}(s)$ at times s, $s \leq 0$. The matrix of input flow coefficients, α, is a function on the past. It is convenient to work with generalized functions. The dynamic input–output model with instantaneous production is recouped by $\alpha = A\delta$, where δ is the Dirac function (unit mass in the origin).

A time profile of inputs or outputs that is not concentrated in the origin implies that commodities are tied up in the productive activity. Such commodities constitute capital. The distributed inputs (α) represent working capital. In ten Raa (1986b) the analysis is applied to the input stock coefficients, modelling Polish investment lead times by distributing matrix B over the past. In a letter, András Bródy wrote the author:

Thank you for sending your interesting new paper with computations for the Polish economy. I have to confess I am less enthusiastic about it than I have been with your former papers.

I rather expected you to forge ahead and to drop the notion of a capital matrix, *B*, altogether. You had a distributed input–point output model, already indicating that the inclusion of stocks can be dispensed with. If you generalize to a distributed input–distributed output model, then our traditional approach becomes truly obsolete. Why don't you do it? It is within your reach.

In this paper I attempt to take up Bródy's challenge. In other words, let me address the question under which circumstances the dynamic input–output model describes a distributed input–distributed output economy without a preconceived distinction between input flows and stocks.

12.2 THE STRUCTURE OF AN ECONOMY

I maintain the state variable of the economy, x, the vector of sectoral capacities. A unit capacity in sector 1 at time zero requires inputs $\alpha_{\cdot 1}(s)$ at times s, $s \leq 0$, and yields outputs $\beta_{\cdot 1}(s)$ at times s, $s \geq 0$. Organizing the sectoral input and output time profiles in a pair of matrix valued (generalized) functions of time, the **structure of the economy** is (α, β). Input and output coefficients α and β are defined on the past and the future, respectively. All commodities are output of some productive activity. Account for stocks: The capacity of sector 1 at time t, $x_1(t)$, contributes $\beta_{\cdot 1}(s)x_1(t)$ to the economy's commodity stock at time $t + s$, $s \geq 0$. By change of time variable, the capacity of sector 1 at time $t - s$ contributes $\beta_{\cdot 1}(s)x_1(t - s)$ to the stock at time t, $s \geq 0$. Summing all contributions of the past ($s \geq 0$) by all sectors, we obtain the commodity stock at time t, $\int_0^\infty \beta(s)x(t - s)ds$. This is **capital**. Since β is confined to the nonnegatives, the domain of integration may just as well be extended to the real time. Thus we obtain the convolution product of β and x, $\beta \star x$, at time t. Capital is thus given by the convolution product of the output coefficients, β, and the sectoral capacities, x. The units of capacity are arbitrary, just like the activity levels of von Neumann (1945). Any rescaling is offset by the output coefficients, and the measure of capital is invariant; it is determined by the physical units of the commodities.

Capital at time t can be allocated to future capacity utilization, $x(t - s)$, where $s \leq 0$. In fact, $x(t - s)$ requires commodities $\alpha(s)(t - s)$ at time t, $s \leq 0$. The total allocation of capital at time t to future production amounts $\int_{-\infty}^0 \alpha(s)x(t - s)ds$ or $\alpha \star x$ valued at time t.

The residual capital constitutes the household stock of commodities, $Y(t)$. Consequently,

$$\int_0^{\infty} \beta(s)x(t-s)ds = \int_{-\infty}^{0} \alpha(s)x(t-s)ds + Y(t) \tag{2}$$

or, in short

$$(\beta - \alpha) \star x = Y \tag{3}$$

This is the distributed input–distributed output model of the economy. The purpose of this paper is to determine the structure of the economy for which the dynamic input–output model, (1), is submitted by the distributed model with no preconceived flow-stock distribution (3).

12.3 THE MATERIAL BALANCE

If the total mass of the net output coefficients, $\int(\beta - \alpha)$, is an M-matrix (Minc, 1988), then any nonnegative stock of household commodities can be sustained by nonnegative capacities. However, interesting economics is in terms of flows rather than stocks. The material balance is usually defined in flows, see equation (1) for example. The transition to flow is by differentiation of equation (2) with respect to time. Differentiating the left–hand side (capital), we obtain

$$\begin{aligned}\frac{d}{dt}\int_0^{\infty} \beta(s)x(t-s)ds &= \int_0^{\infty} \beta(s)\frac{d}{dt}x(t-s)ds \\ &= -\int_0^{\infty} \beta(s)\frac{d}{ds}x(t-s)ds = \\ &= -\beta(s)x(t-s)|_0^{\infty} + \int_0^{\infty} \frac{d}{ds}\beta(s)x(t-s)ds \\ &= \beta(0)x(t) + \int_0^{\infty} \dot{\beta}(s)x(t-s)ds\end{aligned} \tag{4}$$

where $\dot{\beta}$ is the reduction of output of the capacity units, that is **depreciation**. It takes negative values. Differentiating the first term on the right hand side of equation (2), we get $\int_0^{\infty}\alpha(s)\dot{x}(t-s)ds$. Lastly, we have $\dot{Y}$, the additions to the household stock of commodities, a commodity flow vector. Thus (2) can be rewritten as

$$\beta(0)x(t) = -\int_0^{\infty} \dot{\beta}(s)x(t-s)ds + \int_0^{-\infty} \alpha(s)\dot{x}(t-s)ds + \dot{Y}(t) \tag{5}$$

This is the material balance of the economy. It is a rewrite of the simple distributed input–distributed output model, (3). No assumptions have been made. On the left-hand side we have the instantaneous rates of output of current sectoral capacities. On the right-hand side we have, first, replacement investment, second investment in new capacity, and third additions to the household stock.

12.4 THE SUBSUMPTION OF DYNAMIC INPUT–OUTPUT

Replacement investment, $-\int_0^\infty \dot{\beta}(s)x(t-s)ds$, equals the amount of depreciation of capacity s time units old, $-\dot{\beta}(s)$, times the level of capacity at that time, $x(t-s)$, summed over ages s. Thus, to determine replacement investment one must know the life pattern of output, β, and the past distribution of capacity, x. In dynamic input–output analysis, one makes the simplifying assumption that one must know only the current stock of capital. The latter is given by the convolution product of β and x valued at time t (see section 12.2). Now it is well known that replacement investment is independent of the age structure of capital (x) if and only if the life pattern (β) is given by the exponential decay function and independent of the sector of installation:

Assumption 1. $\beta_{ij}(s) = \beta_{ij}(0)e - p_i s$

Then depreciation is, in absolute value,

$$-\dot{\beta} = \rho\beta \tag{6}$$

where ρ is the diagonal matrix with elements ρ_i. Under assumption 1, replacement investment is $\rho \int_0^\infty \beta(s)x(t-s)ds$, the direct product of the matrix of depreciation rates and the stock of capital.

As a matter of fact, the dynamic input–output model incorporates replacement investment in the material inputs term, Ax. This requires a second step. Replacement investment must not only be proportional to the current stock of capital (irrespective its age structure), but the latter, on its turn, must be proportional to the current level of capacity. In general, the amount of capital allocated to production depends on the entire path of future capacities, through the convolution product with the input time profile, α (see section 12.2). When is only the current level of capacity relevant? Well, if production takes no time, but is instantaneous:

Assumption 2. $\alpha(s) = \alpha(0)\delta(s)$

Here δ is the Dirac function, the unit mass in the origin. In the Introduction it was noted that this assumption reduces my distributed input model to the traditional one. Thus, what remains crucial now is the distribution of output. Now let us trace the implication of the assumptions on the structure of the economy on the material balance. Substituting assumption's 1 consequence (6) and assumption 2 into balance equation (5), we obtain

$$\beta(0)x(t) = \rho \int_0^{\infty} \beta(s)x(t-s)ds + \alpha(0)\dot{x}(t) + \dot{Y}(t) \tag{7}$$

Now replace the capital term by the expression given in equation (2) and substitute assumption 2. Then equation (7) becomes

$$\beta(0)x(t) = \rho\alpha(0)x(t) + \alpha(0)\dot{x}(t) + \rho Y(t) + \dot{Y}(t) \tag{8}$$

This, then, is the material balance equation under assumption 1 and 2. It coincides with the dynamic input–output model, provided secondary products are absent: $\beta(0) = I$, the identity matrix. Note the household demand comprises household stock replacement investment as well as additions to the stock. It is interesting to relate the dynamic input–output coefficients matrices to the structure of the distributed input–distributed output economy:

$$A = \rho\alpha(0), \quad B = \alpha(0) \tag{9}$$

Consequently,

$$A = \rho B \tag{10}$$

That is, the dynamic input–output model is consistent with a distributed input-distributed output model of the economy if the flow coefficients are **proportional** to the stock coefficients, where the proportions are the rates of depreciation. This relationship between circulating and fixed capital was first noted by Bródy (1974).

I do not wish to subscribe to this relationship as an absolute requirement on technical coefficients matrices. However, an important corollary to the analysis is that if equation (10) fails, then the dynamic input–output model, (1), is misspecified. The simplifying assumptions made on the structure of the economy will not be valid and one must resort to the general formulation of the material balance: (3) (in stocks) or (5) (in flows).

12.5 CONCLUSION

In this paper I have attempted to carry out András Bródy's programme to dispense with the distinction between flows and stocks in dynamic input–

output analysis by modelling the time profiles of the input and output components of the structure of an economy. The traditional model is retrieved when capital decays exponentially and production is instantaneous. However, the flow and the stock coefficients must be consistent with Bródy's capital equation. If this is not the case, the model better be replaced by the distributed input–distributed output material balance equation derived in this paper.

REFERENCES

BRÓDY, A. (1974) *Production, Prices and Planning*, North-Holland, Amsterdam.

LEONTIEF, W. (1970) 'The Dynamic Inverse', in A. P. Carter and A. Bródy (eds), *Contributions to Input–Output Analysis*, North-Holland, Amsterdam, pp. 17–46.

MINC, H. (1988) *Nonnegatieve Matrices*, Wiley, New York, 1988.

VON NEUMANN, J. (1945) 'A Model of General Economic Equilibrium', *The Review of Economic Studies*, 13, pp. 1–9.

TEN RAA, Th. (1986a) 'Dynamic Input–Output Analysis with Distributed Activities', *The Review of Economics and Statistics* 68, 2, pp. 300–10.

TEN RAA, Th. (1986b) 'Applied Dynamic Input–Output with Distributed Activities', *European Economic Review* 30, 4, pp. 805–31.

13 Towards a Tenable Concept of 'Warranted Supply'

Francis Seton

13.1 INTRODUCTION

Among the comprehensive portrayals of economic structure, the integrated *tableaux économiques* that have engaged the attention of economists in recent decades, the most outstanding is undoubtedly Leontief's input–output table, both for its eloquence and rigour and its fecundity as a tool of economic analysis. Some of its statistical robustness, veracity, and adequacy may have been called into question in various contexts, but it is still a conceptual template which, consciously or unconsciously, underlies much of macroeconomic thinking, whether of an abstract or policy-oriented kind.

In the field of pure economic research it has shown its power most clearly in studies encompassing different economic systems which resist direct comparisons owing to different market- and price-structures, and a number of valuable studies on their comparative performance have been offered with its aid. The famous International Comparison Project (ICP) under the aegis of the United Nations (Kravis *et al.*, 1975) dealing with costs and purchasing powers in their variation across national frontiers is undoubtedly one of the most seminal among them and has been extensively used to compile league tables of GNP, GDP per head, and the more important components of final demand. As so many similar attempts however, it has come up against the perplexities and inherent uncertainties that all index-number analysis is heir to, whether based on Laspeyre, Paasche, or Geary-type indexes.

This has thrown a number of researchers back to clutch at the straws of Input–Output analysis in an attempt to construct theoretical price-models, often with ideological overtones, to make unbiased comparisons possible without resort to the inevitable arbitrariness of index-number construction. In my view these straws have turned out to be strong safety-ropes in enabling – and indeed forcing – their users to make their assumptions crystal clear instead of obscuring them in a welter of statistical conventions, devices, and stratagems. The most prominent among them were no doubt to be found in the former Soviet Union and the Peoples' Democracies of Eastern Europe where a chaotic price system enjoined an almosty frantic search for some ideologically inspired order based on Marxian labour values, 'production prices' (Seton, 1957) or the historic compromise of 'multi-channel prices' (Sekerka *et al.*, 1967, and Bródy, 1965).

Nor has there been any lack of Western attempts at such price modelling, if only in criticism of the ideologies underlying their Eastern counterparts (Morishima, 1974), but often also based on neo-classical foundations or the tenets of Western market-clearing theories (Seton 1985, 1992). The latter were mainly inspired by the desire to make valid comparisons between price-systems and ratios internal to each economy. Only comparatively few efforts at direct quantitative comparisons of absolute aggregates appear to have been published, the most prominent and comprehensive of them being undoubtedly undertaken under the aegis of the Vienna Institute for Comparative Economic Studies (WIIW) within the framework of the 'European Comparison Project' of 1990 (ECP), itself an offshoot of ICP (see Müller, 1994). These latter efforts were based on conversions by means of exchange rates or purchasing power parities and thereby fell victim to all the difficulties inherent in index-number computations.

All this was undertaken in the search for valid comparison between countries, systems, or time-periods. It is surprising however, how rarely the quantitative structure of GDP, the supply of goods and services for final use as it emerges from Input–Output tables has been directly evaluated in terms of criteria furnished by these tables themselves for its relevance or adequacy to the general welfare which it is being produced to serve.

When such an assessment is undertaken it invariably relies on a separate form of analysis dependent on a 'welfare function', conceived in isolation from the input-output system and grafted on to it like a *deus ex machina* from outside. Is there nothing in the input-output system itself which marks off one 'final bill of goods' (list of 'finals' or 'final supply') as better or more appropriate to the economy than others, a benchmark which could serve to judge GNP structures planned or actually achieved by their departure from that norm?

It is the quest for a diagnostic tool of this kind which has prompted this author to cast about for criteria derivable uniquely from features intrinsic in the system that might fulfil such a function. As may be expected, the criterion has more of the characteristics of an equilibrium than of an optimum *tout court*, albeit of an equilibrium defined by essential features of the neoclassical paradigm reflecting an optimum. If factors of production were rewarded in each market by an allocation corresponding to their marginal product in that market, and the pattern of final output precisely adapted to the resulting demand to clear all markets, this pattern would certainly ensure an equilibrium more appropriate to the economy than any other. Can such a pattern be uniquely defined within the confines of a Leontief economy (in which marginal and average products are equal)?

13.2 THE MODEL

13.2 Factor-Contributions to GNP

An attempt at such a definition is bound to start with a synopsis of the usual input–output table in terms of current prices, simplified here – without loss of generality – to three production sectors, say Agriculture (1) producing 'grain', 'Heavy Industry' (2) producing 'steel', and 'Light Industry' (3) producing 'cloth' as typical homogeneous products. The allocation of total output (z_r) to the various processing branches (x_{rs}) and to final uses (y_r) can then be shown in tabular form as

$$\begin{array}{rll} \text{Grain} & x_{11}+x_{12}+x_{13}+y_1 & = z_1 \\ \text{Steel} & x_{21}+x_{22}+x_{23}+y_2 & = z_2 \\ \text{Cloth} & x_{31}+x_{32}+x_{33}+y_3 & = z_3 \\ \text{Labour (wages)} & w_{11}+w_{12}+w_{13} & = w_1 \\ \text{Capital services} & w_{21}+w_{22}+w_{23} & = w_2 \\ \text{Total factors } (w+w) & w_1+w_2+w_3 & = w \end{array} \qquad (1)$$

With $\mathbf{i}$ representing the all-unit column-vector $(1\ 1\ 1)'$, this can be written in matrix form as

$$\begin{aligned} \mathbf{Xi}+\mathbf{y} &= \mathbf{z} \\ \mathbf{Wi} \quad &= \mathbf{w} \end{aligned} \qquad (2)$$

or, using the familiar Leontief input-coefficients a_{rs} ($\equiv x_{rs}/z_s$) and b_{rs} ($\equiv w_{rs} / z_s \equiv \ell_s, k_s$):

$$\begin{aligned} \mathbf{Az}+\mathbf{y} &= \mathbf{z} \\ \mathbf{Bz} \quad &= \mathbf{w} \end{aligned} \qquad (3)$$

where $\mathbf{B} \equiv (w_{rs})$ stands for $\begin{pmatrix} l_1 l_2 l_3 \\ k_1 k_2 k_3 \end{pmatrix}$

As is well known, these last equations can be made explicit with respect to $\mathbf{z}$:

$$\mathbf{z} = (\mathbf{I}-\mathbf{A})^{-1}\mathbf{y} \qquad (4)$$

and with respect to the 'full' (direct and indirect) factor coefficients c_{rs} ($\equiv\lambda\ \kappa$) which emerge from

$$\begin{aligned} \lambda' A + l' &= \lambda' \\ \kappa' A + \mathbf{k}' &= \kappa' \quad \text{as} \end{aligned}$$

$$\mathbf{C} = \begin{pmatrix} \lambda' \\ \kappa' \end{pmatrix} = \mathbf{B}(\mathbf{I} - \mathbf{A})^{-1} \tag{5}$$

When this is post-multiplied by the diagonal matrix $\hat{\mathbf{y}}$, we obtain the full factor costs of final output

$$\mathbf{C}\hat{\mathbf{y}} = \begin{pmatrix} \lambda_1 y_1 & \lambda_2 y_2 & \lambda_3 y_3 \\ \kappa_1 y_1 & \kappa_2 y_2 & \kappa_3 y_3 \end{pmatrix} \tag{6}$$

Finally, pre-multiplying this by the all-unit row-vector $\mathbf{i}'$, we obtain

$$\mathbf{i}'\mathbf{C}\hat{\mathbf{y}} = [(\lambda_1 + \kappa_1)y_1\ ,\ (\lambda_2 + \kappa_2)y_2\ ,\ (\lambda_3 + \kappa_3)y_3] \tag{7}$$

the total 'full' factor-contributions to final supply due to be returned to the factor-owners under what might be described as a 'rational' regime.

13.2.2 Commodity and Factor 'Norms'

The expression $\mathbf{i}'\mathbf{C}\hat{\mathbf{y}}$ of equation (7) may now be analysed to isolate a special matrix of conceptual significance: Replacing $\mathbf{i}$ by $\hat{\mathbf{w}}^{-1}\mathbf{w}$, we obtain the factor demands warranted under the rational regime as

$$(\hat{\mathbf{y}}\mathbf{C}'\hat{\mathbf{w}}^{-1})\mathbf{w} = \mathbf{N}\mathbf{w} \tag{8}$$

where the pre-multiplier in brackets replicates the 'norm matrix' $\mathbf{N}$ exhaustively commented and interpreted in the author's book (F. Seton, 1992, Sections 3.3 and 3.4, pp. 43 *et seq.*). This interpretation may be briefly repeated here by splitting the matrix into two factors deriving from the definitions of $\mathbf{A}'$ and $\mathbf{B}'$as components of $\mathbf{C}'$ (see 2, 3 and 5 above):

$$\begin{aligned} \hat{\mathbf{y}}\mathbf{C}'\hat{\mathbf{w}}^{-1} &= \hat{\mathbf{y}}(\mathbf{I} - \mathbf{A}')^{-1}\mathbf{B}'\hat{\mathbf{w}}^{-1} = \hat{\mathbf{y}}(\mathbf{I} - \hat{\mathbf{z}}^{-1}\mathbf{X}')^{-1}\hat{\mathbf{z}}^{-1}\mathbf{W}'\hat{\mathbf{w}}^{-1} \\ &= \hat{\mathbf{y}}(\hat{\mathbf{z}} - \mathbf{X}')^{-1}\,\mathbf{W}'\hat{\mathbf{w}}^{-1} = \mathbf{V}'\mathbf{E}' \end{aligned} \tag{9}$$

where $\mathbf{V}'$, i.e. $\hat{\mathbf{y}}(\mathbf{z} - \mathbf{X}')^{-1}$ is evidently the transposed solution of

$$\mathbf{X}\mathbf{V} + \hat{\mathbf{y}} = \hat{\mathbf{z}}V$$

and thus measures the 'full' (direct and indirect) contributions of the various commodities to the total production of each commodity in turn (column by column), representing what we have called the 'commodity norms', while $\mathbf{E}'$, i.e. $\mathbf{W}'\hat{\mathbf{w}}^{-1}$ expresses the direct contribution of each factor to the production of each commodity. $\mathbf{V}'\mathbf{E}'$ therefore explains the matrix **N** as the conspectus of the full contributions of the various factors to the several production sectors, the 'factor norms' n_{rs} measuring the full productivities of all factors on which, in a rational system, their individual compensations would be based. The vector **Nw** of (8) thus lists the final outputs which must be produced to secure to each factor its 'rational' reward. If it is further assumed that a uniform margin on top of this ($1/\varphi$) is required from each branch to satisfy collective or government requirements, the list of total demands which the system would be making on its production sectors is

$$\mathbf{d} = 1/\varphi \cdot \mathbf{Nw} \tag{10}$$

13.2.3 Market Clearing

The list of final demands (10) may be expressed in terms of the final outputs that have conditioned them (via rational factor productivities and compensations) by recalling that w or Bz could by virtue of (3) be written as $B(I - A)^{-1}y$, i.e. as Cy (4). The demand which a rational structure of final outputs, say, y^*, would therefore have to meet must obey the equations

$$\mathbf{y}^* = \mathbf{1}/\varphi \cdot \mathbf{NCy}^* \quad \text{or} \quad (\varphi\mathbf{I} - \mathbf{NC})\mathbf{y}^* = \mathbf{0} \tag{11}$$

In fact, the 'warranted supply' of the system y^* is the right-hand eigenvector of the 'Norm-Cost matrix' **NC**. Like all eigenvectors however, its elements are determined up to a multiplicative factor only and need to be 'scaled' to give them absolute values. The most convenient scaling factor is normally the one which leaves the total GNP invariant, and in what follows it will be assumed that all elements of the warranted supply are scaled up or down in conformity with this.

Further, since by virture of (10) and (11) $\mathbf{Nw} = \mathbf{y}$ and $\mathbf{w} = \mathbf{Cy}$,[1] we must have

$$\mathbf{CNw}^* = \mathbf{Cy}^* = \varphi\mathbf{w}^* \quad \text{or} \quad (\varphi\mathbf{I} - \mathbf{CN})\mathbf{w}^* = \mathbf{0} \tag{12}$$

an equation defining $\mathbf{w}^*$ as the 'warranted employment structure' which under the conditions assumed will create a demand for commodities whose factor-input requirements is identical with that structure, i.e. an employment structure which will 'create its own demand'.

13.2.4 The link with Eigenprices

Equations (11) and (12) have shown that the warranted structures $\mathbf{y}^*$ and $\mathbf{w}^*$ are the duals of the eigenprices $\mathbf{p}^*$ and eigenrentals $\mathbf{r}^*$ respectively as defined in F. Seton (1992) (equation 3.29, p. 53) as the left-hand eigenvectors of the same matrices. These are themselves 'rational prices' in the sense of equating cost- and use-values, just as the 'warranted' quantities equate supply and demand.

As has been shown in *ibid* (p. 100) moreover, the elements of the warranted structures are in every case equal to the *actual* final outputs (or factor uses) multiplied by the relevant eigen-prices or -rentals,[2] i.e.

$$\mathbf{y}^* = \hat{\mathbf{y}}\mathbf{p}^* \quad \text{and} \quad \mathbf{w}^* = \hat{\mathbf{w}}\mathbf{r}^* \tag{13}$$

The eigenprices and -rentals are therefore themselves ratios between the warranted and actual supplies (or employments) in each production sector and can thus function as indicators of 'scarcity' in this special sense. The construction of eigenprices as a synthesis of cost- and use-values thus opens the way to investing them with this additional feature usually taken to be characteristic of valid value-concepts.

13.3 SOME RESULTS

13.3.1 Statistical Estimation

From (13) it also follows that, given the eigenprices as computed in ECUV, we can calculate the warranted structures for the economies under review by a simple process of multiplication, without going to the trouble of computing new eigenvectors for every case. We have taken advantage of this in this section. The original data used were compiled from an official UN source (Eurostat, 1986) and the author's previous eigenprice calculations in F. Seton (1992, pp. 126 and 128). The results below are vitiated by a number of serious defects, chief of which are the acknowledged unreliabilty and non-comparability of the data, the author's necessarily cavalier treatment of undefined or insufficiently defined statistics, and the fact that eigenprices were computed on the basis of disaggregations into 29–76 sectors only and subsequently consolidated into the 9 sectors distinguished here.

In view of the deficiencies listed above the coincidence of the eigencost ratio (ϕ) as computed here with the result of the disaggregated computation

Table 13.1 Actual and warranted GNP contributions in 1980

(in mln of local currency)

	Belgium		*Netherlands*		*W. Germany*		*UK*	
Sectors	*Act'l*	*Warr'd*	*Act'l*	*Warr'd*	*Act'l*	*Warr'd*	*Act'l*	*Warr'd*
Agr., etc.	104.7	103.3	12.9	12.9	19.0	17.5	2.0	3.0
Mining	59.8	59.2	52.6	52.0	104.6	99.7	19.3	17.9
Food	412.2	383.4	46.3	46.2	132.8	117.6	21.7	19.5
Chem'l	350.6	348.9	27.8	27.6	74.4	74.3	8.0	8.1
Engin'g	174.9	817.1	60.0	62.1	345.9	363.2	41.4	44.6
Textiles	243.9	249.5	15.7	16.5	70.2	74.4	8.2	8.8
Other Mf.	280.2	289.5	16.0	16.7	62.5	64.4	6.9	7.5
Constr'n	470.2	476.3	36.7	37.7	173.2	181.8	21.3	23.2
Services	2149.6	2143.2	226.1	222.7	781.8	770.8	142.0	139.1
Tot. GNP	5403.2	5402.8	494.2	494.4	1764.4	1763.8	271.8	271.8
Labour	2071.0	2141.4	197.8	200.2	840.7	950.0	137.1	140.9
Profit	778.5	768.3	74.4	72.2	304.3	287.0	30.7	28.9
Imports	2179.3	2201.1	178.6	191.7	364.9	373.3	55.7	57.2
Tax (Res.)	374.4	291.9	43.4	30.3	254.4	153.5	48.3	44.7
Factors		5110.9		464.1		1610.3		227.1
Factors/ GNP		.946		.939		.913		.836
F. Seton 1992 (p. 125)		.945		.919		.913		.836

Associated branches are included everywhere, i.e. Agr. includes Forestry and Fishing, Mining Quarrying and Fuel, Food Drink & Tobacco, Chem'l Plastics and Rubber, Engin'g Metal-Working, Textiles Leather & Clothing, Services Utilities, Transport & Trade.
Act'l = Actual
Warr'd = Warranted

from eigenprices in (F. Seton, 1992, p. 125) is remarkable. Equally remarkable is the slightness of the discrepancy between actual and warranted quantities, although this hides much greater discrepancies in computations based on more disaggregated sectors not shown here. In any case, the reader should be warned once again that the figures are to be taken as illustrative only, and that no reliance is to be placed on them as reflections of any economic reality, whether descriptive or normative. The list of 'warranted supplies' is of course a direct emanation of the arbitrary scaling of results to produce an invariant GNP.

To the extent that the figures may be accepted, there appears to be a consistent (slight) 'overproduction' of agricultural goods in all countries except the Netherlands, and a slightly greater one in the Food, Drink and Tobacco industries everywhere. Equally striking is the universal shortfall in Textiles, Leather and Clothing and in the Engineering and Metal Working industries. Labour appears to be underemployed and/or underpaid everywhere compared with entrepreneurship (Profits, etc.).

13.4 A TENTATIVE VERDICT

13.4.1 The Hidden Hand

By no stretch of the imagination could the warranted structure of final output as defined and computed here be identified with the most 'desirable' or 'desired' assortment, even though it is intended to correspond to the demand structure generated in the process of production. Nothing but personal or collective preferences such as may be embodied in welfare functions of some sort, supplemented by social or moral aspirations, can in the last analysis define such an ideal. The question that remains to be answered therefore is whether any mechanism might be at work capable of shifting the 'warranted equilibrium' into closer proximity with the desired goal, whether the latter can in practice be defined or not.

A mechanism of this sort may be discerned in rough outline when the influence of current prices on the warranted equilibrium is subjected to closer scrutiny, provided we may assume that a shortfall of final output, say z_r, below the desired quantity, even when not 'effectively demanded' may create a tendency for the price of the affected commodity to rise and thereby increase the measured final demand y_r, thus changing the Norm-cost matrix **NC** $(= \hat{\mathbf{y}}\mathbf{C}'\hat{\mathbf{w}}^{-1}\mathbf{C})$ in the *r*th row while leaving its other elements undisturbed. Will such a change push its right-hand eigenvector y^* towards greater emphasis on $\mathbf{y}_r^*$ relatively to its other elements?

The following argument[3] may lend some credence to the mechanism we are looking for:

Let **x** and α be respectively the right-hand eigenvector and dominant eigenvalue of a non-negative and irreducible matrix **A** subject to disturbance, say in its first row only, turning it into $\bar{\mathbf{A}}$ (also assumed to be non-negative and irreducible); the following two equation systems will then be valid:

$$\mathbf{Ax} = \begin{pmatrix} \mathrm{a} & \mathbf{b}' \\ \mathbf{c} & \mathbf{E} \end{pmatrix} \begin{Bmatrix} \mathrm{u} \\ \mathbf{v} \end{Bmatrix} = \alpha \begin{Bmatrix} \mathrm{u} \\ \mathbf{v} \end{Bmatrix} \quad \text{and}$$

$$\bar{\mathbf{A}}\bar{\mathbf{x}} = \begin{pmatrix} \mathrm{a} & \mathbf{b}' \\ \mathbf{c} & \mathbf{E} \end{pmatrix} \begin{Bmatrix} \mathrm{u} \\ \mathbf{v} \end{Bmatrix} = \bar{\alpha} \begin{Bmatrix} \mathrm{u} \\ \mathbf{v} \end{Bmatrix}$$

implying

$$\alpha\mathbf{v} = \mathbf{c}\mathrm{u} + \mathbf{E}\mathbf{v} \quad \text{and} \quad \bar{\alpha}\bar{\mathbf{v}} = \mathbf{c}\bar{\mathrm{u}} + \mathbf{E}\mathbf{v} \tag{14}$$

Now let x_R be the element of **v** subject to the greatest proportional disturbance ($\widehat{x}_R \equiv \bar{x}_R/x_R$)* among all the elements of **v**, i.e.

$$\widehat{x}_r < \bar{x}_R \quad \text{for all } r > 1 \tag{15}$$

Since equations (14) are valid for all elements of **v**, we also have

$$\alpha v_R = c_R u + \mathbf{e}'_R \mathbf{v} \quad \text{and} \quad \alpha \bar{v}_R = c_R \bar{u} + \mathbf{e}'_R \mathbf{v} \tag{16}$$

where $\mathbf{e}'_R$ is the Rth row of **E**.

Furthermore, since increases in any element of a non-negative matrix will increase its dominant eigenvalue,[4] we have $\hat{\alpha} > 1$, and therefore (15) implies *a fortiori*:

$$\widehat{x}_R < \widehat{\alpha}\widehat{x}_R \quad \text{or} \quad \bar{x}_r < \widehat{\alpha}\widehat{x}_R x_r, \tag{17}$$

Since this applies to all r>1, it must apply to any positive linear combination of them, in particuar to

$$\mathbf{e}'_R \bar{\mathbf{v}} < \widehat{\alpha}\widehat{x}_R \mathbf{e}'_R \mathbf{v} \tag{18}$$

and this, by virtue of (16) implies

$$\bar{\alpha}\bar{v}_R - c_R\bar{u} < \widehat{\alpha}\widehat{v}_R(\alpha v_R - c_R u) = \bar{\alpha}\bar{v}_R - \widehat{\alpha}\widehat{v}_R c_R u \quad \text{or} \quad \widehat{\alpha}\widehat{v}_R u < \bar{u} \tag{19}$$

It follows, finally, that

$$\widehat{u} \equiv \widehat{x}_1 > \widehat{\alpha}\widehat{x}_R > \widehat{x}_R > \widehat{x}_r, \quad \text{i.e. } \widehat{x}_1 > \widehat{x}_r \quad \text{for all } r > 1 \tag{20}$$

We have thus proved that any increase in the current price of a commodity (in this case exemplified by commodity 1) will increase the warranted final demand for that commodity more than any other warranted final demand,[5] in fact that there exists a tendency causing the warranted demand structure to approach any ideally desired structure that is capable of exerting a normal influence on current prices. Whether this justifies a claim for the 'warranted structure' to be any more than a sterile equilibrium condition must be left to further research work beyond the scope of this chapter.

13.5 CONCLUSION

13.5.1 Caveats

So far the bare bones of theory. Unfortunately the author lacks the resources and expertise to put the flesh of empirical findings on them. Even though he is well aware that only this would entitle him to the full attention of professional colleagues, he must leave this task to others. It behoves him however, to point out the difficulties likely to be found. First and foremost, the scarcity and inadequacy of relevant statistics and the frequent obscurity of their origin and precise definition would place a severe burden of selection and interpretation on the most undaunted researcher. How can the borderline between intermediate and final output be validly drawn? What factors of production can be identified and independently measured? Are the intermediate flows measured uniformly in producer prices purged of all trade- and service-margins which would falsely credit industries with the contributions of other sectors? Are the observed flows gross or net of taxes and unrequited charges (VAT, employers' contributions to social insurance funds, etc.)? Are import and exports measured in the right currency or at the right exchange rate, – gross or net of tariffs?

All this would no doubt face the researcher with unresolvable conundrums and force him into arbitrary decisions as each Gordion knot has to be cut in turn. The result may well be an amalgam of erratic choices as redolent of uncertainty as any offering brewed in the witches' cauldron of index-number computations. While this is the fate of any new theory, it must be conceded that it is unlikely that any empirical application of the theory set out here will in the near future be seen as a serious competitor of conventional analysis in the search for truth. Direct policy recommendations based on intuition, index-number based comparisons and league tables based on the ICP and ECP method will – and should – continue to be the order of the day and engage the honest toil and sweat and the ingenuity and scholarship of first-rate brains for many years to come. The author of the theory set out here would be foolish indeed to seek to replace them. He merely seeks to offer an alternative which, though possibly inapplicable at the moment, is at least explicit in what it aims at, and might help to confirm or invalidate the findings of conventional methods at some future date. Till then it can claim no more than to be a conceptual framework which might point up useful ways in which improvements in statistics and critical theory might profitably move. It is as such that it is offered here.

NOTES

1. $\mathbf{Cy} = \mathbf{B}(\mathbf{I} - \mathbf{A})^{-1}\mathbf{y} = \mathbf{Bz} = \mathbf{W}\hat{\mathbf{z}}^{-1}\mathbf{z} = \mathbf{Wi} = \mathbf{w}$
2. By virtue of (11), (7), and (14) it may be stated that

$$\mathbf{NC\hat{y}p}^* = \hat{\mathbf{y}}\mathbf{C}'\hat{\mathbf{w}}^{-1}\mathbf{C\hat{y}p}^* = \hat{\mathbf{y}}\mathbf{C}'\mathbf{N}'\mathbf{p}^* = \hat{\mathbf{y}}\mathbf{C}'\mathbf{r}^* = yp^*$$

   I owe this insight to Dr E. Dietzenbacher of Groningen University.
3. A general theorem bearing on this was first proved by Elsner, Johnson and Neumann in the *Czechoslovak Mathematical Journal*, 32, pp. 99–109, 1982, and subsequently sharpened by E. Dietzenbacher in *Zeitschrift für Nationalökonomie*, 1988, vol. 48, No. 4, p. 389. The proof given here is an extreme simplification of the latter.
4. The proof that the dominant eigenvalue of a positive matrix is a monotonically increasing function of each matrix element, along with other classical theorems on such matrices, was originally given by G. Frobenius in *Sitzungsberichte der preussischen Akademie der Wissenschaften*, 1908, vol. I, p. 471.
5. The converse of this theorem, i.e. that a reduction in the price of a commodity will reduce its warranted final demand proportionately more than any other, may be proved analogously.

REFERENCES

AUGUSZTINOVICS, Maria (1993) Review of Seton, F. (1992), in *Structural Change and Economic Dynamics*, vol. 4, no. 1.

BRÓDY, A. (1965) 'Three Types of Price Systems', *Economics of Planning*, vol. 5.

BRÓDY, A. and CARTER, A. P. (eds) (1970) *Contribution to Input/Output Analysis* (North-Holland, Amsterdam).

BRÓDY, A. (1970) *Proportions, Prices and Planning*, (North-Holland, Amsterdam).

BRÓDY, A. (1988) Review of Seton, F. (1985), in *Acta Oeconomica*, vol. 39, no. 1–2.

KRAVIS, I. B. et al. (1975) *A System of International Comparisons of Gross Product and Purchasing Power* (Johns Hopkins University Press, Baltimore).

MORISHIMA, M (1974) 'Marx in the Light of Modern Economic Theory', in *Econometrica*, July.

MÜLLER, W. (1994) 'Wirtschaftsvergleiche zwischen West und Ost' *Internationale Wirtschaft, Statistische Nachrichten*, 24, 4/1994

SEKERKA, B., *et al.* (1967) 'Price Systems Computable from Input/Output Coefficients', Research Paper no. 15 of the Mathematical EGconomics Laboratory of the Czechoslovak Academy of Sciences, Prague.

SETON, F. (1957) 'The Transformation Problem', in *Review of Economic Studies*, June.

SETON, F. (1977) 'The Question of Ideological Obstacles to Rational Price Setting in Communist Countries', in A. Abouchar (ed.), *The Socialist Price Mechanism* (Duke University Press, Durham, N.C).

SETON, F. (1985) *Cost, Use, and Value* (Clarendon Press, Oxford)

SETON, F. (1992) *The Economics of Price, Use, and Value* (2nd edn. of above) (Clarendon Press, Oxford)

SRAFFA, P. (1960) *The Production of Commodities by Means of Commodities* (CUP, Cambridge)

14 The Elusive Standard Commodity: Eigenvectors as Standards of Value

Albert E. Steenge

14.1 INTRODUCTION

Eigenvectors and eigenvalues are among the most useful tools for analyzing properties of input–output systems. At present, undoubtedly, they are used mainly to analyze dynamic systems, in which they define the von Neumann balanced growth path and the corresponding growth rates. It is precisely in this field that some of Andrew Bródy's greatest contributions to economics are found. His work on the structure and the normative implications of the von Neumann growth path has become one of the cornerstones of economic analysis. Here, Bródy was one of the first authors to realize the importance of matrix theory to economic analysis. This in itself is quite remarkable, because in those days many developments in linear algebra were often hardly accessible to economists.

The 1970s and 1980s were periods of rapid development in linear algebra and its applications. It might have been expected, in view of this, that eigenvectors and eigenvalues would have a dominant position in economic analysis. And partly this is the case, of course. Yet, twenty-five years after Bródy's seminal *Proportions, Prices and Planning*, published in 1970, we see something odd. In sharp contrast to their dominant role in *dynamic* models, eigenvectors and eigenvalues only have a very modest place in *static* models; here they play only a minor role in certain *closed* forms, where they are used simply to define equilibrium outputs and the corresponding prices. There seems to be no generally accepted 'use' for eigenvectors and eigenvalues in analysis in the static field. Yet their absence is not total. Specifically in the field of income distribution studies, they serve as the vehicles for expressing the insights of one particular author, Piero Sraffa. In the context of an *open* static input-output model, Sraffa (1960) proposed a simplification in income distribution analysis by introducing a particular eigenvector, his 'Standard commodity', as a system numeraire.[1]

Unfortunately, Sraffa's work has remained isolated from the main field of economic science. This also means that his views on the role of eigenvectors and eigenvalues remained isolated. In this contribution we shall try to establish a connection. This then may result in a new demand for eigenvectors and eigenvalues as instruments in input–output analysis.

14.2 STANDARDS OF VALUE IN STATIC INPUT–OUTPUT MODELS

Let us start with the traditional *open static input–output model*. The model, in its usual specification, consists of two sub-models, one representing the real output side, the other the price side. We have, respectively,

$$x = Ax + f \tag{1}$$

and

$$p = pA + wl \tag{2}$$

Here A, the input coefficients matrix, and l, the vector of direct labour input coefficients, represent the economy's technology, f and x the final demand and corresponding total output vector, p the vector of prices and w the wage rate.[2] Solving for x and p, we obtain

$$x = (I - A)^{-1}f \tag{3}$$

and

$$p = wl(I - A)^{-1} \tag{4}$$

We have distinguished only one primary factor, labour. Correspondingly, relative prices are in terms of embodied labour, expressed by the vector $\underline{l} = l(I-A)^{-1}$ where matrix $(I-A)^{-1}$ is the Leontief-inverse. The wage rate w fixes absolute prices. Labour, clearly, is the standard of value, i.e. a special commodity, the amount of which 'embodied in' or 'imputed to' each good or service in the system under study determines the system's prices or price proportions; so here we are dealing with a labour theory of value.

The above, of course, is straightforward. However, the situation changes quite rapidly if we consider other specifications. Let us turn to the *closed static input–output model*. For the real output side we have

$$z = Mz \tag{5}$$

and for the price side[3]

$$p = pM \tag{6}$$

We can view M as an extended input coefficients matrix obtained by endogenizing labour (see e.g. Seton, 1977 or Pasinetti, 1977, ch 4). Our assumptions regarding the input coefficients matrix M imply that the equilibrium sustaining price vector in (6) is a positive left-hand Perron–Frobenius eigenvector; similarly, the output vector z is a right-hand eigenvector. But what can we say about the standard of value here? To answer this question we must have some rule telling us how to calculate how much of a particular good is embodied in each good or service being produced in the system. Such a rule clearly is lacking here. So, how should we proceed in this case? Obviously we cannot use the expressions for the open form because M's dominant eigenvalue is equal to unity.

14.3 THE SRAFFIAN MODEL

The situation rapidly becomes more complex if we introduce a second factor, capital. Let us return for a moment to the open static model (1). Introducing capital, our price equation may read in 'Marxian' form

$$p = (1 + r)[pA + wl] \tag{7}$$

or in 'Sraffian' form

$$p = (1 + r)pA + wl \tag{8}$$

where in both models r is the rate of profits. These models have given rise to a large body of literature on the nature of equilibrium prices, culminating in the 'transformation problem'. Central here is the distribution of incomes. We know that, distinguishing two factors, this distribution is generally not linear, which implies that analysis of the system will become very complicated (Pasinetti, 1977). As a matter of fact, we only encounter 'simple' labour theory of value prices in the trivial case where r equals zero or in the case where the proportions of l happen to be those of the left-hand Perron–Frobenius eigenvector of A. So, in the general case, which type of prices are we dealing with?[4]

This is where Sraffa comes in. Sraffa is the author of one of the most intriguing and most commented-on books in the history of economics. His 1960 publication *Production of Commodities by Means of Commodities* discussed the income distribution problem in a model of the form {1,8}. He introduced the so-called Standard commodity, which is in fact (as was shown later) a right-hand Perron–Frobenius eigenvector of A, the system's matrix of input coefficients. Sraffa stated that adopting this vector as the system's numeraire will make the distribution issue transparent by generating a linear trade-off between the distributive shares. (The corresponding Perron–Frobenius eigenvalue of A obtained an interpretation in terms of the highest possible profit rate.) So, surprisingly, Sraffa's solution is based on eigenvectors and eigenvalues, which traditionally only played a role in *closed* models! There have been many interpretations of Sraffa's work (see e.g. Roncaglia, 1978). Nevertheless, there still is an embarrassing lack of integration with traditional input–output theory.

Central to our discussion will be the Sraffian price model (8), or, more precisely, the relation between w and r. Sraffa starts with introducing a peculiar real output system, his Standard system. This system has the property that its final demand vector is proportional to the vector of aggregate intermediate inputs, i.e., f is proportional to Ax in (1). It is not difficult to see that this implies that both f and x have the proportions of the right-hand Perron–Frobenius eigenvector of matrix A. Denoting vectors with this property by an asterisk, we thus have

$$x^* = Ax^* + f^* \tag{9}$$

This is the Sraffian Standard system where f^* is known as the Standard commodity. We now put the value of the Standard commodity at unity, so $pf^* = 1$. Correspondingly, the size of the total labour force L is put at unity. The wage rate is measured as a share of the national income, and denoted by w^*, so $0 \leq w^* \leq 1$. Our price model, substituting w^* for w, now reads

$$p = (1 + r)pA + w^*l \tag{8'}$$

Following Sraffa, we shall concentrate on the situation where the relation between r and w^* becomes linear

$$r = (1 - w^*)R \tag{10}$$

Here R, the maximal rate of profits, is determined by μ_1, the Perron–Frobenius eigenvalue of A, via

$$R = \frac{1 - \mu_1}{\mu_1} \tag{11}$$

Sraffa states that adopting the Standard commodity as a standard of value will generate (10). Unfortunately, Sraffa's work is not very accessible. Later authors had to provide a mathematical presentation of what 'adopting the Standard commodity as a standard of value' means. The traditional proof of (10) is as follows (Pasinetti, 1977, p. 115, or Abraham-Frois and Berrebi, 1979, p. 52). Starting from

$$pf^* = p(I - A)x^* = 1$$

and

$$lx^* = 1$$

post-multiplication of (8′) by x^* gives

$$px^* = pAx^* + rpAx^* + w^*lx^*$$

So

$$\begin{aligned} rpAx^* &= px^* - pAx^* - w^*lx^* \\ &= p(I - A)x^* - w^* \\ &= 1 - w^* \end{aligned}$$

But

$$\begin{aligned} RpAx^* &= px^* - pAx^* \\ &= p(I - A)x^* \\ &= 1 \end{aligned}$$

So

$$(1 - w^*) = \frac{r}{R}(RpAx^*),$$

or

$$(1 - w^*)R = r$$

(In section 14.6 we shall come back to this interpretation.)

Clearly, the relation to work in mainstream input–output analysis is not easily established. Yet, as we shall show, there are connections. Although Sraffa, naturally, discussed an open model, below we shall start with a *closed* model.

14.4 COMMODITY BUNDLES AS STANDARDS OF VALUE IN CLOSED MODELS

Eigenvectors as standards of value have received virtually no interest thus far in mainstream input–output analysis. Partly, this may have to do with the fact that indirect inputs do not play a significant role in many model specifications. They do play, of course, an important role in analyzing price and quantity effects in open models via the powers of the input coefficients matrix. In closed models a corresponding analysis is lacking, however. This is a pity as an analysis of indirect inputs leads to new theoretical insights including a new view on the role of eigenvectors as value standards (Steenge, 1990a). In fact, *closed* input–output models seem most appropriate to introduce them. Therefore, let us return to model {5,6} of section 14.2.

The interpretation of the elements of matrix M, by definition, is in terms of the direct or 'first order' inputs necessary for unit production of each commodity. However, just as in the open model, we then also have an interpretation for the dual systems $z = M^2z$ and $p = pM^2$; matrix M^2 then gives 'second order' inputs, i.e. the inputs necessary for the production of the inputs of the first round. Continuing in this way, we also have an interpretation for the dual systems $z = M^3z$ and $p = pM^3$, etc. Taking limits, we obtain

$$z = M^{\infty}z \tag{12}$$

and

$$p = pM^{\infty} \tag{13}$$

where the elements of the rank one matrix M^{∞} now stand for the 'infinite order' or 'all-in' input coefficients for unit production of each commodity. Since M is primitive, indecomposable and primitive, we have $M^{\infty} > 0$.[5] All columns of M^{∞} being proportional to z, we see that in (12), inputs for each commodity are given in terms of a scalar multiple of the output vector z. Likewise, from (13) we see that individual commodity prices are given in terms of the prices of the same scalar multiples of z. Because all prices are expressed in terms of scalar multiples of the same commodity bundle z, this bundle can be interpreted as a system *standard of value*. That is, we can view each price as being expressed in terms of (the price of) a commodity bundle having the proportions of the right-hand Perron–Frobenius eigenvector of M.

We may obtain the same expression via another approach, i.e. via spectral decomposition properties.[6] Vectors z and p being, respectively, right- and left-hand Perron–Frobenius eigenvectors of M, we straightforwardly have

$$z = M_1z \tag{14}$$

and

$$p = pM_1 \tag{15}$$

with $M_1 > 0$ the standardized outer product of both eigenvectors (i.e. the constituent matrix associated with the Perron–Frobenius eigenvalue of M).

Clearly, $M_1 = M^\infty$, so also the system given by equations (14) and (15) can be interpreted as representing a closed input–output system written in terms of a Perron–Frobenius eigenvector serving as a standard of value. We may note that from our original system {5,6} we can obtain {12,13} or {14,15} by pre- or postmultiplying with M_1; for example, from (6) we have $pM_1 = pMM_1$. But $pM_1 = p$, so (15) results straightforwardly. In this price system, therefore, postmultiplication with M_1 results in the required expression.

So, a right-hand Perron–Frobenius eigenvector can be straightforwardly introduced as a standard of value for a closed input–output model. But how about open models? As we have seen, in Sraffian analysis eigenvectors are explicitly introduced in *open* models to obtain a linear income relation. Before turning to that problem, we shall first consider a very special case of an open model, i.e. the case where the direct labour inputs coefficients vector l in (1) is proportional to the left-hand Frobenius eigenvalue of A. We already briefly mentioned this case in section 14.3 after having introduced the model {7,8}.

As an illustration, let us consider Sraffa's two-product system, where wheat (G_1) and iron (G_2) produce wheat and iron (Sraffa, 1960, ch 1). We have, in familiar notation, the following real output system in closed form

$$\begin{bmatrix} \frac{280}{400} & \frac{120}{20} \\ \frac{12}{400} & \frac{8}{20} \end{bmatrix} \begin{bmatrix} 400 \\ 20 \end{bmatrix} = \begin{bmatrix} 400 \\ 20 \end{bmatrix}$$

We see that the input matrix M is indecomposable and primitive. Calculation gives that

$$M^\infty = M_1 = \begin{bmatrix} \frac{2}{3} & \frac{20}{3} \\ \frac{1}{30} & \frac{1}{3} \end{bmatrix}$$

which can be written in the form

$$M_1 = [\bar{z}\bar{p}]$$

with $\bar{z}$ and $\bar{p}$ right- and left-hand Perron–Frobenius eigenvectors normalized to $\bar{p}\bar{z} = 1$. For example, admissible is the pair

$$\bar{z} = \begin{bmatrix} \frac{2}{3} \\ \frac{1}{30} \end{bmatrix}$$

and

$$\bar{p} = [1 \quad 10]$$

That is, the price of G_1 is (equal to the price of) one bundle $\bar{z}$ and the price of G_2 is 10 bundles $\bar{z}$.

14.5 THE STANDARD COMMODITY AS STANDARD OF VALUE: A SPECIAL CASE

In this section we shall discuss the special case where the vector of direct labour input coefficients l in (8′) has the proportions of the left-hand Perron–Frobenius eigenvector of A. This case is unlikely to be found in reality but, as we shall see, will be of central importance from the theoretical point of view. We shall also see that the Sraffian Standard system can be interpreted as a system dual to this special case.

In the particular case considered by us here, also the price vector p is an eigenvector of A. Denoting these vectors here by the symbols l^* and p^*, respectively, we thus have

$$p^* = (1 + r)p^*A + w^*l^* \tag{16}$$

As is well known, in this particular case the income distribution mechanism is linear (Pasinetti, 1977). Now let us take a look at the right-hand side of (16). p^* being an eigenvector, the first term can be written as $(1 + r)\mu_1 p^* A_1$. Because $r = (1 - w^*) R$, we also have $l^* = (1 - \mu_1)p^*A_1$. So we obtain

$$p^* = (1 + r)\mu_1 p^* A_1 + w^*(1 - \mu_1)p^*A_1 \tag{16′}$$

The columns of A_1, the first constituent matrix of A (see n. 6), are scalar multiples of the right-hand Perron–Frobenius eigenvector of A. Earlier we have standardized the value of the Standard commodity at unity, so we have $p^*f^* = 1$. p^* and f^* being left- and right-hand Perron–Frobenius eigenvectors, we thus have

$$A_1 = [f^*p^*]$$

Thus, clearly, p^* can be decomposed in an intermediate inputs part given by $\mu_1 p^* A_1$, an interest part $r\mu_1 p^* A_1$ and a wage part $w^*(1 - \mu_1)p^*A_1$, all expressed in terms of the columns of matrix A_1. Therefore, these columns can be viewed as scalar multiples of a system standard of value of the type discussed in section 14.3 for the closed model.

In addition, we may note that our price equation (16) can be reformulated as the price equation of a closed model with input coefficients matrix

$(1/\mu_1)A$. Substituting $l^* = [(1-\mu_1)/\mu_1]p^*A$, we obtain

$$p^* = (1+r)p^*A + w^*[(1-\mu_1)/\mu_1]p^*A$$

or

$$p^* = (1/\mu_1)p^*A \tag{17}$$

So, we see that the price equation of this special open model is remarkably similar to the closed model case of section 14.2. This implies that we can employ the same argument to obtain an interpretation of (16′) in terms of the 'infinite order' input coefficients introduced in that section. From

$$p^* = p^*A_1$$

we also obtain

$$p^* = \mu_1 p^*A_1 + (1-\mu_1)p^*A_1$$

that is, (16′) with $w^* = 1$ (or $r = 0$). So, in this special case, $100\mu_1$ percent of our value standard is 'used up' in the intermediate production part and the remaining 100 $(1-\mu_1)$ percent in the value-added part.

Let us now consider a numerical example of an economy having the property $l = l^*$. Let us take for our matrix of input coefficients the following[7]

$$A = \begin{bmatrix} \frac{1}{2} & \frac{1}{9} & \frac{1}{12} \\ \frac{2}{3} & \frac{5}{18} & \frac{1}{12} \\ \frac{1}{3} & \frac{1}{3} & \frac{5}{12} \end{bmatrix}$$

Calculation gives that the left-hand Perron–Frobenius eigenvector of A has proportions 11 : 4 : 3. So let us assume that the vector of direct labour input coefficients in our economy is

$$l^* = [\tfrac{11}{6} \quad \tfrac{4}{6} \quad \tfrac{3}{6}]$$

Calculation gives that A has Frobenius eigenvalue $\mu_1 = \frac{5}{6}$. The price vector then is seen to be

$$p^* = [11 \quad 4 \quad 3]$$

Calculation also gives that the right-hand Perron–Frobenius eigenvector of A has proportions 2 : 3 : 4. So let us define as our Standard system a (sub-) economy producing as total output vector[8]

$$x^* = \frac{1}{920}\begin{bmatrix} 240 \\ 360 \\ 480 \end{bmatrix}$$

(Note that this sub-economy has net output vector $f^* = \frac{1}{6}x^*$.) We find straightforwardly

$$A_1 = \begin{bmatrix} \frac{11}{23} & \frac{4}{23} & \frac{3}{23} \\ \frac{33}{46} & \frac{6}{23} & \frac{9}{46} \\ \frac{22}{23} & \frac{8}{23} & \frac{6}{23} \end{bmatrix}$$

Now (16) gives

$$[11 \quad 4 \quad 3] = (1+r)[11 \quad 4 \quad 3]\begin{bmatrix} \frac{1}{2} & \frac{1}{9} & \frac{1}{12} \\ \frac{2}{3} & \frac{5}{18} & \frac{1}{12} \\ \frac{1}{3} & \frac{1}{3} & \frac{5}{12} \end{bmatrix} + \\ + \quad w^* \quad [\tfrac{11}{6} \quad \tfrac{4}{6} \quad \tfrac{3}{6}]$$

or (16′)

$$[11 \quad 4 \quad 3] = (1+r)\{\frac{5}{6}[11 \quad 4 \quad 3]\}\begin{bmatrix} \frac{11}{23} & \frac{4}{23} & \frac{3}{23} \\ \frac{33}{46} & \frac{6}{23} & \frac{9}{46} \\ \frac{22}{23} & \frac{8}{23} & \frac{6}{23} \end{bmatrix} +$$

$$+ \quad w^*\{\frac{1}{6}[11 \quad 4 \quad 3]\}\begin{bmatrix} \frac{11}{23} & \frac{4}{23} & \frac{3}{23} \\ \frac{33}{46} & \frac{6}{23} & \frac{9}{46} \\ \frac{22}{23} & \frac{8}{23} & \frac{6}{23} \end{bmatrix}$$

The right-hand side of (16′) tells us precisely how many standard commodities are 'used up' in, respectively, intermediate production and in value-added creation. Also, we should notice that in (16′) the proportions between the parts of its price going to intermediate outlays (here 5/6) and to value-added (here 1/6) are identical for each good over the full range of w^* and r.

It is interesting to note that the Standard system can be viewed as a case dual to the previous one. In the Standard system we have $f^* = (1 - \mu_1)x^*$, and

$$\begin{aligned} x^* &= Ax^* + (1 - \mu_1)x^* \\ &= Ax^* + [(1 - \mu_1)/\mu_1]Ax^* \\ &= (A + [(1 - \mu_1)/\mu_1]A)x^* \\ &= (1/\mu_1)Ax^* \end{aligned} \tag{18}$$

So, total output in the Standard system also can be analysed as a closed input–output model with input coefficients matrix $(1/\mu_1)A$. Analogous to our previous case, we also have

$$\begin{aligned} x^* &= A_1x^* \\ &= \mu_1A_1x^* + (1 - \mu_1)A_1x^* \end{aligned}$$

The Standard system, again in the proportions adopted by us, thus can be written as

$$\frac{1}{920}\left[\begin{bmatrix} 240 \\ 360 \\ 480 \end{bmatrix} = \begin{bmatrix} \frac{1}{2} & \frac{1}{9} & \frac{1}{12} \\ \frac{2}{3} & \frac{5}{18} & \frac{1}{12} \\ \frac{1}{3} & \frac{1}{3} & \frac{5}{12} \end{bmatrix}\begin{bmatrix} 240 \\ 360 \\ 480 \end{bmatrix} + \begin{bmatrix} 40 \\ 60 \\ 80 \end{bmatrix}\right]$$

or

$$\frac{1}{920}\left[\begin{bmatrix} 240 \\ 360 \\ 480 \end{bmatrix}\right] = \left[\frac{5}{6}\begin{bmatrix} \frac{11}{23} & \frac{4}{23} & \frac{3}{23} \\ \frac{33}{46} & \frac{6}{23} & \frac{9}{46} \\ \frac{22}{23} & \frac{8}{23} & \frac{6}{23} \end{bmatrix} + \right.$$

$$\left. + \frac{1}{6}\begin{bmatrix} \frac{11}{23} & \frac{4}{23} & \frac{3}{23} \\ \frac{33}{46} & \frac{6}{23} & \frac{9}{46} \\ \frac{22}{23} & \frac{8}{23} & \frac{6}{23} \end{bmatrix}\right]\left[\begin{bmatrix} 240 \\ 360 \\ 480 \end{bmatrix}\right]$$

We observe that by decomposing total production in terms of our adopted standard of value, the underlying output relations become very transparant. We see, for example, precisely in which way final demand has been built up in terms of outputs from the three sectors we have distinguished. We also notice that direct labour input proportions are irrelevant in our process of 'allocating' scalar multiples of our value standard to the sectors. That implies, as we shall see below, that equilibrium prices have specific properties in Sraffian type systems.

14.6 THE GENERAL CASE

In this section we shall take a look at our economy in a slightly different way. We shall employ the earlier introduced spectral decomposition of the matrix of input coefficients to take a further look at the properties of the system. Starting from (1) we obtain immediately

$$px = pAx + pf$$

Output is distributed according to

$$pf = rpAx + w^{*}pf$$

So

$$px = pAx + rpAx + w^{*}pf \tag{19}$$

We now focus on the links between the price and output vectors.

Sraffa affirms that 'imposing' the Standard commodity will produce a linear income distribution for all input–output systems, irrespective of technology and the prevailing composition of final demand. Regarding this statement, we should realize that until now we have not 'imposed' anything. Thus far we only have given, in section 14.5, a numerical illustration of a decomposition where the Standard commodity playes a very specific role. That section, however, only discusses a special case. So, let us now turn to the general case where the vector of direct labour coefficients l is not proportional to the left-hand Perron-Frobenius eigenvector and where output proportions can take any value.

Let us start from

$$p = (1+r)pA + w^*l \tag{8'}$$

and postmultiply by A_1 to obtain:

$$pA_1 = (1+r)pAA_1 + w^*lA_1 \tag{21}$$

or

$$pA_1 = (1+r)\mu_1 pA_1 + w^*lA_1 \tag{21'}$$

With $pf^* = 1$ and using $lf^* = l(I-A)x^* = (1-\mu_1)lx^* = (1-\mu_1)$, we straightforwardly have

$$p^* = (1+r)\mu_1 p^* + w^*(1-\mu_1)p^*$$

or

$$p^* = (1+r)p^*A + w^*(1-\mu_1)p^* \tag{22}$$

Using $(1-\mu_1)p^* = l^*$, we observe that via our transformation we – again – meet a familiar equation:

$$p^* = (1+r)p^*A + w^*l^* \tag{16}$$

Thus, by postmultiplying the price vector (8′) by A_1, we obtain a new price vector (i.e., p^*) each element of which is a scalar multiple of the price of the Standard commodity evaluated at prices p. So, by the above desribed transformation, we have obtained a new way of introducing the Standard commodity in our model. The price vector now is in terms of (the price of) a basket of commodities having precisely the proportions of the Standard commodity. Formulated somewhat differently, by introducing the Standard commodity in this particular way, weights are attached to each individual commodity price such that the resulting vector of prices is equal to p^*.

Consequently, the transformation A_1 replaces p by p^* in our original price equation. Here it is important to note that A_1 is technologically determined, being completely independent of prices or final demand. Because of our adopted standardizations, l simultaneously is transformed into l^* and we obtain the characterizing equation of the very special case discussed in section 14.5. That is, by our transformation we have obtained a mechanism to 'induce' the property $r = (1 - w^*) R$ in the general case. A corollary here is that if l happens to have the proportions of l^*, as in section 14.5, prices are 'automatically' also in terms of the Standard commodity. We shall return to the issue of the system numeraire further below.

Above we have discussed a method of 'creating' new commodities, the price of which is equal to the price of the Standard commodity. This, in our view, is the real point of introducing the Standard commodity. What, then, has been missing thus far in the many comments on the Sraffian system? To answer this question we should observe that the literature up to now has 'used' the special vectors f^* and x^* – which define the Standard system – in two standardizations

$$pf^* = 1$$

and

$$lx^* = 1$$

(see also the derivation of (10) in section 14.3). What was lacking was a 'dual' side, linking them to the vectors p^* and l^*. In our approach this link is introduced by imposing $p^*f^* = 1$ which standardizes p^*, and gives a straightforward link with our spectral decomposition. Following Sraffa in standardizing the total labour force at unity, we have $l^*x = 1$. This gives $p^*f = 1$ from $l^*x = (1 - \mu_1)p^*x = p^*(I - A)x = p^*f$. A 'dual' treatment thus is needed to see that Sraffa's 'imposing the Standard commodity' can be understood as a transformation which turns an ordinary price system into the special system of section 14.5. A situation is thus created *as if* the vector of direct labour coefficients has the proportions of the Perron–Frobenius eigenvector of A.

The transformation imputes to each industry inputs precisely in the proportions of the Standard commodity. The proportion between intermediate inputs part $\mu_1 p^*A_1$ and income part $(1 - \mu_1)p^*A_1$ is, as would be expected, $\mu_1/(1 - \mu_1)$. Here we find the same proportions as between the intermediate inputs part and the income part for the Standard system: $pAx^*/pf^* = \mu_1 px^*/[(1 - \mu_1)px^*] = \mu_1/(1 - \mu_1)$. So, on the industry level the proportions of the Standard system are repeated over and over again, as in the earlier cases given in sections 14.4 and 14.5. Equations (21) and (22) show that by imposing a transformation of prices, we 'force' the system to a rearrangement, such that the fractions of each price going to intermediate outlays and value-added part are identical to the corresponding fractions in the special price system discussed in section 14.5. It is this rearrangement that accomplishes the linear income distribution. This, in our view, is the correct interpretation of the term 'imposing the Standard commodity'.

It is important to note that we do also have a labour theory of value here, although its foundations are quite different from the more traditional approaches. The quantity of labour now being imputed to each good being produced is defined in terms of the quantity of labour required to produce the Standard commodity. Because our approach transcribes the economy's production processes in terms of the Standard commodity, it simultaneously imputes quantities of labour to each good being produced. Therefore, the dimensional homogeneity of, say, (21) is always guaranteed. In fact, it can be interpreted both in terms of the Standard commodity and in terms of embodied labour.

We may also observe that our approach contains an interesting way of approaching the numeraire problem in systems incorporating (8′), or a similar equation. Above, we have in fact adopted as our numeraire a scalar multiple of the output vector of the Standard system *plus* the associated labour force, L. So, we also may argue that, in fact, we have been working with a commodity bundle of the form:

$$k^* = \begin{bmatrix} x_1^* \\ x_2^* \\ \cdot\cdot \\ \cdot\cdot \\ \cdot\cdot \\ x_n^* \\ L \end{bmatrix}$$

with x_i^* the ith element of x^*. It will be interesting to see if other commodity bundles, in combination with a desired set of properties for the price system, will generate specific systemic properties in terms of the income distribution as well. This, however, must be left for a later occasion.

Above we have introduced a transformation of the price system. An obvious question is: Is there a need to transform the real output system as well? Actually, we still have to see to what kind of transformed commodities the new prices correspond, and how the – appropriately adapted – new input matrix should look like. Fortunately, the structure of the system is such that this second step, the creation of new commodities, is not necessary. To see this, let us postmultiply (21) by x, the output vector:

$$pA_1x = [(1+r)pA + w^*l]A_1x \qquad (23)$$

Because A_1 is idempotent, we may also write

$$pA_1A_1x = [(1+r)pA + w^*l]A_1A_1x \qquad (24)$$

Equation (24) can be interpreted as the product of transformed prices (pA_1) and goods (A_1x) transformed via *premultiplication* of the output vector by A_1. Postmultiplication of p by A_1 means that the (elements of the) price vector now represent the prices of a specific commodity bundle, the Standard commodity. Premultiplication of the output vector x by A_1 means that this vector is replaced by, precisely, the Standard commodity, the new value standard. By these transformations, clearly, all input proportions become equal, thus eliminating all sectoral differences. However, as we easily observe by comparing (23) and (24) – which give exactly the same result – the particular weights as given by A_1 have the extremely useful property that we can work with the *transformed* prices *without* having to transform the real output system correspondingly. *Because of A_1 being idempotent we can successively introduce a transformation that only involves a transformation of the price system.* This corresponds precisely to the Sraffian 'prescription': transforming the price forming mechanism is sufficient to produce the required linearity of distribution.

Let us return for a moment to our numerical example. Suppose the system's vector of direct labour input coeffcients is not proportional to the left-hand Perron–Frobenius eigenvalue of A, say

$$l = [5/6 \quad 3/4 \quad 15/16]$$

Clearly, this will not affect the linearity of distribution. If we adopt the Standard commodity as our system numeraire, we proceed by calculating from our input coefficients matrix the matrix A_1. Imposing the Standard commodity as we have formulated it, then transforms the price equation so that (21) results. So, again, our methodology attributes inputs precisely in the proportion of the Standard commodity to the production of each good. The production of the first good, for example, requires 11 of our Standard commodities, distributed in proportions 5/6 and 1/6 between intermediate production and value-added requirements.

The Sraffian analysis, interpreted in the way we have suggested, imputes commodities and labour to the production of each good precisely in the proportions of the output bundle of a very specific macroeconomic system, the Standard system. To each good a fraction of this bundle is imputed, together with the amount of labour required to produce this bundle. The amount of labour, in its turn, is transscribed in terms of this same bundle, now serving as a real wage bundle. So, in this sense, Sraffa was right in stating that his system's essential characteristic is 'production of commodities by means of commodities'. Of course, we can visualize the practical mechanics of our system in various ways. One possibility is to imagine that each sector contributes to a 'wage fund' in proportion to the quantity of labour 'imputed' to it. If each sector acts accordingly, the wage fund contains precisely the wage sum needed; the relation between w^* and r will be linear.

14.7 FURTHER REMARKS AND CONCLUSION

In this contribution we have presented a method for dealing analytically with eigenvectors and eigenvalues in open static input–output models. We have shown that with each input–output model a positive matrix of rank one can be associated, the columns of which represent the amounts of the system's adopted value standard, the Standard commodity, to be imputed to each commodity. We also have seen that the value-added part of the model can be treated similarly. In our framework, wages and profits thus are 'transcribed' in terms of commodity bundles of specific composition. In this sense, we are really discussing the 'production of commodities by means of commodities', as formulated by Sraffa in his famous 1960 publication.

Subsequent work will have to explore the relation between our interpretation of the Sraffian idea of introducing the Standard commodity as a system numeraire and the classic Marxian problem of the transformation of values into prices of production. It is not difficult to see that by introducing the Standard commodity in the way we have proposed, we obtain a system where *by construction* the vectors of direct and embodied labour are proportional to each other. By the same construction they also are proportional to the vector of production prices, having created a situation of a uniform 'organic composition of capital'. Our approach thus suggests that the Sraffian approach to the income distribution problem may provide a solution to the transformation problem as well!

Application to related model types must be considered. The most obvious way to proceed may be to look for further structure in dynamic models. For example, it is not difficult to see that the closed dynamic Leontief model in its Bródy equilibrium form

$$x(t) = [A + \lambda B]x(t)$$

where A and B are, respectively, the flow and stock coefficients matrices, $x(t)$ the output vector in period t, and λ the growth factor (Bródy, 1970 or Steenge, 1990a) can be viewed along similar lines. Also joint production models should be considered, but here application may require substantial additional effort because the relation between single and joint production models is still not fully understood (for issues involved, see Steenge, 1990b, or Konijn and Steenge, 1995).

We could venture even further, by stating that part of the above-described problems can be attributed to the fact that there – still – is no generally accepted view on the relation between prices and output in the various types of input–output models that are available at present. The study of specific vectors serving as composite numeraires clearly should play a role in such investigations. To make further progress it may be necessary for us to return to our 'roots', in the wake of innovative authors such as Seton (1985, 1992). In this respect, it may be particularly useful to study earlier writers such as Dmitriev (1974) or the rediscovered Charasoff (1910). The dominant role of Perron–Frobenius calculus also may be questionable. In fact, it may well be that in the light of a renewed research program we should turn rather to results of Markov probability theory.

NOTES

1. Strictly speaking, Sraffa only provided a verbal description of these ideas. Later work provided the transcription into concepts of linear algebra. Nevertheless, we shall proceed as if Sraffa himself introduced these concepts.
2. Throughout (observed) input–output coefficients matrices are assumed to be indecomposable, primitive and of full rank.
3. To avoid a proliferation of symbols, we again use the symbol p for the vector of prices here.
4. We shall only discuss the Sraffian form because, mutatis mutandis, for the Marxian form the same analysis applies.
5. From Markov theory we have that matrix M^{∞} can be written as the standardized outer product of (scalar multiples of) z and p.
6. We have $A = \mu_1 A_1 + \mu_2 A_2 + \ldots + \mu_n A_n$, with the μ_i the eigenvalues of A and the constituent matrices A_i the outer products of the bi-orthonormalized right-hand and left-hand eigenvectors of A. Properties of the A_i include $\sum_{i=1}^{n} A_i = I$, $A_i^2 = A_i$, and $A_i A_j = 0$ for $i \neq j$. For simplicity, we assume that all eigenvalues are simple. If A is an indecomposable input coefficients matrix, its left- and right-hand Perron–Frobenius eigenvectors are strictly positive. Denoting them, as in the text, and after standardization, by p^* and f^*, we then have $A_1 = [f^* p^*]$, with $p^* f^* = 1$.
7. This coefficients matrix is derived from the system discussed by Sraffa (*Production of Commodities*, pp. 18–20).

8. Sraffa's Standard commodity is 920 times ours. The size of the Standard commodity in our case has been adopted to avoid, given our standardizations, very small equilibrium prices.

REFERENCES

ABRAHAM-FROIS, A. and E. BERREBI (1979) *Theory of Value, Prices and Accumulation* (Cambridge: Cambridge University Press).

BRÓDY, A. (1970) *Proportions, Prices and Planning*. (Amsterdam: North-Holland).

CHARASOFF, G. (1910) *Das System des Marxismus: Darstellung und Kritik* (Berlin: Hans Bondy).

DMITRIEV, V. K. (1974) *Economic Essays on Value, Competition and Utility*, D. M. Nuti (ed.) (Cambridge: Cambridge University Press).

KONIJN, P. J. A. and A. E. STEENGE (1995). 'Compilation of Input–Output Data from the National Accounts', *Economic Systems Research*, 7, pp. 31–45.

PASINETTI, L. L. (1977) *Lectures on the Theory of Production* (New York: Columbia University Press).

RONCAGLIA, A. (1978) *Sraffa and the Theory of Prices* (Chichester: Wiley).

SETON, F. (1977) 'The Question of Ideological Obstacles to Rational Price Setting in Communist Countries', in *The Socialist Price Mechanism*, A. Abouchar (ed.) (Durham: Duke University Press), pp. 10–39.

SETON, F. (1985) *Cost, Use and Value, The Evaluation of Performance, Structure, and Prices across Time, Space, and Economic Systems* (Oxford: Clarendon Press; 2nd edn, 1992).

SRAFFA, P. (1960) *Production of Commodities by Means of Commodities* (Cambridge: Cambridge University Press).

STEENGE, A. E. (1990a) 'On the Complete Instability of Empirically Determined Dynamic Leontief Models', *Economic Systems Research*, 2, pp. 3–16.

STEENGE, A. E. (1990b) 'The Commodity Technology Revisited: Theoretical Basis and an Application to Error Location in the Make–Use Framework', *Economic Modelling*, 7, pp. 376–87.

15 Joint Production in a Two-Sector Model

Branko Horvat

15.1 INTRODUCTION

When analyzing price and quantity relationships in input–output models almost exclusively single-product industries are used. There are only few contributions in which it is inquired what difference it makes if single-product industries are replaced by joint production. The inquiry usually ends in complications which make the further analysis intractable and the result agnostic (Pasinetti, 1980; Schefold, 1989). It is shown that if the theoretical background is the same as in Horvat (1989), the ensuing analysis is relatively simple. Two sectors are considered: production of baskets of consumer goods and production of machinery with an unchanging structure of production. The first sector represents the net output and the second a subsidiary one catering for itself and for the first sector. Duality between price and quantity is utilized. The simplicity is not disturbed when fixed capital and expanding economy are considered. At the end the wage-profit curve is derived.

15.2 STATIONARY ECONOMY

Let there be two industries, each of them producing jointly two commodities. The commodities are baskets (of consumer goods) and machines (durable producer goods). The two industries continue to specialize in their original products. Thus each industry produces one main and one subsidiary product. In industry I baskets (of consumer goods of constant quality and structure, for short: baskets) are the main and machines the subsidiary product and in industry II it is the other way round.

15.2.1 Price Equations

It will be convenient to start our analysis by writing down new value balances:

$$
\begin{aligned}
p_2R_1 + wL_1 &= p_1X_1^1 + p_2X_2^1 \\
p_2R_2 + wL_2 &= p_1X_1^2 + p_2X_2^2
\end{aligned}
\tag{1}
$$

where p_i is price, R_i is replacement, w_i is wages, L_i is labour and X_i^j represents quantity i produced by industry j. X_1^1 and X_2^2 are the main products, X_2^1 and X_1^2 are the subsidiary ones. Let us define technical coefficients in relation to main products and add coefficients defining the relations between main and subsidiary products;

$$
\begin{aligned}
\rho_1^* &= \frac{R_1}{X_1^1}, \quad \rho_2^* = \frac{R_2}{X_2^2} < 1 \\
\lambda_1^* &= \frac{L_1}{X_1^1}, \quad \lambda_2^* = \frac{L_2}{X_2^2} \\
a &= \frac{X_2^1}{X_1^1}, \quad b = \frac{X_1^2}{X_2^2}
\end{aligned}
\tag{2}
$$

Since industry II specializes in producing machines, it produces more machines than necessary for its own reproduction, $X_2^2 > R_2$ and consequently $\rho_2^* < 1$. Taking labour as a numéraire ($w = 1$) and dividing the first equation by X_2^1 and the second one by X_2^2, we get the following price equations:

$$
\begin{aligned}
p_2\rho_1^* + w\lambda_1^* &= p_1 + p_2\frac{X_2^1}{X_1^1} = p_1 + p_2a \\
w &= 1 \\
p_2\rho_2^* + w\lambda_2^* &= p_1\frac{X_1^2}{X_2^2} + p_2 = p_1b + p_2
\end{aligned}
\tag{3}
$$

Note that λ_1^* and ρ_1^* are not labour and replacement coefficients comparable with those of the single product industries since they include also labour and replacement attributable to subsidiary products.

The technology of the system may now be represented as follows:

		Activities at unit levels	
Outputs	X_1	1	b
	X_2	a	1
Inputs	L	$-\lambda_1^*$	$-\lambda_2^*$
	R	$-\rho_1^*$	$-\rho_2^*$

(4)

There is also a subtle change in the dimensional characteristics of X_1 and X_2. So far X_1 meant the number of *baskets* and X_2 the number of *machines*. In defining **a** and **b**, they become indices of the levels of activities, i.e. *pure* numbers. Activity I will run at level X_1 and will, of course, produce X_1 baskets (and also aX_1 machines) and activity II will be operated at level X_2 and produce X_2 machines (and also bX_2 baskets).

A standard activity analysis does not distinguish primary factors from produced factors. For our purpose this distinction is vital and so the input matrix will be composed of technical coefficients of produced factors only.

The input (A) and output (B) matrices look as follows:

$$A = \begin{bmatrix} 0 & 0 \\ \rho_1^* & \rho_2^* \end{bmatrix} \quad B = \begin{bmatrix} 1 & b \\ a & 1 \end{bmatrix}$$

The price system (3) may now be written in a compact form

$$pA + \lambda^* = pB, \ w = 1 \tag{3a}$$

The solution of this matrix equation is a row vector of prices

$$p = \lambda^*(B - A)^{-1} \tag{3b}$$

Since $B \neq \mu I$, ($\mu >$ dominant root of A), matrix $(B - A)^{-1}$ is not necessarily semipositive and there is no guarantee that all prices will be positive. Alternatively we may write $(B - A) = (I - A^*)$, where

$$A^* = \begin{bmatrix} 0 & -b \\ \rho_1^* - a & \rho_2^* \end{bmatrix}$$

As A^* is not semipositive, $A^* \ngeq 0$, there is no guarantee that the solution vector will be positive. This is the standard conclusion concerning joint production. Let us investigate the problem in some more detail.

The two price equations (3) determine the two labour prices and their ratio

$$\begin{aligned} p_1 &= \frac{\lambda_2^*(\rho_1^* - a) + \lambda_1^*(1 - \rho_2^*)}{b(\rho_1^* - a) + (1 - \rho_2^*)} w \\ p_2 &= \frac{\lambda_2^* - \lambda_1^* b}{b(\rho_1^* - a) + (1 - \rho_2^*)} w \\ \frac{p_1}{p_2} &= \frac{\lambda_2^*(\rho_1^* - a) + \lambda_1^*(1 - \rho_2^*)}{\lambda_2^* - \lambda_1^* b} \end{aligned} \tag{5}$$

Since X_2^1 is a subsidiary product $X_2^1 < R_1$ and consequently $\rho_1^* - a > 0$. If it were the case that $X_2^1 \geq R_1$, the second industry would not be necessary, and the economy would be reduced to one industry. From (2), $\rho_2^* < 1$ and consequently $(1 - p_2^*) > 0$. Thus the labour price of baskets must be positive, $p_1 > 0$. As it stands, the price of machines may become negative. For it to be positive it is necessary that $\lambda_2^* > \lambda_1^* b$, i.e.

$$p_2 > 0 \quad \text{if} \quad \frac{L_2}{L_1} > \frac{X_1^2}{X_1^1} \quad \text{or} \quad \frac{X_1^1}{L_1} > \frac{X_1^2}{L_2} \tag{6}$$

the ratio of the number of workers employed in the two industries must be higher than the ratio of outputs of baskets in the two industries. Or, main output per worker in the first industry must be higher than subsidiary output per worker in the second industry. Suppose, it was not. Then the machine industry would produce more baskets per worker than the basket industry, while at the same time producing more than necessary for the replacement of old machines, $X_2^2 > R_2$. Consequently, net output (production of baskets) would be maximized if all labour were allocated to the second industry. This means that the inferior technology of the first industry would not be used and the entire economy would consist of the second industry only which would produce a surplus of machines. Barring that degenerate case, both industries will be operating and both prices will be positive. In general, if an economy operates both industries, prices will be positive. Negative prices could appear only if one or the other industry is not operating because that industry uses an inferior technique. This is not likely to occur in practice because specialized industries are more productive and relation coefficients **a** and **b** are not rigidly fixed but can vary within certain intervals. The availability of alternative techniques eliminates inferior techniques and makes possible specialization. If condition (6) is satisfied in a stationary economy it will always be satisfied in a growing economy because growth implies relative expansion of industry II and, therefore, an increase in the ratio L_2/L_1.

If we are interested in a possible generalization to a multisectoral economy, the conditions for positive prices must be presented in the matrix form. From (3b)

$$(B - A)^{-1} = \frac{1}{(1 - \rho_2^*) + (\rho_1^* - a)b} \begin{bmatrix} 1 - \rho_2^* & -b \\ \rho_1^* - a & 1 \end{bmatrix}$$

The multiplicative term is clearly positive, but the adjoint of the matrix $(B - A)$ is not semipositive because of the presence of the term $-b$ (the same as in A^*). For that reason also labour coefficients must be examined. The multiplication λ^*x adjoint gives

$$\lambda_1^*(1 - \rho_2^*) + \lambda_2^*(\rho_1^* - a) > 0 \implies L_1(1 - \rho_2^*) + \lambda_2^*(R_1 - X_2^1) > 0$$

$$-\lambda_1^* b + \lambda_2^* > 0 \quad \Longrightarrow \quad \frac{L_2}{L_1} > \frac{X_1^2}{X_1^1}$$

The first condition is clearly satisfied which means that the price of the consumer good is always positive. The second condition is equal to (6).

Joint production technology is depicted in Figure 15.1. Two industries are now two processes using technologies α and β to produce the same pair of goods in the quantities A and B given labour resources $\bar{L}$. Rays α and β define a convex polyhedral cone that determines producible combinations of outputs. Given labour $\bar{L}$, any combination of outputs can be produced within the triangle OAB. Technologies α and β are efficient, i.e. no process can produce more of both products, and so the labour constraint line HG is downward sloping.

Suppose the required combination of goods is C, then technology γ represents the linear combination of technologies α and β, $\mu\alpha + (1 - \mu)\beta = \gamma$, $0 < \mu < 1$. Prices and quantities must be positive. The line HG represents also linear combinations of the same vectors, except that μ is not restricted to values below unity. Suppose very little replacement is required, so that even process α produces too many machines. The required proportion is δ, but such a technology does not exist. Formally, D can be reached by expanding

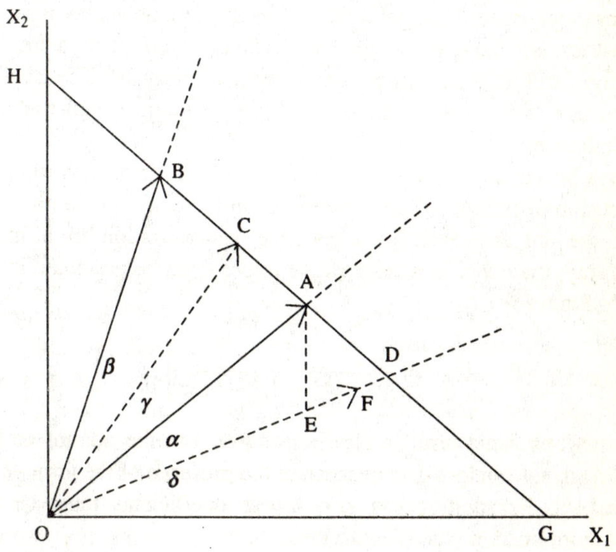

Figure 15.1 Joint production with two industries

labour in α ($\mu > 0$) and allocating negative labour to β. This is equivalent to saying that equations (1) must be solved by using *both* processes. Since using both processes produces too many machines, the solution will show negative p_2. Negative quantities of labour and negative prices are meaningless. Thus, instead of using equalities we must work with inequalities and use the programming format.

It is immediately obvious that only α (i.e. the process specializing in baskets) will be used, that quantities E can be produced and that EA machines are superfluous. If the unnecessary machines can be freely disposed off, $p_2 = 0$. If the handling of waste incurs costs, an additional process must be added which produces negative machines. That makes sense.

In the case of single product industries, at any time one best (or several equally good) process(es) was (were) operated regardless of demand changes. This constant technology theorem holds no longer in joint-production economy where changes in demand require the use of different technologies. Suppose technology δ existed. It is clearly inferior to α when C is demanded but it is superior to α when F is demanded. The reason why we do not encounter this problem in an economy with one-product industries lies in the fact that output vectors are represented by coordinate axes and so the cone represents the entire positive quadrant.

With *n commodities there will be an n-dimensional convex polyhedral cone within which output proportions will generate positive prices,* $C = \{b \in B, b \in R^n, BX^* = X, \lambda^* X^* \leq L\}$ where X^* represents the vector of main products and the components of each vector **b** consist of one main and n-1 subsidiary products. In the real world any change in demand proportions will stimulate research and development which will produce a new cone with positive prices. Also, in the real world of *n* industries producing $m \geq n$ single and joint products, not all industries produce the same assortment of joint products, which, together with the production of substitutes (sheep produce meat and wool, cows produce meat and leather, plastics may partly substitute leather, etc.) which enormously increase the possibility of adjusting aggregate output proportions to those of demand.

Note that for $n > m$, the system in overdetermined and competition will eliminate $n - m$ inferior processes making $m = n$. If $m > n$ and $m - n$ products are not wanted (because they are harmful or produced in excess quantities) additional $m - n$ disposal processes will close the model. If $m - n$ products are wanted, $m - n$ additional processes will be introduced in order to adopt proportions of commodities produced to requirements of consumption. In case of a corner solution, the most profitable process may produce commodities in exactly that proportion what market demands. Then the number of processes is smaller than the number of commodities but that, of course, is a fluke. Thus, in general, the number of processes and commodities will be equal, $n = m$.

If subsidiary products are eliminated, system (5) is reduced to single product industries with $\rho_j = k_j/n$.

$$p_1 = \lambda_1 + \frac{\rho_1\lambda_2}{1-\rho_2}, \qquad a = b = 0$$

$$p_2 = \frac{\lambda_2}{1-\rho_2}, \qquad b = 0 \tag{5a}$$

$$\frac{p_1}{p_2} = \frac{\lambda_1}{\lambda_2} + \frac{\lambda_2\rho_1 - \lambda_1\rho_2}{\lambda_2}, \qquad a = b = 0$$

It is of some interest to note that the original p_2 of the single product industry system does not change even if industry I applies a joint-products technology. This asymmetry results from X_2 being a means of production and X_1 net output. Since X_2 is used in industry I while X_1 is not used in industry II the dependence is unilateral and the conditions of production in I do not influence prices in II.

One additional characteristic of the price system (3) is also of some interest. It follows immediately from the first and the second equation

$$\begin{aligned} p_1 &= \lambda_1^* + p_2(\rho_1^* - a) > \lambda_1^* \\ p_2 &= \lambda_2^* + p_2\rho_2^* - p_1 b \gtreqless \lambda_2^* \end{aligned} \tag{7}$$

The price of the basket is always greater than the corresponding labour coefficient. The same cannot be said for the price of the machine which depends on the difference $(p_2\rho_2^* - p_1 b)$. For $p_2 > \lambda_2^*$, this difference implies

$$p_2R_2 > p_1X_1^2 \text{ and } p_2X_2^2 > wL_2$$

i.e., value of replacement investment is greater than value of subsidiary output in machine industry which implies that the value of the main product is greater than the wage bill in the same industry. The condition is satisfied for single-commodity industries because $X_1^2 = 0$. In the case of joint production it depends on the technology used. One should also bear in mind that λ_1^* and λ_2^* do *not* represent direct labour per unit of commodity 1 and 2.

15.2.2 Quantity Equations

We shall next consider balances of labour and capital resources

$$L_1 + L_2 = L$$
$$K_1 + K_2 = K$$

Since machines last n years, we may replace capital stock engaged by capital used, i.e.

$$R_1 + R_2 = R$$

and total replacement in a stationary state is equal to total output of machines, $R = X_2$. Applying technical coefficients defined in (2) we obtain quantity equations

$$\begin{aligned} \lambda_1^* X_1^1 + \lambda_2^* X_2^2 &= L \\ \rho_1^* X_1^1 + \rho_2^* X_2^2 &= X_2 \end{aligned} \tag{8}$$

to which we must add two technologically determined relations

$$\begin{aligned} X_1^1 + bX_2^2 &= X_1 \\ aX_1^1 + X_2^2 &= X_2 \end{aligned} \tag{9}$$

Now we have four equations from which we can determine four unknowns, X_1, X_2, X_1^1 and X_2^2.

$$X_1^1 = \frac{(1-\rho_2^*)L}{\lambda_1^*(1-\rho_2^*) + \lambda_2^*(\rho_1^* - a)}, \quad X_2^2 = \frac{(\rho_1^* - a)L}{\lambda_1^*(1-\rho_2^*) + \lambda_2^*(\rho_1^* - a)},$$

$$X_1 = \frac{b(\rho_1^* - a) + (1-\rho_2^*)}{\lambda_1^*(1-\rho_2^*) + \lambda_2^*(\rho_1^* - a)} L, \quad X_2 = \frac{a(1-\rho_2^*) + (\rho_1^* - a)}{\lambda_1^*(1-\rho_2^*) + \lambda_2^*(\rho_1^* - a)} L \tag{10}$$

$$\frac{X_1^1}{X_2^2} = \frac{1-\rho_2^*}{\rho_1^* - a}, \quad \frac{X_1}{X_2} = \frac{b(\rho_1^* - a) + (1-\rho_2^*)}{\rho_1^* - a\rho_2^*}$$

All quantities are clearly positive when both industries are operating. We also see that

$$\frac{L}{X_1} = \frac{p_1}{w} = p_1, \quad w = 1 \tag{11}$$

as it should be: p_1 is labour time spent on the production of one unit of net output as in (5).

If subsidiary products are not produced, $a = b = 0$, (10) reduces to the single product industries case with $\rho_j = k_j/n$.

$$X_1 = \frac{1 - \rho_2}{\lambda_2\rho_1 + \lambda_1(1 - \rho_2)}L, \quad a = b = 0$$

$$X_2 = \frac{\rho_2}{\lambda_2\rho_1 + \lambda_1(1 - \rho_2)}L, \quad a = 0 \tag{10a}$$

$$\frac{X_1}{X_2} = \frac{1 - \rho_2}{\rho_1}, \quad a = b = 0$$

Again as with prices, commodity X_2 is an exception. But this time the joint output of b is allowed without disturbing the total output of X_2. In other words, subsidiary machines ($a > 0$) influence the total output of machines (X_2) but not their price; subsidiary baskets ($b > 0$) influence the price of machines (p_2) but not their output. Output and prices of baskets always change when a subsidiary output appears anywhere in the system.

15.2.3 Other Effects

At the level of an economy $p_1X_1 = L$ represents living labour and p_2X_2 represents embodied labour. Such a distinction cannot be made in a determinate way at the level of separate industries.

It has already been mentioned that λ_1^* and λ_2^* do not represent direct labour coefficients. Consequently, it is impossible to disaggregate labour values into living and embodied (direct and indirect) labour in a determined way. This is due to the fact that we have only two equations:

$$\begin{aligned} \lambda_1X_1 + \lambda_2X_2 &= L \\ \rho_1X_1 + \rho_2X_2 &= X_2 \end{aligned} \tag{13}$$

for the determination of four unknowns, of the coefficients λ_1, λ_2, ρ_1 and ρ_2. It is, of course, always possible to use the available two degrees of freedom in various ways.

The most natural procedure is to impose global proportion to individual industries, i.e. to assume that the ratio of indirect and direct labour be equal throughout the economy

$$\sigma = \frac{p_2 x_2}{p_1 x_1} = \frac{p_2 R}{L} = \frac{p_2 \rho_1 X_1}{\lambda_1 X_1} = \frac{p_2 \rho_1}{\lambda_1} \tag{14}$$

This adds the one missing equation.

The two other equations are simply the price equations.

$$p_1 = \lambda_1 + p_2\rho_1 = \lambda_1(1+\sigma)$$

$$p_2 = \lambda_2 + p_2\rho_2 = \lambda_2(1+\sigma) \tag{15}$$

$$p_2 = \frac{\lambda_2}{1-\rho_2}$$

and the argument is exactly the same as before, $\frac{1}{1-\rho_2}$ being the sum of an infinite series $\sum_{k=0}^{\infty} \rho_2^k$.

Also, $p_1/p_2 = \lambda_1/\lambda_2$ price ratios are equal to labour coefficient ratios.

The ratio $\sigma = p_2R/L$ is a sort of organic composition of capital the difference being that $\omega = p_2K/L$ is the ratio of capital in labour value per unit of labour, while σ is replacement in labour value per unit of labour. Obviously $\omega = n\sigma$. An interesting conclusion follows: while equal organic composition of capital is a serious restriction for single product industries, it is no restriction at all for joint product economies. However, in the latter case it does not apply to industries (which produce joint products) but to products (regardless in which industry are they produced).

It is, of course, always possible to have a mixed case: joint products in one industry and one product in the other. In such a case we have two equations with three unknowns. The available degree of freedom may be used to apply the organic composition of the single product industry to the system as a whole and the above conclusion remains valid.

15.3 EXPANDING ECONOMY

It is now a very simple job to describe a uniformly growing economy without technological progress. Since the labour force is growing at the rate g, so is the output of machines. The quantity equations are

$$\lambda_1^* X_1^1 + \lambda_2^* X_2^2 = L$$
$$\kappa_1^* X_1^1 + \kappa_2^* X_2^2 = K \tag{16}$$

Since capital is being replaced at the rate $\frac{1}{\nu}$ and expands at the rate g, the machine industry must deliver $(\frac{1}{\nu} + g)K = X_2$ machines. Thus the second equation will have to be multiplied by $r = \frac{1}{\nu} + g$

$$r\kappa_1^* X_1^1 + r\kappa_2^* X_2^2 = X_2 \tag{17}$$

A comparison between (16)–(17) and (8) shows that the two systems are formally the same. All we have to do is to replace ρ_1^* by $r\kappa_1^*$ and the solution of the systems follows straightforwardly from (10)

$$X_1 = \frac{b(r\kappa_1^* - a) + (1 - r\kappa_2^*)}{\lambda_1^*(1 - r\kappa_2^*) + \lambda_2^*(r\kappa_1^* - a)} L$$

$$X_2 = \frac{a(1 - r\kappa_2^*) + (r\kappa_1^* - a)}{\lambda_1^*(1 - r\kappa_2^*) + \lambda_2^*(r\kappa_1^* - a)} L \tag{18}$$

$$\frac{X_1}{X_2} = \frac{r(b\kappa_1^* - \kappa_2^*) + (1 - ab)}{r(\kappa_1^* - a\kappa_2^*)}.$$

Price equations represent no difficulty either since the same substitution will do the trick

$$rp_2\kappa_1^* + w\lambda_1^* = p_1 + ap_2$$
$$rp_2\kappa_2^* + w\lambda_2^* = bp_1 + p_2 \tag{19}$$

and

$$p_1 = \frac{\lambda_2^*(r\kappa_1^* - a) + \lambda_1^*(1 - r\kappa_2^*)}{b(r\kappa_1^* - a) + (1 - r\kappa_2^*)} w$$

$$p_2 = \frac{\lambda_2^* - \lambda_1^* b}{b(r\kappa_1^* - a) + (1 - r\kappa_2^*)} w \tag{20}$$

$$\frac{p_1}{p_2} = \frac{\lambda_2^*(r\kappa_1^* - a) + \lambda_1^*(1 - r\kappa_2^*)}{\lambda_2^* - \lambda_1^* b} = \frac{rm^* + (\lambda_1^* - a\lambda_2^*)}{\lambda_2^* - b\lambda_1^*}, \quad m^* = \kappa_1^*\lambda_2^* - \kappa_2^*\lambda_1^*$$

Equal pseudo mechanization ($m^* = 0$) does not render price ratio equal to the ratio of labour coefficients ($p_1/p_2 \neq \lambda_1^*/\lambda_2^*$), although it is equal to the ratio of derived labour coefficients of (15).

We have also to show that prices and quantities are positive. For that we have to examine the two expressions in brackets.

$(r\kappa_1^* - a) > 0$ implies $rK_1 > X_2^1$ which is certainly true because X_2^1 is a subsidiary product and therefore not sufficient to cover the investment needs in its industry. Next, $(1 - r\kappa_2^*) > 0$ implies

$$r\frac{K_2}{X_2^2} < 1$$

which is true because $rK_2 < X_2^2$. The third condition, $\lambda_2^* - \lambda_1^* b > 0$, is the same as before.

For $g = 0$, r reduces to $1/n$ and prices and quantities reflect stationary systems (5) and (10). If subsidiary products are not produced, $a=b=0$, prices and quantities are those of single product industries. In either case for $w=1$ prices are exact labour time prices and $p_1X_1 = L$.

If (19) is transformed into value balances by multiplying the first equation by X_1 and the second one by X_2

$$rp_2K_1 + wL_1 = p_1X_1^1 + p_2X_2^1$$
$$rp_2K_2 + wL_2 = p_1X_1^2 + p_2X_2^2 \tag{21}$$

it becomes obvious that the exchange between the two industries remains indeterminate. All we know is that wages must buy consumption goods,

$$w(L_1 + L_2) = p_1(X_1^1 + X_1^2),$$

and that rentals must buy machines,

$$rp_2(K_1 + K_2) = p_2(X_2^1 + X_2^2).$$

But that may be done in many different ways. One possibility to close the system is to assume that each industry first covers its own needs and exchanges only the surpluses. In that case industry I will exchange its surplus in baskets for the surplus in machines of the industry II

$$p_1X_1^1 - wL_1 = p_2X_2^2 - rp_2K_2 \tag{22a}$$

That, of course, implies the equality of deficits as well

$$rp_2K_1 - p_2X_2^1 = wL_2 - p_1X_1^2 \tag{22b}$$

15.4 THE WAGE CURVE

The wage curve for joint production has essentially the same characteristics as for single product industries. The main difference is that, for obvious reasons, it touches the two axes at different points.

From (18) we have

$$\frac{X_1}{L} = \tilde{w} = \frac{r(b\kappa_1^* - \kappa_2^*) + (1 - ab)}{rm^* + (\lambda_1^* - a\lambda_2^*)}, m^* = \kappa_1^*\lambda_2^* - \kappa_2^*\lambda_1^* \qquad (23)$$

We cannot find maximum $\tilde{W}$ and R by simply putting $r = 0$ and $\tilde{w} = 0$ because that would have no economic meaning, even when only one industry is operating it produces both products and so neither $\tilde{w}$ nor r can be zero.

If only machine industry is operating, the quantity equation for labour reduces to

$$\lambda_2^* X_2^2 = L, \quad X_1^1 = X_2^1 = 0 \qquad (24)$$

At the same time per capita output of baskets will be

$$\tilde{w} = \frac{X_1^2}{L} = \frac{bX_2^2}{L} \qquad (25)$$

Substituting X_2^2/L from (24) we get

$$\tilde{w} = \frac{b}{\lambda_2^*}$$

which is the new abscissa axis.

Similarly when only basket industry is operating, the quantity equation for capital reduces to

$$K_1^* X_1^1 = K, \quad X_2^2 = X_1^2 = 0$$

The rental (investment) rate is

$$r = \frac{X_2^1}{K} = \frac{aX_1^1}{K}$$

Substitution gives

$$r = \frac{a}{\kappa_1^*}$$

which is the new ordinate axis. The curve is shown in Figure 15.2.

If $r = a/\kappa_1^*$ is substituted into (23), the maximum wage turns out to be $\tilde{W} = 1/\lambda_1^*$ and if $\tilde{w} = b/\lambda_2^*$ is substituted, the maximum rental is found to be $R = 1/\kappa_2^*$. Both are formally the same as in single product industries but λ_1^* and κ_1^* are no longer single direct technical coefficients since they are calculated with respect to main and not with respect to total products.

Per analogiam with the single product industries, $m^* = \kappa_1^*\lambda_2^* - \kappa_2^*\lambda_1^*$ may be taken as describing relative mechanization in the two industries. Note that $m^* \neq m$, but $m^* = 0$ when $m = 0$. If the degree of mechanization in both industries is the same, $m^* = 0$, the wage function (23) becomes linear, but not so simple as the Sraffa function:

$$r = r^0 R\left(\frac{1 - ab}{r^0 - abR} - \frac{\tilde{w}}{\tilde{w}^0\tilde{W}}\frac{\tilde{w}^0 ab\tilde{W}}{r^0 - abR}\right) \tag{30}$$

$$m^* = \lambda_2^*\kappa_1^* - \lambda_1^*\kappa_2^* = 0,\ \tilde{W} = \frac{1}{\lambda_1^*},\ R = \frac{1}{\kappa_2^*},\ \tilde{w}^0 = \frac{b}{\lambda_2^*},\ r^0 = \frac{a}{\kappa_1^*}$$

If subsidiary products are eliminated, $ab = 0$, the function (30) reduces to Sraffian function $r = R(1 - \tilde{w}/\tilde{W})$.

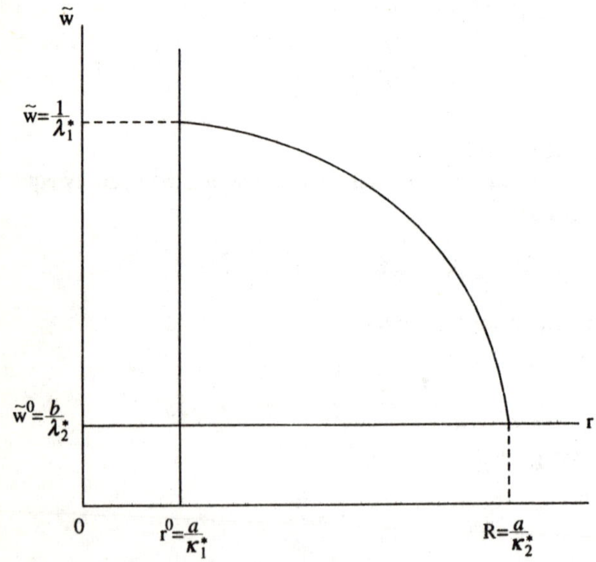

Figure 15.2 The wage curve for joint production in both industries

Note that either a or b may remain positive, $a > 0$ or $b > 0$. In other words, the Sraffian result holds even if one of the industries produces joint products.

The distribution curve has the negative slope

$$\frac{d\tilde{w}}{dr} = \frac{(b\kappa_1^* - \kappa_2^*)(\lambda_1^* - a\lambda_2^*) - (1 - ab)m^*}{[rm * +(\lambda_1^* - a\lambda_2^*)]^2} < 0$$

if the condition for nonnegative price (6) and for nonnegative quantities (18) of machines are satisfied ($\lambda_2^* > \lambda_1^* b$, $\kappa_1^* > \kappa_2^* a$).

The sign of the second derivative again depends on the index of relative mechanization m*

$$\frac{d^2w}{dr^2} \gtreqless 0 \quad \text{if} \quad m^* \lesseqgtr 0$$

Figure 15.2 is drawn on the assumption m* < 0, i.e. that the machine industry is more mechanized. Clearly, for m* = 0 the distribution curve becomes a straight line.

We easily find that both prices increase if the rental (investment) rate increases and that the price ratio p_2/p_1 increases, decreases or remains constant depending on whether the machine industry is more, less or equally mechanized. The output ratio X_1/X_2 always decreases as the investment rate increases. Thus, all findings for the single product industries remain in force. If the technical constraint (6) is satisfied, joint production economy behaves in the same way as single product industries.

REFERENCES

HORVAT B. (1989) 'The Pure Labour Theory of Prices and Interest', *European Economic Review*, pp. 1183–203.

PASINETTI L. L. (ed.) (1980) *Essays on the Theory of Joint Production*, London: Macmillan.

SCHEFOLD B. (1989) *Mr. Sraffa on Joint Production and Other Essays*, London: Unwin Hyman.

16 Price Scheme Cones*

Ian Steedman

It goes without saying that, in any linear model of production, relative commodity prices are determined by the conditions of production, on the one hand, and by wage, rent and profit rates, etc., on the other. It may therefore be useful to be able to 'separate out' the two sets of influences – production conditions and distribution, in brief – and the object of this essay is to show how that can be done.

A VERY SIMPLE CASE

It may be helpful to begin with the very simplest case which can be treated in the way to be proposed here. Consider a single product system with just three commodities, using a single kind of homogeneous labour which is paid *ex post*. (It would make no relevant difference to what follows to suppose *ex ante* payment of wages.) Then

$$p = we + (1 + r)pA \tag{1}$$

where the price vector, p, and the employment vector, $e > 0$, are both (1×3). Of course, w is the scalar wage rate, r the scalar profit rate and A the (3×3) input matrix. It is assumed that e is not orthogonal to any right-hand vector of A. Define the singular, skew symmetric matrix S by

$$S = \begin{bmatrix} 0 & e_3 & -e_2 \\ -e_3 & 0 & e_1 \\ e_2 & -e_1 & 0 \end{bmatrix}$$

It will be clear that $eS \equiv O$. On post-multiplying (1) by SA^tp^t, where t denotes transposition, one thus obtains

$$pSA^tp^t = (1 + r)pASA^tp^t \tag{2}$$

But the R.H.S. of (2) is identically zero (since $vSv^t = 0$ for any vector v when S is skew symmetric), so that

$$pSA^tp^t = 0$$

and

$$p(SA^t - AS)p^t = 0 \tag{3}$$

for *all* w and for *all* r. (*Note*: we do not mean 'for all economically relevant w and r' – we mean for *all* w and r.) Since (3) has non-trivial solutions for p, from the meaning of the problem, (3) is the algebraic equation of a *Euclidean cone*. For all (w, r) the price vector must always lie on the surface of the cone defined by (3), where that cone itself depends only on A and (via S) on e. The technical conditions (A, e) alone define the cone on which prices always lie, distribution being quite irrelevant to the determination of that cone. Distribution simply determines *where* on the cone the price vector must lie. Thus the influences on relative commodity prices of production conditions, on the one hand, and of distribution, on the other, have been 'separated' from one another.

It is to be noted that our 'cone' can degenerate. For example, if only commodity 1 is a produced input, so that $a_{ij} = 0$ for $i = 2, 3$, the 'cone' (3) collapses to the plane:

$$(e_3a_{12} - e_2a_{13})p_1 + (e_1a_{13} - e_3a_{11})p_2 + (e_2a_{11} - e_1a_{12})p_3 = 0$$

We assume away such 'collapsing' in what follows. (Note, however, that one does not need two or more Sraffa-basics to avoid 'collapse': if $a_{23} > 0$ but $a_{21} = a_{22} = a_{31} = a_{32} = a_{33} = 0$ then a genuine cone is obtained.)

Since prices must lie on the cone for *all* r, it follows that, on any commodity – numeraire plane, prices will trace out some conic section as r takes all possible values. It may be shown, for example, that on Sraffa's Standard Commodity numeraire plane, prices will trace out a hyperbola if A has three distinct real roots, or an ellipse if A has one real root and a pair of complex roots. (A parabola or a pair of straight lines will be traced out in the 'marginal' case of a repeated real root.) This point will not be pursued further, however, since the knowledge that prices always lie on a given cone makes the choice of a numéraire irrelevant to the study of relative prices.

ALITER

While the above argument may be thought quite neat for the (3×3) case, it may not be clear how to generalize it; by contrast, the following two alternative presentations of the simple case have rather obvious generalizations (which will be exploited later).

The 'first alternative' is to rewrite (1) as

$$[-1, (1+r), w]\begin{bmatrix} p_1 & p_2 & p_3 \\ pA_1 & pA_2 & pA_3 \\ e_1 & e_2 & e_3 \end{bmatrix} = 0 \qquad (1a)$$

and to note that if the matrix in (1a) were ever non-singular we should obtain an immediate contradiction; hence it is always singular. Setting the determinant of that matrix equal to zero leads quickly to (3) again.

The 'second alternative' begins by noting that we can choose at most two vectors which are both orthogonal to each other and to 'e'. For consistency with our later argument, denote such vectors by v_2 and v_3. From (1),

$$(pv_2) = (1+r)(pAv_2)$$

and (1b)

$$(pv_3) = (1+r)(pAv_3)$$

Hence

$$(pAv_3)(pv_2) = (pAv_2)(pv_3)$$

or

$$pA(v_3v_2^t - v_2v_3^t)p^t = 0 \qquad (1c)$$

Relation (1c), in which $(v_3v_2^t - v_2v_3^t)$ is of course a skew symmetric matrix, can quickly be changed into the standard form of equation for a Euclidean cone.

A LITTLE MORE GENERAL

The above very simple example of how to 'separate' production-condition influences from distribution influences on relative commodity prices is, indeed, so simple that the reader is unlikely to be sure which of our many simplifications has made the separation possible. The small numbers of commodities and of primary inputs are not in fact relevant; nor is the fact that joint production has been ignored. Nor again – and more strikingly – is it necessary to assume a number of activities equal to the number of commodities (a 'square' system of production). Consider, then, the following generalization of (1):

$$pB = wE + (1+r)pA \qquad (4)$$

where p is now $(1 \times k)$, the output (B) and input (A) matrices are $(k \times n)$, the primary input matrix E is $(m \times n)$ and the *vector* of 'wage rates', w, is $(1 \times m)$. Note that throughout this section $k \neq n$ is allowed.

Suppose that matrix E happens to be of rank $(n-2)$. [That vector e was of rank $1 = (3-2)$ was, in fact, the crucial simplification of the previous sections.] By suitable labelling of the different kinds of labour, we may partition E horizontally so that the first $(n-2)$ rows of E, represented by E_*, are linearly independent. Let the remaining rows of E be given by TE_* and rewrite (4) as

$$[-1, (1+r), (w_1 + w_2 T)] \begin{bmatrix} pB \\ pA \\ E_* \end{bmatrix} = 0 \tag{4a}$$

where w has been partitioned appropriately. Now (4a) simply generalizes (1a) and we see at once that the determinant of the $(n \times n)$ matrix in (4a) must always be zero. It will be clear that this yields a homogeneous, second degree equation in the k prices and hence a Euclidean cone on the surface of which the price vector must always lie, for *all* w and *all* r. That cone is defined entirely by the technical conditions expressed by (B, A, E_*); the role of w and r is simply to determine *where* on the technically defined Euclidean cone the price vector will be found.

The argument of the previous paragraph runs parallel to that of the 'first alternative' in the preceding section; we present now the parallel to that of the 'second alternative'. The matrix E, being of rank $(n–2)$ by assumption, admits a singular-value-decomposition of the form

$$E = U \begin{bmatrix} e_1 & & & & & \\ & e_2 & & & O & \\ & & \ddots & & & \\ & & & e_{n-2} & & \\ & O & & & 0 & \\ & & & & & 0 \end{bmatrix} V^t \tag{SVD}$$

where U is $(m \times m)$ and orthogonal, V is $(n \times n)$ and orthogonal and $e_1 \geq e_2 \geq \ldots \geq e_{n-2} > 0$. Denote by v_{n-1} and v_n the last two columns of V; then $Ev_{n-1} = Ev_n = 0$. Hence, from (4), for all values of w,

$$(pBv_{n-1}) = (1+r)(pAv_{n-1})$$

and (4b)

$$(pBv_n) = (1+r)(pAv_n)$$

which generalizes (1b). On defining the skew symmetric matrix $K \equiv (v_{n-1} v'_n - v_n v_{n-1}')$, we quickly derive from (4b) that

$$p(BKA' - AKB')p' = 0 \tag{5}$$

where (5) is the equation of a Euclidean cone. That cone is fully determined by (B, A, v_{n-1}, v_n).

Thus when E is of rank $(n - 2)$ there is a sharp separation of the production-condition influences on relative commodity prices from the distribution (w and r) influences thereon.

A SOMEWHAT MORE GENERAL ANALYSIS

Naturally one cannot be satisfied with an argument turning on the convenient but arbitrary assumption that matrix E just happens to be of rank $(n-2)$. To proceed further we now consider rather more closely the above (conventional) treatment of (w and e) and of (w and E). In our simplest case, we accepted the common assumption that labour in the three different productive activities was homogeneous. And even in our second case, with m primary inputs, we treated each 'kind' of primary input as being the same across the various activities. It is not self-evident, however, that this conventional approach is satisfactory. The labour of sewing machine operation in the men's shirt making activity is *not* precisely the same as the labour of sewing machine operation in the women's trouser making activity. Even the labour of floor sweeping in the former activity is not precisely the same as that of floor sweeping in the latter. (In the terminology of the subsequently eminent Victorian, Dr K. H. Marx, 'concrete' labour necessarily differs from activity to activity.)

Each activity, then, ought to be thought of as employing primary inputs which are specific to that activity. (At least with respect to labour; the position with respect to land might be different, perhaps, and that with respcct to imported inputs certainly is.) We may suppose, then, that E has more rows than columns and is of full column rank, n. In this case, of course, the singular-value-decomposition of E will differ from (SVD) above by having a full set of positive singular values $(e_1, ..., e_n)$ and for no j will $Ev_j = e_j u_j$ be zero. Rather than (4b), we can now derive only, say,

$$(pBv_i) = e_i(wu_i) + (1 + r)(pAv_i)$$

and (6)

$$(pBv_j) = e_j(wu_j) + (1 + r)(pAv_j)$$

If we now impose the restrictions $(wu_i) = (wu_j) = 0$ we can naturally derive a Euclidean cone as before. Now, however, this will be a cone defined by the technical conditions *in conjunction with* our choice of i and j, a cone on which the price vector must lie for all r and for all w satisfying $(wu_i) = (wu_j) = 0$. While it is true both that only two restrictions are placed on the large number of wage rates and that those restrictions reflect the technical conditions themselves, the fact remains that our result is now more qualified than in the case of rank $E = (n - 2)$.

If rank $E = (n - 1)$, then $(pBv_n) = (1 + r)(pAv_n)$ will hold for all w. We need then only impose *one* restriction $(wu_j = 0)$, for some $1 \leq j \leq (n - 1)$, in order to derive a Euclidean price cone; the general remarks immediately above apply again *mutatis mutandis*. (Notice that we are not obliged to restrict w by $(wu_i) = 0$, etc.; that choice was made only to maximize the influence of technical conditions on the resulting cone. The interested reader will easily see how the insertion of constraints $(w_1 + w_2T)c_1 = 0$ and $(w_1 + w_2T)c_2 = 0$ – or just the former – into (4a) will allow one to handle the case rank $E = n$, or rank $E = (n - 1)$.)

If rank $E = n$ or $(n - 1)$, then, our Euclidean cone construction is still possible but must be understood in a somewhat qualified way. It remains true, however, that the structure of the cone is entirely independent of r and of the *permitted* values of w. Since, in capital theory, one is generally interested in the dependence of relative commodity prices on r (rather than on w), this 'partial' separation of influences on commodity prices should still be of interest.

RANK $E < (n - 2)$

It has been argued above that a good *economic* case can be made for regarding the step from rank $E = (n - 2)$ to rank $E = n$ as the important one. Whether that argument be accepted or not, it remains true that from a formal point of view the case rank $E < (n - 2)$ should also be considered. Suppose then that rank $E = (n - t)$, where $3 \leq t \leq (n - 1)$. An obvious extension of the argument leading to (4b) above yields

$$\begin{aligned} (pBv_{n-t+1}) &= (1 + r)(pAv_{n-t+1}) \\ &\;\;\vdots \\ (pBv_n) &= (1 + r)(pAv_n) \end{aligned} \tag{7}$$

where (7) involves t equations. Far from needing to restrict w to obtain a cone, we are now faced with an *embarras de choix*, since any pair of the equations in (7) yields a Euclidean cone defined by the technical conditions. Hence for all w and all r the price vector lies on the intersection of the $(t-1)$ independent Euclidean cones which can be derived from (7). That intersection is itself a cone, of course, but only in the 'modern' more abstract sense; it is not a Euclidean cone. To give a simple example, suppose that $t = 3$, so that we have two independent Euclidean cones. Any one of the prices may be eliminated from the equations defining those cones (in general) to yield a homogeneous fourth degree equation defining a (non-Euclidean) cone in the remaining $(k-1)$ prices. And so on; while it would naturally be possible to pursue this analysis in general terms, to do so would take us away from our emphasis on specifically Euclidean cones. So would a pursuit of the observation that if the rate of profit is not the same in all processes then, under certain conditions, a fully determinate (non-Euclidean) cone will be defined by the technical conditions; we therefore leave the interested reader with no more than this hint.

AN ACTIVITY-LEVEL CONE

It would be surprising if there were not some 'dual' result yielding a cone on which activity levels must always lie – and indeed there is, as we shall now briefly sketch without entering into the possible elaborations which will be obvious from what has been said above on price cones. (Note that we shall not refer to price and activity-level cones as 'dual cones', since the use of that term is pre-empted by its technical mathematical usage.)

Consider the equation

$$Bx = Cc + (1+g)Ax \tag{8}$$

in which x is an activity level vector and g a rate of steady growth. The consumption vector is expressed as Cc, where the columns of the semi-positive $(k \times n)$ matrix C represent alternative consumption proportions and the semi-positive column vector c shows the weighting applied to those alternative proportions. For simplicity, suppose that rank $C = (n-2)$, so that we may choose two, and only two, mutually orthogonal row vectors, s_1 and s_2, such that $s_1C = 0 = s_2C$. From (8),

$$(s_1Bx) = (1+g)(s_1Ax)$$

and

$$(s_2Bx) = (1+g)(s_2Ax)$$

so that

$$x^t A^t ({s_1}^t s_2 - {s_2}^t s_1) B x = 0 \tag{9}$$

Equation (9) defines a Euclidean cone, determined entirely by (B, A, s_1, s_2), on which x must lie for *all* c and for *all* g.

NEOCLASSICAL PRICE CONES

It is not implicit in the foregoing that a Euclidean price cone can only be found in the case of an economy with fixed production coefficients. Suppose, for example, that each of three commodities is produced directly by two kinds of labour, with wage rates w_1 and w_2, subject to a unit cost function of the 'quadratic square root' form. When price equals unit cost for each commodity

$$p_j = \alpha_j w_1 + \beta_j w_2 + \gamma_j (w_1 w_2)^{1/2}$$

for $j = 1,2,3$. Assume that the matrix

$$\begin{bmatrix} \alpha_1 & \alpha_2 & \alpha_3 \\ \beta_1 & \beta_2 & \beta_3 \\ \gamma_1 & \gamma_2 & \gamma_3 \end{bmatrix}$$

is non-singular and denote its inverse by M, a matrix with columns (M_1, M_2 and M_3). Then it is easily seen that

$$(pM_1)(pM_2) = (pM_3)^2$$

for *all* w_1 and w_2, this being the equation of a Euclidean cone, defined entirely by the technical conditions, on which (p_1, p_2, p_3) must always lie. In this case, as p moves 'around' the cone the input–output coefficients are, of course, always changing.

The example of the last paragraph must not be taken too seriously, it goes without saying. We need only change to an example with three 'translog' unit cost functions to see why. Let

$$\ln (p_j/w_1) = \alpha_j + \beta_j \ln(w_2/w_1) + \gamma_j \ln^2(w_2/w_1)$$

for $j = 1, 2, 3$ and choose units of output such that $\alpha_1 = \alpha_2 = \alpha_3$. Then for *all* w_1 and w_2

$$\begin{aligned} &A[(\beta_3 - \beta_2)\ln p_1 + (\beta_1 - \beta_3)\ln p_2 + (\beta_2 - \beta_1)\ln p_3] = \\ &[(\gamma_2 - \gamma_3)\ln p_1 + (\gamma_3 - \gamma_1)\ln p_2 + (\gamma_1 - \gamma_2)\ln p_3]^2 \end{aligned} \tag{10}$$

where $A = [(\beta_1\gamma_2 - \beta_2\gamma_1) + \beta_2\gamma_3 - \beta_3\gamma_2) + (\beta_3\gamma_1 - \beta_1\gamma_3)]$. While (10) represents a cone in (p_1, p_2, p_3), it is not a Euclidean cone. But we should perhaps focus on a somewhat more general analysis, which is closer to that of previous sections in introducing produced inputs and a uniform rate of profit. Suppose then that

$$p_j = c_j[(1+r)p_1, \ldots, (1+r)p_n; w_1, \ldots, w_m]$$

for $j = 1, \ldots, n$, where each $c_j[\ ]$ is a single-product unit cost function. If $(n-1) = (m+1)$, we may take any $(n-1)$ of these equations and solve for $(1+r)$, $w_1, \ldots, w_m$ (subject to a certain determinant, reflecting input proportions, not being zero). Both $(1+r)$ and each w_j will be a homogeneous function of the commodity prices, the former of degree zero and each of these latter of degree one. Elimination of $(1+r)$ and the *w*s from the remaining 'price = unit cost' relation will yield the equation of the cone, determined entirely by technical conditions, on which the price vector must lie for all r and all w. It will be clear both that the condition $m = (n-2)$ plays a key role here and that the cone in question is unlikely to be a Euclidean one. The reader who has followed the argument thus far will have little difficulty in pursuing its further possible developments.

CONCLUDING REMARKS

While it has been indicated briefly how the analysis can be extended both on to the 'quantity' side and into the 'neoclassical' domain, our main focus has been on price cones for an economy employing fixed methods of production. If the matrix of primary input use E is of rank $(n-2)$ one can, without further ado, immediately derive *the* Euclidean cone, defined purely by production conditions, on the surface of which the price vector must always lie for *all* (w, r); these distributive variables merely fix the position of the price vector on the cone. If E is of rank $(n-1)$ or rank n – and some reason has been given for stressing the latter case – then, after either one or two linear restrictions have been placed on w, one again obtains a Euclidean price cone, dependent now on production conditions and on those restrictions but not on r or on the permitted wage rate variations. If rank $E < (n-2)$ then the price vector always lies on the intersection of known Euclidean cones, each one determined by technical conditions alone. In the sense just defined, the influences of production conditions and of distribution on relative commodity prices have been 'separated'. Perhaps, when hot and bothered, Ricardo and Marx would each have enjoyed a price scheme cone?

NOTE

* Earlier versions of this essay were presented to seminars in Catania, Graz, Manchester and Vienna – but the participants in some of those seminars could readily be forgiven for not recognizing the present version. I am indebted to Ch. Bidard, U. Krause, P. Madden, A. Opocher, N. Salvadori, E. Watson and R. Woods for helpful discussion and am especially grateful to R. W. Farebrother for extensive comments and hints. I am also most grateful to Manchester Metropolitan University for the Honorary Visiting Research Professorship during which the final version of this paper was written.

17 Production Prices and Proportions Revisited

Ernő Zalai

17.1 INTRODUCTION

Despite all ideological debates and disagreements economists tend to agree that the economic analysis and theories of Marx are very much in line with the mainstream of contemporary economic theories based on economic equilibrium analysis. As is well known, the controversial but quite powerful theoretical framework of equilibrium analysis has been introduced into economics and gradually modified during the last centuries under the strong influence of the general scientific revolution. The early contributors used it as a colorful metaphor to describe the emerging commercial society as a system of 'natural freedom', which fully recognizes the rights of individuals to pursue their self-interest and in which free competition (the invisible hand) reconciles these potentially conflicting interests to the best of the society.

Marx, too, adopted – in a definitely less optimistic manner – this model of competition as a framework for his economic analysis. Among other things he, too, assumed that the competition of different industries induces the rational owners of capital to move from less profitable industries to more profitable ones and in this way to reduce the differences in the rates of return in the various industries. Such dynamic forces of competition were assumed to act like a force of gravitation, which constantly moves prices towards and keeps them near their 'centre of gravity', namely, of such 'central prices' which yield equal rates of return on the advanced capital in every industry. Marx called such prices the *production prices*, which he defined as:

> The price of a commodity, which is equal to its cost-price plus the share of the annual *average* profit on the total capital invested ... in its production ...'[1]

I believe the word '*average*' deserves special attention in the above definition, for it is a key to the understanding of the essentially dynamic nature of the Marxian analysis. Unlike Walras and most other classical economists Marx did not maintain that the forces of competition would keep the economy 'reasonably' close to a state of equilibrium. Just to the contrary, for Marx disequilibrium was the natural state of affairs and the dominant force of change and innovation in a capitalist economy. Thus, the Marxian production prices and the general rate of profit are some kinds of moving averages rather than long-term stationary equilibrium values.

In this sense, the Marxian production price theory should therefore be interpreted in my view as an abstract static model of a dynamic phenomenon. In this interpretation production prices are only temporarily characterizing an economy at any moment of time and they are not some equilibrium values resulting from a stationary process. Such an interpretation is, thus, closer to Cassel's view, who suggested to see static equilibrium models as 'out of time mathematical structures', rather than to that of Wicksell, who proposed to view them as 'stationary equilibrium' solutions.[2]

If one accepts this view, then it logically follows that contrary to the general perception the Marxian concept of production prices – or that of the classical 'central prices' in general – has little to do with long-term stationary equilibrium prices, despite all the potential formal similarity of the two. One can name two essential differences that separate these two price concepts from each other. First, as we saw, the definition of production prices is based on 'average' input coefficients, whereas the stationary equilibrium prices are determined by 'marginal' input coefficients, in the sense that they are defined by a subset of individual processes yielding the highest profit rate at the given set of prices. Second, the definition of stationary equilibrium prices rests on the assumption of fixed coefficients, independent of time and scale, whereas the definition and the analysis of production prices do not involve any assumption on the underlying technology.

This interpretation differs in some aspects from the point of view of Bródy,too. He was keen to stress the formal analogies of the models of stationary equilibrium and the Marxian analysis of values, production prices and the proportions of balanced reproduction. As a matter of interest Bródy himself has at the same time emphasized the temporary and average nature of the fixed coefficients of his model at the outset:

> one can observe average proportions for any given historical moment. This average has a certain stability and is considered normal ... Thus average proportions of expenditure, average 'input coefficients', will be fixed technically and institutionally at any given time and place.[3]

In this paper we will stick to the Casselian interpretation and analyze the 'out of time mathematical structure' of the economic data in terms of the production prices. The organization of the paper will be as follows. In section 17.2 we will first introduce and analyze some basic properties of the data assumed to be known. Two basic assumptions will be defined (pure commodity production and indispensability of labour) and as a generalization of Gale's productivity theorems it will be shown that they together guarantee the productivity of the input coefficient matrix. Section 17.3 will be devoted to the analysis of the Marxian production prices in case of money wages, the case not analyzed by Bródy himself. We will prove that in a pure commodity producing economy, where both labour and capital are indispensable, the Marxian production prices are well defined and strictly positive, and the real wage and the rate of profit are inversely related to each other. Section 17.4 will be concerned with Bródy's model of the production prices, extending his analysis to the reducible case. We will show the emergence of Sraffian-type basic commodities and prove a theorem on the existence of positive production prices. Finally, in section 17.5 we will compare two alternative forms of the complete input coefficient matrices (labour included), pointing out their essential equivalence and potential problematic features.

17.2 THE INPUT COEFFICIENTS AND SOME FUNDAMENTAL PROPERTIES OF PURE COMMODITY PRODUCTION

Following Bródy we will assume throughout in our discussion that we analyze the structure and proportions of an economy *ex post*, i.e. we assume that we know the average (or 'normal') expenditure proportions of the economy. Let $\mathbf{A} = (a_{ij})$ denote the n by n matrix of average (flow) input coefficients, where a_{ij} stands for the amount of product i used to produce one unit of product j in the period analyzed. Similarly we assume the knowledge of the average labor input coefficients. Let vector $\mathbf{v} = (v_j)$ designate these latter coefficients, where v_j measures the amount of labour – say, manhours – used to produce one unit of product j.

Apart from the above *flow* coefficients we will also need to know the *stock* coefficients, which measure the 'capital tied up' in the production of the various products. The measurement of these latter coefficients is not simple, because the capital tied up in the production process constantly changes its form (inventories of raw materials, semifinished products, final products, etc.).

Bródy assumed that the *stock* coefficients could be derived from the *flow* coefficients through the notion of *turnover time*.[4] For example, in the case of the *fixed* (as opposed to the *variable*) capital coefficients this means that they can be determined by a simple form as follows: $b_{ij} = a_{ij}t_{ij}$, where $t_{ij} > 0$ is the given turnover time. Thus, if we adopt this definition then the matrix of the *fixed capital coefficients*, $\mathbf{B} = (b_{ij})$ will have exactly the same structure (in terms of the position of the positive and zero elements) as the flow input coefficient matrix. Accordingly, the *variable capital* coefficients can be derived in the same manner from the wage coefficients and thus be represented by a vector $\mathbf{b} = (b_i)$, which is similar in its structure to the vector $\mathbf{v}$. We postpone the further discussion of this issue to the last section of the paper.

At this point we may just conclude that if we want to analyze the Marxian production prices in terms of money wages (or real wages defined by some general price index) then we need to know the above data. Later we will extend our analysis to the case investigated by Bródy in which wages are determined by the *necessary consumption*, i.e. by a real wage basket of commodities. For that case we will of course need to have the data characterizing the reproduction of the labour power as well, which will be introduced later.

Throughout our analysis we will assume that we are dealing with a *pure capitalist production system* in which both *labour and capital are indispensable*. One may also rightly assume that in a pure capitalist production system no commodity is produced if under the average conditions (represented by the average input coefficients) they would make loss. We will show[5] that these features of the economy – if properly defined – will be very powerful in proving the existence and expected properties of production prices.

Among other things they will guarantee that the flow coefficient matrix $\mathbf{A}$ of the economy investigated is productive, i.e. it has a nonnegative Leontief-inverse. Bródy and other authors as a rule simply and directly assume the productivity of $\mathbf{A}$ in their works. Unlike them in this paper we will derive it from some more subtle assumptions made about the economy in question. To this end let us define what we mean by the above concepts and assumptions.

Definition 1 (*Pure commodity production*)

A given set of average flow input coefficients $\mathbf{A}$ and $\mathbf{v}$ correspond to a pure commodity producing economy if there is a set of nonnegative prices ($\mathbf{p}^a$) and a positive wage rate (w^a) such that

$$\mathbf{p}^a \geq \mathbf{p}^a\mathbf{A} + w^a\mathbf{v} \tag{1}$$

that is, there exist such prices that cover at least the cost of materials and labour at a given positive wage rate.

Definition 2 (*Indispensability of labour*)

Labour is said to be indispensable in the observed economy, if there exist no semipositive vector $\mathbf{q}$ and positive scalar α such that

$$\mathbf{q} \geq \alpha\mathbf{A}\mathbf{q} \quad \text{and} \quad \mathbf{v}\mathbf{q} = \mathbf{0} \tag{2}$$

that is, the economy could reproduce itself without using labour.

A few remarks may help the reader to better understand the exact nature of these definitions. First, in the spirit of the Marxian analysis we may assume that the prices in Definition 1 are the average prices of the various products prevailing in the observed period, and similarly, the wage rate is the observed average wage rate. What we assume is thus a weak condition that must be met in any economy in which no product is produced at loss (subsidized) under average conditions. This of course does not exclude the possibility that some producers working under worse than 'socially average conditions' (Marx) suffer losses.

Second, note also that although the assumptions in Definition 1 are very close to Gale's (1960) dual conditions of productivity, they are different. What Gale showed was that the strict inequality $\mathbf{p^a} > \mathbf{p^a A}$, or, if $\mathbf{A}$ is irreducible, the semi-inequality $\mathbf{p^a} \geq \mathbf{p^a A}$ and $\mathbf{p^a} \neq \mathbf{p^a A}$ imply that $\mathbf{A}$ has a nonnegative Leontief-inverse. Since however we do not assume either that $\mathbf{v}$ is strictly positive, or alternatively that $\mathbf{A}$ is irreducible, equation (1) does not imply either of Gale's productivity conditions.

Third, the second definition implies that if labour were dispensable the economy could be *fully automated.* It does not exclude however the possibility that all processes but one are fully automated.

In the following lemma we will show that the indispensability of labour implies a special structural feature for the input coefficients.

Lemma 1

Labour is dispensable if and only if $\mathbf{v} = \mathbf{o}$, or there exists a decomposition of the input coefficients (after suitable rearrangements of the sectors if necessary) such that

$$\mathbf{A} = \begin{pmatrix} \mathbf{A}_{11} & \mathbf{A}_{12} \\ \mathbf{0} & \mathbf{A}_{22} \end{pmatrix}, \quad \mathbf{v} = (\mathbf{o}, \mathbf{v}_2)$$

where $\mathbf{A}_{11}$ and $\mathbf{A}_{12}$ are square matrices. In other words, there is an independent set of sectors that do not require labour power at all.

Proof:

(a) *Sufficiency*. Suppose such decomposition exists. Let $\mathbf{q}_1$ be an arbitrarily chosen positive vector compatible in size with matrix $\mathbf{A}_{11}$. Clearly, we can find a positive scalar α such that inequality $\mathbf{q}_1 \geq \alpha\mathbf{A}_{11}\mathbf{q}_1$ will hold. Thus $\mathbf{q} = (\mathbf{q}_1, \mathbf{o})$ and α would satisfy conditions (2).

(b) *Necessity*. Suppose labour is dispensable and that conditions (2) are met by some $\mathbf{q}$ and α. If $\mathbf{q} > \mathbf{o}$, then clearly $\mathbf{v} = \mathbf{o}$. If not, we can rearrange the data according to the positive and zero components of the semipositive $\mathbf{q}$ and decompose (2) in the following way:

$$\mathbf{q}_1 \geq \alpha\mathbf{A}_{11}\mathbf{q}_1 + \alpha\mathbf{A}_{12}\mathbf{o}$$
$$\mathbf{o} \geq \alpha\mathbf{A}_{21}\mathbf{q}_1 + \alpha\mathbf{A}_{22}\mathbf{o}$$
$$\mathbf{v}_1\mathbf{q}_1 + \mathbf{v}_2\mathbf{0} = \mathbf{0},$$

where $\mathbf{q}_1 > \mathbf{o}$ and $\alpha > 0$. From this it follows that we must by necessity have $\mathbf{A}_{21} = \mathbf{O}$ and $\mathbf{v}_1 = \mathbf{o}$.

QED

In the next lemma we will prove that – if labour is indispensable – any price system that covers at least the cost of materials and labour power must be strictly positive.

Lemma 2

If labour is indispensable and $w > 0$, then any $\mathbf{p} \geq \mathbf{o}$ satisfying the inequality

$$\mathbf{p} \geq \mathbf{p}\mathbf{A} + w\mathbf{v} \tag{3}$$

must be strictly positive.

Proof:

Since $w > 0$ and $\mathbf{p} \geq \mathbf{o}$, indispensability of labour and inequality (3) imply that $\mathbf{p}$ must have at least one positive component. Suppose not all components are positive.

Rearranging the data and decomposing them according to the positive and zero elements in $\mathbf{p}$ we get

$$\mathbf{o} \geq \mathbf{o}\mathbf{A}_{11} + \mathbf{p}_2\mathbf{A}_{21} + w\mathbf{v}_1 \tag{3a}$$
$$\mathbf{p}_2 \geq \mathbf{o}\mathbf{A}_{12} + \mathbf{p}_2\mathbf{A}_{22} + w\mathbf{v}_2 \tag{3b}$$

From (3a) it follows that we must have $\mathbf{A}_{21} = \mathbf{O}$ and $\mathrm{v}_1 = \mathbf{o}$, which in turn would contradict our assumption that labour is indispensable.

QED

Suppose now that the Leontief-inverse of **A** exists and thus the full (direct and indirect) labour requirement coefficients can be defined and calculated according to the well known scheme of

$$\boldsymbol{\upsilon} = \mathbf{v}(\mathbf{I} - \mathbf{A})^{-1}$$

A simple consequence of Lemma 2 is that, if labour is indispensable, this vector will be strictly positive, which in turn means that labour is directly or indirectly required to produce every commodity. To show that one should simply see that the following equation must hold:

$$\boldsymbol{\upsilon} = \boldsymbol{\upsilon}\mathbf{A} + \mathbf{v}$$

Thus, the vector υ fulfils the conditions stated in Lemma 2. It is in fact the vector of the Marxian labour values.

We can now formulate and prove a theorem that generalizes Gale's productivity theorem.

Theorem 1

$(\mathbf{I} - \mathbf{A})^{-1}$ exists and is (semi)positive whenever the input coefficients represent a pure commodity producing economy in which labor is indispensable.

Proof:

It suffices to show that $\lambda(\mathbf{A})$, the dominant eigenvalue of **A**, is less than 1. Suppose $\mathbf{p}^a$ and w^a satisfies the conditions of pure commodity production. From Lemma 2 it follows that $\mathbf{p}^a > \mathbf{o}$. Thus for any $k > 1$ we will have $k\mathbf{p}^a > \mathbf{p}^a\mathbf{A}$. From the Perron–Frobenius theorems we know that this implies: $\lambda(\mathbf{A}) \leq 1$. Let us now suppose that $\lambda(\mathbf{A}) = 1$. If this was the case, there would exist a semipositive eigenvector **x** such that

$$\mathbf{x} = \mathbf{A}\mathbf{x} \tag{4}$$

Multiplying inequality (1) by the above vector **x** we would get

$$\mathbf{p}^a\mathbf{x} \geq \mathbf{p}^a\mathbf{A}\mathbf{x} + w^a\mathbf{v}\mathbf{x}$$

Also, multiplying equation (4) by $\mathbf{p}^a$ we would have:

$$\mathbf{p}^a\mathbf{x} = \mathbf{p}^a\mathbf{A}\mathbf{x}$$

These two relations together and the assumed positivity of w^a would therefore imply that $\mathbf{v}\mathbf{x} = 0$. Since however **x** is semipositive and fulfils equation $\mathbf{x} = \mathbf{A}\mathbf{x}$, this would mean that labour is dispensable, contrary to our assumption.

QED

We can easily see that Theorem 1 implies Gale's productivity theorems. Let us suppose that inequality $\mathbf{p^a} > \mathbf{p^a A}$ holds, which is exactly Gale's condition for the general case. One can clearly find strictly positive $\mathbf{v}$ and w^a such that inequality (1) holds. If $\mathbf{A}$ is irreducible, then Gale's inequality $\mathbf{p^a} \geq \mathbf{p^a A}$ and $\mathbf{p^a} \neq \mathbf{p^a A}$ imply the existence of such a semipositive vector $\mathbf{v}$ and positive w^a that fulfil our conditions. Thus, we may reformulate Gale's conditions for the general case as follows:

Corollary. A nonnegative input–output matrix $\mathbf{A}$ has a nonnegative Leontief-inverse if and only if there exists a nonnegative price vector $\mathbf{p}$ such that $\mathbf{p} \geq \mathbf{pA}$ and positive value added $(\mathbf{p} - \mathbf{p^A})$ is generated in every independent group of sectors.

17.3 PRODUCTION PRICES WITH MONEY WAGES: THE REAL WAGE RATE–PROFIT RATE CORRESPONDENCE

The Marxian production prices – if the wages are given in terms of money rather set by the necessary consumption – can be defined with the data introduced as follows.

Definition 3 (*Production prices with money wages*)
The *production price system* is the nonnegative triple of $\mathbf{p}$, w and π that satisfies the following equation:

$$\mathbf{p} = \mathbf{pA} + w\mathbf{v} + \pi(\mathbf{pB} + w\mathbf{b}) \tag{5}$$

Let us observe that the above definition leaves the general price level undertermined. If some $\mathbf{p}$ and w satisfy the price equation at a given value of π, then $k\mathbf{p}$ and kw will also satisfy it for the same value of π. In most cases therefore it is useful to assume that the above equation is supplemented by some normalization rule (e.g. $\mathbf{p1} = 1$) and to speak of *normalized price systems*.

In the *strict economic sense* we should limit the above definition to such solutions in which the price vector $\mathbf{p}$ is at least semipositive, the money wage rate (w) and the uniform rate of profit (π) are positive.[6] If π is zero the above form defines in fact the *'labour value price system'* (i.e. prices proportional to the labour values). These latter prices are clearly well defined and – if normalized – uniquely determined as long as $\mathbf{A}$ is productive and w is positive. Furthermore, if labour is indispensable, they are all strictly positive.

The zero wage case ($w = 0$) case is from the economic point of view irrelevant, although it has attracted considerable attention in the literature, especially in the von Neumann-model version of the problem. In such case the price determination reduces to a simple form as follows:

$$\mathbf{p} = \mathbf{pA} + \pi\mathbf{pB} = \mathbf{p}(\mathbf{A} + \pi\mathbf{B})$$

and the resulting prices could be called '*capital value prices*'.

Clearly, in order for that system to have a nonnegative solution in $\mathbf{p}$, π must assume such a value that makes 1 an eigenvalue of the matrix $\mathbf{A} + \pi\mathbf{B}$ so that there is a nonnegative eigenvalue associated with it. If $\mathbf{A}$ is productive and π is positive then we can simply rearrange the above equation to get

$$1/\pi\mathbf{p} = \mathbf{pB}(\mathbf{I} - \mathbf{A})^{-1}$$

This form clearly indicates that π will necessarily be the reciprocal of such a positive eigenvalue of the matrix $\mathbf{B}(\mathbf{I} - \mathbf{A})^{-1}$ with which there is some nonnegative eigenvector associated. Let us introduce the following definition:

Definition 4 (*Indispensability of fixed capital*)
Fixed capital is said to be indispensable in a productive economy, if $\mathbf{1B}(\mathbf{I} - \mathbf{A})^{-1} > \mathbf{o}$, i.e. it is directly or indirectly required for the production of any commodity.

It is easy to show that the dominant eigenvalue (λ_B) of the matrix $\mathbf{B}(\mathbf{I} - \mathbf{A})^{-1}$ is positive if fixed capital is indispensable, since

$$\lambda_B \mathbf{1x} = \mathbf{1B}(\mathbf{I} - \mathbf{A})^{-1}\mathbf{x} > 0 \tag{6}$$

where $\mathbf{x}$ is a semipositive eigenvector associated with λ_B. It should also be clear that there might exist multiple feasible profit rates and corresponding normalized 'capital value price' vectors, unlike in the case of the labour value prices. Also, we cannot guarantee the strict positivity of these prices.

Under our assumptions the existence of production prices implies some necessary structural properties for the data characterizing the given economy, which as we will see are in fact also sufficient to guarantee their existence and strict positivity.

Theorem 2 (*Necessary conditions of the existence of the production price system*)
If labour is indispensable and nonnegative production prices exist for some positive values of w and π, then all prices must be strictly positive and the matrix $(\mathbf{A} + \pi\mathbf{B})$, and consequently $\mathbf{A}$, too, must be productive.

Proof:

Since by assumption prices are nonnegative, w and π are positive, we have

$$\mathbf{p} \geq \mathbf{pA} + w\mathbf{v}$$

From lemma 2 therefore it follows that $\mathbf{p} > \mathbf{o}$. From the definition of the production prices we also know that

$$\mathbf{p} \geq \mathbf{p}(\mathbf{A} + \pi\mathbf{B}) \tag{7}$$

The strict positivity of $\mathbf{p}$ and the above inequality imply then that

$$k\mathbf{p} > \mathbf{p}(\mathbf{A} + \pi\mathbf{B})$$

for all $k > 1$. This in turn implies – in view of the Perron–Frobenius theorems – that $\lambda(\mathbf{A} + \pi\mathbf{B}) \leq 1$, where $\lambda(\ )$ denotes the dominant eigenvalue of the given matrix. We have still to show that it cannot be equal to 1 either. Suppose it were equal to 1. Then there would exist a semipositive eigenvector $\mathbf{x}$ such that

$$\mathbf{x} = (\mathbf{A} + \pi\mathbf{B})\mathbf{x} \tag{8}$$

Multiplying both sides of equation (8) by the price vector and similarly the price equation (5) by the vector $\mathbf{x}$ we would conclude that $w(\mathbf{v} + \pi\mathbf{b})\mathbf{x}$ must be zero. Since we assumed that both w and π are positive, the above term can be zero only if $\mathbf{vx}$ and $\mathbf{bx}$ are zero, too. The facts that $\mathbf{vx} = 0$ and equation (8) holds would, however, mean that labour is dispensable, contrary to our assumption.

QED

It is of course more interesting to see what assumptions guarantee the existence of feasible production price systems and to show that if prices are normalized the feasible profit rates and the real (money) wage rates are inversely related to each other (by *feasible profit rates* we mean such nonnegative values of π which are compatible with a positive or zero wage rate and nonnegative production prices).

Theorem 3 (*Sufficient conditions for the existence of the production price system and the wage-profit correspondence*)

In a pure commodity producing economy, in which labour is indispensable, there always exists a range of feasible profit rates $(0, \pi^o - \pi^o)$ possibly being infinite – within which

(a) for any rate of profit and for any given positive wage rate production prices are uniquely determined and strictly positive; furthermore

(b) if fixed capital is indispensable, the range of feasible profit rates is bounded from above (i.e. π^{o} is finite); and

(c) if prices are normalized, then any increase in the profit rate implies a decrease in the (real) money wage rate, and *vice versa*.

Proof:

a) From Theorem 1 it follows that our assumptions secure the productivity of matrix **A**. Since $\lambda(\mathbf{A}) < 1$, we can certainly find such $\pi > o$ that $\lambda(\mathbf{A} + \pi\mathbf{B}) < 1$, too, which means, the matrix $\mathbf{A} + \pi\mathbf{B}$ has a nonnegative Leontief-inverse. For any such value of π and arbitrarily chosen $w > 0$, **p** is uniquely determined and nonnegative since equation (5) can be solved for **p** in any of the following ways:

$$\begin{aligned} \mathbf{p} &= w(\mathbf{v} + \pi\mathbf{b})[\mathbf{I} - (\mathbf{A} + \pi\mathbf{B})]^{-1} = \\ &= w(\mathbf{v} + \pi\mathbf{b})(\mathbf{I} - \mathbf{A})^{-1}[\mathbf{I} - \pi\mathbf{B}(\mathbf{I} - \mathbf{A})^{-1}]^{-1} \end{aligned} \tag{9}$$

From Theorem 2 it follows immediately that under the assumptions of this theorem this solution must be strictly positive.

b) As it is known from the Perron–Frobenius–theorems, the matrix $\mathbf{I} - (\mathbf{A} + \pi\mathbf{B})$ will have a nonnegative inverse as long as $\lambda(\mathbf{A} + \pi\mathbf{B}) < 1$. We have seen that any such value of π that makes 1 an eigenvalue of the matrix $\mathbf{A} + \pi\mathbf{B}$ will necessarily be the reciprocal of a positive (for **A** is productive) eigenvalue of the matrix $\mathbf{B}(\mathbf{I} - \mathbf{A})^{-1}$. Thus, if there exists a (finite) upper bound for the feasible profit rates, then it will be the smallest of all such π values for which $\lambda(\mathbf{A} + \pi\mathbf{B}) = 1$. Since π^{o} is the *smallest* of all these values, therefore its reciprocal, the dominant (the *largest* nonnegative) eigenvalue of $\mathbf{B}(\mathbf{I} - \mathbf{A})^{-1}$ must be also positive. If fixed capital is indispensable, that is, $\mathbf{1B}(\mathbf{I} - \mathbf{A})^{-1} > 0$, then – as we have seen – this dominant eigenvalue (λ_B) will necessarily be positive, thus, the upper bound is finite.

c) Let us now take a closer look at the second part of equation (9). Since labor is indispensable, both $\mathbf{v}(\mathbf{I} - \mathbf{A})^{-1}$ and $\mathbf{b}(\mathbf{I} - \mathbf{A})^{-1}$ are strictly positive vectors. (The vector **b** has – by assumption – the same structure as **v**!) Also, the inverse of the matrix $\mathbf{I} - \pi\mathbf{B}(\mathbf{I} - \mathbf{A})^{-1}$ is nonnegative and strictly positive in its main diagonal. Moreover, its components are increasing functions of π (see for example the matrix power series representation of the Leontief-inverse). From all of these observations it follows that every component of **p** is a strictly increasing function of both w and π. Thus, if prices are normalized, any increase in π – within the feasible region of $(0, \pi^{o})$ – will result in a decrease in the wage rate, and conversely, if w increases, π must decrease.

QED

Theorems 2 and 3 in essence underpin the **conceptual validity of the production prices**. We have demonstrated that in a pure capitalist commodity producing economy, in which one may rightly assume that both labor and (fixed) capital is indispensable, the Marxian production prices are well defined, and that the real (money) wage and the rate of profit are strictly decreasing functions of each other. In the light of these theorems one can easily formulate the necessary and sufficient conditions for the production price system to exist.

Corollary. If labour is indispensable *the necessary and sufficient conditions for a strictly positive production price system to exist*, i.e. $(\mathbf{p}, w, \pi) > \mathrm{o}$ satisfying equation (5), is the productivity of **A**. In addition, if **p** is normalized, the feasible rates of profit and wage levels define a strictly decreasing wage-profit frontier.

One can easily see also that the above analysis can be directly applied to the **Sraffian production prices** as well, for if one sets $\mathbf{B} = \mathbf{A}$ and $\mathbf{b} = \mathbf{o}$, then equation (5) simply reduces to the Sraffian definition of prices. It is interesting to note that the existence of the Sraffian basic commodities (such commodities that are directly or indirectly required to produce any commodity) would automatically imply the indispensability of capital in that model.

As a matter of fact, our analysis so far could be labelled Sraffian in spirit, in the sense that we have not considered labour power as a commodity. We have not addressed the question at all whether or not the wage rate and the corresponding set of prices could secure the reproduction of the labour power. As is well known, Marx treated labour power as one of the reproducible commodities and introduced the concept of *necessary consumption* to represent the input requirements of its reproduction. Bródy, too, analyzed the production prices in this latter augmented framework and it is this complete system of reproduction that we will analyze next.

17.4 PRODUCTION PRICES WITH COMMODITY REAL WAGES AND LUXURY PRODUCTS

Let the vector $\mathbf{c} = (c_i)$ and the scalar ν_0 denote, respectively, the amounts of the common commodities and labour power necessary to reproduce one hour of labour power. We will assume that **c** is at least semipositive ($\mathrm{c} \geq \mathbf{o}$ and $\mathrm{c} \neq \mathbf{o}$) and that $0 < \nu_0 < 1$.

Bródy and other authors do not usually take explicitly into account v_o, i.e. the labour used in the reproduction of labour power itself. Such a solution can be justified, but may be misleading, for it conceals the *specific* features of the labour power commodity. Its main specific feature according to Marx is that its reproduction is partly governed by rules other than those of the market. For example, no surplus or profit emerges in the process of its reproduction.[7] The value of labor (the value wage) in his analysis is nothing but the cost of its reproduction, i.e., a *subsistence wage* defined by the following equation:

$$w = \mathbf{pc} + wv_o \tag{10}$$

Rearranging the above equation for w we get:

$$w = \frac{1}{(1 - v_o)}\mathbf{pc} = \mathbf{pc}'$$

The vector $\mathbf{c}'$ represents how much *consumption* is *necessary* to reproduce one hour of labor power that is '*productively*' employed, i.e. employed in the production of the common commodities. It contains not only the consumption of the workers employed productively, but also that of those workers who are employed in the reproduction of the labour power itself. This is exactly how Marx defined the notion of necessary consumption. In this sense one may think that such a reduction has already been made and assume that $\mathbf{c} = \mathbf{c}'$ and $v_o = 0$. But let us emphasize again, this is not the same as to assume that labour is not directly involved in its own reproduction.

Once we know the reproduction input requirements of the labour power, too, we can augment the input–output coefficient matrix defined originally for the n common commodities with an additional row and column to represent labour power along with the rest of the commodities. This is exactly what Bródy did. In this case, however, special attention has to be paid to the way how one redefines the matrix of capital coefficients. If one analyzes a pure capitalist system – as we do here – the column corresponding to labour power in it could contain nothing but zeros. Otherwise profit would emerge in the production of labour power, too – contrary to the above mentioned specific features of the labour power commodity.[8]

Let us represent the complete system of commodity production by the following pair of augmented matrices:

$$\hat{\mathbf{A}} = \begin{pmatrix} v_0 & \mathbf{v} \\ \mathbf{c} & \mathbf{A} \end{pmatrix}, \quad \hat{\mathbf{B}} = \begin{pmatrix} 0 & \mathbf{b} \\ \mathbf{o} & \mathbf{B} \end{pmatrix}$$

and let $\hat{\mathbf{p}} = (w, \mathbf{p})$ represent the joint vector of prices and wage rate. One can easily see that combining (5) and (10) the complete system of production prices takes the form of the dual of a closed Leontief-model:

$$\hat{\mathbf{p}} = \hat{\mathbf{p}}\hat{\mathbf{A}} + \pi\hat{\mathbf{p}}\hat{\mathbf{B}} = \hat{\mathbf{p}}(\hat{\mathbf{A}} + \pi\hat{\mathbf{B}}) \tag{11}$$

Bródy analyzed the production price system in this form by assuming the *irreducibility* of $\hat{\mathbf{A}}$ (and of $\hat{\mathbf{B}}$, too, which of course – as pointed out – cannot be the case) and that $\lambda(\hat{\mathbf{A}}) < 1$. Bródy has shown that the complete flow input coefficient matrix will be irreducible if every product uses (directly or indirectly) labour and every product is (directly or indirectly) required to reproduce labour power. While the first assumption can be justified (see the indispensability of labour), the second one is a restrictive assumption. Such an assumption excludes pure luxury goods from the analysis, i.e. such goods which are only consumed by the individual or collective capitalists. We will relax this assumption and to this end we introduce the concept of *necessary commodities* in the Marxian sense.

Definition 5 (*Necessary and luxury commodities*)

A commodity is necessary if it is directly or indirectly needed for the reproduction of labour power. A commodity that is not necessary is called a luxury commodity.

Necessary commodities clearly exist (since $\mathbf{c}$ is assumed to be semipositive) and if labour is indispensable than they will include labour power itself as well. It will turn out that the Marxian concept of necessary commodities is very similar to Sraffa's (1960) notion of *basic commodities*, the main difference is that Sraffa's definition did not include labour power as a commodity. We will see that under our assumptions the necessary commodities form an irreducible sub-economy which will play a crucial role in our analysis.

Lemma 3

If labour is indispensable, the sub-matrix of the complete flow input coefficient matrix defined by the necessary commodities is irreducible, and every necessary commodity is – directly or indirectly – required to produce any commodity.

Proof:

Let us decompose the coefficient matrix according to necessary and luxury goods (where the latter may be an empty set):

$$\hat{\mathbf{A}} = \begin{pmatrix} v_0 & \mathbf{v}_1 & \mathbf{v}_2 \\ \mathbf{c}_1 & \mathbf{A}_{11} & \mathbf{A}_{12} \\ \mathbf{o} & 0 & \mathbf{A}_{22} \end{pmatrix} = \begin{pmatrix} \hat{\mathbf{A}}_{11} & \hat{\mathbf{A}}_{12} \\ 0 & \mathbf{A}_{22} \end{pmatrix}$$

It is easy to see that by definition we must have $\mathbf{c}_2 = \mathbf{o}$ and $\mathbf{A}_{21} = 0$ in the above decomposition. Also, $\hat{\mathbf{A}}_{11}$ must be irreducible. Suppose it were not. That would mean that there existed an independent sub-group of necessary commodities that could be produced without the rest. This group should contain labour power, because labour is indispensable and consequently all the commodities that directly or indirectly enter into its consumption. Thus, any good that did not belong to this independent sub-group, could not be a necessary commodity by definition. The assumption that labour is indispensable ensures that labour power, and consequently every other necessary commodity, is directly or indirectly required to produce any commodity. This also means that if $\mathbf{A}_{22}$ is productive, $\mathbf{1}\hat{\mathbf{A}}_{12}(\mathbf{I} - \mathbf{A}_{22})^{-1} > \mathbf{o}$.

QED

Definition 4 (*The possibility of surplus*)

Surplus labour in one manhour (v_s) is defined as the amount of labour left after subtracting the labour required to produce the necessary consumption of the labour power itself. It can be calculated from the given data as follows:

$$v_s = 1 - \frac{1}{1 - v_0}\mathbf{v}(\mathbf{I} - \mathbf{A})^{-1}\mathbf{c}$$

If this surplus labour is positive the economy is said to be *capable of producing surplus.*

It is easy to show that the possibility of surplus is equivalent to the productivity of the complete input coefficient matrix $\hat{\mathbf{A}}$.

Lemma 4

The necessary and sufficient condition for the complete input coefficient matrix $\hat{\mathbf{A}}$ to be productive is the productivity of $\mathbf{A}$ and the positivity of the surplus labour.

Proof:

All we have to show is that $\hat{\mathbf{A}}$ is productive if and only if

$$1 > \frac{1}{1 - v_0}\mathbf{v}(\mathbf{I} - \mathbf{A})^{-1}\mathbf{c}$$

that is

$$1 > v_0 + \mathbf{v}(\mathbf{I} - \mathbf{A})^{-1}\mathbf{c} \tag{12}$$

From Gale's productivity theorem we know that $\hat{\mathbf{A}}$ is productive if and only if there exists $\hat{\mathbf{x}} \geq \mathrm{o}$ such that $\hat{\mathbf{x}} > \hat{\mathbf{A}}\hat{\mathbf{x}}$. We base our proof on this latter condition.

Sufficiency: Decomposing the last inequality we get

$$x_0 > v_0 x_0 + \mathbf{v}\mathbf{x} \tag{13a}$$

and

$$\mathbf{x} > c x_0 + \mathbf{A}\mathbf{x} \tag{13b}$$

The productivity of $\hat{\mathbf{A}}$ implies the same for $\mathbf{A}$ (being one of its principal minors). Thus, we can rearrange the last equation to get

$$\mathbf{x} > (\mathbf{I} - \mathbf{A})^{-1} \mathbf{c} x_0$$

Substituting $(\mathbf{I} - \mathbf{A})^{-1} cx$ for $\mathbf{x}$ in (13a) will yield

$$x_0 > v_0 x_0 + \mathbf{v}(\mathbf{I} - \mathbf{A})^{-1} c x_0$$

Clearly, x_o must be positive and thus dividing the above inequality by x_o we can derive condition (12) which was to be shown.

Necessity: Suppose $\mathbf{A}$ is productive and condition (12) holds. Define $\mathbf{x}$ as follows:

$$\mathbf{x} = (\mathbf{I} - \mathbf{A})^{-1}(\mathbf{c} + k\mathbf{d})x_0$$

where $\mathbf{d}$ is a strictly positive vector, k and x_0 are positive scalars. It is easy to see that such x_0 and $\mathbf{x}$ will always satisfy condition (13b). Because inequality (12) holds, one can choose k sufficiently small so that (13a) would be satisfied, too.

QED

Bródy has shown that if $\hat{\mathbf{A}}$ is irreducible and productive the equation system (11) has one and only one positive solution for π and $\hat{\mathbf{p}}$, the latter assumed to be normalized. If the production system is reducible the determination of the production price system can be decomposed according to necessary and luxury commodities in the following way:

$$\hat{\mathbf{p}}_1 = \hat{\mathbf{p}}_1(\hat{\mathbf{A}}_{11} + \pi\hat{\mathbf{B}}_{11}) \tag{11a}$$

$$\mathbf{p}_2 = \hat{\mathbf{p}}_1(\hat{\mathbf{A}}_{12} + \pi\hat{\mathbf{B}}_{12}) + \mathbf{p}_2(\mathbf{A}_{22} + \pi\mathbf{B}_{22}) \tag{11b}$$

where $\hat{\mathbf{p}}_1 = (w, \mathbf{p}_1)$.

Under our assumptions if the above system has nonnegative solution then the wage rate and the prices of the necessary commodities are either all positive or all zeros in that solution. If they are positive, then the rate of profit is determined alone by the necessary commodity sub-system and the prices of the luxury commodities will also be all positive. If they are all zeros, then the rate of profit is determined by the luxury commodity sub-system and the prices of the luxury commodities will not necessarily be all positive, unless $\mathbf{A}_{22}$ is irreducible. We can formulate the conditions of the existence of positive solution in the general case as follows.

Theorem 4 (*Generalized theorem on the existence of positive production price systems*)

Let $\hat{\mathbf{A}}$ and $\hat{\mathbf{B}}$ characterize a pure commodity production economy, which is capable of producing surplus, and in which labor is indispensable. There exists a positive rate of profit and a corresponding set of normalized positive production prices and a positive subsistence wage if and only if

$$\lambda_1 = \lambda(\hat{\mathbf{B}}_{11}(\mathbf{I} - \hat{\mathbf{A}}_{11})^{-1}) > \lambda_2 = \lambda(\mathbf{B}_{22}(\mathbf{I} - \mathbf{A}_{22})^{-1})$$

Proof:

Since $\hat{\mathbf{A}}_{11}$ is irreducible, equation (11a) uniquely determines such value of π at which the dominant eigenvalue of the coefficient matrix $\hat{\mathbf{A}}_{11} + \pi\hat{\mathbf{B}}_{11}$ will be 1, which in turn is the necessary and sufficient condition for a positive $\hat{\mathbf{p}}_1$ vector to exist. The possibility of surplus ensures that such π exits and is positive. It is the reciprocal of λ_1. If $\lambda_1 > \lambda_2$, as assumed, then the matrix $\mathbf{A}_{22} + \pi\mathbf{B}_{22}$ will have a nonnegative Leontief-inverse, thus (11b) can be solved for $\mathbf{p}_2$. The positivity of $\mathbf{p}_2$ is a direct consequence of the assumption that labor is indispensable.[9]

QED

The eigenvalues λ_1 and λ_2 can be interpreted as the 'overall own-capital intensities' of the two sub-economies. Thus, the production of luxury commodities is compatible with positive equilibrium prices only if the own-capital intensity of that sub-system is smaller than that of the necessary commodity subsystem. Since zero wages are hardly conceivable in a capitalist economy, we can interpret the above condition as a kind of technical condition for pure luxury commodities to be compatible with a pure capitalist commodity production system.

17.5 ALTERNATIVE FORMS OF THE COEFFICIENT MATRICES OF THE COMPLETE SYSTEM

Let us come back once again to the definition of the production price system and subsistence wages:

$$\mathbf{p} = \mathbf{pA} + w\mathbf{v} + \pi(\mathbf{pB} + w\mathbf{b}) \tag{14a}$$

$$w = \mathbf{pc} \tag{14b}$$

using for simplicity of notation the 'reduced' form of wage determination ($\mathbf{c} = \mathbf{c}'$, $v_o = 0$).

In the previous analysis – as Bródy did – we augmented the set of commodities with the labour power. We could proceed in another way and 'eliminate' labour power instead, simply by replacing w in (14a) by its definition given in (14b). In this case we would get

$$\mathbf{p} = \mathbf{p}(\mathbf{A} + \pi\mathbf{B}) + \mathbf{p}(\mathbf{cv} + \pi\mathbf{cb}) = \mathbf{p}(\bar{\mathbf{A}} + \pi\bar{\mathbf{B}})$$

where $\bar{\mathbf{A}} = \mathbf{A} + >\mathbf{cv}<$ and $\bar{\mathbf{B}} = \mathbf{B} + >\mathbf{bv}<$ are the condensed forms of the complete coefficient matrices.

Matrix $\bar{\mathbf{A}}$ rather than Bródy's $\hat{\mathbf{A}}$ has been used in the Marxian analysis by Morishima (1973) and some other authors. One may wonder to what extent the 'augmented' and the 'condensed' forms of the complete coefficient matrices are equivalent to each other from a mathematical or an economic point of view. It is not surprising to find out that the basic mathematical properties of the two forms of the complete flow coefficient matrix are the same. We prove this in the following lemma.

Lemma 5

Let $\mathbf{A}$ be a nonnegative quadratic matrix, and $\mathbf{c}$ and $\mathbf{v}$ be semipositive vectors of the same dimension. Construct matrices $\hat{\mathbf{A}}$ and $\bar{\mathbf{A}}$ in the following way:

$$\hat{\mathbf{A}} = \begin{pmatrix} 0 & \mathbf{v} \\ \mathbf{c} & \mathbf{A} \end{pmatrix}, \quad \bar{\mathbf{A}} = \mathbf{A} + >\mathbf{cv}<$$

For $\hat{\mathbf{A}}$ and $\bar{\mathbf{A}}$ the following properties hold:

a) the dominant eigenvalue of $\hat{\mathbf{A}}$ is less than, greater than, or equal to 1 if and only if the same holds for $\bar{\mathbf{A}}$;
b) matrix $(\mathbf{I} - \bar{\mathbf{A}})^{-1}$ is contained by the sub-matrix of $(\mathbf{I} - \hat{\mathbf{A}})^{-1}$ defined by the common commodities;
c) matrix $\hat{\mathbf{A}}$ is irreducible if and only if the same is true for $\bar{\mathbf{A}}$.

Proof:

a) From the Perron–Frobenius theorems we know that the inequality $\mathbf{x} > \mathbf{Ax}$ has nonnegative (in fact positive) solution if and only if the dominant eigenvalue of the matrix $\mathbf{A}$ is smaller than 1. Suppose the dominant eigenvalue of $\hat{\mathbf{A}}$ is less than 1. In this case we can find a strictly positive vector $\hat{\mathbf{x}}$ such that $\hat{\mathbf{x}} > \hat{\mathbf{A}}\hat{\mathbf{x}}$, i.e.

$$x_0 > \mathbf{vx} \tag{15}$$

$$\mathbf{x} > \mathbf{Ax} + \mathbf{c}x_0 \tag{16}$$

Replacing x_o by $\mathbf{vx}$ in (16) yields

$$\mathbf{x} > \mathbf{Ax} + \mathbf{cvx} = \bar{\mathbf{A}}\mathbf{x} \tag{17}$$

from which it follows that the dominant eigenvalue of $\bar{\mathbf{A}}$ must also be less than 1. Conversely, suppose there is an $\mathbf{x} > \mathbf{o}$ such that $\mathbf{x} > \bar{\mathbf{A}}\mathbf{x}$. Define x_o as $x_o = k\mathbf{vx}$, where k is larger than but sufficiently close to 1. Such a pair of $(x_o, \mathbf{x})$ clearly satisfies inequality (15). Also, choosing k close enough to 1 we can achieve that the inequality

$$\mathbf{x} > \mathbf{Ax} + k\mathbf{cvx}$$

will also hold, because of (17). The two inequalities together imply in turn that the dominant eigenvalue of $\hat{\mathbf{A}}$ is less than 1, which was to show.

From the same theorems we also know that the inequality $\mathbf{x} \leq \mathbf{Ax}$ has semipositive solution if and only if the dominant eigenvalue of $\mathbf{A}$ is greater than or equal to 1. Using similar arguments to those above, we can show that if $\hat{\mathbf{x}} = (x_o, \mathbf{x})$ is semipositive and $\hat{\mathbf{x}} \leq \hat{\mathbf{A}}\hat{\mathbf{x}}$ then the vector $\mathbf{x}$ must be semipositive and inequality $\mathbf{x} \leq \bar{\mathbf{A}}\mathbf{x}$ will also hold, and *vice versa*.

The dominant eigenvalues of the matrices $\hat{\mathbf{A}}$ and $\bar{\mathbf{A}}$ can, thus, be greater than or equal to or less than 1 only simultaneously.

b) By calculating the inverse of $(\mathbf{I} - \hat{\mathbf{A}})^{-1}$, choosing first the upper left-hand block as the pivotal element, we can immediately get the Leontief-inverse in the desired form:

$$\begin{pmatrix} 1 + \mathbf{m}(\mathbf{I} - \bar{\mathbf{A}})^{-1}\mathbf{c} & \mathbf{v}(\mathbf{I} - \bar{\mathbf{A}})^{-1} \\ (\mathbf{I} - \bar{\mathbf{A}})^{-1}\mathbf{c} & (\mathbf{I} - \bar{\mathbf{A}})^{-1} \end{pmatrix}$$

c) Irreducibility is a structural property of the given matrices, therefore, without loss of generality, we may assume that the dominant eigenvalues of the matrices $\hat{\mathbf{A}}$ and $\bar{\mathbf{A}}$ are both less than 1. In such a case irreducibility is equivalent to stating that the Leontief-inverse is strictly positive. From the above form of the Leontief-inverse of matrix $\hat{\mathbf{A}}$ the truth of our statement immediately follows.

QED

From an economic point of view there is one crucial difference between the '*augmented*' and the '*condensed' form* of the complete input coefficient matrix. Namely, the condensed form takes into account only the labour power actually used in the commodity production (representing it by its necessary consumption), whereas the augmented form can account for the total labour power reproduced, some of which might be unemployed. In this sense the augmented form is more general.

It is exactly this more general nature of the augmented form, which may create problems if it is not used with special care. The augmented form treats labour power exactly the same way as any other commodity, does not allow for taking into account its 'special' features discussed earlier. We have seen, for example, that it would be a mistake to define the capital stock coefficients for the labour power sector in the same way as for the common commodities (through the turnover time). We have seen that the corresponding column of the matrix $\hat{\mathbf{B}}$, must be zero otherwise the model would give rise to profit in the production of labour power as well.

Also, if we want to maintain the duality of the model then the representation of the variable capital $\mathbf{b}$ in the row of the matrix $\hat{\mathbf{B}}$ corresponding to labour power gives rise to difficulties again. To see that recall that the production identity of an open Leontief-model takes the following form:

$$\hat{\mathbf{x}} = \hat{\mathbf{A}}\hat{\mathbf{x}} + \hat{\mathbf{y}} + \hat{\mathbf{B}}\triangle\hat{\mathbf{x}}$$

where $\hat{\mathbf{y}}$ represents the vector of final use other than investments. If we use $\hat{\mathbf{B}}$ as defined earlier, the equation corresponding to the labor power commodity takes the following form:

$$x_0 = \mathbf{vx} + y_0 + \mathbf{b}\triangle\mathbf{x}$$

where the last term causes some problem of interpretation. How could one interpret the resulting investment, $\mathbf{b}\triangle\mathbf{x}$ taking place in the form of labour power?

Both of these issues point to the same question: what is the proper representation of tied-up capital in the Leontief-framework, that assumes symmetry (duality) between the production and valuation side. It seems, that one can avoid the emergence of the above awkward situations only if he represents all capital tied up – whether fixed or variable – in the form of common commodities, on the one hand, and allows for capital assets – whether they are used in the reproduction of labor power or not – only in the sectors of common commodity production, on the other. In other words, the elements of the first row and column of the matrix $\hat{\mathbf{B}}$ can contain only zeros.

In the case of the *variable capital* this would simply mean that instead of manhours (or wages) one should represent it through consumption, i.e. by common commodities rather than by labour power. This is exactly what we did when we added the diadic (outer) product $>\mathbf{cb}<$ to the matrix of the fixed capital coefficients (**B**). As a matter of fact one may argue that variable capital takes the form of physical commodity stocks (semi-finished products, product inventories, etc.) when measured at the level of the society. The *fixed assets* tied up in the reproduction of the labour power or other areas of social life could be treated as *collective capital inputs* and also distributed among the productive sectors. Thus, unless we accept such a solution we cannot maintain the nice duality between production and price proportions. Duality has been emphasized rather forcefully by Bródy, which also lent special elegance and beauty to his analysis. Why not to save it then?

NOTES

The author wishes to thank András Simonovits for his useful comments on an earlier version of the paper.

1. Quoted by Bródy (1970, p. 41), emphasis added.
2. See Ingrao–Israel (1990).
3. See Bródy (1970, p. 17).
4. Bródy referred to Lange (1952) and Hawkins (1948) as direct predecessors, but quoted Marx's *Capital* at length to justify this treatment.
5. Some of the theorems that follow in this section have been presented by the author earlier, see, for example, Zalai (1989).
6. Note that if $\mathbf{b} = \mathbf{o}$ the resulting price concept is a generalization of Sraffa's price system, which assumed there was no variable capital, because – in his assumption – labour advanced his own cost. If, however, the production period is relatively long such assumption is not justified.
7. We will see, for example, that this specific feature of labour commodity must be kept in sight when one redefines the capital input coefficient matrix for the augmented case. For more details on this issue and other potential errors see Zalai (1980).
8. Bródy assumed that '*the structural patterns of the two matrices* (i.e. of the augmented flow and stock matrices – E. Z.) *must be analogous*', including their irreducibility as well, see Bródy (1970, p. 37). He failed to realize that this causes problems of interpretation (profit being created in the labour power sector).
9. This proof is a special application of the known Theorem 6 of Gantmacher (1967, Ch. XIII, 4).

REFERENCES

BRÓDY, A. (1970) *Proportions, Prices and Planning* (Amsterdam: North-Holland).

GALE, D. (1960) *The Theory of Linear Economic Models* (New York: McGraw-Hill).

GANTMACHER, F. R. (1967) *Theory of Matrices* (3rd edn, Moscow: Nauka Press, in Russian).

HAWKINS, D. (1948) 'Some Conditions of Macroeconomic Stability', *Econometrica*, 16, no. 4.

INGRAO, B. and G. ISRAEL (1990) *The Invisible Hand. Economic Equilibrium in the History of Science* (Cambridge, Mass.: MIT Press).

LANGE, O. (1952) 'Some Observations on Input–Output Analysis', *Sankhya*, 17, part 4.

MORISHIMA, M. (1973) *Marx's Economics* (Cambridge: Cambridge University Press).

SRAFFA, P. (1960) *Production of Commodities by Means of Commodities* (Cambridge: Cambridge University Press).

ZALAI, E. (1980) 'Heterogeneous Labour and the Determination of Value', *Acta Oeconomica*, vol. 25, no. 3–4, pp. 259–76.

ZALAI, E. (1989) 'Eigenvalues and Labor Values', *Economic Systems Research*, vol. 1, no. 3, pp. 403–9.

Index